Anthology of Korean Studies

VOLUME I

THE KOREAN ECONOMY:
Reflections the New Millennium

Edited by
Korean National Commission for UNESCO

HOLLYM
Elizabeth, NJ · Seoul

Anthology of Korean Studies, Volume I
The Korean Economy:
Reflections at the New Millennium

Copyright © 2001
by Whang In-Joung et al.

First published in 2001
by Hollym International Corp.
18 Donald Place, Elizabeth, New Jersey 07208, U.S.A.
Phone: (908) 353-1655   Fax: (908) 353-0255
http://www.hollym.com

Published simultaneously in Korea
by Hollym Corporation; Publishers
13-13, Gwancheol-dong, Jongno-gu, Seoul 110-111, Korea
Phone: (02) 735-7551~4   Fax: (02) 730-5149, 8192
http://www.hollym.co.kr

ISBN: 1-56591-173-3 (Volume I)
Library of Congress Catalog Card Number : 2001098683

Printed in Korea

Contents

Foreword

Since the seventeenth century when Hendrick Hamel first introduced Korea to the Western world, many Westerners have been drawn to the study of Korea and its rich cultural, literary, and philosophical history. Although important pioneering works on Korea have been produced, however, much research by Western scholars has been shaped by ethnocentric assumptions and interpretive biases, often reproducing preconceptions and simple misunderstandings about Korea. Many Korean scholars, too, have pursued scholarly aims that fall short of objective analyses. Thus, there has long been a need for a forum to bridge the gaps between Korean and non-Korean scholars, to make space for a multiplicity of voices, and to promote an interdisciplinary academic approach to Korean studies.

The *Korea Journal,* an academic quarterly published in English by the Korean National Commission for UNESCO, aims to act as such a forum. Since its foundation in 1961, the *Korea Journal* has attempted to provide grounded and accurate knowledge of Korea by featuring articles by prominent Korean and non-Korean specialists. Fortunately, an increasing number of Korean and foreign scholars and specialists are tackling the study of Korea with a more rigorous, objective, and open-minded outlook, engaging in critical dialogue with each other. The *Korea Journal* has played an invaluable role in developing and deepening this scholarly dialogue.

In 2001, the *Journal* celebrates its 40th anniversary. To commemorate this occasion, we are planning to publish the "Anthology of Korean Studies," a series of six volumes in the fields of economics, politics, anthropology, literature, history, and philosophy. All the articles in the series have been carefully selected from previous issues of the

Journal by the Advisory Committee, composed of six prominent specialists representing each field. The Anthology will be completed in 2004, marking the 50th anniversary of the Korean National Commission for UNESCO.

It is our hope that the Anthology will serve those who seek a comprehensive understanding of Korean society and culture. We recommend that it be used as a textbook at the university level or a standard reference for anyone teaching, studying, or researching in any area of Korean studies.

I would like to express my sincere gratitude to the members of the Advisory Committee, who took part in a one-year process to select the articles for inclusion in the Anthology: Dr. Kim Won Bae for economics, Prof. Kang Jung In for politics, Prof. Han Kyung-Koo for anthropology, Prof. Hwang Jong-yon for literature, Prof. Yi Tae-Jin for history, and Prof. Lee Seung-Hwan for philosophy. I would also like to recognize the editors and proofreaders who have labored tirelessly for the publication of this series, and the authors who have reexamined and revised their original texts. My thanks also go to the Hollym Publishing Company which has made it possible for our Commission to publish this Anthology, thus ensuring its contribution to the continued development of Korean studies.

Yersu Kim
Secretary-General
Korean National Commission
for UNESCO

Preface

The Korean economy has often been touted as a model of "miraculous" economic development which compressed full-scale industrialization into a single generation. Korea pushed forward its rapid economic growth through six five-year economic development plans from 1961-1991, based on extensive export-oriented and government-led policies. These successes, however, have not come without past sacrifices and persisting side effects. The recent 1997 financial crisis in particular can be interpreted as a result of failures in economic management. In order to better grasp the contemporary Korean economy in all its complexity, it is necessary to understand the political and economic terrain as well as the historical context in which it is located. Too simplistic an interpretation of the Korean economy, whether positive or negative, is unedifying at best and damaging at worst. The "miracle" must be carefully unpacked —a task attempted by many of the contributors herein.

This volume, *The Korean Economy: Reflections at the New Millennium*, attempts to provide readers abroad with a balanced introduction to economic issues in modern Korea by presenting a wide range of topics from a diverse group of contributors, including policy analysts, historians, sociologists, and of course, economists. The articles were carefully selected under the guidance of Dr. Kim Won Bae and arranged along four themes. Part I introduces earlier efforts for economic development and discusses their achievements and failures. In Part II, several contributors evaluate the meaning and effects of rapid modernization in relation to the country's social and economic growth. The 1997 financial crisis and the subsequent responses by the government and corporate sector are the focus of Part III, although it is still too early to perform a comprehensive evaluation. Part IV critically examines what role the government, often interpreted as essential for Korea's rapid growth, should play in the new world economic environment.

As a comprehensive compilation of academic articles presenting a diversity of topics and perspectives, we hope that this volume will serve as a textbook and reference manual for scholars, students, specialists, and anyone interested in the Korean economy, and we look forward to further scholarly exchanges.

Guide to Romanization

The Anthology uses the new Romanization system proclaimed by the Ministry of Culture and Tourism for terms in Korean. Outline of the Romanization system is as follows.

The Romanization of Korean

1. Basic Principles of Romanization

1) Romanization is based on standard Korean pronunciation.
2) Symbols other than Roman letters are avoided to the greatest extent possible.

2. Summary of the Romanization System

1) Vowels are transcribed as follows:

• simple vowels

ㅏ	ㅓ	ㅗ	ㅜ	ㅡ	ㅣ	ㅐ	ㅔ	ㅚ	ㅟ
a	eo	o	u	eu	i	ae	e	oe	wi

• diphthongs

ㄱ	ㄲ	ㅋ	ㄷ	ㄸ	ㅌ	ㅂ	ㅃ	ㅍ
g, k	kk	k	d, t	tt	t	b, p	pp	p

Note : ㅢ is transcribed as *ui*, even when pronounced as ㅣ.
Long vowels are not reflected in Romanization.

2) Consonants are transcribed as follows:

• plosives (stops)

ㄱ	ㄲ	ㅋ	ㄷ	ㄸ	ㅌ	ㅂ	ㅃ	ㅍ
g, k	kk	k	d, t	tt	t	b, p	pp	p

• affricates

ㅈ	ㅉ	ㅊ
j	jj	ch

• fricatives

ㅅ	ㅆ	ㅎ
s	ss	h

• nasals

ㄴ	ㅁ	ㅇ
n	m	ng

• liquids

ㄹ
r, l

Note 1: The sounds ㄱ, ㄷ, and ㅂ are transcribed respectively as *g*, *d*, and *b* when they appear before a vowel; they are transcribed as *k*, *t*, and *p* when followed by another consonant or form the final sound of a word. (They are Romanized as pronunciation in [ ].)

e.g.	구미	Gumi	영동	Yeongdong
	백암	Baegam	옥천	Okcheon
	합덕	Hapdeok	호법	Hobeop
	월곶[월곧]	Wolgot	벚꽃[벋꼳]	beotkkot
	한밭[한받]	Hanbat		

Note 2: ㄹ is transcribed as *r* when followed by a vowel, and as *l* when followed by a consonant or when appearing at the end of a word. ㄹㄹ is transcribed as *ll*.

e.g.	구리	Guri	설악	Seorak
	칠곡	Chilgok	임실	Imsil
	울릉	Ulleung	대관령[대괄령]	Daegwallyeong

However, the Anthology exceptionally follow the principle below when romanizing Korean family name starting with ㄱ and family name 이.

1) For family names starting with ㄱ (eg., 강, 권, and 김), *K* will be used instead of *G*.

2) When romanizing the family name 이, *Yi* will be used instead of *I*.

The Anthology follows the *pinyin* system as found in the *Xiandai hanyu cidian* published by the Institute of the Chinese Academy of Sciences (Bejing Shangwuyin Shuguan, 1978) for terms in Chinese and the romanization system used in the *New Japanese-English Character Dictionary* (Kenkyusha, 1990) for terms in Japanese.

PART I

THE KOREAN ECONOMY IN THE EARLY DEVELOPMENT STAGES

Administration of Land Reform in Korea, 1949-1952

Whang In-Joung

Introduction

Land reform in Korea took place in two stages: the redistribution of vested land by the United States Military Government in Korea (USMGK) in 1948; and the land reform program implemented by the government of the Republic of Korea during the period of 1950-1952. Vested lands were those lands owned by the Japanese during the period of colonial rule (1910-1945), and controlled by the USMGK after World War II. In the second phase of land reform, land owned by absentee landlords, or any portion of land owned by owner-farmers in excess of three *jeongbo* (one *jeongbo* is equivalent to 0.992 hectare) was redistributed to the tenants and landless famers.

Although these two programs were implemented by different government authorities and dealt with different land categories, they were based on the same philosophical principle of the "land to the tiller" (MOAF 1970, 335-337). Therefore, an analysis of the land reform process in Korea must include both phases of land reform. Since administrative processes are greatly influenced by the political and social environment, this analysis will cover both the political and social forces which influenced the policy planning and the actual implementation of

* Originally Published Vol. 24, No. 10 (October 1984).

Whang In-Joung (Hwang, In-jeong) is President of Kangwon Development Research Institute (KDRI). He obtained his Ph.D. in Economics and Social Development from the University of Pittsburgh in 1968. He has published numerous books and articles including *Economic Transformation of Korea* (1996) and *Gwagamhan gaehyeok-mani yeoksa-reul changjohanda* (Only a Decisive Reform Can Create History) (1998). E-mail: wij@kdri.re.kr.

the land reform programs.

The purpose of this paper is to provide a descriptive analysis of the administrative process directing land reform and the reform's impact on national development in Korea. Specifically, the administration of land reform will be analyzed in terms of: (a) political and economic background; (b) the policies of the land reform programs; (c) reform targets; (d) management processes; (e) organizational apparatus; and (f) reform leadership and environment.[1] The impact of land reform in Korea will be analyzed for its influence on community power structures, agricultural productivity and modernization, national savings, capital formation, income distribution, patriotism, and political development.

The data for this study are drawn primarily from the existing literature, and in part from interviews with former landlords, tenant farmers and government officials involved in the planning and implementation of Korean land reform.

Political and Economic Background of Korean Land Reform

When Korea was liberated from Japanese rule in 1945, it was primarily agrarian, with nearly three-fourths of its population earning their living from farming. Yet the land distribution, or the ownership, prior to 1945 was highly unequal. At one end of the scale, approximately 2.7% owned no land. The bottom 81% of all farm households owned only 10% of the total land (Klein 1958, 84). This disproportionate and concentrated landownership resulted from two major factors: Japanese colonial land policy and the landowners' economic exploitation of tenant farmers.

In 1910, immediately after the fall of the Joseon dynasty, the Japanese colonial government conducted the land survey projects including the measurement of arable land, and the identification and registration of landownership. With very short notice, usually less than thirty days, all Koreans were required to produce documentary evidence—specified by the Japanese colonial government—proving their ownership of the rice

---

1. These middle-range variables are chosen to provide a meaningful base for cross-country comparative study. For the discussion on the uses of middle-range variables, see Etzioni (1961) and Perrow (1970).

paddies, forest land, fishing grounds, and mines. They were also required to install physical landmarks specifying the extent of their land holdings. However, most farmers failed to understand the importance of the land survey, and were not able to prepare the necessary documents within the given period of time. Consequently, many farmers were forced to give up their claims of landownership. The survey, thereby, contributed to the confiscation of Korean land holdings by the Japanese (Yu 1975, 54-64). The end result was that approximately 15% of the total farmland and 60% of all forest land came under Japanese ownership due to unclear evidence of ownership by the time the survey was completed.

As the lands registered under Korean names were often covertly managed by Japanese, the percentage of Japanese controlled land was much higher. In terms of the land value, Japanese owned the predominant portion of the total land value. 120,000 Koreans owned 32% of the total value of assessed land property, while 8,000 Japanese owned 68% (Klein 1958, 85). The dominance of Japanese ownership is demonstrated by the fact that 365 Japanese owned 100 or more *jeongbo* of land, while only 228 Koreans had such large holdings (Yu 1975, 63; *Japanese Colonial Government Bulletin*, February 1919).

The concentration of landownership in the hands of a few landlords accelerated during the period of high tenancy, in which a nationwide average of 60% of the crop was imposed as rent on tenants, in addition to the payment of land taxes on behalf of their landlords (Klein 1970, 85; Cho 1964, 63-66). As a result, the number of tenants increased from 39% of all farming households during 1913-1917 to 56% in 1938 (MOAF 1967, 15). Moreover, the land area in tenancy also expanded from 1.6 million *jeongbo* in 1914 to 2.6 million *jeongbo* in 1938 (Yu 1975, 92).

Both the historically unequal distribution of land and the pressing social and economic needs of the Korean farmers dictated that the USMGK undertake some type of land reform. Indeed, it was an issue of frequent and in-depth debate by political leaders and intellectuals following liberation in 1945. The idea of a comprehensive land reform consistent with the ideology of equal opportunity was predominant among intellectuals and was later incorporated into the Constitution of the Republic of Korea (Lee 1968, 47). The idea was supported by the USMGK from the very beginning and developed into a concrete program of action under the guidance of U.S. State Department economists, such as Burns, Kinney and Anderson (MOAF 1970, 357).

However, despite the rising social pressure for land reform, there emerged an anti-reform movement among landlords. The Koreans with knowledge of English were mostly of the wealthy land-holding class. During this period of "administration by interpreters" under USMGK, therefore, the decisions of the American officials were greatly influenced by the English speaking elite—many of whom had collaborated with the Japanese and somehow eluded the postwar initiatives to punish all "collaborators and traitors" (Cho 1964, 60-63; Mitchell 1949, 37-40). The members of the land-holding class also exercised their influence on the policymaking process through other channels, including the National Assembly, local governments, and the newly founded political parties. On the other hand, many landlords sold their land to their tenants in an attempt to reap profits before the mandatory reallocation of landownership.

Thus, in spite of the strong popular demand for land reform immediately after World War II, anti-reform forces led by the landlords deliberately delayed and hindered the enactment of land reform. Their political power was based on higher education, knowledge, wealth, organization, and very strong motivation to protect their interests. As seen from this perspective, the land reforms of 1948 and 1949 were the products of a bargaining process between two conflicting social forces: one representing the majority of farmers favoring land reform and the other representing the land-holding minority (Yu 1975, 168-169).

Outline of the Land Reform Programs

Redistribution of "Japanese-owned Farmland"

The first phase of land reform was activated in March 1948, more than two years after the liberation of August 1945. Farmlands formerly owned by the Japanese were acquired by USMGK through Sinhan Gongsa, a public corporation established in February 1946 to manage "Japanese-owned" farmland. The land area administered by this corporation constitutes 282,000 jeongbo, or 13% of the total farmland in South Korea at the time. 554,000 farmers worked the land as tenants of the corporation (Rhee 1980, 325). In 1948, according to Ordinance No. 173 of the USMGK, dated on 22 March, all vested land formerly owned by the Japanese and transferred to USMGK was to be distributed by the newly established National Land Administration (NLA), which took over the properties owned by Sinhan Gongsa. The NLA then began to sell the lands to Koreans in the following manner:

(1) The vested land was to be sold to its present tenants. Priority was given to those who had actually cultivated the land as tenants as of 1 March 1948, and who wished to purchase it. Each tenant was allowed to purchase up to two *jeongbo* of land.

(2) The land price was to be equivalent to 300% of the average annual yield of the land, and was to be paid in fifteen annual installments in kind.[2]

(3) The NLA was to continue to extend production credit and family emergency credit at low interest rates to the tiller-purchasers and also to continue assisting them with the land improvement (Klein 1958, 89-90).

(4) The Vested Land Management Special Account was opened as a separate bookkeeping system designed to properly manage the payments from new landowners and to control land improvement expenditures.[3]

The Land Reform Act of 1949

The Land Reform Act was promulgated by the South Korean government in June 1949 in order to institutionally change the land tenure system. This act was based on Article 86 of the Constitution of the Republic of Korea, which reads:

Farmland shall be distributed to self-tilling farmers. The method of distribution, the extent of possession and the nature and restrictions of farmland ownership shall be determined by law.

Thus, the "land to the tillers" principle was incorporated into the Constitution and the old exploitative form of tenancy became unconstitutional. The land reform enactment was accompanied by two additional presidential decrees on regulation of land commission and application of the land reform law. The objectives of land reform were, as described by

---

2. By the Land Reform Act of 1949, the price of vested land was to be based on the same criteria as the price of Korean-owned land—150% of the annual product to be paid in five annual installments in kind (BOK 1955, 69).

3. This was incorporated into the Land Reform Special Account in 1952 (BOK 1955, 69).

the act, to improve farm living conditions, to balance the national economy, and to increase agricultural productivity. Furthermore, the farmland reform was expected to contribute to social and political stability (which was rendered vulnerable by constant communist propaganda), to the mitigation of class conflicts, to the creation of owner-farmers, and to overall agricultural modernization (KLERC 1966, 77-79). The important features of the act were:

1) The government was to acquire all tenanted lands and the portion of any farm over three *jeongbo*, even if owned by a self-tilling farmer. Therefore, land subject to government purchase for resale to tenants included:
   (a) farmland owned by those who were not farming households;
   (b) farmland which was not personally tilled by the owners;
   (c) the portion of farmland which exceeded the ownership limit provided by the act (three *jeongbo*); and
   (d) nonperennial plantations owned by a person who also personally operated more than three *jeongbo* of perennial plantations, such as orchards, nurseries, and mulberry fields (Pak 1956, 72-73).

2) The compensation to be paid for the farmlands was to be fixed by each city, town, or township land commission at the rate of 150% of the average annual yield of the farmland. The principle of "progressive diminution" was to be applied: the larger the area owned by one family, the lower the rate of paid compensation. The compensation was made in kind by the government in negotiable land bonds to be paid in five annual installments. Cash payments were to be made annually to each landlord at the government confirmed market price, or 30% of the standard or expected annual yield of the land.

3) The farmlands so purchased by the government were to be resold at the same price to the farmers. The order of priority was to be given to:
   (a) the present tillers;
   (b) farmers capable of cultivating more land than what they then actually possessed;
   (c) the families of patriots who had died in their struggle against the Japanese colonizer, if they have experience in farming;
   (d) farm laborers; and
   (e) farm households repatriated from foreign countries, such as Manchuria and Japan.

The distribution of the farmland was to depend on the farming potential of each household, but no household could receive more than three *jeongbo*. The payments were to be made to the government in five annual installments either in cash or in kind as specified by the government. Prior to the payment of all installments, the land so acquired could not be purchased, sold, donated, mortgaged, leased, or cultivated by another farm family.

4) Refusal to comply with, the violation of, or an act of deceit in relation to the law, was to result in the confiscation of land without compensation and the forfeiture of a tenant's right of cultivation, as well as payment of large fines by involved parties.

5) The disposition or donation of non-self-cultivated lands was prohibited, unless the transfer was made to educational, charitable, or other public organizations. Transfer or deprivation of the tenancy right was also prohibited.

All of these provisions were desirable. In land-poor, overpopulated South Korea, there simply was no justification for absentee ownership (Klein 1958, 94-95). The provisions concerning compensation of landlords, however, were rather generous. Landlords were to receive special or additional compensation for reclaimed lands acquired by the government for resale to the tenants. This special compensation was to take into account all of their net costs (gross costs less government subsidies) plus another 10%, in compensation of their entrepreneurial function. Furthermore, the principle of progressive diminution of the rate of payment was not to be applied to such land. In addition, all landlords—those selling reclaimed or non-reclaimed land—might have been permitted to purchase or participate in the purchase of government-owned commercial and industrial properties to the extent of the full value of the compensation for their land. This provision tended to channel capital from the rural areas into the industrial and commercial enterprises which would benefit the economy of South Korea the most.

One provision which detracted from the efficacy of the law was the required payment of an extremely high fee to appeal the decision of a lower-level land commission to a higher-level land commission. Therefore, only the wealthiest in the rural areas could afford to appeal the decision of lower-level land commission. Because of the high cost of appeal, the decisions of the lower-level land commissions stood as the final call for the poorer peasantry, but were not final for the wealthier landholders (Klein 1958, 99-100).

Land Reform Targets

The philosophy and the guidelines described in the USMGK Ordinance of 1948 and the Land Reform Act of 1949 clearly define the target land to be acquired and resold. Therefore, the hypothetical target land area is easily estimated in Table 1. However, the implementation of land reform would require more specific information about the land areas, status of tenancy, beneficiary farmers, and landownership in order to enable the surrender of any land to the government. Furthermore, because of the delay in the enactment of land reform, the statistical data reflecting the immediate post-1945 land tenure system could not serve as actual target figures for administrative purposes.

Table 1. Land Areas and Farm Households under Tenancy
(as of the end of 1945)

	Land Area[a] (1,000 *jeongbo*)	Farm Households[b] (1,000 households)
Japanese-owned land under tenancy (A)	230 (282)[c]	554[d]
Korean-owned land under tenancy (B)	1,240	882[e]
Sub-total (A+B)	1,470 (63%)	1,436 (70%)
Total (South Korea)	2,320 (100%)	2,041 (100%)

Sources: a. BOK (1948), pp. 1-29.
       b. BOK (1948), pp. 1-375.
       c. Including non-farmland, estimated as of February 1946, see MOAF (1970), p. 352.
       d. As of February 1946, see MOAF (1970), p. 340.
       e. Residual number because statistics as of 1945 were not available.

When the USMGK initiated the reform of Japanese-owned land in 1948, NLA had been managing 282 *jeongbo* of land tilled by 554,000 contracted tenants. These figures, therefore, were naturally incorporated into the targets for the land redistribution program by USMGK. However, when Syngman Rhee government initiated the land reform five years later, necessary information for implementing land reform was lacking due to considerable socioeconomic changes that had already taken place. Therefore, it was necessary to conduct a broad farm household survey for land reform during the period from May to December in 1949, through the local government channels. Each farm household was required to answer a questionnaire, which sought to determine the total land area under cultivation, extent of ownership, status of tenancy, annual yields, and family size. Landlords were also required to provide information regarding their land holdings (MOAF 1970, 494-495). The survey ran into much difficulties with false reporting, secret sales contracts (often forced by the landlords upon ignorant tenants who were unaware of the land reform programs), misunderstanding of the survey's purpose, and rumors created by landlords to favor their interests. All the above factors contributed to the distortion of the survey results (Yu 1975, 109-119).

Through this survey, approximately 601,000 *jeongbo* of farmland (equivalent to 29% of the total farmland) became subject to the government acquisition for resale to tenants and landless farmers. The number of beneficiaries was estimated to be more than one million farm households, which was equivalent to 42% of the total farming households in South Korea (MOAF 1970, 495). Hence, there was a large discrepancy between the survey data and the statistics shown in Table 1. The difference implied that a considerable portion of land owned by the landlords had already been sold to the tenants through privately and secretly arranged contracts. In addition, more farmers than actually eligible claimed eligibility as land reform beneficiaries. Indeed, the statistical data regarding target land, beneficiary farmers, and landlords were inconsistent and unreliable. The fact that land reform was carried out, in spite of these problems, indicates that the operational definition of the major concepts involved in the land reform was not essential to the successful implementation of institutional reform.

Land Reform Management

The redistribution of Japanese-owned land was relatively easy, mainly because only the government and contracted tenants were involved in the process, and because written documents were available to help speed up the actual change of ownership in most cases.

However, the redistribution of the Korean-owned land was much more complicated. The process involved a delicate balancing of the interests of three different parties. As the Land Reform Act included the indirect transfer of land from owners to the tillers through the government, and did not allow direct transfer of ownership between the two, the land reform administration had four crucial tasks:

1) The physical redistribution of land, including the acquisition and resale of land by the government;
2) The management of financial transactions in the government's purchase and resale of land with differential parties, including the issuance of land bonds, the transfer of funds to the landowners, and the collection of payments from the new landowners;
3) The adjudication of disputes over land boundaries and inheritance rights over land transactions; and
4) The management of post-reform agricultural assistance services, including off-farm income support, credits and other assistance.

The most critical part, however, was indeed the physical redistribution of land. It involved the following:

(a) Identifying the specific pieces of land subject to redistribution;
(b) Initiating changes in tenancy rights through government land purchase from landlords;
(c) Identifying specific beneficiary farmers and tenants who were to purchase land from the government through the land redistribution; and
(d) Issuing the land titles and enforcing the contracts.

Organizational Apparatus

Who were the involved and responsible parties for the land reform management process? How did they work together to complete each task? In the first phase of the vested land reform, the administrative apparatus was rather simple. Immediately after World War II, Sinhan Gongsa was established to take over the formerly Japanese-owned land. The corporation engaged in tenancy contracts with tillers through its six regional branches. In March 1948, the NLA replaced Sinhan Gongsa. Because the redistribution program of vested land simply involved the land resale contracts with the tenants, the NLA and its branch offices could manage the land redistribution program without much support from local government (MOAF 1970, 339-345). The NLA was reorganized in 1949 as the Bureau of Vested Land Management under the Ministry of Agriculture and Forestry (MOAF).

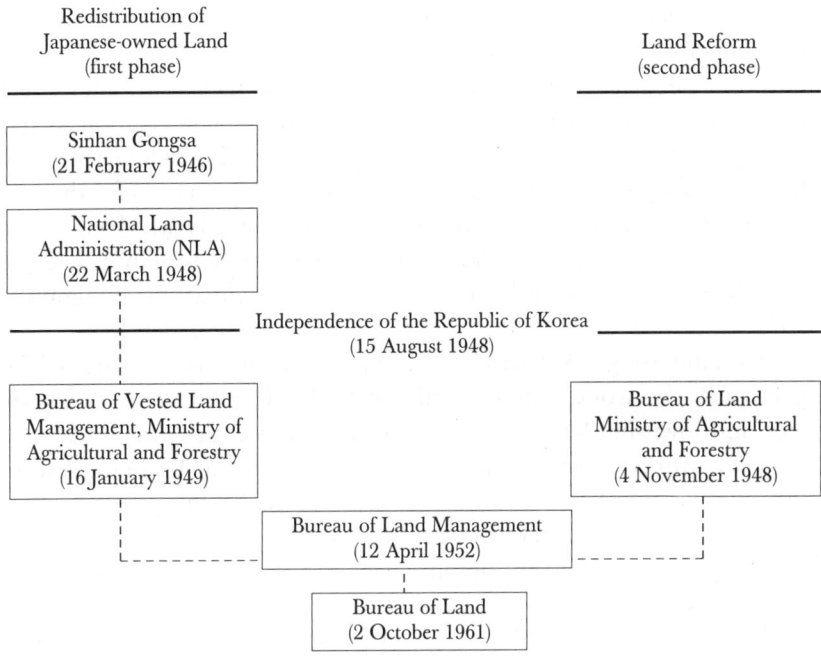

Source: MOAF (1970), p. 353.

Figure 1. Land reform organizations at the central level

In the implementation of the land reform's second phase, however, three major governmental groups were involved in the process of land purchase, resale, transfer of title, and compensation. They were the central government agencies, local governments, and land commissions. As shown in Figure 1, there were two bureaus under MOAF, one of which managed the first phase of land reform—the redistribution of Japanese-owned land—and the other, which ran the second phase—the government purchase and resale of Korean-owned land. But in April 1952, when the physical redistribution of land was almost completed, the two bureaus merged into one as the Bureau of Land Management. The Bureau of Land Management was responsible for making basic policy guidelines with respect to identifying the target land for government purchase, specific beneficiaries, determination of land values, and management of annual installment payments in the implementation process of land reform and in the post-reform land improvement services.

Accordingly, corresponding divisions and sections were set up in local governments at all levels. Discretionary powers were delegated to local governments, particularly with respect to identifying specific land target lands and beneficiaries, enforcing contracts and documentation, determining land prices in terms of annual coverage yields, issuing the land bonds, cashing the bonds, and providing accounting services for the central government. The local officials were also directly involved in the transfer of landownership. This decentralization of land reform had the extra benefit of making local administration more efficient (Montgomery 1972, 65).

One interesting managerial arrangement was the use of para-official personnel who worked closely with local officials, particularly at the village and township levels. This arrangement was made through Decree No. 275, which stated that land commissions were to be organized on five administrative levels: (a) the national level, (b) the provincial and Seoul city level, (c) the county, city and district (of Seoul) level, (d) the township (rural) and town (urban) level, and (e) the village or sub-town level.

The chairmanships of the town and township and higher-level land commissions were to be assumed by local government heads. The members of the commissions were to be appointed " . . . among impartial and unselfish officials and private citizens of good repute and knowledge." One half of the private citizens on the land commissions at the district (of Seoul), city, county, town, and township levels were required to be former landholders with land to be purchased, and the other half had to be those who would receive land.

Although land reform commissions at various levels were to be organized along the guidelines suggested by Decree No. 275, there was no evidence of such implementations. As was the case in the implementation of the program for the sale of vested land, no supervisory or "watchdog" mechanism was set up. Only at the town and township levels did a "reexamination" of the work done at the lower levels take place. In view of the proximity of the commissions at these two levels, it would have been more effective to assign this function to a higher level (i.e., the county or city) so that this process could take place without the elements of personality, personal friendship, or shared interests influencing the results. Why, if landowners were going to lose their land, was it necessary to give them equal representation with the tenants who were going to gain under the program? This question is especially pertinent to the operation of the lower-level commissions, where intensity and speed in the enforcement of the program were essential for success (Klein 1958, 98).

The most critical role of the land distribution administration was performed by the township land commission and the village commission. The township commission's eight members were responsible for providing advisory services to the township head on the following issues:

(a) Reexamination of appeals from the lower-level land commissions;
(b) Review of compensation rates for acquired land;
(c) Physical rearrangement of land plots, if necessary; and
(d) Protection of land after the land reform.

The village land commission's seven members would be responsible for identifying specific land to be acquired, naming owners and beneficiaries, and for services related to the protection of land after the reform.

While specific land to be purchased by the government for redistribution was identified mostly by land commissions, the portions of land exceeding three *jeongbo* were left out to be identified by the landlords themselves. These landlords had the privilege of choosing which of the land they would retain, up to three *jeongbo*. This arrangement benefited the landlords since they certainly chose their best land; indeed, there could be little reason to do otherwise. Why did the village or township commissions not assign land to these landlords which would have been representative of the average quality of their land holdings rather than allow them to select personally the very best lots? This procedure of self-selection by the landlords was neither based on economic considerations neither on political necessity (Klein 1958, 99).

In short, the use of local commissions under the local community leadership made less use of any professional bureaucracy and began to have permanent authority over one or more administrative aspects of land reform (Montgomery 1972, 66). Through local commissions, the beneficiaries certainly had opportunities to participate in the decision-making process of land reform administration.

As for the adjudication of disputes arising from land reform, local land commissions and courts functioned as the major judicial organizations. Disputes were arbitrated by the local commission in proper courts and failure to comply with the provisions of the Land Reform Act was punished. Violators were fined a maximum of one million won ($12.25

at that time) and the court could confiscate their land or take away their right to cultivate the land.

As the long-term success of the land reform depended on improvements in agricultural productivity and modernization, the post-reform administration played a crucial role in the land reform process. MOAF had the primary responsibility for post-reform policies and services, such as land improvement, irrigation, agricultural credit, pesticides, fertilizers, extension services, and other input management.

Although there were many local irrigation management associations, due to a fund shortage their role was extremely limited during the immediate post-land reform period. Since 1952, when the government set up the Land Improvement Program Special Account using the proceeds from sales of vested lands and counterpart funds generated from foreign aid, a series of agricultural improvement programs was organized. Extensive irrigation projects, farmland improvement, and drought protection measures were further strengthened after the establishment of the Federation of Farmland Improvement Association in 1961, which increased the effectiveness of the irrigation associations (NACF 1965, 103-108).

Agricultural credit for the purchase of fertilizer, machinery, and other farming tools was indeed crucial for improving the agricultural productivity of the new owner-tillers, especially as they were suffering from the heavy burden of annual installment payments for the newly-distributed land. The first agricultural credit organization was the Agricultural Finance Associations, continued from the Japanese colonialists. After 1949, when the government first released funds generated by Industrial Rehabilitation Bonds, the associations only provided short-term credit to farmers. Their credit function was gradually expanded through the supply of government funds in the Land Improvement Program Special Account in 1952. The Agricultural Finance Associations later developed into the government-owned Korea Agricultural Bank which was in operation from 1959 until 1961 when it was incorporated into the National Agricultural Cooperative Federation. The major funding sources for agricultural credit during the 1950s were the counterpart funds, proceeds from vested land sales, Industrial Rehabilitation Bonds, and several other government sources (NACF 1965, 354-360).

The Agricultural Technical Institute was founded under MOAF in 1949 to provide agricultural extension services and to conduct research and development in farming technology, but it was not until 1953 that its branch offices at the township level began to operate. In 1957 this organization was renamed the Office of Agriculture, and in 1961 became the Office of Rural Development. Since then agricultural extension services in Korea have been well developed in terms of structure and efficiency (NACF 1965, 432-446). MOAF itself became responsible for other agricultural inputs such as fertilizer, machinery, and pesticides after the land reform. However, the ministry did not become effective in providing or supervising these services of the agricultural cooperatives until the mid-1960s (NACF 1965, 122-131). In brief, although all major agricultural input services formerly provided by the landlords were to be carried out by the government, the actual level of government services during the initial period after the land reform (1953-1961) was lower than the level of same services provided in the 1930s (Ban et al. 1980, 293).

When all the preliminary stages of land reform, including the farm household survey and the promulgation of supporting decrees, were completed in the early 1950s, MOAF constructed a timetable for the implementation of land reform (Land Reform Act of 1949; Cho 1964, 90):

April 30, 1950:
Information on the land to be distributed is to be disseminated to all parties involved (i.e., landlords, tenants, land commissions, and government officials). The purchase and sale price of the farmlands is to be established.

May 30, 1950:
Reports are to be made to those landlords selling their land to the government so that they can be given land bonds for the land.

June/July, 1950:
Adjustments are to be made, and all disputes concerning the purchase and sale of land are to be settled.

December 31, 1954:
Cashing land bonds issued to the landlords and collecting the payment of annual installments by tenant-purchasers must be completed.

About two months after the reform administration got started, however, the Korean War broke out. This delayed the land reform, and the government purchase of land and resale did not begin until January 1951.

Land Reform Leadership[4] and Environment

Except for the financial settlements, the entire program of land reform was implemented during the Korean War and was completed by August 1952. This demonstrates a strong commitment of the newly established government to the land reform and hence it is worthy of special attention. Indeed, a competent and committed leadership was a critical determinant in the successful implementation of any major institutional reform.

The reform was under the leadership of President Syngman Rhee, a man of upper class origin who was educated in a Protestant missionary school in Seoul during his childhood, and who was once a young reformist in the Dongnip Hyeophoe (Independence Club), one of the major Korean political groups seeking modernization (Lee 1968, 79). Hence, upon assuming the presidency, his reformist orientation might have been the source of the government's genuine commitment to the land reform administration in midst of the war. This commitment might also have resulted from the necessity of land reform for the collection of crops to be supplied to the Korean Army during the war. Thus, in October 1950, after the North Korean forces had been driven back, President Rhee announced that the land tenure reform would be resumed in South Korea, and that the first of the five annual payments in kind was to be made by the tenant-purchasers in the fall of 1951 as planned.

President Rhee's motivation and zeal for the nation-building programs in the early days of the Republic were consistent with the policies initiated by USMGK and supported by the intellectuals working with the U.S. State Department. Although the Syngman Rhee administration was characteristic of a coalition government in its incorporation of a broad spectrum of political groups (ranging from conservative nationalists to non-communist socialists), the cabinet was dominated by the bourgeoisie who spoke strongly for the interests of the landlord class (Rhee 1980, 327-328). The only exception was Jo Bong-am, minister of agriculture, who was a well-known socialist. Minister Jo had laid the groundwork for the land reform. He initiated the draft of the Land Reform Act and lobbied for its enactment from the very beginning of the newly independent Republic in 1948. Returning to the National Assembly after the reorga-

---

4. The analytical framework of this variable is that of Esman (1972, 159-182).

nization of the cabinet, he continued to push for land reform throughout the whole process of the enactment.

The idea of land reform was supported by leading conservative intellectuals who understood the strategic advantages of land reform and its potential to mitigate the communist-agitated social unrest and to contribute to nation-building. In addition, because Korea had only recently been freed from colonial "landlordism," both the common public sentiment and the guilty conscience of the Korean upper class contributed to a political environment heavily in favor of land reform. Therefore, the Korean landholders could not openly resist the process of land reform but could only indirectly influence the process in ways designed to protect their own interests as much as possible.

Therefore, the combination of the support of the USMGK, the political ideology and doctrine of the new Korean government, a reformist leadership, and political circumstances allowed the government to introduce a program of relatively "comprehensive reform" (Lee 1970, 17-18).

The Impact of Land Reform

Physical Consequence of Land Reform

In the first phase of land reform, approximately 245,000 *jeongbo* or 87% of the total Japanese-owned land was distributed to 596,000 farm households (equivalent to 38% of all Korean farmers) at the end of 1952. During the six-month period from March to September 1948, all land sales to tenants were completed, and 183,000 *jeongbo* of land previously owned by 505 farmers were sold. Out of the total available land for NLA sale, only 7,000 *jeongbo* were still unsold as of September 1948, and the rest were in the process of being sold or were tied up in legal disputes (Klein 1958, 102-103). The tenants' desire to purchase the land was overwhelming. The NLA's sale of vested land to its tenants took place on a considerably larger scale than the Korean-owned land redistribution, and had better results. Such efficiency is probably the result of smooth cooperation between the government (NLA) and tenant-purchasers without the landlords' involvement.

In the case of the Korean-owned land reform, however, the land redistribution program was complicated by the different interests of the three parties. Many years of inaction and delay on the part of an unstable government had encouraged the landowners to act in their own interests. Their main concern had been to find the means to dispose of their ten-anted land before the government could come up with a viable land reform program, and they thought that privately negotiated land sales might prove to be more lucrative than the government-imposed sales. This resulted in a very active trading in the free land market during the period between 1945 and 1951 (Cho 1964, 91-92).

Therefore, despite the fact that the government succeeded in enforcing the land reform program even during the Korean War, a considerable portion of the land had already been privately redistributed. Out of 601,000 *jeongbo* of land identified by the preliminary land holding survey of 1949, a total of 332,000 *jeongbo* of farmland had been distributed to 915,000 tenant-tillers by 1954. Discounting the small portion of land in the process of distribution or tied up in legal disputes, approximately 204,000 *jeongbo* of land must have been sold by the landlords directly to the tenants in a free market or in other disguised ways during the period between 1949 and 1953 (Pak 1956, 81). The amount of privately trans-ferred land could be as high as 700,000 *jeongbo* during the entire period from 1945 to 1953 (Cho 1964, 92).[5] It is also possible for some land holdings to escape from the reform enforcement through the disguised transfer of landownership to their relatives (KLERC 1966, 94).

The administrative target of the land area to be distributed by the two government programs was 834,000 *jeongbo* (including the vested land), or approximately 40% of the total arable land in South Korea. The total land area actually redistributed was only 577,000 *jeongbo*, or 69% of the target. When Korea was liberated in 1945, however, the total land area available for redistribution through land reform was theoretically 1,470,000 *jeongbo*. Therefore, the land area reformed by the government programs was only 42% of the total farmland to be redistributed through land reform.

Improvement in the Land Tenure System

The "land to the tillers" reform certainly succeeded in reducing the power of the landlords and rich owner-farmers by redistributing the land

---

5. However, another estimate of the private sale is 573,000 *jeongbo* (Ban et al. 1980, 286).

to the actual cultivators and reducing the land holdings to less than three *jeongbo*. Through these two land reform programs, approximately 1.5 million farmers (70% of the total farm households) received land to become owner-tillers. As shown in Table 2, about 50% of the farmers who did not own land under the tenancy system became landowners, and other partial tenants also received additional land formerly owned by the landlords (Cho 1964, 93).

The land reform, with its more egalitarian distribution of land, also changed the mode of land cultivation. The percentage of the tenant-operated land in the total farmland decreased from 65% in 1945 to 2% in 1952 as shown in Table 3.

Therefore, the land reform introduced the owner-tiller farming system. Tenants and half-tenants were legally free independent farmers. However, it was difficult for most of them to establish themselves as financially independent farmers without special governmental protection. With the increased financial burdens and vulnerability, new owner-

Table 2. Distributions of Farmland Ownership, 1944 and 1956

Period	% of Household	% of Farmland	Area per Household (ha.)
Pre-reform (1944)	48.6	0.0	0.0
	48.5	36.6	0.8
	2.9	63.4	26.0
Post-reform (1956)	42.8	17.6	0.3
	51.1	64.8	1.1
	6.1	17.6	2.6

Source: Cho (1964), p. 94; BOK (1948), pp. 1-29; and KAB (1959), pp. 1-63.

Table 3. Owner-operated Area vs. Tenant-operated Area

(1,000 *jeongbo*)

Year	Owner-operated	Tenant-operated (B)	Total (A)	% (B/A)
1945	778	1,447	2,226	65
1949	1,240	847	2,087	40
1952	2,044	43	2,087	2

Source: Pak (1956), p. 81.

farmers had to rely on loans. Because the main private source of farm loans was money-lenders whose interest rates were extremely high, small owner-farmers began to suffer from a new form of exploitation. As a result, a high percentage of small farmers delayed their land payments and some of them sold their lot, becoming tenant farmers once again (Pak 1956, 123-135; Bak 1980, 8-43). Nevertheless, the land reform significantly changed rural life. Centuries-old traditions of feudalistic land-lordism had been destroyed and many farmers began to enjoy the status of free independent farmers. Both the size of farms and the standard of living increased from what they were during the Japanese occupation.

Perhaps the most important result of the land reform was the establishment of a more egalitarian rural society. During the initial period after the land reform, the mutual interactions between the former landlords and tenants continued to follow traditional lines. However, the second generation witnessed a breakdown of these values, and former owners and tenants tended to perceive each other as close neighbors who shared common interests. This change in perception provided a basis for cooperation among village members which contributed to the success of the Saemaeul undong (New Community Movement), the Korean version of integrated rural development in the 1970s (Whang 1981, 250-251).

Agricultural Modernization and Economic Development

In comparing the farm household composition by the size of land under cultivation before and after the land reform, it is revealed that the percentage of households farming less than one *jeongbo* increased from 75% in 1947 to 79% in 1953 (Table 4). In other words, the land reform contributed to the fragmentation of farmland in Korea. The deterioration of the agricultural economy during the Korean War and natural disasters in 1952 further accelerated the subdivision of farmland. The recent decline in small farms is not the result of the land reform but of the migration of marginal farmers to urban areas (Ban et al. 1980, 297).

It seems that the three *jeongbo* clause of the land reform "was of little assistance in making the landless tenant farmers become independent farmers. If the ceiling had been set at four *jeongbo* instead of three, most holdings of the self-tilling farmers would have been unaffected by the law" (Cho 1964, 86).

From the viewpoint of economies of scale, the fragmentation of farm

Table 4. Farm Households by Category of Farm Size under Cultivation

Category of Farm	1945	1947	1951	1953	190	1970	1973
under 0.5 *jeongbo* (A)	72.1	42.2	42.7	44.9	42.9	31.6	32.4
0.5–1.0 *jeongbo* (B)		33.3	35.8	34.2	30.1	31.7	31.5
1.0–2.0 *jeongbo* (C)	23.8	18.8	17.1	16.5	20.7	25.8	26.3
2.0–3.0 *jeongbo* (D)		5.3	4.2	4.3	6.0	5.0	4.8
3.0 *jeongbo* and over (E)	4.1	1.4	0.1	0.1	0.3	1.5	1.5
non-crop farms	–	–	–	–	–	4.4	3.5
Total farm household	100	199	100	100	100	100	100
(A+B)	72.1	75.5	78.5	79.1	73.0	63.3	63.9

Source: Pak (1956), p. 82; MAF (1974), pp. 28-29.

units did not lead to the development of commercial farming or agricultural modernization. Small farmers had little possibility of purchasing new tools, livestock, fertilizers or pesticides in order to increase farm productivity. The small size of the farms kept many farmers at the subsistence level, unable to accumulate savings after payment of annual installments for the newly purchased land. Furthermore, the farmers tended to consume more of their own product than ever before, and rural savings dropped to a record low (Cho 1964, 96). No longer bound by the severe demands of the landlords, and feeling the pressures of a population increase, the farmers had to retain a larger share of the farm output for personal use than they did under tenancy.

Because many independent factors influenced the agricultural productivity, such as weather, fertilizer, insecticides, irrigation, drainage, and farming technology, it is difficult to measure the improvement in agricultural productivity solely attributable to the land reform. The improvement, if any, might have resulted from the increased level of motivation under owner-farming and through the hard work of the new owners. Indeed, agricultural productivity during the period of 1953-1961 grew at 3.6% a year, well over the 2.9% growth in the 1930s (Ban et al. 1980, 291).

According to interviews with eighty-five farmers who had been cultivating since the pre-reform period, however, the contribution of the motivational factor to the overall productivity increase was minimal. The farmers pointed to the increased use of chemical fertilizers and pesticides, and improved farming techniques as the major factors behind the productivity increase after the land reform (KLERC 1976, 105-107).

It was also expected that the land reform would provide an opportunity for the movement of capital out of agriculture and into modern industries. Because of only partial payment of the government land bonds and the decreasing value of the bonds in the inflation-ridden economy, however, the excess rural capital gradually evaporated over time and was not transformed into industrial capital. Of those landlords who did invest in industrial business, most of them experienced failure due to poor managerial skills.

In spite of the short-run disadvantages and negative effects of the land reform, it certainly had a significantly positive impact on both rural communities and the national economy. Rural farmers, though suffering from the financial hardship of annual installment payments, contributed greatly to the national savings and capital formation by developing human capital through the education of their children (Bak 1980, 5-10; Ban et al. 1980, 310-314). Agricultural productivity during the 1960s and 1970s tended to increase as a result of improved farm technology accumulated through highly motivated owner-farming, with the assistance of extension services provided by the government.

When the land reform was introduced, farmland was Korea's largest capital asset. The redistribution of land greatly increased the equality of opportunity and popular access to this productive asset. Therefore, both the land reform and the increase in public education fostered the development of and equal access to the two major factors of production: land and knowledge. The redistribution of land promoted rapid economic growth and increasing social equity in Korea (Singer 1980, 8-9). In other words, the land reform definitely had positive outcomes in the long run, such as the improvement in farm technology and agricultural productivity, equitable distribution of income, and dynamic change in rural communities, which all contributed to rapid economic growth and modernization.

Social and Political Development

The land reform also contributed considerably to the post-liberation political stability. As tenants became free of the feudalistic ties of the traditional rural society, their political and social awareness increased. The improvement in both the economic and social status of farmers indeed provided a basis for equal participation and cooperation among village members and promoted further development of grass-roots democracy. Rural attitudes toward the state became more positive. The patriotic devotion which motivated rural youth to fight against the North Korean invasion might have been rooted in a changed perception of their society, democratic institutions, communities, and land brought about by successful land reform.

The land reform caused significant changes in the community power structures. Former landlords were no longer as powerful in the rural communities and all village members began to share a sense of relative equality and sought to claim equal opportunities and rights. As the difference between "haves" and "have-nots" within the villages decreased, farmers came to recognize their common interests with regard to community issues. It was this type of shared identity among rural dwellers which became the basis for the community participation and cooperation among farmers.

It is more important to note that the land reform provided a conceptual basis for cooperation, self-help and participation, which in turn contributed to the success of the New Community Movement in the 1970s (Whang 1981, 251) and also paved an avenue toward grass-roots democracy in the long run (Whang 1984). However, it should also be noted that it took almost one generation following the land reform to effectively bring about the change of farmers' perceptions—among both the previous landlords and the tenant farmers—toward real cooperation and participation with respect to community action programs. The change of farmers' perception and attitudes stimulated by the land reform eventually expedited the take-off from the tradition-bounded agrarian society toward self-reliant rural development in the 1970s.

Summary and Conclusions

Like everything else in the post-liberation period, the politics of land reform in Korea were complex and confusing. The U.S. Military Government in Korea, unfamiliar with Korean ways and the native Koreans lacking experience in self-government, sought to formulate a coherent land reform program in a chaotic political environment. In essence, land reform in Korea became a product of a political bargaining process between reformist liberal and entrenched conservative forces. In spite of an apparent show of positive unanimity to the idea of land reform, there was a strong undercurrent of resistance determined to protect the interests of the landlords. While the political and social environment after the liberation from Japanese rule strongly favored a vigorous and comprehensive land reform program, conservative resistance delayed the initial enactment of the land reform, distorted the effect of its implementation and reduced its overall efficiency. Thus, the actual area of land redistributed under the government programs made up only 19% of the total farmland in South Korea. However, if one includes the land area privately sold in order to avoid forced redistribution, the land reform movement certainly caused a far-reaching change in the pattern of landownership in Korea.

The administrative power charged with implementing the government land reform program was decentralized by granting discretionary powers to the local governments. Nonprofessional para-bureaucratic personnel were utilized by local governments throughout the organization of local land commissions enabled the collection of fair and specific information required by the land reform administration and provided a forum for popular participation in the nation-wide reform administration. These innovative arrangements indeed made the land reform administration in Korea successful in spite of various difficulties. The administrative leadership under Syngman Rhee and his political party gave the land reform movement enough strength and direction to carry out its objectives even during the Korean War.

The immediate results of land reform were the destruction of the centuries-old feudalistic land tenure system and the establishment of an owner-farming system. The short-term impact of the land reform on agricultural productivity, farm modernization, and rural savings tended to be rather negative. The fragmentation of farmland still impedes the growth of Korean agriculture, and is the target of future structural adjustment policies designed to cope with industrial modernization. However, the long-term benefits of the land reform are enormous: an increase in agricultural productivity through improved farm technology, human capital formation through the education of farm children, and an equitable distribution of income through relatively equal access to land. The egalitarian distribution of landownership indeed provided a social foundation for the cooperation and participation of farmers in the Saemaeul rural development drive in the 1970s. Although the land reform failed to contribute to the formation of industrial capital in the short run, the acquisition of industrial assets formerly owned by the Japanese eventually led to the emergence of a new class of industrialists. It can be concluded that the land reform, in part, provided a base for Korea's rapid economic "growth with equity" during the 1960s and 1970s.

REFERENCES

Ban, Sung Hwan, Moon Pal-lyong, and Dwight Perkins. 1980. *Rural Development.* Cambridge: Harvard University Press.

Bak, Jin-hwan. 1980. "Nongeop munje" (Agricultural Problems). Korea Agricultural Cooperative College, mimeo.

Bank of Korea (BOK). 1948. *Joseon gyeongje yeonbo* (Korean Economic Yearbook). Seoul: Bank of Korea.

_____. 1955. *Gyeongje yeon-gam 1955* (Economic Yearbook 1955). Seoul: Bank of Korea.

Cho, Jae Hong. 1964. "Post-1945 Land Reforms and Their Consequences in South Korea." Ph.D. diss., Indiana University.

Esman, Milton. 1972. *Administration and Development in Malaysia.* Ithaca: Cornell University Press.

Etzioni, Amitai. 1961. *A Comparative Analysis of Complex Organization.* New York: Free Press.

Klein, Sidney. 1958. *The Pattern of Land Tenure Reform in East Asia after World War II.* New York: Bookman Associate Inc.

Korea Agricultural Bank (KAB). 1959. *Nongeop yeonbo* (Agricultural Yearbook). Seoul: KAB.

Korea Land Economics Research Center (KLERC). 1966. *A Study of Land Tenure System in Korea.* Seoul: KLERC.

Lee, Hahn Been. 1968. *Korea: Time, Change and Administration.* Honolulu, Hawaii: East-West Center Press.

Lee, Hahn Been, and Abelardo G. Samonte, eds. 1970. *Administrative Reform in Asia.* Manila: Eastern Regional Organization for Public Administration (EROPA).

Ministry of Agriculture and Fisheries (MOAF). 1967. *Nongji jedo-ui gaehwang* (Outline of Land Tenure System). Seoul: MOAF.

_____. 1970. *Nongji gaehyeok sa* (The History of Land Reform). Seoul: MOAF.

_____. 1974. *Yearbook of Agriculture and Fisheries Statistics.* Seoul: MOAF.

Mitchell, C. C. 1949. "Land Management and Tenancy Reform in Korea under the U.S. Army Occupation." Ph.D. diss., Harvard University.

Montgomery, John. 1972. "Allocation of Authority in Land Reform Programs. A Comparative Study of Administrative Procedures and Outputs." *Administrative Science Quarterly*: 62-75.

National Agricultural Cooperative Federation (NACF). 1965. *Hanguk nongjeong ishim nyeon* (Twenty Years of Agricultural Administration in Korea). Seoul: NACF.

O, Ho-seong. 1981. *Gyeongje baljeon-gwa nongji jedo* (Economic Development and Land System). Seoul: Korea Rural Economic Institute.

Pak, Ki-hyuk. 1956. "Economic Analysis of Land Reform in the Republic of Korea, 1954-55." Ph.D. diss., University of Illinois.

Perrow, Charles. 1970. *Organizational Analysis: A Sociological View*. London: Tavistock Publication.

Rhee, Sang Woo. 1980. "Land Reform in South Korea: A Macro-level Policy Review". In *Land Reform*, edited by Inayatullah, 319-349. Kuala Lumpur: APDAC.

Singer, Hans, and Nancy Ratter. 1980. *Young Human Resources in Korea's Social Development*. Seoul: Korea Development Institute.

Yu, In-ho. 1975. *Hanguk nongji jedo-ui yeon-gu* (The Study of Korea's Land System). Seoul: Geunmundang.

Whang, In-joung. 1981. *Management of Rural Change in Korea: The Saemaeul Undong*. Seoul: Seoul National University Press.

_____. 1984. "Policy Response of Local Government to Social Change." Seoul: Korea Development Institute.

The Korean Take-off

Paul W. Kuznets

The "take-off," one of the five stages of economic growth distinguished by Walt W. Rostow, is ". . . the great watershed in the life of modern societies . . . [when] growth becomes [a] normal condition."[1] This aeronautical metaphor is employed as a synonym for "industrial revolution," for Rostow notes that "the take-off is defined as an industrial revolution, tied directly to radical changes in methods of production, having their decisive consequence over a relatively short period of time."[2] Both the empirical validity and analytical worth of Rostow's analysis have been severely criticized.[3] It is by no means evident either that economic growth has typically conformed to Rostow's stages, or that recent economic developments place the Republic of Korea in the take-off stage.

Yet in the years after the Korean War (1950-1953), something has happened to transform the virtually stagnant economy in Korea into one

* Originally published in Vol. 12, No. 1 (January 1972).

Paul W. Kuznets is Professor Emeritus of Economics at Indiana University. E-mail: kuznets@indiana.edu. He has authored many books and articles including *Korean Economic Development* (1994).

1. W. W. Rostow, *The Stages of Economic Growth: A Non-Communist Manifesto* (Cambridge University Press, 1960), p. 7.
2. *Ibid.*, p. 57.
3. The main lines of criticism are as follows: a) modern growth has generally been continuous rather than discontinuous, with few clearly defined "stages"; b) stage theory imposes specious uniformity on economic history, whose essential characteristic is diversity; c) the analysis is nonoperational. That is, one can only confirm that the "preconditions" for take-off existed after the fact, or that a take-off actually occurred if growth were subsequently sustained. see W. W. Rostow, ed., *The Economics of Take-off into Sustained Growth* (London: Macmillan & Co.; New York: St. Martin's Press, 1963).

of the world's most rapidly growing economies in the 1960s.[4] When Professor Rostow visited Seoul in the spring of 1969, he was quoted to the effect that "Korea might save four or five years in completing the take-off stage."[5] The country's remarkable growth in the last few years (real output rose 13% in 1968, almost 16% in 1969, and almost 9% in 1970) has begun to attract widespread attention.[6] This growth has also raised the question of whether the economy is "taking off" or not, a question which would never have been asked before 1963.

This question is essentially speculative. Rostow's take-off is considered to be a take-off into, not an abortive flight followed by a crash landing. By 1981, observers should be able to answer the question, but today they cannot. The interesting and fruitful issues now, in 1971, lie elsewhere. In particular, what is the evidence of a shift from stagnation to growth? To what extent has change in the tempo of development been accompanied by a restructuring of the economy? Changes in the pace of growth are likely to be marked not only by more of the same, but also by differences in kind. What are the causes of accelerated growth? The costs and the benefits? Finally, what are the prospects for the future? Some of these questions, particularly the last, are no less speculative than that of whether Korea is now in the take-off stage or not. The questions posed here are different, however, in kind from the take-off question, for evidence exists at present which can be used to provide answers to such questions, even if only limited or intuitive.

The Evidence

Analysis of economic growth in Korea is usually limited to South Korea in the period after liberation from the Japanese in 1945. Though today's Republic was once part of a unified Korea which, in turn, was a major link in the Japanese Empire, independence and division have created a new economy. This economy cannot be legitimately compared either

---

4. Figures on GNP growth rates during 1960-1967 for most countries can be found in the United Nations, *Yearbook of National Accounts Statistics* (1968), vol. II, table 5-B.
5. *The Korea Times,* 20 June 1969. The take-off stage normally takes several decades, according to Rostow.
6. For instance, see an article on Korean economy in the "South Korea: Asia's Newest Growth Economy," *Morgan Guaranty Survey* (October 1970).

with all of Korea or the southern provinces before 1945. The sum of the parts, for once, does not equal the whole. Since continuous and reasonably reliable economic data extend back only to 1953 or even later, this analysis is limited for practical reasons to the period after the Korean War.

Gross national product (GNP) measured in constant 1965 prices is shown in the chart and table at the end of the paper (Table 1). Constant-price or real GNP is used here to isolate the effects of price increase from output growth on GNP measured in current prices. This is particularly necessary when rates of inflation vary sharply from year to year (compare the 1962-1963 with the 1963-1964 price indexes shown in the Table 1, column 3). Real GNP is related in the chart to the GNP which would have resulted if output had grown evenly (at a constant percentage rate) from 1953 to 1969. Comparison reveals a gap which opened in 1962 before closing in later years.[7] With the exception of 1957, growth before 1963 is of a different and lower order of magnitude than growth afterward (This is confirmed by the annual increase rates shown in the Table 1, column 2). The annual rate of increase in GNP averaged 4.6% from 1953 to 1962. The average more than doubled (to 10.9%) after 1962.[8]

Private consumption and gross domestic capital formation, two major components of expenditure on national product, are given in columns 5 and 7 of the table. The consumption figures, divided by population estimates (column 4), show that the increase in average per capita consumption was insignificant from the mid-1950s until the early 1960s. Individual consumption has risen almost 50% since then. International comparison of consumption and other expenditure components is known to be problematic, but it is noteworthy that an average consumption of 23,300 won in 1965, for example, was equivalent to less than $90 at the prevailing exchange rate. An increase of 50% from such a level can only have

---

7. A logarithmic scale, which assigns equal distances to the same percentage changes, would perhaps have been more appropriate here. The absolute gap does not begin to close until 1966 (see chart), but the percentage gap (see Table 1, column 1) begins to narrow in 1963 as annual percentage increases rise above the 1953-1969 average.

8. Though three stages might be distinguished from column 2 (slow growth from 1953 through 1958 or 1959, stagnation from 1960 through 1962, and rapid growth thereafter), simplicity of exposition and examination of causal factors both suggest that two stages are sufficient.

profound and welcome welfare effects.

The increase in per capita consumption is a product of offsetting factors. On the one hand, GNP and total available resources (GNP plus net borrowing and transfers from the rest of the world) have risen sharply in recent years while the annual rate of population increase has declined from 3% in 1955-1960 to 2.6% in 1960-1966 and 1.9% in 1966-1970. The share of resources (and GNP) going to capital formation (i.e. investment), on the other hand, has increased too. This is not entirely at the expense of consumption since capital formation today increases output available for consumption or further investment tomorrow. Nevertheless, the rapid increase in domestic investment from 10-12% of GNP in 1959-1961 to almost 30% in 1967-1969 (see Table 1, column 10) has probably held down consumption in recent years.

Capital formation and the share of capital formation in total output (the investment ratio) both began to accelerate in 1963. The rate of capital formation is generally considered the primary determinant of economic growth in modern growth theory. To the extent that investment actually determines the rate of increase in GNP, the rapid growth of investment to over a third of GNP in 1969 has been responsible for Korea's remarkable growth rates in recent years.[9]

This investment has been financed from foreign and domestic sources (see Table 1, columns 8 and 9). Domestic saving was negligible and even negative (when measured in constant 1965 prices) in earlier years, but began to increase in 1963, almost doubled between 1965 and 1966, and has risen since then to account for more than half of total saving each year since 1965. Foreign saving increased to 1957, and then decreased

---

9. Investment and increase in output are conventionally linked by the incremental capital/output ratio. This measure is too unstable to be a useful policy parameter, and too aggregate to reveal the sectoral shares or shifts in investment which are major determinants of the investment-output relationship. The incremental ratio is designed to show the number of units of investment required to increase the annual product flow (GNP) by one unit. The average annual rate of increase in real GNP for the United States in 1963-1969 was 4.8%, for example. The investment ratio in 1967-1969 averaged 15%. Though the implied aggregate incremental capital/output ratio (3.8: 1) was considerably higher than Korea's (2.0: 1), when one tries to explain the difference, it is necessary to examine variation between the two countries in the sectoral allocation of investment, amount of excess capacity, and in relative prices and inputs of labor and capital. The aggregate capital/output ratio hides more than it reveals here.

until 1966 before rising once more.

"Foreign saving" is calculated here by subtracting exports from imports (and net tractor income from abroad); it is pretty much equivalent to Korea's current-account balance of payments which, in turn, is dominated by merchandise exports and imports (see Table 1, columns 11 and 12). The current-account balance (a deficit each year since 1953) has been covered by foreign aid, particularly from the U.S., and by private lending. American aid and United Nations Korean Reconstruction Agency (UNKRA) supplies totaled $4.3 billion between 1945 and 1969. Approximately $1.8 billion was received in the form of commercial loans and direct private investment from 1959 through early 1970, mainly in 1966 and afterward. The decline in foreign saving since 1957 and its subsequent recovery reflects the gradual reduction in aid levels and the more recent increase in commercial borrowing.

Export growth since 1963 has been phenomenal. Exports doubled from 1963 to 1965, and almost doubled again from 1965 to 1967 and from 1967 to 1969. Less than a fifth of total exports were manufactures in 1957-1959, but manufactures made up more than three-fifths of the total by 1969. The rapid growth of manufacturing, the main component of the secondary sector (see Table 1, column 15), has essentially been export-led growth since 1963 or 1964.[10]

Agricultural output has increased too, but at a lesser rate since output has had to rise from a much larger base.[11] The result has been a change in industrial structure which accelerated in the mid-1960s. The share of

---

10. The index of manufacturing production (1965=100) rose most rapidly after 1964. Production doubled during the five-year period from 1959 to 1964, and then tripled between 1964 and 1969. By 1969, exports accounted for roughly half of value added in manufacturing.

11. Gross national product originating in agriculture (forestry and fisheries) was almost three times that originating in manufacturing in 1963. In addition to arithmetic reasons for slower growth, agricultural output has grown less rapidly than manufacturing production because investment in agriculture has been much lower (fixed capital formation, in constant 1965 prices, totaled 125 billion won during 1963-1969; the figure for manufacturing was 418 billion), and labor input declined (from 4.8 million in 1963 to 4.7 million in 1969) while manufacturing employment doubled. Agriculture has also suffered from the well-known difficulties of applying new technology to small-scale, widely dispersed production units. Limited access to credit and adverse cost-price relationships are other factors in Korea which have served to limit growth of agricultural output.

the secondary sector rose almost 10 percentage points during the decade from 1953 to 1963-1964. It rose another 10 points during the five years from 1964 to 1969. This increase has been almost wholly at the expense of the primary sector (predominantly agriculture), since the share of the "other" sector (trade, transport, government, and the remaining service industries) has remained quite stable.

Shifts in sectoral output shares are only one sign of the massive forces in Korea that are transforming an agricultural, rural society into an urban, industrial one. Changes in labor force composition, the widening gap between farm and non-farm incomes, and urban immigration are other signs.

Manufacturing employment doubled from 1963 to 1969. The number of persons employed in agriculture actually dropped during the period. Value added per worker in agriculture averaged 127,000 won in 1968; the figure for manufacturing was 340,000. With a difference in productivity of this magnitude, clearly economic development is not only a matter of increasing output per worker in each sector, but also a process in which the center of economic gravity shifts from low-productivity to high-productivity activities.

This shift has been accelerated in Korea by increasing urban-rural income disparity. Average annual farm-household income equaled 179,000 won in 1968. Annual incomes of urban wage-earner families averaged 221,000 won. Urban wages quadrupled from 1963 to 1968; farm-household income rose 92%. The standard of living (real income) of urban workers doubled during this period while farm families were no better off in 1968 than they were in 1963.[12] Is it surprising that the number of non-farm households has increased four times as fast as the number of farm households in recent years? Or that Seoul's population rose from 2.4 to 5.5 million persons during the past decade?

The evidence here, to summarize briefly, shows a marked acceleration in the pace of economic growth after 1963 or 1964 which distinguishes more recent years from the decade 1953-1962. This acceleration is seen in annual rates of increase in GNP, per capita consumption, capital for-

---

12. These figures are based on employment and wage data from the Economic Planning Board (EPB), *Annual Reports on the Economically Active Population*; EPB, *Annual Reports on the Family Income and Expenditure Survey*; Ministry of Agriculture and Forestry (MOAF), *Reports on the Results of Farm Household Economy Survey*; and MOAF, *Production Cost Survey of Agricultural Products*.

mation, and in the investment ratio. It is also found in the shifting sectoral distribution of output. The share of manufacturers, led by exports, has risen while agriculture's share has fallen. This shift has its counterpart in the labor force, where a larger proportion of workers now work in factories rather than in the fields, and in population distribution, as Korea becomes increasingly urbanized. Insofar as the process described here, to quote Rostow, " . . . [is] tied directly to radical changes in methods of production, having their decisive consequences over a relatively short period of time," then Korea's take-off began seven or eight years ago. The take-off concept itself, as noted earlier, is subject to major reservations. Moreover, that this acceleration in the tempo of economic activity really constituted a take-off is also debatable, since we have not yet had the benefit of sufficient hindsight to test the hypothesis adequatelly. Whatever one wishes to call it, the major shift in Korea's economic situation deserves an explanation. An explanation is offered in the next section of this paper.

The Causes

Any evaluation of the acceleration in the rate of Korea's economic development in the early 1960s must explain why growth was slow from the end of the Korean War to approximately 1963, what happened at the time to change the situation, and why subsequent growth has been so rapid.

Slow growth after the Korean War is difficult to understand in the immediate historical context. The war was responsible for about one million casualties in the South from a population of 20 million. Physical damage was estimated to almost equal the value of total output in 1953.[13] Reconstruction of the shattered economy should have resulted in high growth rates if only because output reached very low levels during the war. The answer to this apparent paradox is that the battle line stabilized in early 1951, while agricultural and industrial output recovered to pre-war levels by 1953. Recovery was remarkably swift, a tribute to the Korean people, but earlier output levels were low and the basic problems

---

13. Bank of Korea, *Annual Economic Review* (1955), appendix tables 8-9.

which had bedeviled the economy still persisted.[14]

Liberation from Japan and division of the Korean peninsula in 1945 had left the South a truncated part of the former Japanese Empire. Korea's comparative advantage within the Yen Bloc in producing rice, iron ore, chemicals, and other products ended with liberation in 1945. Separation of the country into North and South broke up a highly complementary economy in which rice and barley were mainly grown in the South, beans and cereals in the North. Most textiles and machine tools were manufactured in the South, while metal and chemical (especially fertilizer) production was centered in the North.

The division of an interdependent economic system clearly caused many problems. For example, light bulbs manufactured in Korea used tungsten filaments imported from Japan. Korea had exported the tungsten ore to Japan, but now had no filament-making facilities. Similar examples of disrupted economic ties could be listed indefinitely, but the major case in the South after liberation was in agriculture, and the immediate results were hunger and rice riots.

Though "starvation exports" of rice no longer had to be shipped to Japan, the domestic supply was inadequate because fertilizer could not be obtained from the North. Also, there were more mouths to feed. The population of the South rose from 16 million in 1944 to over 20 million in 1948-1949 as many Koreans returned from Japan and Manchuria and others emigrated from the North.[15] The U.S. Military Government in Korea under General Hodge, faced with severe economic and political problems it was not adequately prepared to handle, eventually established compulsory rice collection and brought fertilizer to replace that no

---

14. Output in the fiscal year ending in March 1954 was virtually back to the pre-war level reached in 1949-1950: "This is a remarkable recovery by any standard." John P. Lewis, *Reconstruction and Development in South Korea* (National Planning Association, December 1955), pp. 18-19.

15. Migration from Korea before liberation was so large that "at least 10% of the Korean population was abroad." Yi Jeong-myeon, "Population Movement of Korea—International Movement," *Korean Affairs* (1963): p. 21. By 1940, Osaka contained the third largest Korean population after Seoul and Pyeongyang. Irene B. Taeuber and George W. Barclay, "Korea and the Koreans in the Northeast Asian Region," *Population Index* (October 1950): p. 287. Return migration was heavy at the end of World War II but the official statistics published by the South Korean Interim Government (SKIG) and the Supreme Allied Commander for Japan (SCAP) are too incomplete to estimate gross flows.

longer available from the North. In addition to the major problem of feeding an enlarged population, the U.S. Military Government faced a host of other immediate problems. One was that plant and equipment had been run down and the economy cannibalized to meet war needs.[16] Korea's capital stock was consequently in poor shape. Limited productive capacity and severance of former economic ties combined to cause massive unemployment.[17] Also, the Japanese had monetized their assets (life insurance policies were paid out in full, etc.) in preparation for departure. Monetization plus shortages of necessities led to rampant inflation in 1947.[18] The United States responded to these problems during the occupation with a series of relief measures. Aid imports, for example, were composed mainly of food and raw materials rather than equipment. This was essentially a holding operation rather than a development program.[19]

After the occupation forces left, an independent Republic of Korea was established under the presidency of Syngman Rhee in August 1948. It was now becoming evident that this dismembered former colony would have to be transformed into a viable, independent economy. As a result, American aid policy began to shift from direct reliance to longer-term development aid.[20] The issues now were how to develop economic independence and what to do first.

---

16. "Even the iron water mains and fire plugs were taken up during the war and concrete pipes substituted." Earnest J. Fisher, "Korea Today," *Far Eastern Quarterly* (May 1946): p. 263.
17. Almost 900 thousand were listed as unemployed (from a population of 20.2 million) as late as May 1949. The actual number was probably higher. See Bank of Korea, *Annual Economic Review* (1949), table 173.
18. The Seoul wholesale price index rose almost 800% between April 1945 and September 1945. These were official prices. Black market prices were 20 or 30 times official prices immediately before the war's end. George M. McCune, *Korea Today* (1950): p. 103.
19. This is hardly surprising since Korea's importance to United States national interests had never been defined. See Cho Soon Sung, *Korea in World Politics, 1940-1950: An Evaluation of American Responsibility* (Berkeley, CA: University of California Press, 1967), chapter 12. Also, until it became evident that Korea was to remain divided, there was no basis for embarking on a program to develop one portion of the peninsula.
20. The ECA (Economic Cooperation Administration, predecessor to AID) was scheduled to begin a three-year, $350 million development program in Korea during fiscal 1950. Funds for expanding coal and electric-power output and building fertilizer plants were included in the program. See W. A. Brown, Jr. and R. Opie, *American Foreign Assistance* (Washington: Bookings Institution, 1953), pp. 375-376.

The basic outlook in 1948 appeared bleak. Only a fifth of the land area was arable yet Korea had one of the world's highest population densities. The economic structure was lopsided, with redundant export industries on the one hand and insufficient capacity to meet domestic needs on the other. Three-quarters of the population was illiterate at the time of liberation. After the Japanese were repatriated, Korea was left with virtually no administrative, managerial, or technical manpower.

When the Korean War erupted less than two years after the founding of the Republic, too little time had passed and the political situation was too turbulent to expect much economic progress or the establishment of economic programs. The period from the armistice in July 1953 to the student revolution in April 1960 was sufficiently long, however, for government economic priorities to be set and for development efforts to show results. Land reform was completed by 1958; food production rose roughly 50% from 1949 to 1959; illiteracy was sharply reduced, and primary education greatly expanded. Industrial production doubled from 1955 to 1960, largely through import substitution.[21] Despite these gains, the overall pace of growth was unsatisfactory. Real output rose at an annual average rate of 5% from 1953 to 1959, but three-fifths of this increase was eaten up by population growth.

Given the basic outlook in 1948 and the havoc of the Korean War, one may argue that any progress was sufficient and that satisfactory rates of development could not be expected for several generations. This argument is simplistic because it fails to recognize the favorable factors. Korea had been well along the road to industrial development by 1939-

---

21. Food production (rice and other grains, pulses, and potatoes) rose from 3.5 million metric tons in 1949 to 5.4 million tons in 1959. See UNKRA-FAO, *Rehabilitation of Agriculture, Forestry, and Fisheries in South Korea* (1954); and MAF, *Yearbooks of Agriculture and Forestry Statistics*. Estimates of agricultural output are especially liable to error and bias, while sharp year-to-year variation in weather conditions makes single-year output estimates potentially misleading indicators of trend. Nevertheless, output in the late 1950s was considerably above that in 1949, the best post-liberation, pre-war year.

A literacy drive after the war helped to reduce the proportion of illiterates to less than 30% by 1960. The number of primary school students rose from 1.9 million in 1945 to 3.6 million in 1960 so that two-thirds of all children aged 6-11 were enrolled in primary schools in the latter year. Central Education Research Institute, *Education in Korea* (1966): p. 105; and EPB, *Korea Statistical Yearbook* (1966).

Available supply (domestic output plus imports less exports) of cement, flat glass, newsprint, and tires was largely produced in Korea by the late 1950s.

1941.[22] Though higher-level talent was missing, the more basic skills were available. Also, the United States was already committed in 1948 to help Korea become "a display window of democracy."[23] The commitment was strengthened by the Korean War so that large-scale aid in the 1950s gave Korea one of the world's highest levels of per-capita assistance.[24]

What progress occurred before 1960 was achieved despite the lack of any coherent government economic program and despite the handicap of mistaken economic policies.[25] These can be blamed on inexperienced administration, but the basic cause was President Rhee. He knew little of economics and had no plans for economic development.[26] The first opportunity for any sort of coordinated government economic policy occurred when the Rhee regime was overthrown in May 1960. The successor government of Chang Myon was too brief and unstable for new economic policies to be adopted before it was turned out the Military Coup of 16 May 1961.[27] The military junta, led by General Park

22. The share of mining and manufacturing in next commodity product (e.g. the net output of goods originating in agriculture, forestry, fisheries, mining, and manufacturing) had reached 35-40% by 1939-1941. See Suh Sang-chul, "Growth and Structural Changes in the Korean Economy Since 1910" (Ph. D. dissertation, Harvard University, 1966), table II-4.
23. Brown and Opie, *op. cit.*, p. 373.
24. Korea received over $1.7 billion in official grants and loans from 1955 through 1960, which amounts to a little over $73 per person.
25. The list of policy failure is endless, but insistence on overvaluation of the won, use of multiple exchange rates, finance of continued government deficits by borrowing from the central bank, and artificially low interest payments on savings are the main ones.
26. President Rhee evidently believed, for instance, that inflation was caused by exchange devaluation. My judgment of Rhee's economic policies may be too harsh, for the sort of institutional change and educational reform required for economic growth is likely to be slow, and later progress can be traced back in part to developments under Rhee. Still, "his tragedy is that a lifetime devoted to his country should have left so little of lasting value." Richard C. Allen, *Korea's Syngman Rhee: An Unauthorized Portrait* (Rutland: Tuttle, 1960), p. 235.
27. This is not to say that there was no economic planning or any attempts to coordinate development policies. A three-year economic plan was approved three months before the Rhee government was overthrown. A new five-year plan was prepared by the Jang government. Given Rhee's anti-planning bias, however, it is unlikely that the plan would ever have been implemented had he remained in power. See David C. Cole and Young Woo Nam, "The Pattern and Significance of Economic Planning in Korea," in *Practical Approaches to Development Planning: Korea's Second Five-Year Plan,* ed. Irma Adelman (Baltimore: Johns Hopkins University Press, 1969), pp. 12-16.

Chung-hee, was succeeded in 1963 by civilian government under General (now President) Park. The government since 1961, unlike that in earlier years, has been a stable, continuous force with pronounced economic goals.[28]

The economic slowdown in 1959-1962 (see Table 1, column 1) was due to poor crops in 1959-1960 and again in 1962, and the disruption and uncertainty which followed the student revolution and military coup in 1960 and 1961. A poorly conceived currency reform in June 1962 also had a depressing effect on economic activity. By 1963, however, better harvests and heavy investment in First Five-Year Plan (1962-1966) projects caused GNP to rise substantially.

Rapid growth from 1963 on can be attributed to planning, new policies, accidental factors, and basic sources of economic strength. Five-year plans have been endowed with powers they do not possess and made the subject of much economic science fiction. To be taken seriously a plan must be more than a shopping list of projects, and more than an exercise in futility by government economists who either lack the information needed to draw up an adequate plan or whose government is unwilling or unable to implement one. If a plan meets the necessary conditions for credibility, then it can be used like a map on which the course of the economy is plotted for the next five years. As is often the case with maps, however, the map may prove misleading, there may be detours due to unforeseen circumstances, or one may miss signs and either overshoot or stop short of the destination.

In Korea, unlike other developing countries, the five-year plans can be taken seriously. The Second Plan (1967-1971), with annual modification, has served as a guide to the country's economic future and so, to a lesser extent, did the First Plan. The Third Plan (1972-1976) will undoubtedly perform the same function. The First and Second Plans established aggregate growth rate targets and sectoral output goals. The amounts of foreign and domestic investment needed to meet the various targets

---

28. Economic achievement has also served political ends. The ruling Democratic Republican party sponsored a referendum in the fall of 1969 to revise the constitution so that the president might serve a third term. President Park, campaigning for revision, said "I proposed the referendum because I thought that retaining the present system . . . will contribute to economic development. . . . I wanted to . . . add the finishing touch to the vast enterprises of construction I started," *The Korea Times,* 11 October 1969.

were specified. Less detailed information on savings sources and labor requirements was also provided. Each plan, despite inclusion of a proposal to achieve self-sufficiency in food grains production, has emphasized industrialization with particular stress on the expansion of manufactures.[29]

The plans set targets but usually do not specify how they are to be reached. This appears, at first sight, to be dodging the issue. When plans are being constructed, however, the appropriate choice of policies needed to implement them is not readily apparent. Nor is the quantitative effect of a particular policy decision likely to be known in advance, though attempts are of course made to predict such things. A "stabilization program," or set of new policies adopted in 1963-1965, does not appear in the plans. This program had a major impact on plan achievement and subsequent growth.

Government deficits, financed mainly by borrowing from the central bank, had been the main factor responsible for increase in the money supply and a chronic cause of inflation since 1954. Beginning with the budgets of 1963-1964, budgets were adjusted—first by holding down expenditure, later by increasing revenues—so that the government would be a net saver rather than a net borrower. This new role of government as saver has limited inflation which, at Korean rates, has probably retarded development.[30] To the extent that the increase in government saving is greater than the reduction in saving of those whose taxes rose, and insofar as government funds are used more productively than the same funds would have been were they still in private hands, greater government saving has also contributed directly to economic growth.

A major devaluation of the won took place in June 1964 (from 130 to 255 per dollar). The won has since depreciated to 370 per dollar by mid-

---

29. See P. W. Kuznets, "Korea's Five-Year Plans," in Irma Adelman, ed., *op. cit.,* pp. 41-54.

30. Most economists regard price increase as inevitable and moderate rates of increase as possibly desirable. But when rates of increase rise above 5 or 10% a year, price relations become increasingly distorted and the cost of such distortion is likely to outweigh possible benefits. In Korea, annual price increases averaged over 20% in 1953-1960, 19% in 1960-1965, and 12% in 1965-1979. See Graeme S. Dorrance, "The Effect of Inflation on Economic Development," *IMF Staff Papers* (1963); and Harry G. Johnson, "Is Inflation the Inevitable Price of Rapid Development or a Retarding Factor in Economic Growth?" *Malayan Economic Review* (April 1966).

1971. The 1964 devaluation, and the simultaneous elimination of multiple-exchange rate devices and relaxation of quantitative import restrictions, all made export more attractive relative to domestic sales for Korean producers. The import liberalization which accompanied devaluation expanded government revenues (from duties on imports), sustained counterpart fund receipts, and reduced the profiteering and resource misallocation which occur when the price of foreign exchange is too low to reflect its actual scarcity. Liberalization has also limited the growth of noncompetitive, low-productivity industries which flourish like weeds behind the protective import barriers used to prop up an overvalued currency.

The interest-rate "reform" of September 1965 was another dramatic policy move. The basic loan rate (on bills) was doubled, while rates on some term and saving deposits more than doubled.[31] Like devaluation, the purpose of the reform was to correct unrealistic prices, in this instance the prices paid to savers and charged to borrowers. The average annual rate of inflation (19%) had been above the bill rate (14%) and payments on savings deposits (15% or less) in 1960-1965. Savers were being asked to subsidize borrowers, which is patently ridiculous in a capital-scarce country like Korea.

The results were predictable. Demand for loans exceeded supply, and supply was limited because savers placed their funds in the unorganized money market. With reform, savings deposits in banks doubled between September 1956 and April 1966. As with fiscal stabilization, the interest-rate reform could be evaluated according to how much it increased the savings and whether savings were better utilized after the event than before. Most of the new deposits in banks were probably transferred from the private (unorganized) market. Since private lending is illegal, the size and loan characteristics of the unorganized market are unknown. It is probable, however, that the reform increased saving and improved the overall utilization of loans.

Devaluation and the interest-rate reform both constituted readjustment of administered prices which had gotten out of line. In addition, a series of more positive measures were adopted to promote exports and encourage foreign lending. Tax exemption, easy access to low-cost loans,

---

31. The yield on 18-month saving accounts went to 2.5% a month, or more than 34% a year.

and direct subsidies have been used to encourage export. By the spring of 1969, when the exchange rate was 285 won per dollar, these incentives were estimated to be worth from 40 to 52 won per dollar's worth of exports.[32]

Foreign lending has been encouraged by political stability, rapid growth of exports (which provide the foreign exchange needed to repay loans), and Korea's limited foreign-debt service obligations. In addition, the Bank of Korea and more recently the Korea Exchange Bank have guaranteed repayment of foreign loans. The results can be seen in the foreign currency liabilities (guarantee acceptances) of these banks. Acceptances totaled 26 billion won in 1965; they reached 413 billion won by August 1970. The increase in exports has already been seen (Table 1, column 11).

Random or exogenous events with major consequences for the Korean economy have included atypical weather and war in Vietnam. In 1964 and 1966, for example, harvests were unusually good because weather conditions were particularly favorable. Drought was largely responsible for a drop in the GNP growth rate from 13.4% in 1966 to 8.9% in 1967. The influence of weather on growth should diminish as agriculture's share in total product declines.

Merchandise exports to Vietnam reached a peak of almost $14 million in 1966 before declining more recently. Most of the war-related dollar earnings, however, have come from "sales to U.N. forces" (mainly to the two U.S. divisions stationed in Korea, but also an unspecified amount of receipts from Vietnam) and U.S. offshore procurement, which includes payments to Korean contractors in Vietnam and costs of maintaining Korean troops stationed in Vietnam since 1966. Receipts from these sources (presumably included under "government, i.e., military transactions" in the balance of payments) doubled from 1966 to 1967. They accounted for a little over 20% of total exports of goods and services in 1969.[33] As Japan benefitted from the Korean War, so has Korea benefit-

---

32. *The Korea Times*, 27 April and 20 May 1969. For a more detailed description of policy measures, see S. Kanesa-Thasan, "Stabilizing an Economy: The Korean Experience," in Irma Adelman, ed., *op. cit.*

33. Balance-of-payments categories which combine receipts from sales to U.N. forces in Korea with service payments earned by Korean contractors or troops in Vietnam were not designed for use in determining Korea's earnings from war in Vietnam. Similarly, annual reports of the Agency for International Development show military assistance programs (MAP's) by country, but not by activity, so Korea's receipts can-

ted from war in Vietnam.[34] Basic resources or elements of economic strength, most of which existed before 1963, have permitted Korea's rapid growth in recent years. Without such resources, the best planning, most sophisticated policies, or simple good luck are likely to prove ephemeral. Their possession may be a necessary condition for rapid growth, but it is not a sufficient condition since these resources were part of Korea's economic endowment during the earlier era of unsatisfactory progress.

A literate, relatively well-educated labor force is perhaps the main element of Korea's economic strength. Expenditure on education of 7 to 8% of GNP, which is undoubtedly above the international average, has given Korea an educational system on par with semi-advanced countries like Norway.[35] Stress in education has been on quantity rather than quality, but Korean workers have probably been better able than most to adopt the new techniques and develop the new skills required by rapid industrialization.[36]

A second element is Korea's relatively well developed infrastructure.

' not be obtained from the MAP budget for Vietnam. Recent testimony before the U.S. Senate revealed that military equipment originally valued at $3.4 billion had been given to allied governments (Korea was a major recipient) between 1951 and 1970 for a small fraction of cost, and that nearly $1 billion had been paid to finance Korean combat troops in Vietnam since 1965. *The New York Times*, 29 March 1970, p. 1., and 1 April 1970, p. 1; *The Korea Times*, 13 September 1970. One may conclude that Korea's earnings from the war in Vietnam are hard to define (what is a ten-year old destroyer worth?), that the balance-of-payments figure used here is too low to measure such earnings (government, n.i.e., military credits totaled only $942 million from 1965 through mid-1970) and that the actual amount—if it were known—would probably be much higher.

34. Credits under the "government, i.e., military" category in Japan's balance of payments rose from $49 million in 1949 to $803 million in 1953. This item, which includes sales to military personnel stationed in Japan as well as sales to U.N. forces under special procurement programs in connection with the Korean War, made up 37% of Japan's total earnings from sales of goods and services in 1953.

35. The expenditure estimate, for 1967, includes private as well as public outlays. It was released by the Office of Planning and Control. See *The Korea Times*, 21 November 1968. International comparison of educational expenditure is difficult because the share of private outlays in total expenditure varies widely, and because private expenditure data are often inaccurate or not available. One comparison, which includes Korea, is given in Frederik Harbison and Charles A. Myers, *Education, Manpower and Economic Growth* (McGraw-Hill, 1964).

36. That emphasis in Korea has been placed on quantity rather than quality was noted in the 1965 report of a UNESCO advisory team for educational planning.

Though the transport and communications networks inherited from the colonial era were oriented toward North-South traffic, and East-West movement became more important after partition, the networks have been expanded to meet the increased demand generated by a growing population and increasing levels of economic activity. The recently completed Seoul-Busan expressway is a noteworthy case in point. Similarly electric output has risen sharply in recent years (generation doubled from 1962 to 1966, and doubled again from 1966 to 1969). Inadequate infrastructure could have easily constituted a crippling bottleneck for industrialization in Korea. That it has not is largely due to the construction industry. The supply of skilled workers and production of construction materials have both been sufficient to meet most of the demand for new overhead facilities in recent years.

Other elements which deserve more attention than can be given here are Korea's size, ethnic and linguistic homogeneity, location, and social and political structure. Size in this context refers not only to area (about equal to Indiana), but also to population, now almost 32 million. Neither area nor population are so large as to hamper communication or overtax administration, as in India or China, nor is the country so small that the internal market cannot support specialization or economies of scale. Imagine Korea with the population density of Sierra Leone; its population would then be only 4 million.

Korea has also benefitted in recent years from proximity to "the economic miracle," Japan, one of the villains in Korea's tragic modern history. This proximity has provided access to new ideas, new technology, and new markets, particularly after the signing of the normalization treaty between the two countries in 1965. Though blocked from trade with the North, China, and Russia, location near Japan means that Korea is not nearly so economically isolated as countries like Nepal or Burma.

Because the population is quite homogeneous, there has been none of Ceylon's linguistic strife, Malaysia's ethnic conflict, Northern Ireland's religious battles, or Nigeria's separatist warfare. Political power is highly centralized because the government has not had to cater to local or regional interests, as in Pakistan, nor is Korea saddled with a rigid social structure or tenure system in which ancestral origin or very skewed land holding determine individual status and prospects, as in much of Latin America. One consequence is that the government can govern. Korea is not a "soft state" like many of the South Asian countries Myrdal describes in his *Asian Drama*.

The Consequences

Evidence of a shift from slow to fast growth in the early 1960s was found in the behavior of GNP, consumption, and other broad economic aggregates. The industrialization and urbanization which accompanied this shift were seen in sectoral-share estimates and demographic data. Such aggregate data have their counterpart in individual experience. Accelerated growth has provided sufficient food and shelter, opportunities for worthwhile employment, and an optimistic outlook for many persons who had none of these in earlier years.[37] Though the average Korean is still quite poor by international standards, he/she is demonstrably better off now than a decade ago.[38]

Statistical aggregates do not reveal the physical transformation which has accompanied rapid growth, however, nor do they show qualitative changes. Any foreign visitor who stays long enough or returns over a

---

37. The term "sufficient" in this context, particularly with regard to food, may be misleading. Nutritional standards are controversial and the published estimates are inconsistent. See Marguerite C. Burk and Mordecai Ezekiel, "Food and Nutrition in Developing Countries," in *Agricultural Development and Economic Growth,* ed. Bruce F. Johnston and Herman M. Southworth (Ithaca, NY: Cornell University Press, 1967). The Ministry of Health and Social Affairs announced recently that the national average caloric intake was 2,105 per day. *The Korea Times,* 20 December 1970; an earlier study gives a figure of 2,438 as the national average for 1958-1959. See E Hyock Kwon, et. al., *A Study of Urban Slum Population* (1971). Still, there is undoubtedly less hunger—and better housing—than there was a decade ago (Data on housing from the 1970 census of population and housing are not yet available).

   Unemployment statistics are suspect because they are based on quarterly surveys which cannot adequately reflect seasonal swings in agricultural work. Also, underemployment is more of a problem than unemployment in Korea and most other developing countries. Both employment and wage statistics show rapid growth of employment and wages, though, especially in manufacturing. Such expansion of employment in manufacturing and other industrial activities is atypical, and suggests that unemployment and underemployment have lessened. See, for example, Charles R. Frank, Jr., "Urban Unemployment and Economic Growth in Africa," *Oxford Economic Papers* (July 1968).

38. Korea ranked 71st of 80 countries included in a study of real per capita consumption in 1960. With the United Kingdom assigned a value of 100, Korea's index was 6. See W. Beckerman and R. Bacon, "International Comparisons of Income Levels: A Suggested New Measure," *Economic Journal* (September 1976). If all other countries maintained their 1960 consumption levels, Korea's index would have advanced from 6 to 9 in 1969, but its rank would only rise from 71st to 61st.

period of years can see the new buildings and highways. Increased traffic congestion and air pollution are also visible, though not acknowledged in the national income statistics. We know that one of every 14 Koreans lived in Seoul in 1949; the figure is now one in six. We do not really know, though, how urbanization and industrialization have influenced the pace of life, family structure, or the individual's sense of identity.

There are clearly noneconomic as well as economic costs and benefits of rapid economic expansion. The realistic alternative to rapid growth is slow growth rather than no growth. Given past rates of population increase in Korea, slow growth entails little or no improvement in individual welfare.[39] It is not clear how the balance of costs and benefits changes as growth accelerates. The economist's efficiency criteria are essentially static (one chooses among alternatives when everything else is "given") and provide no answers here. We all know that "haste makes waste," and every beginning economics student is taught that supply is more elastic in the long run than in the short run. Still, given the choice, most people—and governments—in developing nations would choose rapid rather than slow growth. With low living standards and high rates of population increase, this is hardly surprising.

Cost-benefit considerations of the sort raised here tend to be speculative because there is no actual alternative to use as a measuring stick, and intuitive because the costs and benefits are essentially incommensurable.[40] Prospects for the future, surprisingly, are more certain. This becomes less surprising, however, when one considers that the press is already carrying articles on the Third Plan (1972-1976) and that previous events have future consequences.

Extrapolation of past trends is normally used to predict future developments, and there is no reason why Korea's progress in the 1970s

---

39. Rates of population increase and economic growth are probably related, however. Interaction between economic and demographic factors is largely ignored by economists and demographers. Better medicine and sanitation may explain the practically universal decline in mortality which has occurred during the last few decades, but little is known of the factors, some economic, which determine fertility. It hardly seems coincidental that rapid economic growth in Japan, Taiwan, and Korea has been associated in recent years with declining rates of population increase, and unlikely that these rates would have declined or declined as much if economic growth, urbanization, and industrialization had been less rapid.

40. How, for example, are the costs of breaking up the extended family system to be weighed against the benefits of more to eat for people living at subsistence levels?

should not resemble that in the second half of the 1960s if allowance is made for the effects of an even larger base for growth rates. Past successes and neglect of particular problems are likely to alter the future path of development, however.

Agricultural modernization and manpower development, for example, are to receive more emphasis in the Third Plan period than in the past. These are cases of previous neglect. The costs of backward agriculture are evidently beginning to outweigh the benefits (more resources available for allocation elsewhere), while the previous assumption that the labor supply would impose no constraints on growth is probably no longer true.[41]

A moderate growth rate (8.5% per year) is projected in the Third Plan. Development of the heavy machinery industry is to be encouraged. Greater reliance on domestic saving and an improved balance of payments are additional, related targets.[42] These are, in a sense, goals which result from past success. Rapid growth has been led by exports of light manufactures. The equipment and much of the materials used to produce these exports have been imported, and financed in large part by borrowing abroad, which has increased dependence on foreign saving and led to current-account deficit in the balance of payments. Insofar as heavy machinery and other investment goods are produced locally, less foreign borrowing will be necessary. The net result, then, will be to increase the importance of domestic saving and reduce current-account deficits in the balance of payments.

Export-led growth of light manufactures has provided access to foreign exchange, created opportunities for employment, built manufacturing capacity, and generated impressive growth rates. The rising opportunity costs of emphasis on export promotion are reflected in Korea's increasingly overtaxed infrastructure, comparative neglect of agriculture and manpower requirements, and the postponement of previous plans for developing a petrochemical complex, integrated steel mill, and other heavy, import-substitute manufactures like machinery.[43] Preliminary evi-

---

41. See Roger D. Norton, "Planning with Facts: The Case of Korea," *American Economic Review* (1970): pp. 62-63. Shortages of particular skills can be seen in sharp wage increases. Housing repair wages in Seoul, for example, rose more than any other component of the Seoul consumer price index from 1965 through 1969.

42. See, for instance, *The Korea Times*, 18 March, 16 April, and 3 September 1970.

43. New emphasis on any target necessarily implies previous neglect or revaluation of opportunity costs. Problems caused by neglect and those due to success can both be

dence indicates that the new elements in the Third Plan are designed to reduce these costs.

The sort of investment required to meet the new plan goals tends to be more expensive than investment in production for export. That is, capital requirements (capital/output ratios) are much higher in the transport, communications, or power industries, for example, than in building export capacity. Agricultural modernization and manpower development require overhaul of an educational administration, creation of an effective extension service, and other kinds of institutional change which may take decades to achieve. The really cheap sources of growth, in short, have already been exploited. This is one reason that the Third Plan's projected growth rate is below rates achieved in recent years.[44]

The main single determinant of Korea's growth in the near future is likely to remain export expansion. Either more exports or fewer imports will be required to right the balance of payments and reduce dependence on foreign saving. Import substitution, as experience elsewhere indicates, has proven to be a poor alternative to export expansion in closing the trade gap.[45] Until this gap is closed, growth will not be "self-sustained," to revert to Rostow's terminology.

Export expansion has benefitted from diversification, both in markets and in products, and from a combination of low labor costs and a technological base which have allowed Korean exporters to exploit comparative advantage in producing relatively simple, labor-intensive manufactures. Diversification has kept market shares small and thus reduced the likelihood of trade restriction. It has also limited the risk associated with instability in markets for particular products. Although protectionist sen-

---

subsumed under the opportunity-cost concept. The distinction between the two types of problems is raised here because their causes are different. In one case a positive, successful program created new difficulties. In the other, continued neglect and a changing situation increased existing problems.

44. Other reasons are credibility (it is hard to believe that the phenomenal rates of the late 1960s can be sustained) and opposition from the central bank and potential foreign aid donors. These last are concerned with possible inflationary consequences of overinvestment, and tend to discourage ambitious growth targets. On the other hand, underestimate of actual growth in the First and Second Plans has led to transport and power bottlenecks because too little investment was allocated for expanding the infrastructure.

45. See, for example, Albert O. Hirschman, "The Political Economy of Import Substituting Industrialization in Latin America," *Quarterly Journal of Economics* (February 1968).

timent in high-wage countries is still a potential threat to Korean exports, as are the winding down of war in Vietnam and the U.S. troop withdrawals from Korea, the main problem is internal.[46]

Korean exports are maintained by subsidy. The amount of a subsidy needed to bring forth exports depends, in turn, on producers' costs and productivity. Manufacturing output more than doubled between 1965 and 1969 while employment rose only 70%. Productivity (output per worker) clearly increased, but so did the wages, almost two-and-a-half times. This wage increase has outstripped productivity growth so that unit labor costs rose, profits fell, and more subsidy has been needed.[47] Such developments cannot continue indefinitely.

Agricultural modernization, education and training, and the government's ability to meet social needs are among the more important internal factors which should influence the pace of economic development and levels of individual welfare in the long run. "Agricultural modernization" requires the raising of wages and productivity in rural areas to approximate industrial levels. Increased productivity will probably not lead to self-sufficiency in food production, however, nor is it clear that such self-sufficiency is desirable.[48] Modernization may or may not has-

---

46. Opposition to free trade in the United States, one of Korea's major trading partners, has come mainly from shoe and textile producers in the last few years. The unions were strangely silent, but this has changed. The electrical workers' union recently joined the opposition, citing the growth of imports produced by cheap labor in American-owned plants abroad, including a TV manufacturing plant in Korea. See *New York Times*, 3 January 1971, section 3, p. 12.

47. Value added (GNP originating in the manufacturing sector, in constant prices) increased 125% from 1965 to 1969. The index of manufacturing output (1965=100) was 265.3 in 1969. Manufacturing employment grew from 800 to 1,222 thousand during the period. The average monthly wage for production workers in manufacturing rose from 4,600 won in 1965 to 11,270 won in 1969. The increase in the wage bill (number of employees times average wage) divided by the increase in output indicates that unit labor costs rose at least 40% from 1965 to 1969. This increase was partly but not entirely offset by devaluation. The won fell from approximately 272 per dollar in 1965 to 285 per dollar by mid-1969. The Bank of Korea's financial statements show that profit ratios, however defined, fell from 1965 through 1968.

48. Each five-year plan has announced the goal of agricultural self-sufficiency, but none has provided the means to achieve it. Given Korea's high man-land ratio, industrial base, and access to foreign food grains, a program of "self-sufficiency" makes little economic sense. The term is evidently a shibboleth which the government feels obliged to honor for political reasons.

ten the farmers' cityward flight, depending upon the labor-intensity of new production techniques, but it should reduce the disparity between farm and non-farm incomes. This disparity is a likely cause of increasing income inequality which, in turn, is a potential source of political unrest.

The demand for new skills, like that for electricity, seems to increase more than proportionately with economic growth. Korea's trained manpower has been a major asset in the past, to the point that doctors, nurses, miners, and construction workers have been sent abroad to induce foreign-exchange earnings. Yet manpower projections indicate both shortage and surplus of particular skills (in particular, a shortage of technicians) that show no sign of abating. Korea is also a major victim of the "brain drain." The relative economic status of teachers has probably declined in recent years, while the educational system suffers from administrative inflexibility. The system clearly needs to be reformed if manpower bottlenecks are not to strangle growth in the future.

Korea's pattern of government expenditure differs from that of other Asian countries (and more economically mature nations as well) in that outlays for social services are quite modest. There are historic and social reasons for this; moreover, private foreign agencies have assumed part of the welfare burden in the years after the Korean War. Yet rapid urbanization has raised the social or external costs of living for many city dwellers while the extended family, the individual's traditional shelter in the time of need, has been eroded by city life-styles. Again, as in the case of agricultural modernization, recent trends carry the threat of political disturbance. Government action will be necessary to meet social needs, if only to maintain political stability.

Economists will probably note the absence of reference to market allocation or stabilization programs here. The reason is simple. Korea's basic economic problems are problems of growth rather than stability, the government's economic role is pervasive, and conventional market allocation criteria are generally inapplicable. Others may wonder why nothing was said of administrative, ecological, or health problems, all of which have economic effects. The need for brevity and the tenets of comparative advantage both argued for the omissions.

Questions of procedure and coverage or discussion of particular economic problems should not be allowed to obscure the essential finding here: A basic shift in the pace of growth took place during the early 1960s that transformed Korea from just another stagnant, underdeveloped country into one of the world's fastest growing economies. Whether this was the "take-off" or not, as Rostow has used the term, is debatable. Whatever the term, rapid growth experienced in Korea is most unusual, and merits the attention it has begun to receive.

Figure 1. Gross national product in 1965 price:
actual and constant-increase rate*

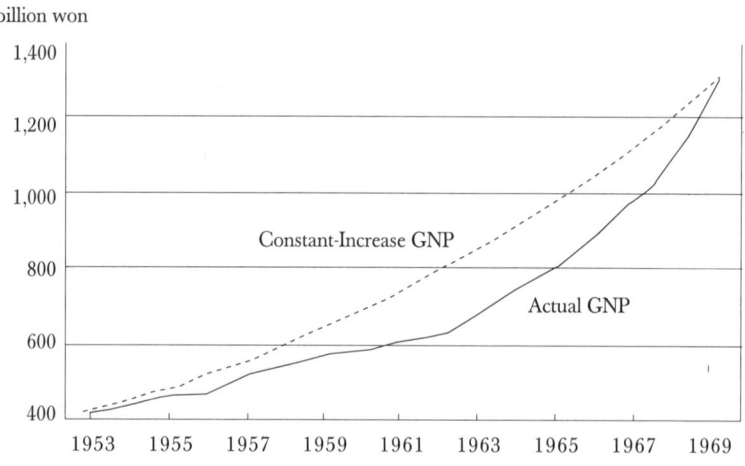

billion won

* Assumes GNP grew a steady 7.32% a year.

Table 1. The Korean Economy Since 1953*–1

	Gross National Product	Annual Increase (%) in (1)	Price[a] Index: 1965=100	Population[b] (thousands)	Private Consumption Expenditure
	(1)	(2)	(3)	(4)	(5)
1953	422		11.4	21,546	362
1954	447	6.0	15.0	–	381
1955	475	6.1	24.5	21,502 (C)	423
1956	480	1.2	31.7	22,307	445
1957	523	8.8	37.8	22,949	471
1958	552	5.5	37.6	23,611	486
1959	576	4.4	38.4	24,291	509
1960	589	2.3	41.9	24,989 (C)	523
1961	614	4.2	48.4	25,700	528
1962	635	3.5	54.9	26,432	569
1963	693	9.1	70.4	27,184	588
1964	750	8.3	92.9	27,958	620
1965	806	7.4	100.0	28,670	669
1966	914	13.4	112.9	29,193 (C)	717
1967	995	8.9	124.8	29,784	784
1968	1,127	13.3	139.8	30,469	874
1969	1,306	15.9	156.7	31,139	970
1970	1,422	8.9	178.9	31,461 (C)	1,077

* All figures are billions of won, expressed in constant (1965) market prices, unless otherwise indicated.

a) Implicit deflator for GNP.

b) Census figures for 1 September (1955), 1 October (1966, 1970), 1 December (1960), others are end-of-year estimates, except for 1967-1969 (1 July estimates).

Table 1. The Korean Economy Since 1953 (Continued)–2

| | Per Capita Consumption (1,000 won) | Gross Domestic Capital Formation | Saving | | Investment Ratio (%) |
			Foreign[c]	Domestic	
	(6)=(5)÷(4)	(7)	(8)	(9)=(7)÷(8)	(10)=(7)÷(1)
1953	16.8	70	70	0	16.5
1954	–	58	50	8	12.9
1955	19.7	61	71	–10	12.9
1956	19.9	57	87	–30	11.9
1957	20.5	88	103	–15	16.8
1958	20.6	78	83	–5	14.1
1959	20.9	58	60	–2	10.0
1960	20.9	62	69	–7	10.6
1961	20.6	73	53	20	11.9
1962	21.5	78	77	1	12.3
1963	21.6	137	107	30	19.8
1964	22.2	114	59	55	15.2
1965	23.3	118	52	66	14.7
1966	24.6	207	86	121	22.7
1967	26.3	242	111	131	24.3
1968	28.7	344	177	167	30.5
1969	31.1	451	211	240	34.6
1970	34.2	456	213	243	32.0

c) Foreign saving was derived by subtracting exports plus net factor income from imports.

Table 1. The Korean Economy Since 1953 (Continued)–3

	Exports[d]	Imports[d]	Merchandise Balanced[d]	Industrial Origin of GDP[e] (%)		
				Primary[f]	Secondary[g]	Other
	(11)	(12)	(13)=(11)–(12)	(14)	(15)	(16)
1953	39.7	347.1	–307.4	51.2	8.9	39.9
1954	25.1	241.2	–216.1	51.8	9.7	38.5
1955	17.7	327.0	–309.3	50.1	11.1	38.8
1956	25.3	380.1	–354.8	47.0	13.0	40.0
1957	19.5	390.4	–370.9	47.0	13.3	39.7
1958	17.3	343.7	–326.4	47.5	13.7	38.8
1959	19.8	273.4	–253.6	45.2	14.4	40.4
1960	32.9	305.4	–272.5	44.3	15.4	40.3
1961	40.9	283.1	–242.5	46.5	15.1	38.4
1962	54.8	390.1	–335.3	42.5	17.0	40.5
1963	86.8	497.0	–410.2	41.7	18.2	40.1
1964	120.0	364.9	–244.9	44.6	17.8	37.6
1965	175.1	420.3	–245.2	41.3	20.2	38.5
1966	250.3	679.9	–429.6	40.7	20.6	38.7
1967	334.7	908.9	–574.2	35.8	23.6	40.6
1968	486.2	1,322.0	–835.8	32.0	26.1	41.9
1969	658.3	1,655.9	–997.6	30.9	27.6	41.5
1970	882.2	1,761.3	–879.1	28.6	29.2	42.2

d) Millions of U.S. dollars.
e) Gross domestic product at 1965 constant factor cost.
f) Agriculture, forestry, and fisheries.
g) Mining, manufacturing, electricity and gas.

Sources: Bank of Korea, *Economics Statistics Yearbook*; Bank of Korea, *Monthly Economic Statistics*; and Economic Planning Board, *Korean Statistical Yearbook*.

Social and Economic Costs of Industrialization in Korea

Lim Youngil

Introduction

The South Korean economy has been recognized in recent years as a successful example of rapid industrialization. Indeed, the economy has achieved a remarkable growth rate of the Gross National Product (GNP) and unprecedented structural changes toward industrialization. On the other hand, such rapid industrialization was accompanied by side effects. The discussion of these problems in relation to the success story, however, is scanty. Objectivity requires a balanced analysis and evaluation; the costs of rapid industrialization and development should be examined alongside the benefits. This paper will discuss the social and economic costs incurred by the Korean economy in the process of industrialization since the end of Korean War (1953) to the end of the Second Five-year Economic Development Plan (1971).

The costs will be discussed in terms of (1) income distribution, (2) efficiency in allocation of investment resources, (3) inflation, (4) balance of payments and foreign debt, and (5) rapid urbanization and related social costs. Based on statistical evidence and its interpretation, this paper will argue that these aspects of industrialization in Korea have been neglected partly because of intellectual inconsistency on the level of economic planning, and that a substantial part of these costs arises from the neglect of the agricultural sector. The analysis will demonstrate that

---

* Originally published in Vol. 13, No. 10 (October 1973).

Lim Youngil (Im, Yeong-il) was a professor at the East-West Center of the University of Hawaii.

more investment in the agricultural sector would have eased, at least partially, the social and economic costs in all five categories listed above. These costs still remain as challenges to be faced by policymakers during the 1970s.

The International Bank for Reconstruction and Development (IBRD) estimated a per capita GNP of $250 for Korea in 1970, placing Korea in the 75th rank out of 122 countries (IBRD 1973, 26-27). By this standard, Korea is still an underdeveloped nation. In terms of growth indicators, however, the rates of change since the Korean War have made impressive records, some of which are listed in Appendix I. Both the rates of GNP and GNP per capita have increased, indicating an acceleration, especially during the 1960s. It is noteworthy that the mining and manufacturing sectors spearheaded all other growth rates. The rapid pace of these changes brought about an entirely different productive composition by 1971 compared to 1953. For instance, GNP contribution by the agricultural sector decreased from 47.1% to 26.5%, whereas GNP contribution by the manufacturing sector increased from 6.1% to 23.3% in 1970 constant prices. This is a significant achievement by any standard.

The rapid growth of the manufacturing sector was in turn led by a vigorous export promotion policy. Especially during the 1960s, the export of manufactured goods grew at an annual rate of over 40% (Balassa 1971, 66-67). This trend of development appears to be well suited to its economic context, since Korea is not well endowed with resources, except abundant labor, and is limited in market size due to low income. Advocacy of export-driven industrialization is in vogue today. There is substantial merit to this view and I concur with the applicability of such a policy to Korea. The issue at stake, however, is the question of costs, and whether such costs can be mitigated. These are difficult questions requiring in-depth investigation to provide answers. Despite the absence of such investigation, these questions should still be raised among scholars and given serious consideration.

Income Distribution

There are no official data on income distribution—this itself is an indication of negligence—and hence serious research has been impossible to undertake. This is likely due to the politically sensitive nature of economic development. Yet, needless to say, the ultimate purpose of economic development is to improve the welfare of the people. Income distribution is an important variable determining welfare, which cannot be revealed by average per capita income. The only possible statement to be made with an increasing per capita income is that the potential for greater economic equality increases. However, indications show that inequality of income distribution increases with the growing per capita GNP. What is needed is an explicit directive as to how income distribution should be traced in the planning process. This is lacking at the moment. The relationship between the growing GNP and the enhancement of welfare is the issue at hand, and development economics is increasingly concerned with this problem.

Income disparity can be indirectly observed in the urban-rural income distribution. This distribution portrays roughly the impact of industrialization—a phenomenon which takes place in urban areas. Evidence indicates that on the average, agricultural family income is about one-third of urban family income, even though the majority of the Korean population is engaged in agriculture. According to statistics provided by the Bank of Korea, per capita income in Seoul was 63,223 won (or $230), while that in agricultural areas was 20,364 won (or $75) in 1966 (Bank of Korea 1967, 68-70). The concern is that such an income differential may further widen in the future with continued industrialization. Some evidence shows the widening of this gap already (Kim and Choe 1971, 5-7). Furthermore, an econometric study concludes:

> Despite a very high degree of factor mobility, especially compared to Japan between 1955 and 1960, the regional economic growth path lies outside the area of stability. In that year (1968) of rapid growth, the Korean economy experienced more polarization of economic activity in the more dynamic regions (Renaud 1973, 439).
>
> The important point is that, under the present conditions of rapid growth of the national economy, the existing regional growth patterns are not capable of achieving income equality among provinces or even of maintaining the existing level of disparity (Renaud 1973, 443).

Such a growing income disparity and unbalanced growth seem to have made obvious the potential benefits arising from interdependency between the agricultural sector and the industrial sector. The interaction between the two sectors in providing each other with a market, in consumption and in production, would have resulted in greater income distribution equality and increased output. Outward-looking policy is recommended, but such a policy should not limit the expansion of domestic markets. In Korea's case, the agricultural development potential still exists, despite often-expressed pessimism. The agricultural sector has been growing in spite of neglect, and this development can be accelerated with a proper policy measure (Ban 1971, 27-31). This would alleviate the problem of the limited domestic market for industrial goods, thereby relieving the burden of the agricultural sector on the industrial sector.

In this sense, the Korean economy should learn from Taiwan's experience, which John Fei and Gustav Ranis have extensively examined (Fei and Ranis 1972, 27-31). While Taiwan is self-sufficient in food supply, Korea's importation of food, largely financed by exportation of industrial output, has increased. More investment of resources in the agricultural sector is needed.

Efficiency in Allocation of Investment Resources

The investment policy, which heavily favored the manufacturing sector, partially explains the urban and rural income disparity. Throughout the period between 1953 and 1971, investment in the manufacturing sector was about three times greater than that in the agricultural sector (see Appendix II). Is this pattern of investment allocation consistent with the objective of maximizing GNP growth? In order to answer this question, it is necessary to compare the marginal productivity of capital in the two sectors. One rudimentary way to measure the efficiency of investment would be to compute the ratio of incremental sectoral output (value added) over investment, allowing one year for gestation. This is shown in Appendix III. Another way to test comparative productivity of capital is to estimate a production function for each sector and compare the capital coefficients. Irma Adelman's estimation is used for this purpose (Adelman 1969, 80-81):

Agriculture:
$$V^a = 192.08 + 9.183D^w + 1.812K^a \quad R^2 = 0.963$$
$$\qquad (9.342) \quad (3.016) \qquad (0.152)$$
Manufacture:
$$V^m = -2.723 + 0.329M^i + 0.931K^m \quad R^2 = 0.985$$
$$\qquad (6.701) \quad (0.102) \qquad (0.066)$$
where V refers to value added,

D^W refers to weather dummy (0, 1, or −1)
K refers to capital
M^i refers to imports of input material, and figures in parentheses are
the standard errors of estimation.

Both tests suggest that the output per unit of capital would be twice as
high in the agricultural sector as in the manufacturing sector. Through
the results of these calculations, one may infer that the actual investment
patterns were not consistent with the objective of GNP maximization.
Greater investment in the agricultural sector would have yielded a
greater gross national product. An equilibrium analysis based on the
Adelman-Kim aggregate model produces the same conclusion. A matrix
inversion of this model reveals that the investment-output multiplier is
greater for the agricultural sector. One dollar investment in agriculture
will result in approximately two dollars of total income, while one dollar
investment in manufacturing will result in 1.32 dollars in total income.
It appears that the benefits from the lost opportunities may be greater
than what was gained through actual investment, despite rapid industrialization.

Some degree of inefficiency in allocation is also observed in the utilized capacity within the manufacturing sector. According to one study,
the sector utilized only about 68% of capacity in fixed capital (Han 1970,
84-103). This may be attributed to many reasons, such as shortages of
input material, working capital, market demand, and skilled management. Nonetheless, in some parts, various subsidies to encourage investment may also be responsible. Whatever the reason may be, the unuti-
lized capacity seems to be high, especially since 1978 when a high rate of
growth was recorded.

This begs the question of why such an investment policy has been
pursued. There may be noneconomic reasons which I am not well qualified to discuss; however, several reasons can be located, especially in
terms of conceptual difficulties and analytical inconsistency in the planning process. First, a consistency test by planners was performed sepa-
rately for manufacturing and agricultural sectors. Furthermore, planners
did not attempt to analyze the maximization or optimization (Norton
1970, 63-64). Second, the so-called "external diseconomies" of industrialization were not considered. Air, water, and noise pollution, congestion,
and other public costs had been entirely disregarded. Third, there was
no plan for income distribution.

Inflation

The industrialization in Korea was accompanied by inflation throughout the period under study. Specifically, the years immediately following the Korean War and the early 1960s witnessed high rates of inflation. The wholesale price index rose from 15.4 (1965=100) in 1954 to 145.9 in 1970, a nine-fold increase, although fluctuation of inflation rates was recorded in the intervening years. The Korean inflation can be largely explained in terms of increased money supply, which, in turn, is attributable to government deficits (Lim 1971, Table 2). In order to finance the development projects, the government partly relied on deficit financing by creating credit at the Bank of Korea. This was a convenient but costly way to raise government funds in light of the state's inability to levy sufficient tax revenues. One study shows that state investment and loans amounted to more than half of the total fixed capital formation in the economy during the 1950s and early 1960s (Lee 1966, 329ff).

One result of this development policy and the resulting inflation was a reduction of real income for fixed income earners. Since wages and salaries are fixed by contract, the workers' real income is reduced by inflation until they can be adjusted to catch up with inflation. Statistics indicate that the proportion of employees' compensation to national income is negatively correlated with the rate of inflation (Lim 1971, Figure 1). Thus, it can be said that the burden of inflationary financing for development has been placed on the contractual income earners. This method of forced saving is usually regressive where money is not held for wealth accumulation, and the Korean case was not an exception. Government workers and military personnel were especially hard hit by inflation, since their income lagged behind inflation for a long period.

Even as the government pursued inflationary financing for industrialization, it often adopted a policy of regulating grain prices in an effort to counteract inflation. Such a policy is counterproductive to the purpose of price stabilization and agricultural development for self-sufficient food supply. Evidence suggests that low grain prices induce farmers to shift acreage to cultivation of other crops. The regulation of grain prices as part of the anti-inflation policy exacerbates inflation because it reduces grain supply. Policymakers seem to believe that uncontrolled grain prices are a main cause of inflation through a cost push spiral, or by expectation of further inflation with increased the price of grain. Statistical analysis does not, however, support this position (see Appendix IV).

The outcome of the grain price policy in combination with the investment policy is the unbalanced growth of the agricultural sector and the manufacturing sector. As a result, a large quantity of food grains had to be imported to meet the annual increase in food demand. The burden of financing such imports had to be placed on the industrial sector's capability to earn foreign exchange or on America's P.L. 480 grains. In some years, food imports amounted to about half of net dollar export earnings of manufactured goods. Such importation has been increasing steadily over the period under study, and has added to the difficulties in the balance of payments. In this sense, the agricultural sector appears to be a potential candidate for a policy of import substitution. Dollar earnings so saved would facilitate further industrialization. Of course, rapid inflation is a major culprit in the balance of payment difficulties, in addition to rapid industrialization requiring an increased importation of capital and input materials.

Balance of Payments and External Debts

The annual excess of imports over exports averaged around $300 million, with some fluctuations, during the ten year period 1955-1965. However, this excess has increased rapidly since 1966, reaching over the billion dollar mark in 1968. A large part of the increase may be due to the importation of capital goods and raw material input to support industrialization, in addition to the importation of food (see Appendix V). The trade deficits were financed mainly by foreign aid (largely non-reimbursable) in the earlier years. As foreign aid dwindled, however, the trade deficits had to be financed increasingly by reimbursable loans, commercial or otherwise. Between 1959 and 1971, the sum of external debt amounted to about $2.9 billion, approximately one-third of the nation's GNP. This increasing rate of such foreign debt is indeed troubling (EPB 1971, 81).

Though exports of manufactured goods reached over $1 billion at an impressive growth rate in 1971, it should be noted that the ratio of net earnings (not of imported raw materials) is just about half the value of exports. In contrast, the net earnings ratio of agricultural exports is close to one hundred percent according to a study conducted by the Korea Traders Association (KTA 1968, 196). This shows the potential of the agricultural sector to earn foreign exchange if it develops to the point of exporting products on a large scale. But the current situation is that imports of agricultural goods (food plus industrial raw material for agricultural purposes) have been growing at a rapid rate. The dollar amounts of such imports increased six fold between 1960 and 1970.

In addition, domestically manufactured items were found to have been exported at a price below their production cost. This deficit has been covered by various government subsidies. On average, the export price was found to be 10.3% below the production cost according to one survey (IBRD 1971, 77). Roger Norton noted that "the consequences of subsidized exports are beginning to appear: for example, the import content of export goods appears to be increasing, and some firms have raised prices on their domestic sales in order to offset the export losses" (Norton 1970, 64). Such protection and subsidies tend to prolong the existence of inefficient firms which would have gone bankrupt otherwise. Further costs may be incurred when the inefficient firms fail in spite of the subsidies, because the government usually underwrites the foreign loans for the firms. Though such incidences were publicly reported in the latter half of the 1960s, the exact amount of government-held responsibility is not known.

Foreign exchange could be saved not only in productive activities but also in investment activities, in addition to the development of the agricultural sector. It is generally recognized that the import content of capital formation is larger for the manufacturing sector than for the agricultural sector. This means that relatively less foreign exchange is required to finance agriculture (Myrdal 1968, 1356-1366). Furthermore, a labor intensive method of capital construction can be utilized in the agricultural sector since it has a pool of underutilized labor resources, especially during the off-season. Although not much evidence is available in this regard, the inverse coefficient matrix of the Adelman-Kim model shows that one dollar investment in agriculture would induce $1.27 worth of total imports, while one dollar investment in manufacture would induce $2.18 worth of total imports.

Rapid Urbanization and Related Social Costs

Social costs related to rapid urbanization are difficult to define or quantify, as the conventional GNP approach is not able to capture social costs. I will briefly illustrate the nature of the problem facing South Korea.

Rapid industrialization was accompanied by urbanization, at great environmental cost, such as water, air, and noise pollution, traffic congestion, housing shortages and poor sanitation. These are the so-called "external diseconomies" which should be weighed against the external economies which tend to cause urbanization. However, nowhere in planning documents can the discussion of the adjustment in benefit calculation be seen. Truly rational planning would require a quantification of these costs in order to arrive at a net benefit from investment allocation.

The extent of the urbanization problem can be assumed by the rapidity of urbanization. Over the past ten years, for instance, the population of Seoul has been increasing at a rate between 7 and 8% annually. At this rate, the population will double every decade. The question to be addressed is: Would the existing infrastructure be doubled every decade? This would just maintain the current proportional relationship of infrastructure to population, without any improvement. An indicator of this problem is the housing shortage. According to one study, 43% of the households in Seoul were living in substandard or slum-like dwellings (Ro 1971). In Busan, the country's second largest city, about 50% of the households were in a similar condition.

Another example is the problem of urban unemployment (and underemployment). The massive migration from rural areas constitutes the main source of population growth in Seoul. The rate of job creation in the urban areas is inadequate to keep up with the rapid inflow of labor force. The result is a high urban unemployment rate in comparison to the rural areas. "The data given for 1970 show 193,116 unemployed persons. If we define the total labor force as including employed workers plus the recorded unemployed, then open unemployment represented 13.3% of the labor force" (Nelson 1972, 12). Underemployment is more difficult to define and measure. Nelson defines it as: "Ill-paid workers with little prospect of advancement [who] constituted just about one-quarter of Seoul's employed labor in 1970" (Nelson 1972, 13).

Yet another problem is the movement of rural savings into urban areas. The majority of the rural-urban migrants seek either jobs or education. They are often supported by their rural families. The period of job-seeking may be a lengthy one, and even more prolonged support is usually necessary for the education of rural young men in the urban areas. The quantity of such a flow of savings is unknown. In-depth research is necessary, since this flow tends to exacerbate the urban-rural income disparity. Decentralization of job availability and educational opportunities may be required to improve the regional disparity of income and cultural opportunities.

Concluding Remarks

The existing evidence suggests that the past emphasis on industrialization and the neglect of the agricultural sector should be seriously reexamined. I have argued that greater gains may have been obtained if more investment had been made in the agricultural sector. The gains include a greater GNP, more equality of income distribution among sectors and regions, mitigation of price instability, and reduction of the balance of payment difficulties and other social costs of rapid urbanization.

I have also argued that the planning process should be reexamined for greater consistency in all sectors. Maximization (or optimization) models should be constructed to test the guidelines for investment allocation. Some attempts should be made to determine various welfare or social costs for alternative policy actions. An explicit statement with respect to hitherto neglected variables such as income distribution, employment, and external diseconomies is required. Only then can the calculation of development be consistent with the ultimate objective of development—enhancement of welfare for all economic units.

These arguments should not be construed as a deprecation of past achievements in Korea's phenomenal industrialization. It is only that a small fraction of the all-out effort devoted to export manufacturing would be capable of releasing the great potential of the agricultural sector to contribute to national development. The central issue is that the unbalanced growth since 1954 involved forgoing an opportunity to minimize the economic and social costs. The decade of the 1970s, with its Third Five-Year Economic Development Plan, may be the crucial time to correct such an imbalance.

BIBLIOGRAPHY

Adelman, I., and Kim Mahn-je. 1969. "An Econometric Model of the Korean Economy (1956-1966)." In *Practical Approaches to Development Planning, Korea's Second Five-Year Plan,* edited by I. Adelman, 77-108. Baltimore: Johns Hopkins University Press.

Balassa, Bela. 1971. "Industrial Policies in Taiwan and Korea." *Wiltwert-schaftliches* Archiv, Band 106, Heft 1. 55-76.

Ban, Sung-hwan. 1971. "The Long-run Growth of Aggregate Input and Productivity in Korean Agriculture." *Journal of Agricultural Economics* XIII (October): 11-31.

Bank of Korea. 1967. *Monthly Statistical Review* (December). Seoul: Bank of Korea.

Economic Planning Board (EPB). 1971. *Major Economic Indicators*. Seoul: Economic Planning Board.

Fei, John C. H., and Gustav Ranis. 1972. "A Model of Growth and Employment in the Open Dualistic Economy: The Case of Korea and Taiwan." Paper presented at the SEADAG Ad Hoc Seminar for South-East Asian Economies, Atlanta, Georgia, 7-9 December 1972.

Han, Kee-Chun. 1970. *Estimates of Korean Capital and Inventory Coefficient in 1968*. Seoul: Yonsei University Press.

International Bank of Reconstruction and Development (IBRD). 1973. *Finance and Development* (March). Washington D.C.: IBRD.

Kim, Dong-hi, and Choe Yang-boo. 1971. "Regional Imbalance in Economic Growth and Its Implication for Agricultural Development." *Journal of Agricultural Economics* (October) 13: 1-10.

Korea Traders Association (KTA). 1968. *Current Status and Prospect of Export Industries and Export Promotion*. Seoul: Korea Traders Association.

Myrdal, Gunnar. 1968. "The Problem of Labor-intensive Investments in Agriculture." In *Asian Drama*, Vol. II, 1356-1366.

Lee, Chang-nyol. 1966. *Korea Monetary System and Capital Resource Mobilization*. Seoul: Korea University Press.

Lim, Young-il. "Inflation and Capital Formation: Post War Korea." *Economia Internationale* 24.2.

Nelson, Joan M. 1972. "Migration, Integration of Migrants, and the Problem of Squatter Settlements in Seoul, Korea." Harvard Center for International Affairs and Woodrow Wilson Center, Smithsonian Institution.

Norton, Roger. 1970. "Planning with Facts: The Case of Korea." *American Economic Review* (May).

Renaud, Bertrand. 1973. "Conflicts between National Growth and Regional Income Equality in a Rapidly Growing Economy: The Case of Korea." *Economic Development and Cultural Change* 21 (April).

Ro, Chung-hyun. 1971. "Population and the Asian Environment." Paper presented at the Conference on Asian Environment, University of Michigan, Ann Arbor, June.

Appendix I. Some Indicators of Development

	1953–57	1958–61	1963–66	1967–71
(1) Growth rate of GNP (%)[a]	4.8	4.0	7.8	10.5
(2) Growth rate of per capita GNP[a]	1.8	1.1	4.9	8.5
(3) Growth rate by industry[a]				
Agriculture[b]	3.4	3.9	5.3	2.5
Manufacture[c]	14.7	8.0	14.2	20.3
Other Sectors[d]	4.5	3.2	8.4	12.3
(4) Gross investment ratio to GNP[c]	12.9	11.9	16.6	26.3
(5) Foreign savings ratio to GNP[c]	7.9	8.0	8.7	10.5
(6) Ratio of exports to GNP[c]	2.5	4.1	8.0	15.8
(7) Ratio of imports to GNP[c]	10.4	12.1	16.7	26.3
(8) Annual rate of inflation (WPI)[e]	37.0	4.8	16.4	7.8

Source: Bank of Korea, *National Income Statistics Yearbook* (1972), p. 177.
Note: (a) Based on series at 1970 constant market prices;
　　　(b) Includes agriculture, forestry, and fishery;
　　　(c) Based on series at current market prices;
　　　(d) Includes social overhead capital and other services;
　　　(e) Based on the wholesale price index series published by the Bank of Korea, *Economic Statistical Yearbook.*

Appendix II. Gross Domestic Capital Formation for Agriculture and Manufacturing

(billion won in 1965 constant prices)

Year	Investment Agriculture	Cumulative Investment	% of Total Investment	Investment Manufacture	Cumulative Investment	% of Total Investment	Domestic Capital Formation
1953	4.04	4.04	5.8	6.99	6.99	10.0	69.56
1954	3.45	7.49	6.0	6.44	13.43	11.1	57.87
1955	4.53	12.02	7.4	12.74	26.17	20.8	61.34
1956	5.07	17.09	8.8	16.71	42.88	29.2	57.29
1957	6.48	23.57	7.4	18.27	61.15	20.8	87.91
1958	5.35	28.92	6.9	16.64	77.79	21.4	77.72
1959	5.99	34.91	10.4	12.77	90.56	22.1	57.83
1960	6.97	41.88	11.2	14.85	105.41	23.8	62.48
1961	8.35	50.23	11.4	13.84	119.25	19.0	72.95
1962	6.72	56.95	8.6	17.76	137.01	22.8	77.99
1963	10.28	67.23	7.5	24.08	161.09	17.5	137.27
1964	10.66	77.89	9.3	22.37	183.46	19.6	114.41
1965	13.67	91.56	11.5	30.46	213.92	25.7	118.48
1966	23.16	114.72	11.2	61.72	275.64	29.7	207.38
1967	19.24	133.96	7.9	64.22	339.86	24.4	246.72
1968	23.82	157.78	6.9	79.71	419.56	23.2	344.12
1969	24.26	182.04	5.4	90.74	510.31	20.1	451.47
1970	26.97	209.01	5.9	91.75	602.06	20.1	455.58
1971	34.36	243.37	7.0	98.52	700.58	20.1	491.34

Source: Bank of Korea, *Economic Statistics Yearbook*, annual.

Appendix III. Sectoral Capital Efficiency 1954-1971 (1965 Constant Price: Billion Won)

Year	(1) Value-Added Incremental Output	(2) Agriculture Investment t-1	(3) (1)/(2)	(4) Cumulative Ratio	(5) Value-Added Incremental Output	(6) Manufacturing Investment t-1	(7) (5)/(6)	(8) Cumulative Ratio
1954	15.66	4.04	3.08	3.88	6.18	6.99	0.88	0.88
1955	4.94	3.45	1.43	2.75	8.10	6.44	1.26	1.06
1956	−6.95	4.53	−1.51	1.14	7.91	12.74	0.62	0.85
1957	18.27	5.07	3.60	1.87	5.99	16.71	0.35	0.65
1958	15.60	6.48	2.41	2.02	4.54	18.27	0.25	0.53
1959	−2.57	5.35	−0.48	1.55	5.41	16.64	0.33	0.49
1960	−0.31	5.99	−0.05	1.28	5.08	12.77	0.40	0.47
1961	24.76	6.97	3.55	1.65	2.01	14.85	0.14	0.43
1962	−16.10	8.35	−1.93	1.06	11.14	13.84	0.80	0.47
1963	18.12	6.72	2.70	1.25	19.90	17.76	0.84	0.52
1964	43.56	10.28	4.24	1.71	4.62	24.08	0.19	0.47
1965	−2.67	10.66	−0.25	1.44	23.52	22.37	1.05	0.54
1966	34.13	13.67	2.50	1.60	20.73	30.46	0.68	0.59
1967	18.93	23.16	0.82	1.12	35.75	61.72	0.58	0.58
1968	3.93	19.24	0.20	0.98	52.10	64.22	0.81	0.63
1969	39.34	23.82	1.65	1.08	52.90	79.71	0.66	0.63
1970	−2.95	24.26	−0.12	0.92	52.00	90.74	0.57	0.62
1971	11.34	25.06	0.45	0.87	61.55	86.16	0.72	0.64

Appendix IV. Is an increase in grain price the cause of general inflation? A test.

We note in the following table that the lag effect for prices seems to be slightly longer in the agricultural sector than in the manufacturing sector, with respect to the money supply variable. This finding seems inconsistent with the hypothesis that non-grain prices follow (or lag behind) grain prices. Further tests regressing non-grain prices against prices with a lag pattern can clarify this hypothesis. The following linear equation has been devised and fitted with quarterly percentage data:

$$(dp/p)_t^{ng} = F\ ((dp/p)_t^g, (dp/p)_{t-1}^g, (dp/p)_{t-2}^g, \ldots$$

where: $(dp/p)_t^{ng}$: quarterly percentage changes in non-grain wholesale price index at period t;

$(dp/p)_t^g$: quarterly percentage changes in grain wholesale price index at period t;

$(dp/p)_{t-1}^g$: $(dp/p)_t^g$ lagged by one period;

$(dp/p)_{t-2}^g$: $(dp/p)_t^g$ lagged by two periods, etc.

The rationale for this regression is that there should be some lag between the change in grain prices and the change in non-grain prices, if grain prices truly push up non-grain prices in the manner predicted by the cost push hypothesis. Instantaneous adjustment between the two prices is unlikely. If, on the other hand, the concurrent change is observable with a high correlation between these two price series, then this can be regarded not as instantaneous adjustment but as both series being caused by a third factor—in our case, the increase in money supply which influences both simultaneously. The result of the regression is presented in the second table below.

As can be seen, the lagging explanatory variables have negligible effect, while there is a small correlation for the current explanatory variable. This evidence (in addition to our previous finding that agricultural prices have a larger lag period than manufacturing prices with respect to the money supply variable) leads us to conclude that the two markets are not significantly related in the price formation process. In other words, supply-demand behavior in each market is different and not connected in any economically meaningful sense, lending support to the so-called cost-push variation. It is hard to believe, therefore, that an increase of grain prices would push up non-grain prices, as has often been suggested. The time sequence of a rise in grain prices preceding non-grain prices, if at all observable, does not mean very much. I suspect that reversing the independent and dependent variables might reveal a higher correlation because the agricultural sector is slower to adjust its prices with respect to increased money supply than the manufacturing sector. But this should not be construed as non-grain prices causing grain prices to rise.

Appendix IV (a). Sectoral Price Formation Function (1953-1966)

$(dp/p)_t$	Constant	$(dM/M)_{t-1}$	$(dI/I)_t$	$(dE/E)_t$	S	R	F
1. WPI all goods	0.17	0.26	0.18	0.06	16.67	0.75	3.77
		(0.21)	(0.27)	(0.09)			
2. WPI grain	1.94	0.59	0.17	-0.11	36.79	0.59	1.58
		(0.46)	(0.60)	(0.20)			
3. WPI non-grain	0.48	0.20	0.11	0.19	7.32	0.95	27.23
		(0.09)	(0.12)	(0.04)			
4. Deflator agr.	4.12	0.30	0.11	0.04	29.18	0.51	1.08
		(0.36)	(0.48)	(0.16)			
5. Deflator mfg.	7.25	0.05	0.04	0.21	11.10	0.84	7.10
		(0.14)	(0.18)	(0.06)			
6. Deflator serv.	2.79	0.17	0.21	0.05	5.4	0.94	22.93
		(0.07)	(0.09)	(0.03)			

$(dM/M)_{t-1}$: Percentage change in money supply lagged by one year.
$(dI/I)_t$: Percentage change in investment expenditures for fixed capital.
$(dE/E)_t$: Percentage change in exchange rates.

Appendix IV (b). Relation between Grain and Non-Grain Prices:
Regression with 1953-1966 Quarterly % Change Data

Constant	$(dp/p)_t$	$(dp/p)_{t-1}$	$(dp/p)_{t-2}$	$(dp/p)_{t-3}$	S	R
5.28	0.12				10.08	0.29
(1.50)	(0.05)					
5.59		0.03			11.36	0.08
(1.60)		(0.06)				
5.54			0.08		11.29	0.19
(1.60)			(0.06)			
5.62				0.08	11.39	0.19
(1.63)				(0.06)		
5.30	0.11	0.02			11.01	0.29
(1.55)	(0.05)	(0.05)				
5.49		0.02	0.07		11.39	0.20
(1.62)		(0.06)	(0.06)			
5.44			0.07	0.07	11.34	0.26
(1.63)			(0.06)	(0.06)		
5.10	0.13	0.01	0.09		10.92	0.37
(1.57)	(0.06)	(0.05)	(0.05)			
5.35		0.03	0.06	0.07	11.43	0.27
(1.66)		(0.06)	(0.06)	(0.06)		
5.01	0.12	0.01	0.08	0.05	11.01	0.40
(1.60)	(0.06)	(0.06)	(0.06)	(0.06)		

Appendix V. Total Imports, Total Exports, and Imports of Agricultural Goods

(Unit: $1000)

Year	(1) Food and Live Animal SITC (0)	(2) Crude Material Inedible SITC (2)	(3) Non-Material Oil & Fats SITC (4)	(4) (1) (2) (3) Less SITC (27) & (28)*	(5) Total Imports	(6) Total Exports
1955	17.468				341.416	17.966
1956	43.964				386.063	24.599
1957	107.568				442.174	22.202
1958	65.435				378,165	16.451
1959	27.344				303.807	19.812
1960	31.564	68.504	2.528	102.000	343.527	32.827
1961	40.128	63.294	3.949	106.885	316.142	40.878
1962	48.647	89.690	3.856	139.069	421.782	54.813
1963	120.607	107.074	4.781	223.962	560.273	86.802
1964	68.237	97.064	3.886	160.923	404.351	119.058
1965	63.505	110.021	3.764	167.435	463.442	175.082
1966	72.365	153.924	5.491	213.446	716.441	250.334
1967	94.115	208.473	6.945	276.376	996.246	320.220
1968	167.538	267.123	8.293	399.308	1462.873	455.401
1969	301.675	332.383	12.313	575.623	1863.974	835.185
1970	319.362	404.526	15.250	645.508	1983.774	835.185
1971	399.536	462.728	21.278	792.631	2394.400	1067.600

Source: Bank of Korea, *Economic Statistics Yearbook.*
* Notes: SITC (27): Crude fertilizers and crude minerals.
       SITC (28): Metalliferous ores and metal scrap.

Achievements and Failures of the Korean Economy in the 1970s

Jeong Ki-Jun

Introduction

During the initial stage of development, the Korean economy was characterized as a dualistic and labor-abundant economy with poor natural resources. On the one hand, it was a dualistic economy in the sense that the traditional agricultural sector and the modern industrial sector were not well integrated into industrial relationships nor was the socioeconomic behavior of the individuals in these two sectors synchronized. On the other hand, it was a labor-abundant economy as the labor-land ratio and the labor-capital ratio were unusually high. Korea had a population density of 380 persons per square kilometer in 1979 and continues to be one of the most densely populated developing countries in the world.

The story of the economic development of Korea may be told as a process of transforming the dualistic and labor-abundant economy into a capital- and skill-abundant one. And the objectives of development policies are to help achieve this transformation. The purpose of this paper is to describe and analyze the major achievements and failures in the development of the Korean economy during the 1970s. A number of different approaches are possible in delineating the major points of economic growth, but perhaps the most fruitful way to understand this

* Originally published in Vol. 20, No. 1 (January 1980).

Jeong Ki-Jun (Jeong, Gi-jun) is Professor of Economics at Seoul National University. He received his Ph.D. in Economics at Claremont Graduate University in 1976. He has written many articles on economic theory and Korean economy. His main interests include the theory of cooperation and the theory of games. E-mail: kjjeong@plaza.snu.ac.kr.

process in a given country is to first examine it from a historical perspective. In the next section, I will provide an overview of the general economic environment of Korea.

General Economic Environment of Korea before 1970

Viewed historically, the patterns of Korea's economic development between 1946 and 1970 can be most aptly summarized as follows.

The Post-World War II and the Korean War Period (1946-1953)

The first phase is one of economic calamity brought on by the aftermath of World War II and the Korean War (1950-1953). The Korean economy during the prewar period was almost totally dependent on the Japanese economy as a result of the long Japanese colonial rule from 1910 to 1945. Not only did the malformed economy completely collapse after liberation in 1945, but the economic calamity worsened with the division of the country into North and South. In the midst of this economic chaos, in 1948, the government of the Republic of Korea was founded in the South. The interval between the foundation of the government and the outbreak of the Korean War in 1950 was too short for the state to undertake any projects to rebuild the economy.

The three years of the Korean War devastated the entire peninsula. The war cost the country approximately one million lives and destroyed production facilities in the magnitude of three billion dollars, which was equivalent to twice the annual gross national product of Korea for the early 1950s. Production was almost completely paralyzed, the supply of basic materials was in acute shortage, and the government financed the war through enormous deficits. As a result, inflationary tendencies, inherited from the period of colonial rule, accelerated.

Rehabilitation and Import Substitution with U.S. Aid (1954-1961)

The Korean government had the great task of rehabilitating the economy when the cease-fire was signed in 1953. A financial stabilization program was instituted in 1954 with U.S. aid. Facilities for producing basic materials were established, and inflation was gradually brought under control. The economic aid provided by the United States was the most important external factor that facilitated the rehabilitation of the devastated economy. It helped to establish a framework of import-substituting industries and social overhead capital such as systems of transportation, communication, and public health, as well as educational facilities.

During the 1950s, the Korean government showed little insight into the pressing problem of how to develop the national economy. The government was preoccupied with the task of reducing inflation, using all available measures for this task. It ultimately failed to formulate and execute a well-coordinated plan to promote national economic growth.

The administration adopted three main lines of policy from which it never deviated throughout this period. The three lines were: 1) to maintain low prices for agricultural products, 2) to preserve a low interest rate at organized financial institutions, and 3) to maintain the low foreign exchange rate so as to maximize the amount of foreign exchange received from the U.N. forces. These policies may have been justified as anti-inflationary measures, but they can hardly be regarded as well-conceived development policies.

The economic consequences of these policies were unmistakably clear: they were highly favorable to business investments, particularly those related to U.S. aid. The low interest rate in the midst of high inflation often rendered the effective rate of interest negative which, in turn, favored borrowing from banking institutions. The low exchange rates were advantageous to those end users to whom the foreign funds provided by aid were allocated. As well, low agricultural prices were beneficial to business because they held down the wage rate within the industrial labor sector.

By virtue of these policies, the manufacturing industries were established primarily in the areas of food-processing, textiles, leather, and some chemical products. These industries were heavily dependent on raw materials provided by the U.S., and were not closely related to developing the domestic resources. Moreover, the low price of agricultural products contributed to the retarded growth of agriculture, while the low interest rates at financial institutions hindered the healthy development of financial institutions and resulted in the misallocation of loans. Finally, the exchange rate overvaluing local currency mitigated against the development of export industries. Under the regime of strictly controlled interest rates and low foreign exchange rates with import licences, the allocation of bank loans and foreign exchange to the so-called end users constituted a form of subsidy. The industrialists who were the end users of foreign exchange and bank loans emerged as the propertied class during this period.

With the decrease of foreign aid in 1958, the Korean economy began to slow down. The demand for industrial goods also dwindled as the small domestic markets became quickly saturated. Simultaneously with the onset of an economic recession, there developed political unrest which culminated in the overthrow of the government by students in 1960 and a military coup in 1961.

Import Substitution and Export Promotion in Light Industries (1962-1969)

The military regime announced the First Five-Year Economic Development Plan in 1961. The First Five-Year Plan was imbued with a sense of purpose and urgency, and purported to establish the foundation of a viable economy during period of 1962-1966. The main objectives of the plan were declared as: 1) the development of energy industries such as coal production and electricity, 2) the expansion of agricultural production aimed at increasing farm income and correcting the structural imbalance of the economy, 3) the development of basic industries and infrastructure, 4) the maximum utilization of idle resources, 5) an increase of employment, 6) the conservation and utilization of land, 7) the improvement of the balance of payments through export promotion, and 8) the promotion of science and technology.

Above all, the First Plan emphasized the fostering of social overhead capital. For this purpose, a frugal life-style of living was advocated to maximize the domestic rate of savings. In addition, the plan aimed at an annual rate of economic growth of 7.1%, a very high rate relative to the past economic performance. To achieve this growth rate, the ratio of investment to GNP was slated to increase from 20.1% in 1962 to 22.7% in 1966, or twice the rate as that of the previous period.

The plan, though carefully formulated and implemented, met early setbacks. Consecutive poor harvests in 1962 and 1963, together with the excessive growth of the money supply, caused inflation to rise. Furthermore, the unfavorable balance of payments drastically reduced the foreign exchange holdings. Under these adverse conditions, the government had to revise the original targets and change its main policy directions. In the revised version, the target rate of annual economic growth was reduced from 7.1% to 5%, and the policy was reoriented towards economic stabilization.

The three most outstanding policy measures were the inducement of foreign capital, the devaluation of the Korean won, and the raising of interest rates. The government also implemented reforms in the tax system, and liberalized foreign trade. The adoption of the first two measures signified a departure from the main policy directions that were adopted throughout the 1950s. The raising of interest rates greatly contributed to increasing deposits at banks as people switched from demand deposits and currency to savings deposits, thereby reducing the quantity of money which otherwise would have grown much more rapidly due to the increased inflow of foreign capital.

The U.S. aid grants decreased markedly during the First Plan period, and official government aid came largely in the form of loans. Short-term private commercial loans also started flowing in, and with these loans a large number of factories were established particularly for the production of consumer goods.

Based on the experiences of the First Plan, the basic objectives of the Second Five-Year Plan (1967-1971) were to promote the modernization of an outmoded industrial structure and to build up a solid foundation for a self-supporting national economy. The major targets were stated as follows: self-sufficiency in food production; increased output of chemical, machinery, and iron and steel industries; export expansion and further import substitution; encouragement of family planning and higher employment levels; substantial income growth with a special emphasis on increasing farmers' productivity and income through diversification; and the enhancement of manpower resources by improving scientific knowledge and management skills. The key strategies adopted to achieve these targets consisted of a greater emphasis on export promotion and the development of agriculture and heavy industry.

Overall, the Second Five-Year Economic Development Plan was enormously successful: the achievements exceeded the targets in nearly all respects. The average annual growth rate of the GNP was 12% (plan target was 7%), and that of exports 38% (plan target was 17%). Industrial production and foreign capital imports were much greater than originally envisaged in the plan. This dynamic economic growth, however, was achieved at the cost of domestic and international economic equilibrium. The inflationary trend never subsided, the balance of payments deteriorated, and foreign debts increased.

The vigorous investment activities, financed by borrowing from abroad as well as from domestic banking institutions, placed increasing pressure on the meager absorptive capacity of the economy. These activities were partly nurtured as undervalued foreign exchanges started to subsidize, as various kinds of bottlenecks developed. A number of "unstable" enterprises also emerged. Due to the heavy borrowing from both foreign and domestic sources, the financial structure of business enterprises deteriorated and the rate of profit declined steadily as the domestic market gradually became saturated. Thus, beneath the surface of prosperity, the signs of economic recession became steadily more apparent toward 1968-1969.

Economic Performance in the 1970s

As stated above, the vigorous growth during the 1960s was not without its costs. In the late 1970s, the state began to adopt a series of measures that would lead to economic stabilization. Tight monetary and fiscal policies as well as import restriction measures were adopted.

Realizing the importance of stability and equilibrium of the economy, the government emphasized balance between growth and stability in the development process in the Third Five-Year Development Plan for 1972-1976. The plan also included the goal of achieving a balance in regional development. Despite this new emphasis, the basic characteristics of the Third Five-Year Plan were the same as those of the previous plans: rapid economic growth through vigorous promotion of exports. The pursuit of balance between growth and stability, however, was a difficult goal for the Korean economy, especially after the international oil crisis of 1973-1974.

Although the Korean economy suffered setbacks due to the oil crisis, the weakness of the international monetary system, and the economic nationalism of the Third World during the period of the Third Plan, it succeeded in achieving a high economic rate of growth. The average annual GNP growth rate was 10.9% compared to the target rate of 8.6%, though the rate of annual growth was highly uneven mostly due to the oil crisis and its effects.

While the Third Plan accomplished the primary goal of maintaining a high rate of growth, it was highly unsuccessful in achieving economic stabilization. The regime issued a strong stabilization decree in August 1972 to impress businesses, consumers and the administration alike of the need for economic structural readjustment. Structural adjustment was to be achieved through healthier management practices, sounder consumption, and tighter fiscal and monetary policies. The decree suppressed inflation rates in 1972 and 1973, but the stabilization measures were nullified by the international oil crisis; only in 1976 did the inflation rate return to normal.

In the Fourth Five-Year Development Plan for 1977-1981, a new concept of social and economic development was introduced to improve the national quality of life. While the plan also emphasized the establishment of a self-supporting structure in the economy, it showed no substantial changes from the development strategies adopted in the previous plans. The Korean economy succeeded in achieving a high rate of economic growth in 1977 and 1978. Beneath the successful economic expansion, however, factors detrimental to the stability of the economy mounted, and rapid economic growth was no longer sufficient to justify the costs paid by the Korean people.

The Mechanism of Korean Economic Development

The main policy objective for the Korean economy consistently pursued through the series of five-year development plans since 1962 has been a high rate of economic growth. In the early stage of development, this objective was pursued through the domestic market, but it soon turned out to be an impossible goal in an economy with scarce natural resources and a limited domestic market. Therefore, the development strategy turned toward foreign markets, both for supply of raw materials and purchase of manufactured products. This may be called the development strategy of export-led rapid economic growth.

The main aspects of the implementation of this strategy were as follows. First, the ratio of exports to GNP increased from 7.2% in 1966 to 15% in 1970, and again to 37% in 1978. The increase in exports deepened the dependence of the Korean economy on the international economy through the importation of raw materials and capital. Second, without a foothold in foreign economies or technological advantages, the international competitiveness of export goods had to be created artificially by sustaining a low wage rate. Therefore, the low wage rate policy was intimately linked with the strategy of export-led economic growth. To generalize, we may say that a typical export industry is constructed by foreign capital with foreign technology—it imports raw materials from abroad and processes them into final products which are then exported. The only advantage of the domestic industry is the low wage rate of relatively well-educated labor. In many cases, a low wage rate is insufficient for an industry to be competitive abroad. An export industry typically enjoys special favors from banking institutions and domestic markets; moreover special favors for entrepreneurs are also needed for a high rate of investment and a high rate of export expansion and economic growth. Third, Korea's export-led economic growth was also state-led economic growth. The state interfered in private business at every level of activities by controling the investment decisions, production quantities, and price of products.

The most important achievement of the strategy of the export promotion has been the high rate of economic growth. The strategy increased the average annual growth rate of the GNP from 4% to the order of 10% in the early 1960s. The GNP may not be the sole, nor the best performance indicator for an economy, but there is no doubt that the steady and high growth of the GNP has increased the material well-being of the Korean people during the last decade. Another achievement of the export-led economic development plan has been an increase in employment levels. In the early 1960s, the unemployment rate was around 10% excluding substantial hidden unemployment. Now it has dropped to less than 5%.

The rapid economic growth powered by export expansion has, nevertheless, created undesirable effects. The accelerated growth policy based on foreign capital, foreign raw materials, and foreign export markets has made the Korean economy more dependent on foreign economies, particularly those of the United States and Japan. The Korean economy relies on these two countries for 50% of its export markets, and 60% of its import markets. More specifically, 40% of total imports come from Japan. This high level of dependence makes the Korean economy excessively vulnerable to international economic fluctuations as seen during the oil crisis, the international monetary instability, and the raising of trade barriers.

Another adverse outcome of the rapid economic growth policy has been the deterioration of the income distribution. One the one hand, the export-led economic growth has been based almost exclusively on a low wage rate, which, in turn, has been based on low agricultural prices and labor restrictions. On the other hand, high economic growth has required high investment, which, in turn, has generated opportunities for capital accumulation. Entrepreneurs have been offered various ways to accumulate capital and have given diverse inducements to invest.

The pursuit of export-led growth has weakened the inter-sectoral relations among domestic industries and has helped to create a malformed industrial structure. An export industry dependent on foreign raw materials and foreign markets needs only location and a labor force from the domestic sector, and does not need any industrial relations with other production sectors. The agricultural sector, which no longer supplies raw materials to the export industry, now loses its role of supplying food to the urban laborers. The primary role of the domestic consumer is not as a buyer of export industry products, but rather it is to supplement the industry's loss. Biased support for an export industry and against a domestic good industry has led to a deformed industrial structure unfavorable to domestic consumers.

The state-led economic growth policy has grown more and more ineffective as the size of the economy has increased. When the economy was small, as in the early 1960s, direct government control of the major industries could be an efficient method of management, but as the economy expanded, rigid state control over the economy has become increasingly ineffective and has been overwhelmed by corruption.

A considerable part of investment funds has been borrowed from abroad, but domestic investment funds have been financed, mainly by forced savings through inflation. The high rate of inflation has discouraged voluntary savings. This is a vicious circle of high inflation and low savings.

Suggested Directions for the 1980s

Korea made great strides on the path of industrialization during the 1970s, as in the 1960s, against tremendous odds. Partly due to the success itself, the Korean economy has developed a number of problems which must be solved if the economy is to sustain its growth in the 1980s.

First, we should revise the measure of economic performance. Explicitly or implicitly, the economists have treated economic growth as synonymous with GNP growth. GNP is a measure of the level of economic activity, and when the activity level is low, it is usually proportional to economic performance or economic welfare. When the activity level is high, however, it does not necessarily correspond to economic performance or economic welfare. A multi-dimensional measure of economic performance rather than a uni-dimensional one is now needed.

Second, we should decrease the level of foreign dependence and the resulting international vulnerability. An economy with a high GNP and a high level of foreign dependence can not be called a self-supporting economy. The reduction of foreign dependence may cost a temporary decrease in the GNP, but in terms of a multi-dimensional measure of performance, a lower GNP will not necessarily imply a worsened economic situation.

Third, it is necessary to accord much greater emphasis to the problem of income distribution in formulating economic policies. The assumption that growth in per capita income will somehow and someday create a more egalitarian distribution of income does not seem warranted. In the Korean economy, the low wage rate has been the foundation of rapid economic growth led by exports. That basis should be changed.

Fourth, the state intervention in the private sectors of the economy should be selectively reduced, as price mechanism may be more efficient in generating detailed decisions.

Last but not least, we should be more alert to the problem of environmental pollution, which is becoming increasingly serious as industrialization proceeds. Clean air and water, and a pleasant environment are perhaps more important than the conveniences of industrialization which the people could easily dispense with.

Exports and Business Conglomerates

Kim Cae-One

The Transformed Economic Picture

The Korean economy has seen major quantitative as well as qualitative changes during the past 30 years. Rapid growth and structural changes, since the early 1960s in particular, have had a decisive effect on development in all aspects of society.

Let us first review the changes through looking at the economic indicators as shown in Table 1. In constant price of 1975, the GNP increased by 6.7 times during the 1954-1982 period. The average annual growth rate for the ten years since 1962 exceeded 9% and a growth rate of 7 to 8% was registered even in 1974 and 1975, when most countries, including developed ones, had zero or minus growth. The year 1980 was an exception when Korea marked a growth rate of –6.2%. Taking into account population growth, the average annual growth rate in per capita GNP remained at about 1% from 1954 to 1962, but exceeded 6% from 1962 and sustained major increases in real income.

Such quantitative expansion was accompanied by changes in the industrial structure itself. The component ratio of manufacturing in GNP, which stood at less than 9% until 1962, when the First Five-Year Economic Development Plan was launched, marked a sharp upturn and has approached 34% in recent years. When manufacturing alone is reviewed, based on the value added, the distribution ratio between light

* Originally published Vol. 26, No. 10 (October 1986).

Kim Cae-One (Kim, Se-won) is Professor of Economics at Seoul National University. He obtained his Ph.D. in International Economics from Brussels University. His publications include *Yuro hwa-ui chulbeom-gwa hanguk gyeongje* (1999). E-mail: caeonek@plaza. snu.ac.kr.

and heavy industries was reversed from about 81:19 in 1961 to 48:52 in 1982. If industrialization is defined as "a production structure centered on secondary industry," one can say that Korea is approaching the level of industrialized countries.

Rapid economic growth achieved by a number of developing countries, including Korea, created a new economic zone in the world economy in the 1960s. The 1979 OECD Report identified these countries as "newly industrializing countries" (NICs), and they are also known as the "fast-manufactured goods exporting countries," "semi-developed countries," and "semi-industrialized countries." Various reports now cite Korea as a representative model of an economy growing out of underdevelopment.

Table 1. Korea's Major Economic Indices (1954-1982)

	1954	1962	1972	1982	Average Annual Increase Rate (%)		
					1954-62	1962-72	1972-82
Population (in millions)	21.8	26.5	33.5	39.3	2.5	2.4	1.6
GNP[1] (one billion won)	2,319	3,071	7,366	15,509	3.6	9.1	7.7
Primary industry (%)	(51.1)	(45.3)	(29.2)	(19.2)	2.0	4.5	3.3
Secondary industry (%)	(5.3)	(9.1)	(20.9)	(34.2)	10.8	18.6	13.2
Tertiary industry (%)	(43.6)	(45.6)	(49.9)	(46.6)	4.2	10.1	7.0
Per capita GNP (dollar)	220	239	454	815	1.1	6.6	6.0
Per capita private consumption (won)	84,775	100,114	116,388	260,359	2.1	5.2	4.6
Investments and savings Total investments/ GNP (%)	11.9	12.8	22.2	27.0			
Investments in secondary industry/Total investments (%)	17.5	20.6	19.4	15.3			
Domestic savings ratio (%)	6.6	3.3	16.5	22.4			
Foreign savings ratio (%)	5.3	9.5	5.7	4.6			

1) Based on the constant price of 1975.
Source: Bank of Korea.

Leaving American Aid Behind

The Korean economy sustained itself with American aid until the latter half of the 1950s. The U.S. offered Korea free aid amounting to approximately $2.15 billion from 1953 to 1961 through various agencies such as the ECA (Economic Cooperation Administration), SEC (Supplies Economic Cooperation), CRIK (Civil Relief in Korea), UNKRA (UN Korean Reconstruction Agency), PL 480 (Public Law 4801), FOA (Foreign Operation Administration), and ICA (International Cooperation Administration). The impact of U.S. aid on the Korean economy is shown in Table 2. The average sum of aid per capita received during this period was $11.18, which is comparable to the Marshall Plan (about $12), which provided for the rehabilitation of Europe from 1948 to 1952. American aid amounted to an average of 2.4 times the amount of Korea's imports from the United States.

As pointed out earlier, however, such American economic aid failed to lay the foundation for a self-sustaining economy. In terms of industrial structure, it gave rise to a light industry system centered on consumer goods. The rapid development of the textile, flour milling, sugar refining, and leather industries in the 1950s was mostly due to American aid, which provided the momentum in the 1960s for some of these industries to grow into competitive export industries.

Table 2. U.S. Economic Aid to the Republic of Korea

Year	Aid per Capita ($)	Aid/ GNP (%)	Aid/Total Trade Balance	Aid/Imports from U.S. (%)
1953	9.59	14.3	–	–
1955	11.05	16.7	73.2	304.0
1956	14.82	22.4	90.4	375.7
1957	16.88	22.9	91.2	349.4
1958	13.77	16.9	88.8	153.7
1959	9.26	11.2	78.2	150.6
1960	9.94	12.3	79.0	183.5
1961	7.90	9.5	73.2	140.6
1953-1961	11.18	15.2	82.0	236.8

Source: Bank of Korea, *Korea Statistical Yearbook.*

Under the Kennedy Administration, the U.S. overseas aid program underwent a major change, and Korea, following the military coup of 1961, began to rely on loans rather than on free aid to implement an ambitious economic development plan. Although loans are also a form of economic aid, because they must be reimbursed, it is possible to say that Korea began to raise the financial resources needed for its economic development on its own.

Deployment of the Development Strategy

Viewed from the supply side, Korea's development strategy pursued extensive growth on the strength of its abundant labor force and its expanded introduction of foreign capital from the early 1960s. On the demand side, increased exports emerged as the most important factor for economic growth in contrast to most developing countries, including Latin American countries, which emphasized import substitution as their strategy of coping with external economies.

The development of the Korean economy is often described as a development model relying on surplus labor. The possibility of supplying a qualified labor force, virtually without limit from the beginning of the 1960s, acted as a force stimulating growth. This is supported by the fact that, while the unemployment rate during the latter half of the 1950s reached 9 to 10%, the average number of years spent in education by the male population of the non-farming sector was more than 7 years, much higher than other developing countries.

The employment increase rate which remained at about 1% until the early 1960s registered a sharp upturn paralleling the remarkable economic growth achieved thereafter. The average annual rate recorded 3.6% during the 1963-1972 period and 3.2% during the 1972-1982 period. Both exceeded the rate of increase in the labor force.

Such a large absorption of the labor force was made possible by active public and private investment. The total investment rate increased from 11.9% in 1954 to 21.6% during the implementation of the First Five-Year Economic Development Plan (1962-1966), and to 31.2% during the Third Five-Year Plan (1977-1981) (See Table 1). The rate, however, has decreased slightly in recent years to 27%.

During the initial development period in the 1960s, Korea relied largely on foreign capital to secure investment capital. The component ratio of domestic savings in total investments in this period fell below 50%. The domestic savings ratio progressively increased and the self-reliance ratio in investment sources reached 90% in the latter half of the 1970s, but has in recent years decreased to around 80%, indicating an increasing trend in the relative weight of foreign capital.

The basic means mobilized to systematically carry out the growth strategy was the economic development plan. The formulation of development plans, mainly by the foreign aid agencies, goes as far back as the Korean War of 1950-1953. A good example is the Nathan Five-Year Plan (1954-1958) which was geared toward economic rehabilitation but rejected by the Korean government. The government under Syngman Rhee later formulated a seven-year plan and the Chang Myon administration a five-year plan, neither of which was implemented. Following the 1961 military coup, government-led development planning was successfully initiated for the first time under Park Chung-hee.

Implementation of the Development Plans

Due to the incompatibility between market and planning, the formulation and execution of an economic development plan in a market economy system face many restrictions and require a high degree of flexibility and skill. France is the only developed country that executes a development plan. As the name "planning indicatif" implies, the French plan is mainly designed to indirectly promote national economic activities. A "bottom-up" formula and a very complicated coordination scheme between various sectors have been adopted so that regional data and prospects are gathered to the center. Furthermore, it is national planning subjected to parliamentary vote.

In the case of Korea, however, partly due to the many restrictions the Korean economy faced, the long-term economic plan featured government involvement from the outset. The government intervened heavily in raising and distributing the limited investment resources. Preferential treatment was given in taxation, finance, and foreign exchange control. From the outset, almost no consideration was given to the inducive and complementary functions of a development plan designed to strengthen the market functions or rectify malfunctioning market mechanisms.

Meanwhile, limited investment resources, a tendency toward ambitious industrialization, and export-oriented growth resulted in the pursuit of unbalanced growth. Preferences were given to the manufacturing sector over the agricultural sector, to export industries over import-substitution and domestic consumption industries, and to large enterprises over small- and medium-sized enterprises. Also, investments were concentrated in specific regions. It may be said that the intention was to foster leading sectors, forming so-called growth-poles, and then to use such sectors to spread growth to other areas.

Strong government-led development plans began to reveal their limits in the mid-1970s when the government prepared its Fourth Five-Year Plan (1977-1981). This coincided with a low unemployment rate in Korea, and therefore the government had to change its previous growth strategy and pursue intensive growth through increased productivity. Among other factors, the enlarged private sector, the need to upgrade efficiency, and the limitations of government capabilities appear to have brought about a shift toward reinforced market mechanisms or an economy led by the private sector.

Of course, no capitalist country relies on the market mechanism in a true sense with respect to the form of ownership, the mechanism of economic decision-making, and resource allocation. And every economy adopts a mixed system consisting of a formula appropriate to its conditions. Whatever the adopted operational formula may be, for a thriving market economy, not only must the philosophy and convictions of policymakers correspond with socioeconomic realities, but also channels must be provided for the participation of diverse interest groups.

A clearer classification of the actual governmental role and the role of the private sector, with respect to economic management, remains as one of the tasks to be resolved.

Export-oriented Strategy and Growth

One of the important driving forces that enabled Korea to achieve such rapid economic growth was its strong will for development. This determination can be seen in the expanded exports.

Exports emerged as the strongest driving force for growth and were directly linked to the domestic business boom. Until recently, the contribution ratio of exports to economic growth was as high as 40% and for employment it once registered as much as 50%, though it has now leveled off at 15-20%.

Korea broke the world record by achieving an average annual export growth rate of nearly 40% for 12 years from the early 1960s, and advanced to the status of a newly industrializing country through its export-oriented growth strategy. Exports thus constitute a factor testifying to the dynamism of the Korean economy.

Until the late 1950s, Korea's total annual exports averaged less than $40 million with considerable fluctuations. The largest export item, then, was tungsten ore, and exports in general were dominated by primary industrial products such as agricultural and fishery products (See Table 3).

The expansion of exports was emphasized from the beginning of the First Five-Year Plan, albeit passively, as more stress was placed on improving international balance of payments. Policymakers, however, began to have confidence as exports increased beyond expectations in the course of the First Five-Year Plan. It is ironic that the majority of developing countries, which sought development through import substitution, desired growth through "not aid but trade," with the 1964 founding of UNCTAD providing momentum. But, most of them could not achieve this goal.

Beginning with the Second Five-Year Plan, "the promotion of industrialization through exports" was heavily stressed. Such determination was supported by the fact that export performance, with few exceptions, far outpaced the annual targets since 1964. Exports in 1971 and 1972 even surpassed their annual targets by 2 to 2.5 times, and exports in 1973 registered a 98.6% increase over the previous year.

Table 3. Major Export Items in the 1950s

Year	1953		1955		1960		1961	
Item and percentage of total	Tungsten	(43.9)	Tungsten	(31.8)	Tungsten	(14.2)	Tungsten	(11.0)
	Laver	(6.9)	Silk	(9.8)	Rice	(11.5)	Iron ore	(10.4)
	Silk	(6.3)	Agar-agar	(5.6)	Iron ore	(7.5)	Silk	(6.9)
	Agar-agar	(4.9)	Graphite	(5.6)	Cotton textiles	(7.4)	Pork	(6.1)
	Fresh fish	(4.8)	Swine bristles	(3.8)	Fresh fish	(4.7)	Dried fish	(6.1)
Total		66.8		56.9		45.3		40.5

Source: Korean Traders Association.

Pursuit of an Export-first Policy

Though Korea has pursued an "outward-looking" industrialization, external transactions have been conducted primarily through export increases. A rapid increase in exports fostered export industries themselves and greatly contributed to industrialization by earning foreign exchange. This, in turn, enabled the import of capital goods and technology by expanding the market to take advantage of "economies of scale." Thus, a "market expansion policy," in particular, was a great advantage over an import-substitution policy.

The export-oriented growth strategy, coupled with a "can do" mentality, was adopted in order to overcome the barriers of a narrow market and a shortage in natural resources, technology, and capital. This strategy worked because of the qualified labor force. The abundance of low-wage, educated labor was a decisive factor enabling Korea to secure a competitive edge in the labor-intensive sectors until the mid-1970s.

In addition, many favors and incentives given to the export industries, such as in the import of capital goods and raw materials, banking credits, and tax breaks, were sufficient to stimulate and invigorate them. The export-first policy emerged at this time and began to be perceived wrongly as an objective in itself that should be attained even at considerable cost, and not as a means of promoting growth, industrialization, and eventually the public welfare. In the meantime, the so-called "target fulfillment" centered economic policy began to show side effects. As a result, Korea's absolute scale of exports (based on current prices) increased by almost 440 times in a 30-year period and the structure of exports underwent a drastic change. The component ratio of manufactured goods in Korea's exports increased from 27% in 1962 to 62% in 1966 and then to more than 90% since the early 1970s.

Under the Third Five-Year Plan, from 1972 to 1976, priority was given to exports in heavy and chemical industries. While many light industries grew in the 1950s and the early 1960s through the process of import substitution, many heavy and chemical industries were established for export purposes from the outset.

The percentage of heavy and chemical industries in the export of manufactured goods, as shown in Table 4, exceeded 50% in the 1970s and machinery topped the list of heavy and chemical industrial exports early in the 1980s. Although textiles are still the single largest export, ships, steel, and electronic products amount to nearly 25% of total exports.

Table 4. Exports in Manufacturing Sector

Industry \ Year	1975	1981	1982	1983
Light industry	61.4	47.4	42.7	38.4
Food and beverage	7.3	4.3	3.1	2.9
Textiles	37.3	27.8	25.3	22.5
Others	16.8	15.3	14.2	13.0
Heavy and chemical industry	38.6	52.6	57.3	61.6
Chemical	11.8	11.3	10.7	10.9
Metal	8.0	15.4	15.2	14.5
Machinery	188.8	25.9	31.5	36.1
Total manufactured goods	100.0	100.0	100.0	100.0

Source: Korean Traders Association.

The Dilemma in Expanded Exports

Like the previous labor-intensive, light industry-oriented export policy (though there is a degree in difference), production and exports focused on the assembly and processing of finished goods and neglected the corresponding elevation of domestic industries, thus increasing reliance on the import of raw materials, capital equipment, and intermediate goods (e.g., parts and components). This inevitably resulted in the increase of imports, thus worsening the international balance of payments (See Table 5).

Table 5. Annual Export and Import Trends

Year	Export		Import		Trade Balance
	Amount ($1 million)	Increase Rate over Previous Year (%)	Amount ($1 million)	Increase Rate over Previous Year (%)	
1962	55	34.1	422	33.5	−335
1965	175	47.1	463	14.6	−240
1970	835	34.0	1,984	8.8	−922
1975	5,081	13.9	7,274	6.2	−1,671
1980	17,505	16.3	22,292	9.6	−4,384
1981	21,254	21.4	26,131	17.2	−3,628
1982	21,853	2.8	24,251	−7.2	−2,594
1983	24,445	11.9	26,192	8.0	−1,655

Sources: Korean Traders Association.

Korea could achieve such a drastic increase in exports partly because the developed countries, Korea's major export markets, enjoyed a record-high economic boom in the 1960s and gave Korea exceptionally favorable treatment as a developing country. As a result, the government could provide export industries with direct subsidies and various incentives.

The situation changed, however, as the world economy suffered from recession in the mid-1970s. Neoprotectionism began to spread in order to protect employment and the balance of payments, and at the same time, Korea gained recognition at home and abroad as a semi-developed country. Korea now has to take part in world competition on a footing almost identical to the advanced countries (officially since the Tokyo Round), and faces protectionist tendencies and a long-term stagnation in international demand. Now it must seek a turning point in its export policy. It is also evident, when compared to other semi-developed countries with similar conditions, that the slowdown in the export increase rate since the late 1970s came not merely because of the above-mentioned changes in the world economy. It is necessary for Korea to promote a readjustment of its export structure on a medium- and long-term basis.

The Image of a Strong Korea in the Construction Industry

On the one hand, Korea's construction industry significantly contributed to the pursuit of export-oriented growth strategy. In particular, the negative impact Korea sustained from the oil crisis, due to its high reliance on imported oil, was largely minimized by a rapid expansion of the construction contracts in the Middle East. The all but miraculous boost in Korea's foreign exchange earnings from these construction projects was another element of the dynamism of Korean economy.

Although the construction projects were stimulated by the 1973 oil shock, overseas projects actually started back in 1965 and 1966 in Southeast Asian markets. Overseas construction contracts amounted to $11 million in 1966 and grew to $233 million by 1972, and most of these were in Southeast Asia. Construction firms had a number of major projects at home in the 1950s, including the construction of military facilities for the United Nations Command. Since the 1960s, these firms were engaged in large-scale infrastructure projects and facilities investments according to the execution of long-term economic development plans at home, and also participated in major construction projects in South Vietnam, Thailand, and Malaysia, thereby building up a supply capability.

Overseas construction contracts registered an annual increase of 220% in 1975, and a 200% increase in 1976. Except for 1979, overseas construction orders jumped sharply year after year at rates well exceeding not only economic growth rates but export increase rates as well. During the 1975-1982 period, the average annual increase rate in overseas construction contracts was about nine times the overall economic growth rate and three times the export increase rate.

In other words, the effects of construction exports on the Korean economy were comparable to commodity exports in that they resolved restrictions imposed by the narrow domestic market. The overseas construction boom since 1975 has been an important driving force in the nation's economic growth through increasing income, improving the international balance of payments, expanding employment, enlarging the scale of enterprises, and diversifying the markets. According to research conducted by the ENR Co. of the United States, Korea ranked second after the United States in the total sum of construction contracts awarded around the world in 1982, and accounted for nearly 14% of the total projects. In addition to the fame involving its export-oriented growth strategy, Korea has thus acquired a name as "the construction country."

On the down side, due to loose monetary policy, the overseas construction boom that grew rapidly since the mid-1960s resulted in chronic inflation. Large enterprises also began to be involved in real estate speculation around this time.

After reaching a peak of around $13.5 billion in 1981 and 1982, the amount of awarded construction contracts decreased to slightly over $10 billion in 1983. The future prospects are not bright.

Such a negative outlook is attributable to a reduction in export revenues on the part of Middle Eastern countries due to a fall in oil prices and to their expanded policy of localization, but a serious problem also lies in the structure of Korea's construction exports. Structural weaknesses can be found in the practice of almost totally concentrating business in a limited number of Middle Eastern countries, in excessive competition among domestic firms, and in contracts focused on simple projects such as public works and housing. For instance, until 1983, Korea won 65% of its accumulated overseas construction contracts from Saudi Arabia alone, with the participation of 49 out of a total of 59 construction firms engaged in overseas construction projects. Excessive competition has resulted in dumping, poor project performance, a fall in profit ratio, and an increase in the amount of receivables. In addition, more than 80% of the overseas construction projects awarded to Korean firms have been labor-intensive, consisting of simple processes. As a result, Korea has been losing its competitive edge to host countries or other developing countries. In short, Korea faces similar difficulties in both commodity and construction exports and therefore a new economic strategy is much needed.

Sources of Growth for Enterprises

It has often been said that the rapid quantitative expansion of the Korean economy since the early 1960s was made possible through an export-oriented growth strategy, based on an abundant and educated labor force, and through the introduction of foreign capital and technology. It should also be pointed out that the spiritual and cultural heritage of Korea has also been instrumental in the efficient use of the above-mentioned resources and the successful implementation of the development strategy.

It is certain that the country's dynamic enterprise activities, whatever their motivation, have been the most decisive factor in economic growth. In the process of development, Korea has created its own business climate, and the expansion of production activities has directly fostered economic growth.

The main objective of capitalist activities is profit-making. Several sources can be identified as spurring the emergence and development of Korean enterprises. To begin with, as mentioned above, American aid significantly contributed to capital accumulation in the rehabilitation process following the Korean War (1950-1953). It was during this period that consumer industries, the parent bodies of some of today's business conglomerates, were established. Such simple processing industries as flour milling, sugar refining, cement, textiles, glass, leather, and fertilizers emerged and developed with the help of various forms of American economic aid. Due to the shortage of goods, these industries enjoyed full support from domestic demand. The demand for military supplies during the war boom also helped to expand the construction sector and some labor-intensive light industries, such as tires, foodstuffs, textiles, leather and radios.

The second source was the introduction of foreign capital, particularly in the form of loans. This was initiated by the Development Loan Fund Agreement, under which free aid was replaced by the loans. The public loans extended during the 1959-1961 period amounted to only $22 million, but contributed greatly to placing the cement and nylon industries on their tracks. A substantial sum of loans was introduced in connection with the launching of the economic development plan in the early 1960s, which played a decisive role in the formation and development of enterprise. The average annual sum of foreign loans, which stood at merely $242 million during the First Five-Year Plan of 1962-1966, jumped to $783 million during the Second Five-Year Plan of 1967-1971. The figure increased to $1.98 billion during the Third Plan of 1972-1976, under which heavy and chemical industries were given priority, and to $5.84 billion during the Fourth Plan of 1977-1981. In 1982 alone, foreign loans reached $7.2 billion. Since 1967, these loans have exceeded 10% of GNP on the average.

The introduction of foreign loans accelerated in 1966 when various laws legislated early in the 1960s were incorporated into the Foreign Capital Inducement Law. The introduction of foreign loans was possible because of the high marginal productivity of capital due to the qualified but the low-cost labor force. But it was also because their large profitability was guaranteed by the discrepancies between market prices and interest rates due to the distorted financial system at home. In addition, the fact that foreign investment was only 5% of the accumulated aggregate of foreign loans introduced until 1981, incomparably below the level prevailing in other developing countries, indicates the degree of policy intervention.

Under such circumstances, foreign loans could not help but be good investments and lead to burgeoning enterprises at a time when almost no industrial base existed in the early 1960s. In addition to light industries, some heavy and chemical industries, such as automobiles, electronics, oil refining, and steel production, began to expand their bases in the mid-1960s.

The third source was the export-oriented growth strategy promoted in earnest from the mid-1960s. It was export achievements that generated an attitude of "You can do it if you try hard," and "You can advance a level further if you succeed in one transaction." Various incentives further encouraged exports. Domestic resources were concentrated around export industries for nearly ten years from the mid-1960s, and this period can be described as the era of exports. Exports were induced by direct and indirect subsidies in public financing, import policies, foreign exchange, and the favorable exchange rate. Faced with international pressure, and in consideration of the ill effects on domestic industrial structure and competitiveness, direct support of exports began to be replaced gradually by indirect support from the mid-1970s. Still, the exports of textiles, plywood, electric appliances, and footwear, leading the manufacturing industries since the early 1960s, increased phenomenally by 224, 102, 646 and 2,080 times respectively during the 11-year period from 1961 to 1971.

As the heavy and chemical industries policy promoted in the 1970s centered around the so-called "strategic industries," enterprises began to take shape as today's business conglomerates. Because tremendous investments in the facilities were needed, centralized policy intervention and large-scale preferences, unimaginable in the light industries, had to be introduced. Due to the limited domestic market, products from the newly-built heavy and chemical plants had to be exported from the very beginning. The heavy and chemical industries, therefore, enjoyed dual or triple preference not only in the process of formation but also in export and loan allocation.

As policy measures were shaped by ambition, without regard for economic feasibility, serious ill effects such as insolvency, economic unrest, and an unsound business climate followed. Heavy and chemical industries had to undergo major readjustment in the early 1980s.

From the early 1970s, electronic goods, steel, ships, metal products, and synthetic resins emerged as the major export items. The exports of these products registered an increase of 6.7 times, 10.7 times, 27.1 times, 4.4. times, and 6.7 times respectively during the 1975-1983 period. Machinery and electric appliances were added to the ten major export items from 1982.

Lastly, the source of expanded domestic demand arising from increased income at home during the mid-1970s must be noted. The 1983 scale of a 40 million people market with a per capita GNP of $1,877 (based on 1980 prices) is by no means small by world standards. Such an expanded market undoubtedly had a remarkable effect on the production of household electronic appliances, clothes, and consumer durables. It should also be pointed out that the contribution of expanded domestic demand to the growth of industries has largely been assisted by import restrictions which limited competition.

The Inevitable Aggrandizement of Enterprises

The factors discussed above have provided some enterprises with the favorable and unique conditions under which they could grow into major business conglomerates in a short time. They are indeed a very rare phenomenon given the fact that today's *zaibatsu* took more than 100 years to form after the Meiji Restoration in Japan, which has a shorter industrial history than any Western nation. The top ten business conglomerates in Korea, on the other hand, have a history of merely 15-30 years, but most of them have been listed among the world's 500 largest enterprises since the early 1980s.

Inevitably, behind the rapid growth of Korean enterprises in a short period, were functioning noneconomic factors such as policy arbitrariness. The country had to be rehabilitated after the Korean War, and some enterprises had to take the lead in economic development as well as compete in the world market in the early 1960s. Thus it seems that "a visible hand" had to intervene in the market. Furthermore, the government, in launching its economic development plan, had to intervene in the mobilization and the distribution of limited resources. It was inconceivable, therefore, to leave the growth of industries purely to the market mechanisms. However, it is possible to debate whether it might not have been possible to consistently promote a more rational and equitable policy conducive to generating a healthy business climate on a long-term basis.

Under such conditions, enterprises could naturally expand themselves whenever opportunities arose. As they sought imbalanced growth, those enterprises that happened to meet the policy directives could enjoy preferences denied to others, while practical and nominal barriers for the new enterprises contributed toward the aggrandizement of business tycoons.

For instance, the percentage of large manufacturing firms with more than 500 workers steadily increased from 0.5% in 1963, to 1.3% in 1972, and to 1.5% in 1982. On the other hand, the percentage of small firms with 50 employees or less declined from 92.4% in 1964, to 88.3% in 1972, and to 81.5% in 1982.

The aggrandizing trend of industries can be seen in their relative contribution to economic growth as well. To cite an example, the average annual increase rate in value added of large enterprises with 500 employees or more, stood between 38 and 39% for about 20 years since the early 1960s, or nearly four times the economic growth rate during the same period. It is undeniable that these enterprises played a leading role in the growth of the nation's economy.

Monopoly and Oligopoly: Concentration of Economic Power

A conspicuous feature of the business climate is that most Korean business conglomerates today have enjoyed the benefits of monopoly and oligopoly from the early stages of development.

In addition to the above-mentioned support measures, participation by other competitive firms has been restricted in order to elevate capital efficiency in view of the small market, and to prohibit excessive competition. Import restrictions have also been a major factor in rendering the market structure noncompetitive by limiting competition from abroad.

Table 6. Structure of Commodity Market

Classification	Year	1970	1981
Monopoly	Number of commodities	442 (29.6)	521 (23.5)
	Sum of deliveries	110 (8.7)	4,878 (11.0)
Duopoly	Number of commodities	279 (18.7)	211 (9.6)
	Sum of deliveries	204 (16.8)	2,070 (4.7)
Oligopoly	Number of commodities	495 (33.2)	1,085 (49.0)
	Sum of deliveries	439 (35.1)	22,500 (49.0)
Competition	Number of commodities	276 (18.5)	397 (17.9)
	Sum of deliveries	498 (39.9)	14,735 (33.4)
Total	Number of commodities	1,492 (100.0)	2,214 (100.0)
	Sum of deliveries	1,253 (100.0)	44,183 (100.0)

Source: Korean Development Institute.

Table 6 shows changes in the commodity market structure from 1970 to 1981, indicating a deepening trend of monopoly and oligopoly. In 1981, 82.1% in terms of the number of commodity items and 66.6% of the sum of services were under the category of monopoly and oligopoly.

Although monopoly and oligopoly have some negative consequences on the economy, some positive elements contributing to the popular welfare, through technological development and economic effectiveness, should not be overlooked. Controversy seems to be centered around the economic benefits from monopoly and oligopoly as well as on the costs.

Next, the rapid growth of industries has resulted in an excessive and exclusive concentration of economic power. As shown in Table 7, the share of large industries both in domestic sales and value added saw a rapid expansion since 1963. The component ratio of their value-added production in GNP increased from 5% in 1963 to 20.5% in 1982. And the component rate in GNP for the total value-added production on the part of the 30 largest enterprises stood at about 14% in 1982, and that of the ten largest enterprises was about 11%, both illustrating the high concentration degree of economic power.

Table 7. Component Ratio in Deliveries and Value Added by Scale of Enterprises

Year \ Scale of Enterprises (Number of Employees)		5-49	50-99	100-199	200-499	500 over
Sum of deliveries	1963	33.6	11.8	10.9	13.5	30.3
	1967	23.2	8.7	8.6	18.2	41.3
	1972	12.3	6.6	9.2	20.5	51.2
	1977	8.3	6.3	9.0	19.8	56.6
	1982	9.2	7.3	9.7	16.8	56.9
Value added	1963	29.2	10.3	10.2	14.2	36.1 (5.1)
	1967	21.9	7.9	8.0	19.8	42.4 (7.7)
	1972	12.2	6.5	8.9	18.3	54.1 (12.7)
	1977	9.1	6.7	9.5	18.6	56.1 (19.1)
	1982	10.5	7.6	9.9	17.1	55.0 (20.5)

* Figures in parenthesis are the ratio of value added to GNP.
Source: Economic Planning Board, "Mining and Manufacturing Census."

Though exports on behalf of other firms were included, it is neverthe-less noteworthy that the share of the five biggest trading firms was 13.3% in 1975, when they were first founded, but the share of exports of the ten biggest trading companies increased to 48.2% in 1982. In con-trast, the share of exports by small and medium enterprises decreased during the same period from 35% to 22.3%.

One of the most controversial issues involving the concentration of economic power is the so-called "octopus-like" expansion. Some argue that such an expansion of business is natural. It can be claimed, on the other hand, that business conglomerates expand the number of their subsidiaries without abiding by the market mechanisms. To cite a few examples, some business conglomerates with unhealthy financial struc-tures may take over other enterprises, invest in real estate speculations, or control banking institutions—even under the pressure of debts. And some large enterprises encroach upon small and medium enterprises' areas of specialization in search of short-term profits.

The top ten business conglomerates in 1984 controlled 194 sub-sidiaries, excluding such nonprofit entities as schools and cultural and welfare foundations. This represents more than double the figure of 80 registered in 1980 (See Table 8).

Table 8. Number of Subsidiaries of Business Conglomerates

Number of Business Conglomerates / Year	1973	1975	1977	1984
5	43	54	81	108
10	80	104	150	194

Source: Economic Planning Board.

Such concentration of economic power is significantly higher than in other developed countries. This not only gives rise to a sense of relative poverty and alienation due to the deepening income disparity, but is also counterproductive to balanced development of the national economy since it generates an unsound business climate based on selfish interests, and it induces insolvency and weakens competitive power.

Desirable Entrepreneurship

It is needless to mention that large enterprises have so far greatly contributed to economic growth, the creation of jobs, and export expansion. In addition, they are engaged in the social welfare activities more actively than their counterparts in the advanced countries.

It cannot be denied that Korean businessmen, in the course of founding and developing business conglomerates, have exercised the capitalist ethical virtues and attributes of initiative, innovation, diligence, and sincerity cited by Weber and Schumpeter. They may have exercised these qualities more so than their counterparts around the world.

At the same time, however, the governmental role which was decisive in the formation and development of large enterprises in the past three decades, such as aid allocation, import permits, loan allocation, export support, and import restriction, cannot be overlooked. More than anything else, these factors have stimulated the growth of large enterprises. Big business received a high level of preferential treatment from the government, but at a cost felt by the entire society.

It was necessary to foster the initial enterprises through policy measures in Korea. It should be pointed out, however, that this practice has been counterproductive toward building the foundation of a market economy. Pursuit of profit and business expansion should be realized through initiative and innovation. In reality, however, the prevailing mentality among Korean businesses is that they should rely on policies and preferences rather than on economic forces.

Controversial behaviors of some large enterprises are attributable both to their tendencies to rely on policy preferences and to their selfish desire for profit-making. Some can be blamed for their excessive debts both at home and abroad, and their unreasonable expansion of heavy and chemical industrial facilities, while for others, it has been investments in real estate, control of small and medium enterprises' product markets, involvement in the banking business, and the "octopus-like" expansion of business. Such business practices have resulted in a higher degree of monopoly and oligopoly than that of the developed countries and have also increased the weight of some business conglomerates in the national economy. They also provide grounds for the fear that an economy led by the private sector, desirable as it is, may have more negative effects as long as the unhealthy business climate continues to exist.

For the proper operation of a market economy, entrepreneurs must conduct business activities within the ethical bounds of capitalism. Inappropriate practices of some business conglomerates produce social distrust. According to one report (*Social Science and Policy Studies* 3.5), business tycoons showed the lowest minus index in a comparison of "comprehensive credence index" according to occupation.

Of course, the undisciplined practices of a few business conglomerates should not be generalized for all large enterprises. What are important are the kinds of values generally held by business tycoons and the kinds of principles under which they engage in production activities. Social perceptions about them are also important. If and when positive perceptions prevail about the business conglomerates, a market economy will take root and the growth potential will be fostered.

Nevertheless, businesses are not charity or welfare organizations, and the social restoration or donation of private property to the state need not be discussed. They can meet social expectations when they fulfil their proper functions as economic entities under given social conditions. Such a role must be stressed more emphatically in view of the process of formulation and development of Korean businesses.

A social climate in which basic logic and ethics prevail must be established. For instance, the following ways of thinking should be accepted in society: that the pursuit of profit is realized only by supplying less expensive and high-quality goods and services; that one should not invest in an "uneconomic" business; and, that one cannot expand one's business so long as it has debts. In the same manner, business conglomerates should raise economic efficiency by maintaining the relationship of specialization and alignment with small and medium enterprises. They also should fully recognize the social and economic harms which their real estate investments, directly unrelated to production, might entail.

On the other hand, the roles of the government and consumers have to be emphasized to rectify the unreasonable behaviors of some business conglomerates. The Fair Transactions Law regulating monopoly went into force in 1981 and the Code of Commerce was revised in 1984 as a way of checking the centralization of economic power. The government has a further role in setting up an indirect framework to foster a market economy. It must also be pointed out that practices of excessive luxuries and the high levels of consumption on the part of some social strata induce unproductive business activities.

Future Tasks

Various side effects and imbalances have accumulated in the course of pursuing fast economic growth since the early 1960s, some of which are considered to restrict the future growth.

Reconsideration of the Outward-looking Strategy

First, the question arises whether Korea should continue its externally-oriented growth. There is fear that the continued pattern of growth will result in a dependent development.

Due to the conditions of the initial developmental period, such as the limitations of capital, technology, natural resources, and market scale, growth was externally oriented and the economy's reliance on trade reached nearly 80% early in the 1980s. Though such initial conditions were partially improved and differences in the degree of emphasis existed in the wake of the expansion of heavy and chemical industries, there has been no change in basic policies. An even greater problem seems to lie in the qualitative management of development strategy, as can be seen from the case of Taiwan and the three Benelux countries whose reliance on trade exceeds 90%.

Export promotion is aimed at not only increasing production and employment, but also at upgrading the industrial structure and elevating the degree of economic autonomy. However, since Korea has stressed only the export of finished products, it was not able to achieve such aims. Thus, for instance, the degree of exports' inducement of imports has remained unchanged at around 65% since the mid-1960s. The further Korea tries to expand exports, the more the imports of raw materials, parts, components, and capital equipment are increased. Expanded exports have thus failed not only to link sectors even within export industries but also to help improve the international balance of payments.

In this sense, a balanced development of exports, import substitution, and even domestic demand is a long-term task in the pursuit of outward-looking development strategy. Accordingly, the government, instead of offering preferences to specific sectors, should implement indirect incentives of inducement under general criteria to stimulate technological development and to increase productivity so that competitive companies may grow as export industries.

To develop exports on a long-term basis and to foster further the potential of economic growth, it is time to reconsider the so-called theory of imbalanced growth. And the review must cover all the economic sectors in order to increase the linkage effects and efficiency between diverse industries by restoring balanced growth in the long run. In connection with the Korean economy's high reliance on overseas markets, the problem of "dependency," most often applied to Latin American economies, can be raised.

The Korean economy, which used to be summed up by the word "poverty," has expanded quantitatively and undergone qualitative and structural changes through transactions with major advanced countries. The export structure has changed into a manufactured goods-centered one, and the developed countries since the mid-1970s have been restricting the import of major Korean products on the grounds that they disrupt their markets. Unlike the developing countries in Africa and Latin America, Korea has not experienced deteriorated market conditions due to the fall in world market prices of primary industrial products. Thanks to a rapid increase in real income, its income gap, which could have widened from the exploitation of economic surplus by the advanced countries, has been narrowed. Although there are some differences of opinion, it is difficult to say that the disparity in income distribution has been considerably worsening. The share of foreign investments, often mislabelled "exploitation," in the aggregate of foreign capital introduced to Korea stands at only 5-6%, an exceptionally low level when compared with other developing countries.

On the other hand, whether Korea can overcome the increasingly accumulated foreign debt and heavy dependence on certain advanced economies (mainly the U.S. and Japan) in the near future remains as critical question. In fact, foreign loans totaled over $40 billion at the end of 1983 and their share in the GNP slightly exceeded 50%. The ability of repayment, depending on which indexes one chooses, is the issue and the situation appears to be optimistic. Generally speaking, Korea can hardly cast off its dependency or subordination so long as it is not free from the vicious circle of foreign debts. The commercial loans, due to their unfavorable terms including high interest rates, entail an outflow of income. As mentioned above, Korea is approaching a stage where enterprises have to pursue production activities based on market principles and improve their weak financial structure, and where other economic bodies also should practice frugality and increase their savings.

Structural and imbalanced concentration on specific markets has also doubly deepened the nation's overseas reliance. For instance, Korea's trade with Japan has consistently been to Korea's disadvantage since the normalization of bilateral relations in 1965. Korea's trade deficits with Japan have mostly exceeded its total deficits in the general trade balance, through the introduction of capital and technology. In 1983, Korea's deficits in trade balance stood at $2.57 billion, whereas trade deficits with Japan reached $2.88 billion, representing a sharp contrast with its trade surpluses with the United States and European countries.

Though such an imbalance is attributable to specific conditions, it nevertheless has to be rectified in consideration of the long-term benefits of economic autonomy. Diversification of markets, as well as improved international balance of payments, remains an important task to be undertaken.

The Need for Economic Stability

Economic instability has become a serious side effect of fast growth. Even until the end of the 1970s, attainment of targets and one-sided growth policy was pursued with the thinking that economic stability hinders growth. Excessive expectations, desire for achievement, enthusiasm, and economic growth have had multiplying effects, but with corresponding consequences. Economic and social side effects, such as sharp wholesale price increase rates which averaged 16.1% annually from 1962 to 1978 and 26.6% from 1979 to 1981, over-heated speculations, disparity in income distribution, deteriorated international balance of payments, excess investments in heavy and chemical industries, and economic concentration in large cities, emerged in the early mid-1980s as factors restricting sustained growth. Because a balanced fulfillment of various economic targets was not realized, it became difficult to achieve even the original targets. Accordingly, restoring and cementing basic economic stability must be emphasized as the next major task.

Economic stability does not simply mean controlling prices, but includes stable changes in such macroscopic variables as production, individual income, consumption, investment, savings and interest. Its aim is to let all economic bodies experience normal economic change and to generate such conditions for them to conduct economic activities in a meaningful manner. The major premises for economic stability are the execution of consistent economic policies, the avoidance of disruptive measures, and the pursuit of social stability in a larger context. Finally, a gradual rectification of the imbalances and side effects accumulated in the economy is necessary to cement a basic stability.

An Inquiry into Factors Affecting the Behavioral Pattern of Korean Enterprises

Ouh Yoon-Bae

Preface

Alfred Whitehead once said that the civilization of America must be pursued by the business class. It would, in fact, not be an overstatement to say that the cultural and social development in the United States is the fruit of creative activities launched by enterprises. This observation is applicable not only to America, but also to development in other Western, capitalist societies. The role played by entrepreneurs in the development of the modern capitalist economic system after the Industrial Revolution was especially important. Their entrepreneurial activities and their nature exerted a critical influence on the formation of political and social systems and managerial methods.

The influence of modern entrepreneurs is undeniably less than that of their predecessors of eighteenth and nineteenth century Western society. Modern entrepreneurs were prevented from playing this role due to following reasons: the strengthened state control over the economy; the state strategies of mobilizing resources during the Cold War; the ideological confrontation that dominated world politics in the Cold War; and the continual hot wars, though limited in scope, which have oc-

* Originally published in Vol. 28, No. 3 (March 1988).

Ouh Yoon-Bae (Eo, Yun-bae) is President of Soongsil University. He received his Ph.D. in Public Administration from New York University. He has authored many books including *Bokji gukga-wa jungso gieop* (Welfare State and Small Business) (1994) and *Sahoe jeongchaek-ui iron-gwa gwaje* (Theory and Major Tasks of Social Policies) (1996). E-mail: ouh@president.soongsil.ac.kr.

curred during the last forty years. Despite of the limitations placed on this business class, it is difficult to deny the vitality in the advanced capitalist world that still springs from the creative and pioneering spirit of entrepreneurs.

The visions and creative activities of entrepreneurs are a constant source of social and economic change. In other words, continuous economic growth or social development on a broad scale cannot be expected without the creative activities of capitalist enterprises. Their creative activities support the existing social values while generating a new order of values. They are indispensable in spurring socioeconomic changes by developing and diffusing new technologies and training skilled workforce. The traits of diligence, frugality, sincerity, creativity, and a spirit of fair competition displayed by entrepreneurs in the process of founding and expanding new industries are the basic values of modern society and economy. This is evident in all advanced capitalist societies.

Taking note of the value-creating function of enterprises and their strategic contributions to national development, nations that achieved independence after World War II regarded promotion of enterprises as essential for national development policies and established the privileges and protective measures necessary for their growth.

In Korea, economic policies were formulated under government direction, and enterprises have been fostered and supported by the state from the First Five-Year Economic Development Plan (1962-1966) to the present. As a result, enterprises, especially large ones, could achieve external expansion in a short period of time. Consequently, various governmental policies and restrictive measures greatly influenced growth and managerial method of Korean enterprises.

Nonetheless, a climate conducive to business did not exist despite the growth of the economy because the enterprises operated as government agencies rather than adhering to the fundamental capitalist logic of managing their own capital, under their own responsibility and on the basis of their own creativity. Even though the government took such steps as the emergency measures announced on 3 August (1972) and 28 June in order to provide special privileges for enterprises even at the cost of great sacrifice on the part of the laborers, the recent pattern of entrepreneurs' operations and their attitudes towards business are far from the people's expectations. The public considers entrepreneurs not as holders of responsibility nor creators and protectors of the public interest, but rather as individuals bent on satisfying their personal greed and accumulating private wealth. For example, entrepreneurs seemed to thrive even though their companies went to ruin. This critical assessment is becoming stronger and emerging more clearly as the years pass.

The primary aim of this paper is to explore the relationship between the irrational behavior of enterprises and the government policies or restrictive measures. This inquiry is based on the premise that the problems connected with irrational behavior of entrepreneurs and their counterproductive functions in the economy cannot be resolved solely by urging them to fulfill their ethical responsibilities. Since enterprises are key constituents of the socioeconomic system, they will be able to properly fulfill their social responsibility and perform their functions only after the related social institutions are reformed.

There are as many instances of irrationality as there are enterprises and their aspects and types are as complex and varied as the businesses themselves. As enterprises adapt to different contexts, irrationalities also change their forms and patterns of action in response to changes in the environment. The previous irrationalities or abnormal methods have lost their practical effect and in their place, new irrationalities have emerged. The background, causes, characteristics, and processes of change in irrationalities are diverse and complex. As all irrationalities do not always destroy moral and legal rules or openly deviate from them, it is not easy to identify the counteractive functions of enterprises. As enterprises adroitly take advantage of the generally accepted system, find loopholes in it, or slip from its grip, it is almost impossible for outsiders to locate and analyze instances of their irrational behavior.

This paper, therefore, will examine the realities of irrational behavior involving Korean enterprises on the basis of the reported instances in newspapers, various surveys conducted by government agencies, academic research, and published records. I will approach this topic using a sociological framework in order to allow a further level of analysis in previously collected data.

Background to the Behavioral Pattern of Korean Enterprises

Sociological Understanding of Irrationalities

When seen from a sociological perspective, irrationalities are a type of deviant behavior defined as actions infringing upon institutionalized expectations.[1] According to theory, deviant behavior arises most frequently when sanctions regulating actions in given social circumstances become contradictory.[2] For example, optional taxation is paradoxically liable to cause tax evasion. In another instance, the government may set the price of certain items below actual market price, causing market scarcity and thereby encouraging black market transactions, or forcing producers to deliver poor-quality products at unreasonable prices. These instances are so numerous that we cannot cite them all. When enterprises are driven into this kind of absurd situation, they face a serious question: how to choose one course of action among many. When specific conditions or demands are imposed on them, enterprises try to find a way out which they regard as "normal" or "rational" under the situation. Repetition of a situation over a period of time gives rise to a structural contradiction in which deviant business activities come to be regarded as normal.

Therefore, irrationalities cannot be defined solely in terms of the behavioral pattern of enterprises; it must be remembered that they originate in imbalance or contradictions in the social order, or more specifically, the set of business regulations. As shown in the above instances, the behavior of enterprises is defined as deviant or normal according to a particular point of view. An action can be justified from the standpoint of particular enterprises in pursuit of maximizing profit, but it can also be defined as deviant from the view of the government which regulates business activities or attempts to protect consumers.

Consequently, deviant behaviors should be seen as the interpretations of third parties, such as the government, citizens, or society, rather than as features inherent in the behaviors themselves.[3] In other words, the specific behaviors of enterprises are defined as irrational because society considers them irrational.

---

1. Albert K. Cohen, "The Study of Social Disorganization and Deviant Behavior," in *Sociology Today: Problems and Prospects*, vol. II, ed. Robert K. Merlon et al. (New York: Harper Torchbooks, 1959), p. 462.
2. Two scholars who have articulated this standpoint most clearly are as follows: Robert K. Merton, *Social Theory and Social Structure*, rev. ed. (Glencoe: The Free Press, 1957); and Talcott Parsons, *The Social System* (Glencoe: The Free Press, 1951).
3. Kai T. Krikson, "The Sociology of Deviance" in *Social Problems: Persistent Challenges*, ed. Edward C. McDonagh and Jon E. Simpson (New York: Holt, Rinehart and Winston Inc., 1966), p. 458.

Here arises the next question: how does society see the specific behavior as irrational? Sociologists have attempted to answer this question with social system theories, which argue that any society permits and controls the behavior of its constituents within a certain frame in order to maintain its existence and normal functions. For this reason, an understanding of the boundaries of permissible behavior is important in defining deviant behavior. Generally, the boundaries are drawn, changed, and reorganized according to the traditions of society,[4] religion,[5] specific political, economic, and social circumstances,[6] general societal conditions,[7] and established customs. Mutual human relations are formed, maintained, and permitted to change within the boundaries. What concerns us here is the following: when the boundaries become obscure, or the function of protecting the boundaries is weakened or develops internal contradictions, the constituents of society become less uniform in their behavior and begin to interpret their situations according to self-interest, thereby bringing about a confusion in values and disorder. In other words, the constituents come to experience social tension and discord, and furthermore, create mutual distrust and begin to experience feelings of social disparity.

Sociologists refer to this phenomenon as social disorganization and locate its main cause in the rapid social transformations. In the processes of industrialization and urbanization, traditional values and social norms were often lost or weakened. The social order of the premodern ages

---

4. The sociologist Edward Shils systematically outlines the characteristics and functions of tradition as it exerts its influence on culture, art, science, and social systems. Edward Shils, *Tradition* (London: Faber and Faber, 1981).

5. As an example showing how the Protestant ethic influenced the development of capitalism, refer to Max Weber, *The Protestant Ethic and the Spirit of Capitalism* (1904-1905), translated by Talcott Parsons (New York: Charles Scribner and Sons, 1958); and R. H. Tawney, *Religion and the Rise of Capitalism, A Historical Study* (New York: Harcourt, Brace & Co. Inc., 1926).

6. A good example is the political and social realities in the early part of the 1960s that made it inevitable for Korea to pursue a growth-first economic policy on the basis of large enterprises, as explained later.

7. As with the natural law that flowers bloom when the time is right, enterprises can grow and develop only in favorable social conditions. See, H. G. Barnett, *Innovation: The Basis of Cultural Changes* (New York: Mcgraw Hill Book Co., 1953); Joseph Schumpeter, *The Theory of Economic Development* (Cambridge: Harvard Univ. Press, 1934), chapters I and II.

became meaningless in modern circumstances, and the old form of human relations consequently disintegrated. A changed society demands a new value system and a new set of norms. The business sector is no exception. Therefore, a continuous regulatory function is required in order to establish business ethics over time in response to the new social demands. Nevertheless, if such a regulatory function is unstable, both politically and socially, irrationality will become inseparable from the structure of enterprises.

In Korea, new business ethics could not take root because the enterprises had such a short history and thus they did not develop with their own capital.

Room for Irrationality in the Growth of Korean Enterprises

1) Characteristics of Korea's Traditional Entrepreneurs

It is a widely held view that modern Korean enterprises were first originated by *yangban*, landlords, and merchants in the late Joseon period.[8] The process of entrepreneurs' capital accumulation was traditionally inseparable from commercial activities. Commercial capital was accumulated by the so-called Gaeseong merchants at the end of Joseon period by operating stores or engaging in local trade on a limited scale. Needless to say, the building of industrial capital through manufacturing was extremely limited. In other words, Korea's traditional entrepreneurs came not from the artisan class or the peasantry as in the case of the Europe but from *yangban*, landlords, and merchants who possessed the attributes of entrepreneurs. This difference in the origin has exerted much influence on the character of today's Korean entrepreneurs.

Under Japanese rule, Korean enterprises were limited to a small number of traditional business activities such as the operation of sawmills, rice mills, and rice wine wholesale stores.[9] According to an investigation

---

8. Byeon Hyeong-yun and Kim Yun-hwan, eds, *Hanguk gyeongje ron* (Theories of Korean Economy) (Seoul: Yupung Publishing Co., 1977), p. 97; Bak Eun-tae, "Gieopga-wa gieop yulli" (Entrepreneurs and Business Ethics), in *Saneop sahoe-ui jigeop yulli* (Industrial Society and Occupational Ethics), ed. Asan Foundation (Seoul: Asan Foundation, 1981), p. 247.
9. This is taken from the gist of statement made by Kim Jong-dae. See Asan Foundation, ed., *op. cit.*, p. 272.

by Im Jong-cheol, at the end of 1940, 94.1% of 14,856 industrial production facilities were owned by the Japanese.[10] Not only is it evident that these industries were intended to exploit Korean labor, resources, and markets, but it is also clear that it was highly difficult for Koreans under these circumstances to learn the techniques of operating industrial plants or managing modern business enterprises. Therefore, among Korea's traditional enterprises which today possess large-scale production facilities, not a single one made a spontaneous start with its own accumulated capital and expertise.

2) Korean Enterprises Which Received Apportioned Privileges

After liberation from Japan on 15 August 1945, the ownership of industrial facilities left behind by the Japanese was returned to Korea, and with the establishment of the government of Republic of Korea in 1948, they were sold to civilians. Thus began the history of Korean enterprises and entrepreneurs growing under the state umbrella of privileges and protective measures. In particular, grant-type aid from the United States after the Korean War (1950-1953) and other foreign assistance until the end of the 1950s were preferentially distributed among a small number of enterprises. This was proven in the disposal of illegally accumulated fortunes after the May 16 Military Coup in 1961, and in statements made by entrepreneurs who forced to submit their fortune to the state.[11]

The number of entrepreneurs competing for a greater share in the allocation mushroomed in a short span of time due to the privileges granted by the new political regime. It is difficult to oppose the view that current acts of injustice, illegality, and irrationality committed by Korean enterprises have their origin in this practice. Whenever one regime was replaced by another, a number of enterprises and entrepreneurs were ruined by charges of the accumulation of wealth by illicit means, tax evasion, or illegal donations to election campaign funds. Unfortunately, this continues to be the case.

---

10. Im Jong-cheol, "Gyeongje gweollyeok-gwa geu biri" (Economic Power and Its Irrationality), *Monthly Chosun* (August 1982): p. 95.
11. Ibid., p. 95. For a detailed explanation of enterprises which volunteered to submit their wealth and the names of their owners and how it was collected, refer to Bak Byeong-ik, *Jaebeol-gwa jeongchi—hanguk jaebeol seongjang imyeon sa* (*Jaebeol* and Politics: An Inside History of Growth of Korean Business Conglomerates) (Seoul: Doseo Chulpan Hanguk Yangseo, 1982), part 4.

As explained above, traditional Korean entrepreneurs started with commercial capital. Perhaps for this reason, since the founding of the Republic of Korea, a considerable number of entrepreneurs have tried and still try to amass wealth more from commercial pursuits than manufacturing. These pursuits include real estate speculations riding high on inflation, imports taking advantage of the low exchange rates and low interest rates, and processing semi-finished goods from overseas which can be finished quickly and yield higher returns. As long as they remain attached to commercial capital, the entrepreneurs have to secure and expand their shares of the limited market and press the government to control and prevent the newcomers from advancing into the market.

Under these circumstances, a number of enterprises are suppressing a free market by making the most of monopolies and oligopolies.[12] The most crucial factor which allows some entrepreneurs to monopolize can be found in the failure to induce them to invest a considerable part of their profits in the development of technology and new products. The result was a low rate of investment, and the degree of contribution by the development of technology to expanding output in the manufacturing industrial sector was far lower in Korea than in all other advanced countries, including Taiwan. It was less than 7% in Korea; 27.1% in Taiwan; and 50-70% in other advanced countries.[13] The wide disparity can be explained by the emphasis Korean enterprises attached to gaining easy returns through the utilization of cheap labor and foreign capital, simple imitation, and the introduction of foreign technology, rather than the development of domestic technology and training of manpower. Therefore, as Byeon Hyeong-yun has commented, whether the Korean economy can successfully achieve a take-off depends on whether it can eliminate its attributes of commercial capital.[14] It is impossible to survive

---

12. Refer to Sin Sang-min, "Gongjeong georaebeop jejeong-ui baegyeong" (The Background of Legislation of the Fair Trade Law), *Shin Dong-a* (November 1980): pp. 198-207. For material describing the formation of prices by corporate monopolies and oligopolies, the pattern of their business management, and how to keep them in check, refer to Korean Economy Research Center, Korea Chamber of Commerce and Industry, "Dokgwajeom cheje-ui gyeongjejeok hyogwa" (Economic Effect of the Monopoly and Oligopoly System) (1976).

13. Korea Chamber of Commerce and Industry, "Gisul gaebal mit seongnyeokhwa siltae josa bogo—ilbon-gwa bigyo bunseok" (A Report on Realities in Technological Development and Utilization—Comparative Analysis with Japan) (October 1982), p. 51.

14. Byeon Hyeong-yun and Kim Yun-hwan, eds, *op. cit.*, p. 97.

in the current climate of intense international competition without technological innovation and capital accumulation. Because of their lack of competitiveness, Korean enterprises cannot sustain themselves without government support in the form of preferential loans and other privileges, in spite of their external growth. As long as they fail to liberate themselves from the influence of political power, they will remain unable to eliminate the causes of irrationality.

3) Growth Pattern of Korean Enterprises under the Economic Growth Policy

In the initial stage of economic growth in the 1960s, the Korean government could not have exercised its administrative function properly without eliminating the vicious circle of poverty and chronic unemployment within a relatively short period of time. For this reason, the formation of a development strategy emerged as an important political issue. This strategy had to be based on industrialization because of the rapid growth in the population, overcrowding, and limited agricultural resources. In fact, it was calculated that the development in the industrial sector rather than in agriculture would be more effective for encouraging employment and national savings. Furthermore, industrialization was a symbol of national strength and modernization and served as an instrument to unify the nation. Industrialization was the logical conclusion for Korea's development.

Korea faced many obstacles to the implementation of the industrialization strategy, including the scarcity of capital, technology, and natural resources as well as limited key facilities. These constituted serious problems for the industrialization plan. The light industry facilities and basic infrastructure for electricity, transportation, and industrial water supply were concentrated in and around the Seoul-Incheon area after the Korean War; furthermore, most of the experienced entrepreneurs were based in Seoul. It was inevitable that the development strategy was pursued around Seoul for the purpose of utilizing resources effectively. Korea had no other means than to introduce capital, technology, and resources necessary for industrialization from overseas. Foreign plants were constructed on a turnkey basis, and Korea had to rely on foreign specialists to operate and manage the plants.

In pursuing industrialization, Korea was dependent on numerous forms of foreign assistance from the outset. In addition, because of

Korea's limited domestic market, the economic growth strategy was implemented with an eye on the foreign markets. This being the case, the Korean economy was destined to be fragile, subject to significant external influences and changes.[15]

In the process of industrialization, the government had to shoulder the task of utilizing the nation's resources, albeit limited and scarce, in the most effective manner. It was also inevitable for Korea to pursue growth by implementing an export-first strategy led by large enterprises, as dictated by practical economic principles that emphasize the need to pursue high productivity and a large scale economy, explore overseas markets, rationalize management practices, and introduce and utilize techniques from abroad.[16] What matters here is that the government had to mobilize enterprises operated by commercial capitalists who could barely maintain their existence since the period of the Syngman Rhee's Liberal Party regime, and even by the so-called political entrepreneurs who accumulated illicit fortune after the April 1960 Revolution and the May 16 Military Coup in 1961. It is ironic that Korean enterprises came to inherit the irrationality that was rampant under the Liberal Party regime.

During the 20-plus years of rule by the Park Chung-hee's regime, a large amount of foreign capital flowed into the country, and the scope of the nation's production, the organization of its enterprises, and the style of business management expanded to unprecedented levels. On the other hand, Korean enterprises engaged in irrational behavior in alarming proportions. As the nation pursued an export-first policy, exporters, under government protection, were entitled to various preferential loans and tax privileges aimed at rapid economic growth.

More than 100 enterprises were founded in the 1970s. It is well-known that most of them grew fat on the special financial measures provided by the government.[17] Furthermore, most of them used low-interest bank

15. Korea Development Institute (KDI), *Long-Term Prospect for Economic and Social Development 1977-1991* (Seoul: KDI, 1978), p. 3.
16. Ouh Yoon-Bae (Eo Yun-bae), "Sahoe jeongchaek-ui gaenyeom jeongnip" (Establishment of Concepts in Social Policies) in *Nonmunjip* (collected papers), ed. by Soongjon University, Vol. 9 (1979), p. 24.
17. Bak Mu, "Jaebeol-gwa geumnyung" (Business Conglomerates and Finance), *Shin Dong-a* (September 1981): pp. 152-167. The article exposes how business conglomerates grew by utilizing the privileges in obtaining bank loans and how their owners amassed personal wealth through real estate speculation utilizing low interest rates on loans and inflation.

loans to invest in the soaring real estate market. This irrational business management practice was disguised under a cloak of legality. It remains one aspect of today's business management that large firms, despite the financial strain, have excessive real estate holdings not serving any business purposes.

Needless to say, all these forms of irrationality arose in the process of exploiting the contradictions inherent in the system. In short, the growth-first policy pursued in the 1970s accelerated the external growth of enterprises and made them recklessly pursue export quotas without considering profitability. The government indiscreetly provided privileges for enterprises only when their export increased. It would not be an exaggeration to say that this resulted in the ability of the large firms to financially sustain themselves. As these firms became increasingly more constrained by the insufficient funds for business operations, they were forced to resort to abnormal methods of generating money, such as tax evasion, unfair competition, and the takeover of small firms.

Examples of Irrationality in Enterprises

As mentioned in the introduction, irrationalities are as numerous as enterprises, and each has its own origin and peculiarities,[18] making it almost impossible to classify them. If we define irrationality only as a clear violation of existing statutes, we are able to analyze acts of irrationality easily. From the theoretical point of view, however, irrationality constitutes acts that destroy socially institutionalized expectations. For this reason, the expectations that society places on enterprises are not limited to the hope that they will abide by the law. Abiding by the law is only a part of the large set of social expectations. I will divide the general expectations on enterprises into several types, and employ several methods of analysis in order to investigate how acts contrary to societal expectations harm business management.

---

18. For instance, the methods and cases of tax evasion are manifold and complicated according to line of business without general commonality. See Kim Dae-su and Byeon Hyeong-yun, *Talse—gieop siltae-wa talse yuhyeong* (Tax Evasion: Actual Conditions of Enterprises and Patterns of Tax Evasion) (Seoul: Geunmunsa, 1968).

Irrationality Stemming from the Closed Nature of Business Management

Enterprises may avoid transparent operations because they lack a sense of responsibility to function as a public instrument in society. Regardless of their scope, they perpetuate internal cover-ups such as tax evasion and improper expenditures. Factors stemming from the tax system infrequently cause the closedness of enterprises.[19]

According to a report on shares held by major stockholders in 154 listed enterprises submitted to the regular session of the National Assembly by the Ministry of Finance in the fall of 1982, the owners of 75 companies, 48.7% of the 154 listed enterprises, possessed more than 25% of the shares in the names of their relatives and other closely connected persons. In eight of the 75 companies, the owners held shares ranging from 49.1 to 70% of the total shares. Ten entrepreneurs held shares in the names of more than 80 persons, and there was even one stockholder who possessed shares in the names of 106 persons. These figures exposed the difficulty of the opening up enterprises to the public.

Korean corporate tax law stipulates that if the percentage of total shares held by major stockholders exceeds 35%, the corporation concerned is subject to a tax rate of 38% applied to corporations closed to the public, three percent higher than 35% applied to an open corporation. Eleven of the 154 listed companies which were opened to the public fell under this category. It was evident that small investors suffered losses on account of this law.

Corporation tax law was amended to unify tax rates for open and closed enterprises at 22%, and only unlisted companies were subjected to the rate of 25%. This change closed the difference between listed and unlisted companies, except for the 35% ceiling on the maximum percentage of shares that large stockholders are permitted to hold.

This created the temptations for major stockholders to increase the size of their shareholdings even further. It is now possible to run counter to the policy of evenly distributing income and wealth through the popularization of stocks and the principle of modern business administration that separates ownership from management.[20] Whereas major Japanese entrepreneurs each possess less than one to five percent of the total

---

19. Byeon Hyeong-yun and Kim Yun-hwan, *op. cit.*, note 18 in p. 525.
20. For detailed reports or comments on this, see *Dong-a Ilbo*, 21 October 1980, p. 5 and *Chosun Ilbo*, 21 October 1982, pp. 1-2.

shares, their Korean counterparts hold a much larger percentage of shares. For one thing, it may be desirable that owners are permitted to hold a high percentage of shares temporarily in the initial stages of development so that they are encouraged to view their enterprises "as their own" and foster their growth accordingly. However, as numerous examples demonstrate, irrationality could be seen in the form of unfair apportionment of dividends through the disguised dispersion of shares and scattered settlements of accounts. It is apparent that this practice weakened corporate dedication to public interest. This attitude stems from the lack of openness in the management of enterprises, which enables the owners to survive even if their enterprises went to ruin. Listed enterprises are not essentially different from properietary companies. For this reason entrepreneurs are free to exercise tyrannical management practices draining the assets of their enterprises.

Irrationality Stemming from Excessive Reliance on Outside Capital

"An Analysis of Business Management 1985" published by the Bank of Korea disclosed the business index in 1984 as follows: the ratio between an enterprise's own and outside capital in the heavy and chemical industries—both dominated by conglomerates—was 48.0% to 52.0% while the debt ratio was calculated at 307.3%. The high degree of reliance on outside capital indicates that entrepreneurs are unable to operate their companies independently. As a result, they have to rely on financial institutions or private money lenders, giving rise to irrationalities that, as exposed in the Jang Yeong-ja Scandal, the heads of big businesses and even bank presidents were judged guilty in court for their issuance of bad checks, the illegal advance of loans, and bribery.

As long as the existence of large enterprises hinges on outside capital, this form of irrationality is liable to recur. In this light, Yi Cheol-seong observed that "in many instances, entrepreneurs, basically because they have no capital of their own, have to maintain their companies by associating themselves closely with political circles, utilizing private loans, indulging in illegal transactions, and resorting to other means such as tax evasion."[21] According to the Bank of Korea's report, expenditures

---

21. This statement is taken from Professor Yi Cheol-seong, who teaches finance at Sungkyunkwan University at one of his lectures in the second symposium sponsored by the Asan Foundation. Asan Foundation, *op. cit.*, p. 261.

other than business operations, including the interest on loans, exceeded the 6.5 percent mark. As a result, enterprises used to absorb the impact by raising the prices of their products to create a profit. This weakens their competitiveness and, furthermore, acts to spur general inflation.

Because of financial pressures, enterprises have been forced by slight but successive business recessions to readjust their employment structure, refuse wage increases, and avoid spending on improving benefits packages for their workers. This causes discord between management and labor, demoralizes the workers, and in the end, lowers productivity. In other words, the unstable financial structure of enterprises affects the national economy, eventually engendering irrationality, illegal practice, and injustice while exerting adverse influence directly or indirectly on management-labor relations, the price structure, and the quality of life itself.

Especially in relations with small and medium enterprises, large enterprises delay payments, interfere in management, indulge in dumping practices, and absorb or amalgamate small business establishments. In other words, large enterprises mistake these irrationalities for normal business practices. The basic cause lies in the weakness of their financial structure.

Irrationality Originating in the Expansion of Enterprises

The greatest irony in the Korean business environment is that an individual without private capital can establish an enterprise with loans and absorb other enterprises. During the recent privatization of the Commercial Bank and liberalization of short-term financing companies, it was revealed that one can buy shares in Bank A with a loan drawn from that bank, or establish an enterprise with the loan one is now free to use as one's own money. Large enterprises are currently engrossed in buying shares of commercial banks or establishing short-term financing companies. All of them are hard pressed by financial concerns and can barely manage themselves with relief loans and are under the protection of the Special Measure of 28 June (1982). Where could firms obtain the capital needed for the purchase of bank shares or the establishment of short-term financing houses? This is certainly one aspect of the irrationality which has become chronic in the Korean business sector. The money that should have been invested in productive activities or in strengthening their financial structure was misused for expanding away from the original purposes of their business. This type of diverted activity has weakened their financial structure and confused the business environment.

As mentioned earlier, these irrationalities were not solely generated by the enterprises and a considerable part of the responsibility should be borne by the nation's financial structure and its regulatory bodies. For instance, creditor banks, while disposing of insolvent enterprises and collecting their credit, entrusted the ailing firms to other large enterprises with the privilege of obtaining preferential loans. As a result, size and scale of large enterprises were increased. We should not overlook this fact. It is necessary to reexamine the government policy of announcing the special measure of 27 September 1980 after the relief steps were taken in order to encourage large enterprises to strengthen their financial structure by disposing of the real estate owned by their affiliate companies.

How were the large enterprises obliged to take over insolvent companies? The answer to this question is simple; banks control enterprises. There is no other answer than to say that the life and death of enterprises hinge on whether they receive loans from banks. It is understandable, however, that large enterprises do not operate themselves without pursuit of profit. Needless to say, large enterprises agreed to take over insolvent companies because it was to their advantage to do so. This expectation of profit was a factor that promoted their irrationality in the process of corporate expansion.

Irrationality Coming from Motives for Profit Outside Business

The guiding principle for enterprises should be the pursuit of increased profits by raising productivity in the strengthened financial structure and a rationalized management system, and by strengthening their international competitiveness through innovated technology and improved products. However, many obstacles, such as the lack of accumulated private capital and indigenous technology, prevented Korean entrepreneurs from creating a business climate in which this principle could dominate. Failure to forge such a business environment has resulted in the irrational and irregular practices we easily observe today: entrepreneurs refuse to abide by standard principles and instead resort to temporary expedients.

For instance, when bank interest rates remain below inflation, it is natural for people to expect that their bank savings cannot increase, and instead focus on "object-economy." Likewise, it is logical for entrepreneurs to invest in low-interest bank loans rather than in modernizing equipment or improving their products—instead, they concentrate on gaining high short-term profits through real estate transactions.

What stands out here is that entrepreneurs utilize bank loans or private loans in real estate speculations; when an excess profit accrues, they pocket it as private gain and when a loss accrues or when it becomes possible that a contract will be signed to fulfill the terms of speculation, they write it off as a company loss to their companies. On account of such irrational business management, a considerable number of enterprises have come to possess real estate not suitable for the business purposes.

Furthermore, entrepreneurs are able to borrow unlimited funds from banks by taking advantage of the name value of their companies. Entrepreneurs then privately invest this money in real estate speculations and shares, or lend it as private loans and pocket the gains accruing from high interest on the loans. As long as environmental factors allowing entrepreneurs to engage in such underhanded business operations persist, acts of acquiring an income without due labor will continue, and companies will remain mere tools for their owners to accumulate personal wealth.

Irrationality Stemming from Relations between Large Corporations and Small- and Medium-sized Enterprises

The relations between large and small- and medium-sized enterprises (hereafter SMEs) should be one of mutual support and reliance. As the existence of large firms depends on SMEs and vice versa, both must develop with a symbiotic relationship. In other words, SMEs should not be placed in a position subordinate to large enterprises. Both can prosper together when they create their own spheres of activity and develop a mechanism of cooperation in technology, capital, and human resources.

As mentioned earlier, however, the reality is that SMEs have not yet secured their own basis of existence or activities even though they have made continuous contributions to the development of the national economy in production, employment, the creation of added value, and expanding exports because government assistance was channeled toward large conglomerates in the pursuit of the growth-first policy of the last twenty years.

Various laws had the unintended consequence of promoting unnecessary competition and friction between large enterprises and SMEs. Even though measures were taken to foster rational affiliation between the two, they are still far from reaping any practical results. Large enterprises always made inroads into the territory of SMEs and dominated the market in order to survive regardless of business conditions. SMEs were always subject to losses because of the manipulations of the quantity and prices of raw materials and components which big firms monopolized. In many instances, products coming from SMEs failed to acquire enough international competitiveness because they were forced to use high-priced Korean-made raw materials on the pretext of import substitution.

SMEs, which entered into supplier contracts with large enterprises, became wholly dependent on orders and payment from the latter. For this reason, SMEs subordinated themselves to large enterprises or risked the casualty of absorption, even against their will. The existence of SMEs is greatly endangered by the interference of large corporations, such as when the latter places an order with their SME subcontractors because of a limit in the corporation's production capacity or because the cost of processing is cheaper at the SME location. Thus, the case often arises that large enterprises become reluctant to issue orders to SMEs which ask for a raise in the unit price of goods to be supplied or increase their general wage scale. In this case, SMEs, which came into being or expanded the scope of their facilities on the basis of a promise for orders from large enterprises, are driven to extreme financial strain and are doomed to perish or be absorbed by the large enterprises. As a result, large firms can easily control a number of SMEs.

We have yet to find even a single case where these abnormal practices brought about legal sanctions in order to help establish a system of fair practice between large and small companies. In the meantime, attracting technical manpower away from small enterprises with higher wages as bait should be considered immoral. To use high wages to lure skilled workers away from the companies that expended resources to train them cannot be tolerated from an ethical standpoint. As long as the irrationality of capitalizing on the weak and disadvantageous position of SMEs is not checked, the development of large enterprises themselves will be hindered. In particular, the wrongful tactics or irrational behavior indulged in by the management of large enterprises in charge of dealing with SMEs remain widely spread.

We have classified acts of irrationality into several types, but this is just the tip of an iceberg. The limited scope of this paper prevents further explanation into other widespread offenses, such as tax evasion, illegality, the flight of domestic assets overseas, and unreasonable layoffs of workers.

Several Proposed Solutions

As we have seen above, irrationality in Korean enterprises can be considered a structural phenomenon molded through the intersection of political, economic, and social factors in the course of historical capitalist growth. The harder we try to cure the disease, however, the more difficult it seems to discover the solution. Despite the numerous political upheavals of the last twenty years that have disposed of a considerable number of entrepreneurs and the politicians and officials who colluded with them, the roots of irrationality in Korean enterprises have been left untouched. History teaches us that irrationality in enterprises cannot be cured before illegality and corruption are extirpated from society.

On the other hand, however, we should not underestimate the many entrepreneurs who, armed with a clear vision and good sense, devoted their lives to fostering their enterprises in the midst of irrational business practices. We should learn from these exemplary entrepreneurs and their business operation and not draw the conclusion that the irrationality in enterprises is attributable only to external environmental factors. What matters here is how to nurture and root in the Korean climate of business a positive entrepreneurial spirit and rationality. In short, to eradicate irrationality in enterprises we must employ positive and creative means of training a new type of entrepreneur. This is the next step beyond targeting only the irrational patterns of behavior, and from a long-term perspective, this is the most effective method for approaching today's problem.

Together with constructing an environment in which entrepreneurs who operate their companies in a rational manner are easily recognized and socially appreciated, we must also exert social pressure so that they revise their understanding of business and cultivate an appropriate philosophy of business management. The fact that this kind of pressure can exert a considerable change in the outlook of entrepreneurs has already been proven.[22] What is important is to persuade entrepreneurs to cultivate a firm conviction that it will become more and more difficult to operate their business without a change in their attitude, and that such a change alone can bring increased profits to themselves as well as to their enterprises. As the primary aim of enterprises is to pursue profits, the government must lead the people in creating favorable social and economic conditions in which entrepreneurs can devote themselves wholly to increasing their profit through normal business management. Several preparatory steps are necessary.

First, political leaders and administrative officials must establish the will to reform. No system can prove effective without convincing its leadership. Throughout the entire process of drafting and implementing the policy, both the goals of eradicating irrationalities and creating a new business climate should be targeted. The government should refrain from extending any preferential treatment to specific enterprises or entrepreneurs. Concerning the problems that may accompany such preferential treatment, the government is advised to listen to public opinion. If the government refuses to spend the necessary time consulting the public before deciding upon its policy, the resulting policy is liable to be criticized as rash. The result will not be the eradication of irrationality but its aggravation.

Second, after resolute political decision and determination are announced and widely enacted, the existing laws must be revised to remove factors leading to irrationality in enterprises, including the numerous contradictions inherent in institutions. The government must also forcefully purify itself if administrative agencies are found more culpable than its laws, policies, or institutions. The proper business climate must be created in which the concerned officials, banks, and other institutions closely connected with business operations thoroughly assume responsibility. In short, when laws are properly enforced, entrepreneurs will be compelled to obey them.

Third, the government should create an institutional climate in which

---

22. For the further reference, see David C. McGlelland, *The Achieving Society* (Princeton: D. Van Nostrand Co., 1961); Everett E. Hagen, *On the Theory of Social Change: How Economic Growth Begins* (Homewood, Illinois: The Dorsey Press, 1962); Alex Inkeles and David H. Smith, *Becoming Modern: Individual Change in Six Developing Countries* (Cambridge: Harvard University Press, 1974).

the influence of ordinary citizens and workers is strengthened to such an extent that they can effectively confront any irrationality in enterprises. When, for instance, major stockholders buy shares in excess of the legally recognized ceiling and small stockholders are subjected to an unreasonably high rate of corporation tax, the latter should be allowed to hold a hearing on irrationality in enterprises without going through the complicated formalities such as convening a stockholders meeting. If this is made possible, irresponsible entrepreneurs will be publicly ashamed and citizens more awakened to the spirit required of them.

Fourth, banks attach greater importance to financial statements than to the entrepreneurs themselves when examining the creditability of enterprises before lending loans or extending credit guarantees. This often leads firms to draw unreasonably large loans illegally or obtain a credit guarantee by fabricating their settlements of accounts. A systematic method must be developed in the future for examining the creditability of entrepreneurs and their executives on the basis of their achievements and character. Such measures are necessary to guarantee bank autonomy. Moreover, bank officials at all levels must be held responsible for the loans.

Last, in accordance with the spirit of ethical market competition, it is necessary to weed out those entrepreneurs with unsound business attitudes, technological backwardness, and irrational management practice. Large enterprises have so far been exempted from this principle. In the future, however, they must not be allowed to live the life of parasites enjoying preferential protection extended by the government and financial institutions.

Conclusion

We cannot expect that a nation will be strengthened and the quality of its people's lives improved without the economic contributions of enterprises. For this reason, the state provided all possible measures and assistance to guarantee their development. At a minimum, enterprises should respect the social expectations placed on them even if they are unable to satisfy all of them. In other words, they should not inflict damage on society even though they may be unable to benefit it. This constitutes the essence of business ethics.

On the other hand, a set of institutional measures must be established and enforced in order to enable society to exercise its right of self-defense against any infringement by entrepreneurs. It is not too much to say that our society has been defenseless against the tyranny of enterprises, which has structurally rooted irrationality in modern business enterprises.

Our future task, therefore, will be to strengthen our self-defense capabilities so as to restrain the irrational acts perpetuated by enterprises on the basis of their formidable organizational strength. This alone will make it possible to create a new climate of sound business.

PART II

ECONOMIC GROWTH AND SOCIO-POLITICAL DEVELOPMENT

The Three "E's" of Economic Development–the Hardest Is Equity:

Thirty Years of Economic Development Planning in the Republic of Korea

Susan A. MacManus

For more than two decades Korea has repeatedly proved its capacity to grow and progress, both economically and socially, while continually adapting to external and domestic change.

Finance & Development (19 March 1989)

Korea's growth over the past 30 years has been referred to as one of this century's economic miracles. When Korea joined the International Monetary Fund (IMF) in 1955, it had a per capita gross national product (in current dollars) of only $65; in 1988, its per capita GNP was over 6,000 (IMF 1989, 18).[1] In the 1980s alone, South Korea reversed its negative

* Origianlly published in Vol. 30, No. 8 and No. 9 (August and September 1990).

Susan A. MacManus is a Distinguished University Professor of Public Administration and Political Science at the University of South Florida, Tampa, U.S.A. Her most recent books are *Young v. Old: Generational Combat in the 21st Century (1996)* and *Targeting Senior Voters: Campaign Outreach to Elders and Others with Special Needs* (2000). She is a member of the Florida Governor's Council of Economic Advisers. She received her Ph.D. in Political Science from the Florida State University in 1975.

1. Excellent discussions of the history of Korean economic development in the post-Korean War period (1960s) are in Cole and Lyman (1971); Jones and Sakong (1980) for the 1960s to mid-1970s; Kuznets (1977) and Mason et al. (1980) for 1945 to mid-1970s; and Kim (1975) and FKI (1987) for the period 1954-1972. E-mail: samacmanus@aol.com.

3.7% gross domestic product rate (1980) to achieve a peak growth rate of 12.2% in 1988, only two years after it recorded its first trade surplus (Willis 1989).[2]

A rigorous, centralized process of formulating and implementing economic development plans is one factor behind this economic success story. The introduction to the Sixth Five-Year Plan (1987-1991) cites successful implementation of the previous five consecutive five-year plans as the factor "lifting the nation up from a state of underdevelopment into a newly industrializing country that has attracted global attention" (Government of the ROK 1986, 2).[3] A close examination of Korea's six five-year economic development plans yields some critical insights into changing elements of economic development policy in newly industrializing countries. Many of these insights are relevant to the reform efforts of Eastern European bloc nations making the transition toward participatory democracy and capitalism.

This work focuses on the changes in economic priorities (from expansion to efficiency to equity) that accompanied changes in Korea's economic and political systems. It also focuses on public sector stimulants to economic development and their consequences over an extended period of time. The longitudinal time frame (1962-1991) of the economic development planning process in Korea affords a unique opportunity to observe the short- and long-term consequences of public sector stimulants to economic growth and development. It also permits a look at the consequences of a shift from a highly authoritarian political regime to a more democratic one.

---

2. Discussions of economic development in the 1980s: FKI (1987); IMF (1989); Yonhap News Agency (1989); Jin (1988), *Korea Business World* (September 1989); and *Korea Economic Report* (September 1989).

3. A number of studies concur with the conclusion that central economic planning has played a major role in Korea's economic development (Kuznets 1977; Mason et al. 1980; and Nahm 1988, among others). A markedly different opinion has been stated by Park (1988, i): "The so-called Korean economic miracle is anything but an orderly development process following a well-cut master plan conceived by a well-informed planning institution. It is rather a product of a series of massive changes and adjustments by the whole economy in response to the rapid dislocations of the world economy during the 1960s and 1970s. Such responses were poorly prepared, frantically conjured, and excessively pursued in the face of massive economic and political change both within and outside the country."

A Brief History of Economic Development Planning in Korea

Modern economic planning in Korea has been a post-Korean War phenomenon (Cole and Lyman 1971; FKI 1987). The reason for its relative infancy is that "throughout most of its modern history, development has been stifled by foreign intervention and occupation" (Government of the ROK 1986, 4).[4] Even between the end of the Korean War and 1962, economic planning efforts were largely formulated and carried out with the assistance of the U.S. The plans primarily dealt with the priorities for spending U.S. foreign aid (the Five-Year Korea Economic Reconstruction Plan 1953/1954-1957-1959; the Three-Year Task Assistance Program recommended by the U.S. in July 1963).

The first Korean-developed plan was drawn up by the Economic Development Council of the Ministry for Reconstruction. It was a Three-Year Economic Development Plan for 1960-1962, the first half of the Seven-Year Economic Development Plan (1960-1966). However, it was never implemented due to the April Revolution of 1960. Consequently, the First Economic Development Plan to be formulated and implemented by Koreans was for 1962-1966. The series of five-year plans has continued to the present (see Table 1).

The responsibility of economic development planning lies with the Economic Planning Board (EPB) created in 1961. This Board has a tremendously wide range of authority and responsibility. "The Board takes charge of matters related to overall planning for development of the national economy, formulation and execution of the government budget, overall coordination of plans for mobilization of resources, investment, technical development, and economic cooperation with foreign countries and international organizations" (Yonhap News Agency 1989, 140). The importance of the Board is evidenced by the fact that the EPB Minister concurrently serves as Deputy Prime Minister and is responsible for coordinating business among all the ministries related to

---

4. Japan controlled Korea from August 1910 to August 1945. Allied forces (U.S.) occupied South Korea from August 1945 to June 1949. Excellent histories of Korean political and economic domination by foreign nations and their impact on future economic development efforts are found in: Nahm (1988); Kim (1975); Lee (1984); Kuznets (1977); Jones and Sakong (1980); Kim (1985).

the economy and finance.

Prior to the Sixth and Revised Sixth Five-Year plans, the formal plan-ning process almost exclusively involved government officials, although consultation of academics and some private citizens has been mentioned since the Second Plan. Responding to the shifting political winds, the two Sixth Plans broadened the public's participation in the process. Rep-resentatives of academia, research institutes, industry, and other private organizations served on 31 ministry-level sectoral planning committees which drafted these plans. They made up over half of the committee membership; one private sector representative served as a committee co-chair with a government official.

The process of drafting such plans also involved solicitation of popu-lar opinions through public hearings and regional policy consultation meetings. These were specifically designed to solicit input from farmers, fishermen, and provincial residents.[5] As stated in the Revised Sixth Plan, "Primary emphasis was placed on sounding out views and opinions of various strata of society and on seeking a national consensus in deter-mining policy priorities" (Government of the ROK 1988, 6). There was also wider dissemination of the plans through the media—a strategy designed to emphasize the new openness of the process. Not surprising-ly, this process yielded plans that placed much more emphasis on eco-nomic equity than the previous ones which emphasized first economic expansion, then economic efficiency.

Changing Priorities of Economic Development

A contrast of the major goals and policy elements of each of the six Five-Year Plans is shown in Table 1. In broad terms, the plans of the 1960s to mid-1970s emphasized rapid economic growth. The plans of the mid-1970s to mid-1980s stressed efficiency through technological improve-ments and productivity gains. The plans for the latter half of the 1980s heavily stressed economic equity (both domestically and internationally).

---

5. There are nine provinces (Gyeonggi-do, Gangwon-do, Chungcheongbuk-do, Chung-cheongnam-do, Jeollabuk-do, Jeollanam-do, Gyeongsangbuk-do, Gyoengsangnam-do, Jeju-do) and six special cities which are given the same administrative status as province (Seoul, Busan, Daegu, Incheon, Gwangju, and Daejeon).

With the exception of the Fourth Plan, the specific economic targets of each plan were achieved.

Plans Emphasizing Expansion

1) First Plan (1962-1966)

The basic objective of this initial plan was to "reverse the decelerating trend in the economy . . . to attain a substantial rise in economic growth rates" by investing an increasingly large portion of the expanding gross national product in the expansion of the means of production. The plan placed emphasis on the development of three basic industrial sectors (energy, agriculture, and public infrastructure) "to build a strong industrial base for the development of a future self-sustaining economy" (Government of the ROK 1962, 24). Its targeted growth rate for the period was 8.3%.

2) Adjusted First Plan (1964-1966)

This plan was adjusted in 1964 to correct the first plan's failures to consider such restraining factors as the repayment of loan principal and interest and the effect of raw material imports on economic growth; lack of attention to the role of public finance in economic growth; insufficient attention to long-term growth potential; neglect of inter-sectoral and inter-project relationships and of individual project feasibility studies; insufficient support measures for actual execution of the Plan; and an inadequate commodity supply and demand schedule (Government of the ROK 1964, 3). The basic change, however, was in the projected growth rate, not in policy direction, with the exception of exports being singled out as an area to be emphasized. The growth rate was revised downward from 8.3 to 7.1%. The actual growth rate was 7.8%.

3) Second Plan (1967-1971)

The basic objective remained "to promote the modernization of the industrial structure and to build the foundations for a self-sustaining economy." The key elements were "export expansion, capital mobilization, and efficient manpower utilization" (Government of the ROK 1966, 33). Emphasis was placed on: achieving self-sufficiency in food production; investment in chemical, machinery, iron and steel industries to accelerate and diversify industrialization; expansion of exports; control of population growth rate through family planning; and raising the level of technology and productivity to accelerate economic modernization of all sectors. This plan was also significant for initiating the New Community Movement (Saemaeul undong) to assist farmers in improving their economic and living conditions (Whang 1987; Yi 1984; Yu 1987; Nahm 1988). The projected growth rate for this plan was 7.0%; the actual rate was 9.6%.

4) Third Plan (1972-1976)

The major emphasis of this plan was on the dynamic development of the rural economy, a dramatic and sustained increase in exports, and the establishment of heavy and chemical industries, which was designed "to avoid dependence on imported raw materials and intermediate goods" (FKI 1987, 5).

Balanced regional development of basic social facilities (electricity, transportation, storage, cargo handling, and communications) and promotion of social welfare programs, along with increased emphasis on food production were also targets of this plan. The projected growth rate for this plan period was 8.6%; the actual growth rate was 9.7%.

In summary, the economic development plans of the 1960s and early 1970s emphasized economic expansion through exports—a very common development path for resource poor countries (Park 1988), "Relying on the vast international markets provides the industrializing LDCs (lesser developed countries) with economies of scale together with the latest and most efficient equipment and machinery to work with" (Park 1988, 13). Nonetheless, despite the overall tendency to rely more on the external markets while maintaining a shallow domestic industrial structure, some deepening of the industrial structure did take place over this period (Park 1988, 5).

Plans Emphasizing Efficiency

The Fourth and Fifth plans were designed to "remedy the structural imbalance in the economy and build up the foundation for economic stability" (FKI 1987, 7). "Social development, technological innovation, and rationalization were new additions to these plans" (FKI 1987, 7).

1) Fourth Plan (1977-1981)

The major goals of this plan were efficiency-oriented: achievement of self-reliance in investment financing; equilibrium in the balance of payments; diversification of the industrial structure (promotion of skilled labor-intensive industries); promotion of social development (job creation, strengthening of education, health care, and vocational education programs); tax reform; rural development; pollution control; more housing; technological innovation; and improvement in efficiency. This plan stated that "increased productivity through technological innovation and improved efficiency are the keys to Korea's continued high rate of economic growth" (Government of the ROK 1976, 12). The projected growth rate for this five-year period was 9.2%. However, the actual growth rate was far short (5.8%), representing the first time the actuals fell below projections. The reasons for this shortfall were two oil price shocks and a period of high inflation (FKI 1987; *Korea Business World* September 1989, 35).

2) Fifth Plan (1982-1986)

The basic objectives of this plan were "stability, efficiency, and balance" (Government of the ROK 1982, 13). Price stabilization (to control inflation), stimulation of domestic savings, promotion of competition (the market model), export growth, development of industries with a comparative advantage in both the domestic and world markets, balanced regional development, and greater social development were all specific objectives. This plan was the first to emphasize "the principles of a market economy encouraging private initiative and creativity" (Government of the ROK 1988, 7). It was also the first to mention greater citizen involvement in the priority-setting process paralleling the political democratization movement. It also represented a shift in emphasis from heavy and chemical industries to technology-intensive industries (FKI 1987, 8). The projected growth rate for this period was 7.5% and the actual was 8.6%.

Plans Emphasizing Equity

Growth rates exceeding expectations under the Fifth Plan, along with changes in the political environment, shifted the emphasis to equity in the two Sixth Plans.

1) Sixth Plan (1987-1991)

This plan, more democratically conceived, also marked a basic shift in purpose. The previous five plans had the broadly stated objective of "developing an economic structure for self-sustained growth." The sixth plan, on the other hand, "represented the first phase of laying a foundation for the nation towards the goal of an industrialized, advanced state in the twenty-first century" (Government of the ROK 1986, 26). The desire to "play in the big leagues" of world industrial powers became the major external goal.

Domestically, the emphasis shifted to improving equity in the economic arena. Exemplary of this new equity emphasis are the three major objectives identified in the plan: 1) competition between government and major sectors of society to establish an economic and social system that will encourage all people to fully develop their potential; 2) cooperation between Korean business leaders and workers to restructure industry and improve technological levels; and 3) government promotion of balanced regional development (to redistribute national income on a fair and equitable basis, especially for the benefit of lower-income groups) to establish a fair market order (Government of the ROK 1986, 26). The projected growth rate for this plan was 7.3%. In the first year of this plan, the actual growth rate so far exceeded projections that it was necessary to formulate a Revised Sixth Plan.

2) Revised Sixth Plan (1988-1991)

This version was deemed necessary for both economic and political reasons. "Economic performance during 1987 (the first year of the Sixth Five-Year Plan) far exceeded the original projections . . . and political reform toward democratization and the subsequent demands voiced by different segments of society made it inevitable that macroeconomic management and the priorities for economic policy be adjusted" (Government of the ROK 1988, 3).[6] The revised plan calls for greater empha-

---

6. On 27 October 1987, Korean voters overwhelmingly approved a new Constitution which went into effect on 25 February 1988. The Constitution called for direct presidential election (a single five-year term), reduction in presidential power, and strengthening of the power of the National Assembly. The revised Constitution "features better protection of human rights and labor interests as well as enhanced separation of powers. . . . People have greater freedom of assembly, association and

sis on qualitative improvement of the economy, private initiative in future economic development, and provision of equal economic opportunities. The plan "stresses institutional reforms designed to enhance autonomy and equal opportunity" and gives priority to support for the underprivileged and lagging sectors of the economy, which have been largely ignored during the past period of rapid economic growth" (Government of the ROK 1988, 9). The plan also stresses increased international economic cooperation, especially with socialist nations (the "Nordpolitik" or the Northern Policy).

The Revised Sixth Plan's call for less governmental involvement in economic development represents a basic change in Korea's economic development philosophy. However, the specific plans for improving equity and balance and competition in the world marketplace (such as tax reform, land reform, rural development, liberalization of the financial market, and liberalization of trade) all are heavily contingent upon public sector involvement. In fact, a common thread running through all the plans is the critical role of government in stimulating economic development (Kuznets 1977; Jones and Sagong 1980; Mason et al. 1980; Mills 1988).

Types of Public Sector Stimulants to Economic Development

In the May 1987 issue of the *Economic Development Quarterly*, Sternberg identifies nine common types of public sector involvement in economic development:

1. Direct subsidy to businesses by distributing public resources to firms through grants in cash or kind, through favoritism in government purchasing, or by relieving private tax obligations;
2. Indirect subsidy (government directs its services or fiscal capabilities at businesses in general or at their sectoral or geographic subdivisions);

---

speech, while workers have the rights of free association, collective bargaining, and striking. Censorship of the press is banned. The political neutrality of the armed forces is also provided for. President Roh Tae-woo was the first president to be elected under the new Constitution—and the first popularly-elected president in 16 years (Yonhap News Agency, 1989).

3. Information and exhortation (government influences business decisions by educating or exhorting businesspersons to change business practices);

4. Regulation (government determines the rules of the game in the behavior of individual businesspersons, in relations between buyers and sellers, and in permissible effects on third parties);

5. Policies to affect crucial industries and institutions (government takes a special interest in banking and transportation through subsidy or taxes, regulation, and guidelines);

6. Shaping of market opportunity and environment (government controls the spatial relation of firms to each other and to markets, and can increase or decrease business risk);

7. Shaping of market structure (government uses regulation, subsidy, and exhortation to affect conditions of competitiveness and monopoly);

8. Defining and limiting forms of enterprise (government defines what makes a firm into a corporation, partnership, or nonprofit organization); and

9. Engaging government in enterprise and expanding government employment (government increases the public work force and establishes public corporations or, to the contrary, privatizes them).

While there is a great deal of research on the extensiveness and effectiveness of many of these different types of policies, the bulk of them have focused on developed nations, particularly the U.S. (Carleton 1983; NASDA, NCED, and UI 1983; Helms 1985; Ahlbrandt and DeAngelis 1987; Warner 1987). Most studies of public sector stimulants to economic development also tend to examine these policies in a decentralized decision-making governmental environment (Conyers 1984: Kee 1977; Wasylenko 1987; the exception is Bahl and Nath 1986). However, most developing nations, including Korea, are characterized by more heavily-centralized public sector policy-making structures (Hicks 1961; Caiden and Wildavsky 1980; Olson 1982; Olowu 1984; Caiden 1985; Lewis and Kallob 1986; Roth 1986; Caiden 1988; Mjkhopadyay 1988; Thai 1988; Lim and Moore 1989). These biases in the existing research on economic development make cross-national studies like this one imperative for a broader understanding of the development process in an interdependent world economy.

Public Sector Involvement in Korea's Economic Development

Throughout the thirty-year period examined here, the Korean government has utilized all nine types of involvement identified by Sternberg. Most pervasive, and perhaps most effective, have been direct subsidies (tax reductions and exemptions, and loans), policies affecting crucial industries and sectors (especially banking and the manufacturing sector), and regulation. But indirect subsidies, information and exhortation ("jawboning"), and, more recently, policies shaping the structure of the market have also played critical roles in the Korean "economic miracle."

Together, these public sector involvements have been instrumental in stimulating economic growth (GNP and GDP), creating more balance among the sectors (agriculture, manufacturing, and service), reducing reliance on foreign investments, improving the social welfare of the populace, promoting regional and rural development, and changing the order of economic power. However, as will be noted, the latter three have changed less dramatically than the others and have been at the heart of recent controversies regarding economic equity.

Recent Examples of Government Involvement

There is little indication that government's role in the economy, using all nine techniques, has declined in the first two years of the Revised Sixth Plan. Heavy involvement has continued despite the explicit language calling for the achievement of a free market economy, using such devices as deregulation, decentralization (local autonomy), privatization, and liberalization of trade and investment policies. The difference, however, is that fairness and equity and redistribution have become critical objectives of the interventionist policies. We turn now to a look at examples of different types of public sector involvement.

1) Direct Subsidies

Government subsidies remain one of the most frequently used techniques to stimulate economic development. There is a great deal of consensus among Korean scholars of economic development that tax incentives are effective. (This is different from the U.S. where the bulk of competition for industry occurs at the state and local levels and incentives are regarded as marginally effective.) Recent uses of tax incentives and loans by the Republic of Korea have been targeted more toward small and medium-sized businesses and businesses in rural areas. (The key elements of the Korea's major tax law, the Tax Exemption and Reduction Control Law, are shown in Table 3.)

Tax incentives have also been a major element of government policy aimed at encouraging overseas investment by Korean businesses, especially in communist and socialist nations (Soviet Union, Poland, Hungary, Vietnam, China, and Czechoslovakia). And tax incentives still play a major role in the development of high technology industries. It is here that foreign corporations have sustained a few tax breaks (the rest were removed in the mid-1980s to promote domestic industries).

Under the Foreign Capital Inducement Law, tax incentives to foreign corporations now can be granted only for qualified companies meeting one of the following criteria: (1) they induce high technology; (2) are located in a free-export zone; (3) are invested by a Korean living abroad; or (4) are approved by the Foreign Capital Inducement Deliberation Committee to receive tax benefits in consideration of diversifying investments or increasing employment (e.g., investment in small and medium-sized companies in designated industries where foreign ownership is less than 50%) (Samil Accounting Corporation 1989, 20).[7]

2) Indirect Subsidies

The most significant evidence of the change in the government's indirect subsidy policies is demonstrated in the government's budget. A greater share of public money has been allocated to the development of human capital (education, welfare, and health) (See Figure 1).

A greater proportion has also been allocated to the more rural provinces, although regional imbalance remains extensive, a problem that will be discussed in more detail later in the paper.

Other recent examples of indirect subsidies have been the creation of the Aerospace Research Institute to develop the aerospace industry and an investment of 37.5 billion won to develop substitute energy sources (solar photovoltaic energy and fuel cells).

---

7. Excellent discussions of the availability of tax incentives and the effect of other tax policies on foreign firms can be found in Samil Accounting Corporation (1984, 1989); Jang (1988); Yu (1988).

3) Information and Exhortation

Government-sponsored information campaigns have played an important role in recent development efforts, especially in light of the expanded freedom of the media. Use of information strategies is evidenced by inclusion of industry leaders, including representatives of the electronic and print media, in officially-sponsored delegations to foreign nations to open up trade and/or increase exports. This has been a popular approach in implementing the Nordpolitik strategy. This policy is aimed at export expansion and diversification of trading partners (reducing reliance on the U.S. and Japan). Nordpolitik is also an important part of both the strategy to gain entry into the United Nations and the long term goal of reunification with North Korea.

Exhortation also has been widely used. The government met with industry groups in late 1989, urging some to stabilize prices (apparel, footwear, and heaters) and others to cut prices in response to falling prices on the world market (zinc ingots, petrochemicals, and steel products). Government "jawboning" was also aimed at the large corporations (*jaebeol*) to "encourage" them to invest less in service and leisure industries (golf courses, hotels, and restaurants) and more in productive industries. The jawboning was followed by an announcement of intensified tax probes into the "nonproductive" investments of the *jaebeol*.

Heavily-publicized jawboning efforts also were aimed at firms importing luxury items. Both they and the *jaebeol* were chided for fueling the flames of consumerism. Another group targeted for government jawboning was the "entertainment" industry (linked to increased crime rates, especially violent crimes against women). In each instance, jawboning was followed by an announcement of more intense tax probes of these industries. In addition, a higher value-added tax was imposed on the entertainment industry (from 2% to 10%).

Another heavy dosage of exhortation has involved the stock market. The government has used exhortation techniques to stimulate large businesses (domestic and foreign) to go public. The government's announcement of capital market liberalization of in the early 1990s has also "boosted the market with the expectation that the opening of the capital market to foreign investors will enhance the stock price levels which are relatively low in terms of a worldwide perspective" (Corporation 1989, 26).

4) Regulation

This remains a common technique for inducing economic change, in spite of the government's Sixth Plan goal of less government regulation. Stepped-up enforcement of existing regulations (tax laws, conflict of interest) by the National Tax Service has taken place. The targeted businesses have been the aforementioned large firms importing expensive consumer items and the entertainment industry. High ranking government ministry officials who traded their positions of influence for personal economic gain also came under closer scrutiny when tougher conflict of interest laws were enforced.

Regulation of the real estate market has been proposed through an extensive land reform package submitted to the National Assembly in late 1989. The regulations prohibiting landownership in excess of "proper" acreage are most controversial. The top 20% of the landowners possess nearly 90% of the privately-owned land. Unequal ownership of land by some big corporations is said to be particularly acute. One report shows that as much as 67.4% of the 4,496km^2 currently owned by 56,000 corporations is concentrated in the hands of 403 corporations. "The lopsided concentration makes it all the more difficult to secure a site for a new factory and contributes to skyrocketing prices" (*The Korea Times*, 12 September 1989).

Three land reform bills have been drafted. Their commonality is reliance on tax policy as the major tool for accomplishing reform. One is aimed at limiting the size of land for each house to 200 *pyeong* (660 m^2) and levying a heavy tax on the amount above the limitation. Another would levy a heavy tax every three years on land whose prices are hiked. The third would levy a tax on 70% of the profits resulting from a hike in the real estate value caused by the development of nearby areas.[8]

Land reform policy (or land tax policy) is exemplary of government efforts to improve economic equity. It is also the epitome of government involvement in economic development. The following outline of the specifics of the reform as they would affect business makes this point:

> Business firms owning excessive land will face various disadvantages in financing and taxation. Firms associated with business groups will be

---

8. Lee Song-Yol, "Parties at Variance over Government Land Reform Bills," *The Korea Times*, 8 September 1989, p. 2.

subject to a prior investigation by the prime credit bank when they plan to buy real estate. If any of the land owned by firms turns out to be of non-business use, the owners will be ordered by the credit bank to dispose of the land. If enterprises have non-business land, the property acquisition tax rate will be 15%, an increase of 7.5 times from the present 2%. A heavier tax will also be imposed on land which reverts to a non-business use within five years after the land was purchased. In addition, money spent for management, repair, insurance, property tax and facilities depreciation will not be recognized as tax deductions. When non-business property is sold, a special capital gains tax of 25% will be imposed. The 25% special capital gains tax will also be levied on enterprises owning real estate in excess of the proper level when they dispose of ranches, golf courses, sports grounds, training institutes, resort villas, parking lots, woods, salterns, and property of entertainment restaurants, even if it has been determined they were used for business purposes. The new implementation system will not accept money used to pay back interest rates as a tax deduction. This will be most effective against a firm whose loans exceed two times its own capital. This measure is aimed at increasing the ratio of equity capital while reducing dependence on credit, thus helping strengthen international competitiveness and stabilize enterprise management. Financial institutions will also be restricted from possessing real estate in excess of the size required for their business. Banking institutions will be permitted to own land equivalent to 50% of their capital, down 25 percentage points from the current 75%. Investment and credit firms along with merchant banking organizations will be authorized to own real estate property equivalent to 50% of their capital. The property that can be owned by insurance companies will be reduced from the current 15% of their total asset value to 10%.[9]

The land reforms will be one of the benchmarks by which the public gauges the sincerity of the government to move in the direction of economic equity. In a Gallup survey taken in September 1989, nearly 85% of the population expressed support for the concept of broad public ownership of land. The same survey showed that over 89% see the problems concerning land and housing as very serious.[10]

In the September 1989 Gallup survey, the same high percentage of

9. *The Korea Times*, 12 September 1989, p. 8.
10. Other studies which highlight the severity of the housing problem are: Hwang Myung Chan (1985); Park Woo Suh (1985); Kim Kyung-Hwan (1988).

Koreans (89%) supported strengthening the regulation on non-business purpose landownership by businesses. More than 80% believe that the proposed land reforms will cool down the speculative investment in land and 63% think it will narrow the gap between the haves and have-nots (*The Korea Times*, 22 October 1989, 8). The major problem with the land reform proposal is that it is seen as conflicting with the tenets of democracy and capitalism. Its opponents regard it as "infringing upon individual rights and betraying the underpinnings of the capitalist system."[11]

5) Policies Affecting Crucial Industries and Institutions

Granting greater autonomy to the financial market is one of the major objectives of the Sixth Plan. As with the land reform proposals, government involvement in restructuring the financial sector has been extensive and designed to induce competition. As a step toward market liberalization, the government announced guidelines designed to permit foreign banks to operate in Korea. Again, the cross-pressures of adopting a pure free market economy while promoting the development of domestic industries are evident in the area of financial market reform. The following account of government restraints on foreign banks makes this point:

> Any foreign bank wishing to open a branch in Korea must be among the top 500 international banks. To qualify for additional branches, the total assets of the main branch of a specific foreign bank must be over 100 billion won, must have been in operation here for more than five years and a new regional branch must make a significant contribution to the development of regional financial markets. To join retail banking services, different criteria will be applied. A foreign bank must be one of the top 100 international banks and it must have at least one main branch in Seoul and one regional bank in Korea. The main branch must have been operating here for more than 10 years and the regional branch must have been in operation for more than five years. At the same time, the total asset of the main branch must exceed 300 billion won. As a way of enabling foreign banks in Korea to generate additional local currency funding, the government will establish a new unified call money market merging banks with short-term finance companies.

---

11. Lee Song-Yol, *op. cit.*, p. 2.

It will also introduce a brokerage system and eliminate the ceiling on the size of call money and permit each foreign bank to expand the issuance of certificates of deposit–twice the paid-in capital or 10 billion won, whichever is greater. The Korean government will maintain its principle of reducing swap line–a vital local currency funding source for foreign banks–but not before alternative sources of local funds are provided to offset such swap reduction. The Korean government will allow foreign banks to increase their capital up to 12 billion won as long as they file an application with the Finance Ministry and the Bank of Korea. But any capital increase beyond 3 billion won will be deducted from the swap facilities. As a new market opening measure, the government has already deregulated telegraphic transfer selling and buying rates for foreign currencies within the limits of 0.4-0.8%. It also allowed foreign banks to expand their foreign exchange position–the maximum amount of foreign currencies each bank can hold. Redundant paperwork is eliminated for currency forward dealings. Another proposal is the consolidation of foreign bank branches as a single entity. For example, five branches of the Citibank Seoul will be treated as one entity in the future.[12]

Insurance is another industry which is being targeted for rapid development. An example of how the government has promoted this industry and tied it to the development of the stock market is a regulation that forces local insurers to own over 20% of their total assets in the form of bonds.

The insurance industry is also part of the land reform equity proposals. While Korean insurance companies can invest only 10% of their total assets in real estate (as mandated by the Ministry of Finance), the government allows insurance companies to purchase real estate equivalent to an additional 5% of total assets if they use the real estate for such public projects as the construction of rental housing units, city redevelopment projects, and other social welfare projects (*The Korea Herald*, 26 October 1989).

6) Shaping of Market Opportunity and Environment, Shaping of Market Structure, and Defining and Limiting Forms of Enterprise

The government's use of these techniques to promote economic devel-

---

12. *The Korea Times*, 27 September 1989, 1.

opment has already been demonstrated. Government regulations, subsidies, both direct and indirect, and exhortations all have the effect of
shaping the market. This has been quite obvious in the case of Korea's
rapidly developing economy. The major issue remains one of balance
and equity in the implementation and impact of such policies.

One of the consequences of Korea's rapid growth has been its success
in joining world economic organizations. Korea's upgraded status under
the General Agreement on Tariffs and Trade (GATT) in 1989 makes
import liberalization an even more important economic goal. The problem is that intense pressure has emerged from the domestic sectors
which will be the most affected by such a policy—agriculture, service,
and finance. A recent statement by the Director-General of the Livestock
Bureau at the Ministry of Agriculture, Forestry & Fisheries reflects this
problem: "Free trade is wonderful but I don't want any industry in any
country to be sacrificed in the name of free trade" (Clifford 1989, 53).
The government is now paying a high price (in terms of increased pressures internally and externally) for the export-based development strategy which initially played second fiddle to the development of the domestic market. It is but one of many examples of how economic development strategies that are extremely effective in the short term may turn
out to be problematic in the long term as the economy matures.

7) Engaging Government in Enterprise and Employment

The Korean government over the years has utilized public corporations
and enterprises rather extensively. As of 1989, there were 90 public
enterprises, including 25 government-invested enterprises and 54 subsidiary companies of government-invested enterprises (Song 1986, 1989;
Kang 1988).[13] But the trend under the Sixth Plan has been to privatize

---

13. There are four categories of public enterprises in Korea: government enterprises,
    government-invested enterprises, subsidiaries of government-invested enterprises,
    and "other" government-backed enterprises. Government enterprises include those
    government-departmental agencies which produce goods and services and are operat-
    ed by officials employed by government ministries and agencies (n=5). Government-
    invested enterprises are those enterprises in which the government holds more than
    50% of their equity and whose top management is appointed by the state (n=25).
    The third type is a subsidiary company of a government-invested enterprise (n=54).
    "Other" are government-backed enterprises or companies in which the government
    is a minority shareholder (n=6) (See Song 1986, 4-7).

these corporations. Two entities were proposed for privatization in 1989: the Korean Electric Power Corporation (KEPCO) and the Korea Heavy Industries Corporation, a firm specializing in the manufacture of power generating facilities. These were selected from a list of ten public enterprises the government identified as "for sale" in its 1987 privatization policy.[14]

The listing of KEPCO on the stock exchange prompted a series of government directives, primarily equity-oriented. Three investment trust companies were authorized to increase the capital of their people's stock funds to a combined 760 billion won from the previous 46 billion won. The Ministry of Finance also announced it would allow the Securities and Exchange Commission to closely monitor speculators in order to keep them from manipulating the initial price of KEPCO shares. To prevent market disruptions, the exchange allowed the trading of KEPCO shares for just five minutes after its opening. Its initial price was decided after averaging out all bid offer prices for the first five minutes. The government also allocated 20% of KEPCO shares to members of the employee stock ownership association and 78% to low-income bracket families with incomes of less than 600,000 won per month.

The privatization of Korea Heavy Industries Construction was less smooth. An economic slowdown made the investment less attractive. Government requirements that at least two bidders take part (which seemed likely to be no problem when the policy was formulated and the economy was strong) proved burdensome. Privatization was delayed.

Perhaps the biggest change in the governmental structure is the planned local autonomy. In 1990, local governments may be able to elect their own officials.[15] If the National Assembly approves this plan, local governments will be given more revenue sources (the cigarette tax already has been transferred to local government to strengthen their revenue base and self-sufficiency). Responsibility for much of the public infrastructure

---

14. See Kang (1988) for an excellent history of privatization efforts in Korea.
15. The local autonomy proposal before the National Assembly calls for local elections of provincial governing bodies beginning in 1990. Local autonomy is a major component of President Roh's campaign platform. While the idea is broadly endorsed in principle, the actual details for how to do it and when are very controversial. Potentially, the details may change the balance of power of political parties in the National Assembly, not to mention regions. For excellent discussions of the local autonomy movement, see Yoo (1987-1988).

development will most likely be shifted downward. It is a classic example of how decentralization emerges as a development priority when centralized authoritarian systems move in the direction of democracy. This is particularly so when there has been a history of regional imbalance, as has been the case in Korea. There has been little change in the proportion of the population living in each province over the past three decades (Figure 2) or in the proportion of the central government's grants to local governments received by each province (Table 4).

These examples of government involvement in the latter half of 1989 are merely among the most publicized. But they show the extensive nature of government involvement in a newly industrialized nation making the transition to political democracy. There are lessons to be learned from the Korean experience.

Lessons from Korea's Experiences

One of the ironies observed in Korea's economic development history is that effective plans in the short term may be counterproductive in the long term. Perhaps most exemplary are government-directed economic initiatives adopted in the early stages of Korea's economic development plans that have caused imbalanced growth (regionally and sectorally) and concentrated support in large monopolistic industries (the *jaebeol*). In a sense, government policies necessary to fuel rapid growth and expansion have produced major inequities that are now extremely difficult to remedy. Yet political democratization has mandated rapid economic democratization—a feat that may be even more difficult to achieve than political democratization.

Korean development over the last thirty years has been described as "unbalanced" (Kwon 1989, 5). Marked schisms have appeared between:

• large firms vs. medium- and small-sized firms;[16]

---

16. Small- and medium-sized businesses have had the toughest time adjusting to the economic downturns. A disproportionate number have failed. And in spite of widely-publicized government efforts to help small and medium-sized businesses, they remain skeptical. For example, despite vociferous claims for months that restrictions on bank loans for the top thirty business conglomerates would not be eased, the government eased them in November 1989, for export and high-tech industries and

- the agricultural, fishing, and mining sector vs. the manufacturing sector;[17]
- foreign firms vs. domestic firms;[18]
- metropolitan provinces (especially Seoul Metropolitan area) vs. rural provinces;[19]
- male vs. female workers;[20]
- young vs. old workers;[21]

---

industries investing in overhead facilities and equipment (i.e., most of the conglomerates). Large firms argue that they have produced the economic growth that has brought Korea to where it is today and that for the government to turn its back on them now is an extremely short-sighted approach.

17. The transition from a predominantly agrarian economy to a more diversified one has been very painful. Farmers are extremely powerful politically and have a lot of sympathy from the average citizen. But subsidy policies and restrictions on land ownership infringing on agricultural land have conflicted with other government policies offering incentives to manufacturing industries to move into rural areas of the country, creating a natural conflict between the agricultural and manufacturing sectors.

18. Foreign vs. domestic firm conflicts have arisen mostly with regard to imports, licensing, and intellectual property rights laws. Domestic firms want domestic industries protected. Foreign firms want less protectionism and more evidence of a free market at work.

19. Regional discrimination has deep cultural, political, and economic roots (Kwon, 1989). Historically, political leaders have come from the urbanized provinces and government spending and educational policies have reflected an urban bias as well.

20. Women's wages still trail those of men (women's wages were 51.4% of men's in 1989). But more at issue are the differences in government-imposed mandatory retirement ages. A study by Professor Lee Eun-Yong reported in *The Korea Herald*, 19 October 1989, found that markedly lower mandatory retirement ages were established for occupations with heavy concentrations of female workers (e.g., secretaries, typists, and telephone operators) than for jobs dominated by male workers. This is in spite of the fact that in August 1988, the Labor Ministry banned all firms with more than 5 employees from discriminating against women in retirement age. However, Lee reports little enforcement of this Act. Women also make up nearly 50% of the work force, but many have college degrees and find it very difficult to get a job, especially in the area in which they were trained.

21. Older workers are more likely to work overtime and less likely to strike. They are also more loyal to the corporation in which they have probably worked throughout their entire period of participation in the labor market. Younger workers, in contrast, are less likely to work overtime, put personal leisure activities at a higher premium than corporate production goals, and are more likely to be at the forefront of strike activities, particularly if they are college graduates.

- banking vs. nonbanking financial institutions;[22]
- management vs. labor;[23]
- non-college graduates vs. college graduates;[24] and
- large landowners vs. small landowners.[25]

Historically, government-promulgated policies have disproportionately benefited: large firms, the manufacturing sector, the metropolitan area (Seoul), foreign firms initially and domestic firms later, male workers, older workers; banking financial institutions; management, non-college graduates, and large landowners (these are generalizations, but there are, of course, exceptions). These schisms have shown up in recent public

---

22. The Korean banking system is made up of commercial banks, specialized banks, non-banking credit institutions, and government-controlled development banks (Samil Accounting Corporation, 1989, 23). Deregulation of the financial industry to promote competition and modernization has created conflicts between different types of institutions as their financial roles have merged.

23. Labor-management conflicts have intensified as political democratization has progressed. The average Korean places most of the blame for conflict on management. In a 1988 survey of the Korean populace, 70% of the respondents laid the blame for labor disputes on employers. This represents attitudes that business got rich through perpetrating low wages for workers. But management lays most of the blame for labor unrest on leftists and has expressed a legitimate concern that continuation of annual wage increases averaging 20% is an unrealistic request on the part of workers. Such wage rate increases have clearly been shown to have affected negatively Korean business exports and domestic prices. Again, workers say domestic prices have been most inflated by business real estate speculation investments and that workers would not push for such sharp increases in wages if domestic prices, particularly of essentials (housing, food, and clothing), were not increasing at that rate.

24. The unemployment rate for university graduates is much higher than for junior college (two-year) graduates or for non-college graduates in general. For example, in 1989, 79.4% of the graduates of two-year institutions (technical colleges) gained employment while only 45.9% of the graduates of four-year institutions were employed. This is extremely distressing to the college graduates who have made it through a highly competitive process to be admitted to a four-year institution. The lack of employment opportunities for college graduates is one source of much of the political turmoil in Korea. On the other hand, those who did not make it through the rather exclusionary university admissions process do not feel much sympathy for college graduates. They often attack an admissions process as discriminatory and biased in favor of the wealthy and powerful in the Seoul Metropolitan area.

25. This schism is a product of increasing land speculation and is a composite of business vs. labor and farmer vs. manufacturer schisms. The current proposed land reforms are aimed at redressing the vast inequities in land ownership perpetrated under past political regimes.

opinion surveys. An excellent article by Seoul National University sociologist Kwon Tai-hwan (1989) analyzes attitudes about social, economic, and political phenomena and finds significant differences by age, gender, education, region, and income. In general, more negative appraisals are made by the "have-nots" (young, female, non-college, rural provinces, workers, or poor). However, most significant was the fact that among all groups, regional conflict between Yeongnam and Honam was identified as the most serious social conflict facing Korea today. It supports the conclusion that the biggest failure of Korea's economic planning thus far has been the inability to achieve balanced regional development. The challenge for continued Korean economic development is to develop policies that diffuse protests about economic inequities but do not stifle economic growth. It is somewhat ironic that at the very time the nation's economic development plan (Revised Sixth) calls for less government intervention in the economy (a pure market model), political demands on the government to iron out inequities have intensified.

A close examination of the specific policy recommendations for 1988-1991 shows that policies aimed at pleasing each of the above groups are included in the Revised Sixth Plan. The issue, however, remains one of the perceptions of imbalance and a deep-seated feeling that the system has served only the very rich. A survey of 1,514 Seoul citizens by the Korea Applied Statistical Research Institute and Munhwa Broadcasting Corporation (MBC) in September 1989 shows that "almost 75% believe the country's instant millionaires earned their money through dishonest means like investments, personal ties with government officials, or the exploitation of employees" (*The Korea Herald*, 9 November 1989, 3). The problem that all democratic nations face is that equity is frequently measured in selfish, subjective terms by individuals, groups, or firms who presume they are competing in a zero-sum game. Under such circumstances, even if government were to implement policies that produced equality in benefits, the competitors would not necessarily see this as an equitable solution. One's views of equity are clearly colored by one's perceptions of past relative deprivations. As a consequence, rates of increase become equally, if not more, important than base comparisons. This is especially true in climates where rapid economic and political changes have occurred—and the change is in the direction of openness and competitiveness. This problem is exacerbated when the political regime changes from an authoritarian to a more democratic one. Public distrust of government-generated social and economic statistics becomes a serious problem. An excellent example of this occurred in Korea with regard to wage rates. A decline in the projected economic growth rate in 1989 (particularly of exports) led government and industry to lay most of the blame on labor. Specifically, they cited the fact that wages had increased an average of 60% over the previous three years. Government and industry leaders legitimately claimed that these steep increases raised the price of Korean goods and made them less competitive, especially with other Pacific Rim nations (e.g. Singapore, Malaysia, Vietnam, Taiwan, and the Philippines). While statistics were generated to show the relative place of Korea in the Asian and world markets,[26] the general populace was reticent to accept these figures at face value. The history of powerful linkages between big business and government was too long. Suspicion of the collusion between government and business among the population-at-large will continue to plague future economic development efforts in Korea for quite some time.

The Korean economic development experience has also demonstrated that while free market principles are widely lauded among business leaders at home and abroad, they are not easily implemented. The pace of market liberalization is frequently perceived as too slow by foreign businesses but too fast by domestic firms, especially those most likely to be directly, and negatively, affected. The implementation of free market principles must be made by government but the more government intervenes, the deeper public perceptions of excessive "government tinkering" become—unless the policy may personally benefit them, then the government is perceived as "not tinkering enough."

Finally, there is a lesson in Korea's biggest economic development failure, namely the failure to achieve regional balance in development, especially of human capital. Biased, exclusionary educational policies and the failure to employ the nation's best and brightest (its college graduates) have sewn the seeds of discontent that have blossomed into cyni-

---

26. A survey by the Korea Trade Promotion Corporation of 958 major importers of Korean-made goods in 69 trade centers around the world reported that 40% are intending to shift their import sources to other Asian countries in pursuit of better prices. The most popular alternatives were: Taiwan (44.9%), Hong Kong (18.9%), Thailand (9.9%), and Singapore (6.8%). Price increases were the major complaint (28.7%), followed by shipping delays (16.3%), slow response to inquiries (15.4%), and rejection of small orders (no figure reported in *The Korea Herald*, November 17, 1989, 6).

cism about accomplishment of the government's goal of economic equity. Educational reform and the development of a balanced local autonomy system may just hold the keys to the future of Korea.

In the end, perceptions of fairness of the system must be shared by a large proportion of the population if a system of economic and political democracy is to prevail. Truly, equity is the hardest hurdle to overcome on the long track of economic development.

Table 1. Strategies of Korean Economic Development Plans

Contents of Plans	Targets	Rates of Planned (Actual) Economic Growth	Development Strategy (Policy)	Principles of Industrialization
First Five-Year Plan (1962-1966)	1. Correction of vicious cycle of social and economic aspects 2. Establishment of the foundation of a self-sustaining economy	7.1% (8.5%)	1. Correction of structural imbalance in national economy caused by increase in agricultural productivity 2. Securing of resources supplying energy 3. Expansion of basic industry and sufficient supply of social overhead capital 4. Utilization of idle resources 5. Improvement of the balance of payments 6. Promotion of technology	Adjustment of the foundation of industrialization
Second Five-Year Plan (1967-1971)	1. Modernization of industrial structure 2. Acceleration of self-sustaining economy	7.0% (9.7%)	1. Self-sufficiency in food and development of water resources 2. Establishment of the foundation for rapid development of industries (chemical, iron and steel, and machinery) 3. $700 million worth export performance and acceleration of import substitution industries—improvement in the balance of payments . 4. Increase of employment and family planning measures, and restraint of population growth 5. Diversification of farming and management technology and increase in productivity	Outward-oriented industrialization
Third Five-Year Plan (1972-1976)	1. Balanced growth, stabilization, and a balanced economy 2. Realization of self-sustaining economic structure	8.6% (10.1%)	1. Self-sufficiency in major food grains 2. Improvement of living standards in farming and fishing villages 3. Promotion of science and technology and development of manpower 4. Promotion of manufacturing through the build-up of heavy and chemical industries 5. Balanced expansion of social overhead capital 6. Efficient development of national land resources and optimum dispersion of industries and population 7. Social security and promotion of national welfare	Build-up of export-oriented heavy and chemical industries

Contents of Plans	Targets	Rates of Planned (Actual) Economic Growth	Development Strategy (Policy)	Principles of Industrialization
Fourth Five-Year Plan (1977-1981)	1. Growth, equity, and efficiency 2. Creation of economic structure of self-sustaining growth 3. Promotion of social development 4. Technological innovation and raising of efficiency	9.2% (5.5%)	1. Self-reliance in investment financing 2. Equilibrium in the balance of payments 3. Change in industrial structure and rapid development thereof 4. Expansion of Saemaeul undong (New Community Movement) 5. Increased investment in science and technology 6. Management of economy and system improvement	Development of technological and skilled labor-intensive industries
Fifth Five-Year Plan (1982-1986)	1. Stabilization, efficiency, and balance 2. Completion of the foundation of economic stabilization 3. Increased opportunity and income 4. Promotion of national welfare	7.6% (8.6%)	1. Price stabilization 2. Nurturing of comparative advantage industries 3. Maximization of investment efficiency 4. Promotion of marketing competition 5. Acceleration of liberalization or market-opening to foreign goods 6. Resolution of management-labor disputes 7. Expansion in social development	Attainment of a stage of advanced industrialization
First Sixth Five-Year Plan (1987-1991)	1. Sustained price stability 2. Promotion of com-petition 3. Improved equity of income distribution and enhanced social welfare 4. Balanced development between regional and economic sectors	7.3%	1. Establishment of new free-market economic order based on autonomy, competition, and internationalization 2. Economic ethics based on principles of equity and rationality 3. Reduction of central government regulatory functions to a minimum; transfer of functions to private sector or local government (privatization; local autonomy) 4. Government encouragement of plant and equipment investment in potentially high-growth manufacturing industries 5. Accelerated development of small- and medium-sized industries to bolster the industrial base 6. Increased investment in science and technology development projects and education	Industrial diversification; balanced regional and sector development

Table 1. Strategies of Korean Economic Development Plans (Continued)

Contents of Plans	Targets	Rates of Planned (Actual) Economic Growth	Development Strategy (Policy)	Principles of Industrialization
			7. Adoption of more rational, professional (less nepotistic) business management 8. Government promotion of different regional economic blocs (in addition to Seoul) by strengthening ability of large local cities to serve as regional growth centers 9. Development of small- and medium-sized industrial estates in areas designated as agro-industrial districts 10. Strengthening of vocational training and lifelong education programs to bolster employment services 11. Promotion of workers' welfare 12. Expansion of the middle class 13. Sustained economic growth 14. Expansion of the medical insurance system 15. Development of a medium- and long-term housing loan system for wage earners 16. Institution of a national pension system in 1988 17. Improved social well-being by strengthening traffic safety, food sanitation, and crime prevention, recreational and cultural activities	
Revised Sixth Five-Year Plan (1987-1991)	1. Sustained economic growth and control inflation 2. Enhanced economic equity 3. Diversified economic base 4. Liberalized and internationalized economy	7.5%	1. Tax reform; make system more progressive 2. Curbed real-estate speculation 3. Greater autonomy for the financial market 4. Balanced development of stimulation of large and small firms by facilitating fair competition and preventing concentration of economic power 5. Cooperative and autonomous labor-management relations 6. Accelerated and expanded rural industrialization	Industrial diversification; balanced regional and sector development; stimulation of small- and medium-sized manufacturing and service firms

Contents of Plans	Targets	Rates of Planned (Actual) Economic Growth	Development Strategy (Policy)	Principles of Industrialization
			7. Alleviated shortages of housing units for working people, especially in urban areas 8. Increased government support for educating children of low-income families 9. Controlled balance of payments surplus 10. Accelerated industrial restructuring and promotion of balanced growth of both the export and industrial sectors 11. Expanded international competition and overseas investment, especially with socialist countries 12. Establishment of round rules for a free market economy that generates equal opportunity and fair competition and stresses autonomy and responsibility 13. Expanded public welfare programs and improved redistribution of income so as to maintain economic stability 14. Opening of domestic markets to promote greater internationalization of the economy	

Notes: The GNP growth rate in 1987 (12.0 %) so far surpassed the projected GNP growth rate (8.0%) that a Revised Sixth Five-Year Plan was deemed necessary. The better-than-expected growth rate was attributed to: "underestimating the effects of exchange rate realignments of major currencies, falling oil prices, and other favorable factors" (Government of the ROK 1988, 3).

The process of developing the Sixth Five-Year Plans, especially the Revised Sixth Five-Year Plan, "marked a major departure from the past practices of government-led formulation" (Government of the ROK 1988, 7). The process here involved representatives from academia, economic and business organizations. "Primary emphasis was placed on sounding out the views and opinions of various strata of society and on seeking a national consensus in determining policy priorities" (Government of the ROK 1988, 6). The participatory nature of the process was promoted by the political democratization of Korea (President Roh Tae-woo was elected in 1987). The Revised Sixth Five-Year Plan in particular reflects the strong public demand for economic democratization.

Sources: The first five plans are from the Federation of Korean Industries (1987), p. 6. Entries for the two Sixth Five-Year Plans were abstracted from Government of the ROK (1986), pp. 26-32; (1988), pp. 9-16.

Table 2. Comparison of First to Sixth Five-Year Plans

(Planned figures are as of target year of each period)

Measure	Unit	Baseline 1962	1st Five-Year Plan (1962-66) Planned	Actual	2nd Five-Year Plan (1967-1971) Planned	Actual	3rd Five-Year Plan (1972-76) Planned	Actual
Gross national product	1980 prices ($100 million)	126.7	137.6	180.6	233.1	309	416	490
	current prices ($100 million)	23		37		94		287
Rate of GNP growth	average annual rate of growth (constant prices: %)	2.2	7.1	7.8	7.0	9.6	8.6	9.7
Per capita GNP	1980 prices ($)	395	471	613	719	941	1,221	1,367
	current prices ($)	87		125		285		800
Industrial structure	current prices (%)	100.0	100.0[1]	100.0	100.0[2]	100.0	100.0[3]	100.0
Agriculture, forestry, & fishery		37.0	34.8	34.8	34.0	26.8	22.4	23.5
Mining & manufacturing		16.4	26.1	20.5	26.8	22.2	27.9	28.4
Social overhead capital & other services		46.6	39.1	44.7	39.2	51.0	49.7	48.1
Investment ratio	current prices (%)	12.8	22.7	21.6	19.9	25.1	24.9	25.6
Domestic savings ratio		3.2	13.0	11.8	14.4	14.6	21.5	23.9
Current account balance	$100 million	-0.6	-2.5	-1.0	-1	-9	-4	-3
Merchandise exports		0.5	1.4	2.5	6	11	35	78
Merchandise imports		3.9	4.9	6.8	9	22	28	84
Increased rate of employed population	average annual rate of increase (%)	–	4.7	3.2	3.3	3.6	2.9	4.5
Unemployment ratio		8.2[5]	14.8	7.1	5.0	4.5	4.0	3.9

(Planned figures are as of target year of each period)

Measure	Unit	4th Five-Year Plan (1977-81)		5th Five-Year Plan (1982-86)		First 6th Five-Year Plan (1987-91)[6]	Revised 6th Five-Year Plan (1987-91)[6]	% Change (1962-91)[7]
		Planned	Actual	Planned	Actual	Planned	Actual	
Gross national product	1980 prices ($100 million)	669	643	933	971	1,381	1,450	—
	current prices ($100 million)		662		940	1,750	2,400	—
Rate of GNP growth	average annual rate of growth (constant prices: %)	9.2	5.8	7.5	8.6	7.3	7.5	+5.6
Per capita GNP	1980 prices ($)	1,723	1,669	2,229	2,344	3140	3,300	600.6%
	current prices ($)		1,719		2,286	4,000	5,500	—
Industrial structure	current prices (%)	100.0[4]	100.0	100.0	100.0	100.0	100.0	—
Agriculture, forestry, & fishery		18.5	15.8	12.2	12.8	10.6	10.1	−71.4%
Mining & manufacturing		40.9	30.7	31.0	30.1	32.7	32.9	+26.1%
Social overhead capital & other service		40.6	53.5	56.9	57.1	56.7	57.0	+45.8%
Investment ratio	current prices (%)	26.0	30.3	29.5	29.5	31.3	31.6	+39.2
Domestic savings ratio		23.9	20.5	21.7	32.5	33.5	33.5	+157.7
Current account balance	$100 million	12	−47	4	45	50	60	—
Merchandise exports		202	207	357	336	554	795	—
Merchandise imports		189	243	351	293	489	765	—
Increased rate of employed population	average annual rate of increase (%)	3.2	2.3	2.5	1.9	2.3	2.3	−51.1%
Unemployment ratio		3.8	4.5	3.8	3.8	3.7	3.5	−76.4%

Note: 1) 1961 prices, 2) 1965 prices, 3) 1970 prices, 4) 1975 prices, 5) 1963 prices, 6) Revised in 1988 due to better-than-projected performance in 1987, 7) Change figures calculated for standardized (% or p.c.) entries only.

Sources: Government of the ROK (1986), pp. 132-133; Government of the ROK (1988), pp. 83, 90-93, 107.

Table 3. Tax Incentives under the Tax Exemption and Reduction Control Law

Criteria for Eligibility	Exemption of Reduction
• Newly organized small- and medium-sized companies having generally no more than 300 employees (200 in the case of the construction industry), and operate in the manufacturing or mining industries. The company's total assets should not exceed a certain limit which ranges between 8 and 30 billion won depending on its industry type. In addition, the industry should be classified as technology intensive or the company should be located in the agricultural or fishery area to qualify for the tax exemption.	• Corporation tax is fully exempted for the period of the first taxable year plus three years thereafter, and reduced by 50% for the subsequent two years. Registration tax, acquisition tax, and property tax are also reduced.
• Small- and medium-sized companies defined as companies having generally no more than 300 employees (200 in the case of the construction industry), operating in the manufacturing, mining, constructions, transportations, or fishery industries.	• A deductible provision for investment up to 15% of the book value of business assets as of the end of the fiscal year. In addition, for the manufacturing and mining industries, special depreciation of 50% (or 100%) of the normal depreciation, or machinery and equipment only.
• Resident or domestic corporations, including foreign-invested companies, operating in the manufacturing, mining, construction, or engineering service industries, who are making expenditures for technology or manpower development.	• A deductible provision for technology development up to 1.5% (or 2%) of gross receipts or 20% (or 30%) of net income, whichever is greater. In addition, an investment tax credit of 10% of expenditures for technology or manpower development.
• A new company starting a business using new technology.	• Either an investment tax credit of 3% (or 10%) of expenditures for technology development, or special depreciation of 30% (or 50%) of the normal depreciation, at the taxpayer's option.
• Resident or domestic corporations, including foreign-invested companies, earning foreign currency.	• The following deductible provisions: – Provision for export loss of the lower of 1 % of foreign currency receipts or 50% of taxable income. – Provision for overseas market development of 1% of foreign currency receipts. – Provision for export price fluctuations of 5% of the value of specified inventory. In addition, special depreciation generally at 30% of the normal depreciation.
• Resident or domestic corporations, including foreign-invested companies, investing in facilities for – Improving productivity – Energy conservation – Pollution control – Prevention of industrial hazards – Distribution industry – Mine safety	• Either an investment tax credit of 3 % (or 10%) of the amount invested in the enumerated facilities, or special depreciation of 30% (or 50%) of the normal depreciation on such facilities, at the taxpayer's option.

Source: Samil Accounting Corporation et al. (1989), p. 21.

Table 4. Subsidies to Local Governments by Province: 1984-1988,
Republic of Korea (%)

Province	1984	1985	1986	1987	1988
Special cities[1]					
Seoul	2.04	1.39	1.64	0.9	1.6
Busan	1.04	1.26	1.5	2.1	3.6
Daegu	1.35	1.15	0.9	0.9	1.0
Incheon	0.34	0.63	0.4	0.5	0.7
Gwangju	–	–	0.6	0.9	1.0
Provinces					
Gyeonggi-do	15.4	14.0	14.7	10.9	13.8
Gangwon-do	11.5	8.1	8.8	7.8	7.4
Chungcheongbuk-do	6.4	7.0	6.2	6.7	6.7
Chungcheongnam-do	11.3	12.0	12.8	20.0	13.3
Jeollabuk-do	9.1	8.8	8.9	7.6	8.8
Jeollanam-do	11.7	15.6	14.5	11.6	13.8
Gyeongsangbuk-do	12.7	14.1	13.9	11.9	12.7
Gyeongsangnam-do	15.4	14.4	13.7	16.8	14.1
Jeju-do	1.8	1.5	1.6	1.4	1.5
	99.9%	100.0%	100.1%	100.0%	99.8%

1) Data for Daejeon were not reported. Percentages do not add up to 100% due to rounding.

Source: NBS (1989), pp. 114-115.

Percent of Budget

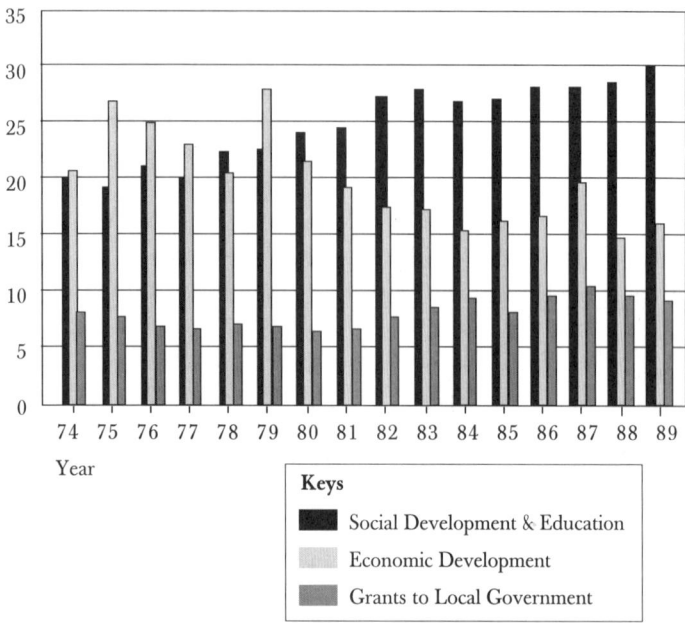

Source: NBS (1989), p. 59.

Figure 1. Percent of budget expended for social development & education, economic development, and grants to local government, Republic of Korea, 1974-1989

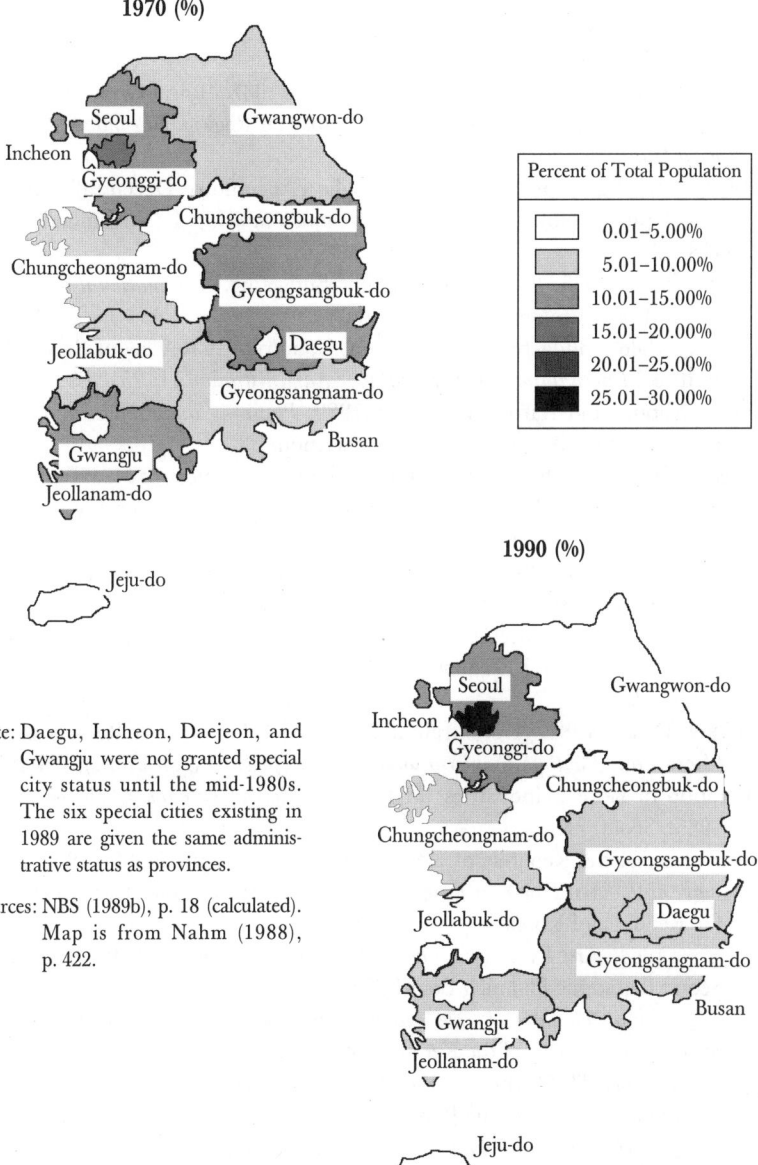

Note: Daegu, Incheon, Daejeon, and
   Gwangju were not granted special
   city status until the mid-1980s.
   The six special cities existing in
   1989 are given the same administrative status as provinces.

Sources: NBS (1989b), p. 18 (calculated).
   Map is from Nahm (1988),
   p. 422.

Figure 2. Change in population composition: Special cities and provinces in
the Republic of Korea, 1970 and 1990

BIBLIOGRAPHY

Ahlbrandt, Roger S. Jr., and James P. DeAngelis. 1987. "Local Options for Economic Development in a Maturing Industrial Region." *Economic Development Quarterly* 1 (February): 41-51.

Bahl, Roy, and Shyam Nath. 1986. "Public Expenditure Decentralization in Developing Countries." *Environment and Planning* 4 (November): 405-418.

Caiden, Naomi. 1985. "Comparative Public Budgeting." *International Journal of Public Administration* 7: 375-402.

_____. 1988. "Budgeting in Developing Countries: A Review of Recent Literature." *International Journal of Public Administration* 11: 251-269.

Caiden, Naomi, and Aaron Wildavsky. 1980. *Planning and Budgeting in Poor Countries.* New Brunswick, N.J.: Transaction.

Carleton, D. 1983. "The Location and Employment Choices of New Firms: An Economic Model With Discrete and Continuous Endogenous Variables." *Review of Economics and Statistics* 65 (August): 440-449.

Clifford, Mark. 1989. "Seoul's Beef Hash: South Korea's Agriculture is Still Mired in the Past." *Far Eastern Economic Review* (7 December): 53-54.

Cole, David C., and Princeton N. Lyman. 1971. *Korean Development: The Interplay of Politics and Economics.* Cambridge, Mass.: Harvard University Press.

Conyers, Diana. 1984. "Decentralization and Development: A Review of the Literature." *Public Administration and Development* 4 (April/June): 187-197.

Federation of Korean Industries (FKI). 1987. *Korean Economic Policies* (1945-1985). Seoul: FKI.

Government of the Republic of Korea (Government of the ROK). 1962. *Summary of the First Five-Year Economic Plan 1962-1966.* Seoul: Government of the Republic of Korea.

_____. 1964. *First Five-Year Economic Development Plan* (1962-1966). Rev. ed. Seoul: Economic Planning Board (EPB).

_____. 1966. *The Second Five-Year Economic Development Plan* (1967-1971). Seoul: Government of the Republic of Korea.

_____. 1971. *The Third Five-Year Economic Development Plan* (1972-1976). Seoul: Government of the Republic of Korea.

_____. 1976. *The Forth Five-Year Economic Development Plan* (1977-1981). Seoul: Government of the Republic of Korea.

_____. 1982. *The Fifth Five-Year Economic Development Plan* (1982-1986). Seoul: Government of the Republic of Korea.

_____. 1982. *The Second Comprehensive National Physical Development Plan* (1982-1991). Seoul: Government of the Republic of Korea.

_____. 1986. *The Sixth Five-Year Economic and Social Development Plan.* Seoul: Government of the Republic of Korea.

_____. 1988. *The Revised Sixth Five-Year Economic and Social Development Plan* (1988-1991). Seoul: Government of the Republic of Korea.

Helms, L. Jay. 1985. "The Effect of State and Local Taxes on Economic Growth: A Time-Series-Cross Section Approach." *Review of Economics and Statistics* 67 (November): 574-582.

Hicks, Ursuba. 1961. *Development From Below: A Study of Local Government and Finance in Developing Countries.* London: Oxford University Press.

Hwang, Myung Chan. 1985. "The Search for Low-Cost Land Development Techniques." In *Administrative Dynamics and Development,* edited by Kim Bun-Woong, David S. Bell Jr., and Lee Chong Bum, 237-251. Seoul: Gyobo Publishing Co.

International Monetary Fund (IMF). 1989. "Korea's Fruitful Cooperation with The Fund." *Finance & Development* (March): 18-19.

Jang, Song-Hyon. 1988. *The Key To Successful Business in Korea.* Seoul: S.H. Jang & Associates.

Jones, Leroy P., and Sakong Il. 1980. *Government Business, and Entrepreneurship in Economic Development.* Cambridge, Mass.: Harvard University Press.

Kang, Shin Il. 1988. *Korea's Privatization Plans and Past Experience.* Working Paper 8823, Korea Development Institute, Seoul.

Kee, Woo-Sik. 1977. "Fiscal Decentralization and Economic Development." *Public Finance Quarterly* 5 (January): 79-97.

Kim, Dong-Hyun. 1985. "The Development of Human Resources and Economic Growth in Korea." In *Administrative Dynamics and Development,* edited by Kim Bun Woong, David S. Bell Jr., and Lee Chong Bum, 32-55. Seoul, Korea: Gyobo Publishing Co.

Kim, Joungwon Alexander. 1975. *Divided Korea: The Politics of Development 1954-1972.* Cambridge, Mass.: Harvard University Press.

Kim, Kyung-Hwan. 1988. "Inefficiency of Housing Finance in Korea." In *Korean Development Into the 21st Century,* edited by Lim Gill-chin, 125-130. Seoul: Consortium on Development Studies.

Korea Business World. 1989. "How Korea Did It." *Business World* 5 (September): 35-37.

The Korea Herald, 8 September–17 November 1989.

The Korea Times, 12 September–22 October 1989.

Kuznets, Paul W. 1977. *Economic Growth and Structure in the Republic of Korea.* New Haven: Yale University Press.

Kwon, Tai-hwan. 1989. "Perceptions of the Quality of Life and Social Conflicts." *Korea Journal* 29.9 (September): 10-32.

Lee, Ki-baik. 1984. *A New History of Korea.* Seoul: Illchogak Publishing Co.

Lewis, J. P., and V. Kallob, eds. 1986. *Development Strategies Reconsidered.* New

Brunswick, N.J.: Transaction Books.

Lim, Gill-Chin, and Richard J. Moore. 1989. "Privatization in Developing Countries: Ideal and Reality." *International Journal of Public Administration* 12.1: 137-161.

Mason, Edward S., Kim Mahn Je, Dwight H. Perkins, Kim Kwang Suk, and David Cole. 1980. *The Economic and Social Modernization of the Republic of Korea.* Cambridge, Mass.: Harvard University Press.

Mills, Edwin. 1988. "The Role of Public and Private Sectors in Economic Development." In *Korean Development into 21st Century,* edited by Im Gill-chin, 21-26. Seoul: Consortium on Development Studies.

Mjkhopadyay, A. 1988. "Issues and Trends of Local Government in the Third World Countries." Paper presented at the IPSA Research Committee Workshop, New Delhi, 16-18 March.

Nahm, Andrew C. 1988. *Korea: Tradition and Transformation: A History of the Korean People.* Seoul: Hollym Corporation.

National Bureau of Statistics (NBS), Economic Planning Board (EPB), Republic of Korea. 1989a. *Korean Economic Indicator 1989 3/4.* Seoul: EPB.

_____. 1989b. *Major Statistics of Korean Economy.* Seoul: EPB.

National Association of State Development Agencies, National Council for Economic Development, and the Urban Institute. 1983. *Directory of Incentives for Business Investment and Development in the United States.* Washington, D.C.: Urban Institute Press.

Olowu, Dale. 1984. "Problems of Human and Financial Resources in the Development of Nigeria's Local Government Areas." *Nigerian Journal of Administrative Science* 1 (December): 27-41.

Olson, Mancur. 1982. *The Rise and Decline of Nations: Economic Growth, Stagflation, and Social Rigidity.* New Haven: Yale University Press.

Park, Woo-Suh. 1985. "An Analytic Study of the Housing Policy for the Improvement of Squatter Settlements: A Case Study of Seoul, Korea." In *Administrative Dynamics and Development,* edited by Kim Bun Woong, David S. Bell Jr., and Lee Chong Bum, 252-277. Seoul: Gyobo Publishing Co.

Roth, Gabriel. 1986. *Private Provision of Public Services in Developing Countries.* Washington, D.C.: IBRD.

Samil Accounting Corporation. 1984. *English Translation of Corporation Tax Law of The Republic of Korea, Including Presidential Enforcement Regulations, 1985.* Seoul: Samil Accounting Corporation, Coopers and Lybrand.

Samil Accounting Corporation, Coopers and Lybrand. 1989. *Republic of Korea: A Guide for Businessmen and Investors.* Seoul: Samil Accounting Corporation, Coopers and Lybrand.

Song, Dae-Hee. 1986. "The Performance Evaluation of Korean Public Enterprises: Policy, Practice, and Experience." Working Paper 8601, Korea

Development Institute, Seoul.

_____. 1989. "Three Essays on Korean Privatization Policy: An Overview of Privatization Policies, the People's Share Program, and A Case Study of POSCO Privatization." Working Paper 8922, Korea Development Institute, Seoul.

Thai, Khi V. 1988. "Public Budgeting and Financial Management in Developing Countries: A Symposium." *International Journal of Public Administration* 11: 243-250.

Warner, Paul D. 1987. "Business Climate, Taxes, and Economic Development." *Economic Development Quarterly* 1 (November): 383-390.

Wasylenko, Michael. 1987. "Fiscal Decentralization and Economic Development." *Public Budgeting & Finance* 7 (winter): 57-71.

Hwang, In Joung. 1985. "Popular Participation in Community Development Projects." In *Administrative Dynamics and Development*, edited by Kim Bun Woong, David S. Bell Jr., and Lee Chong Bum, 348-367. Seoul: Gyobo Publishing Co.

_____. 1987. *Management of Rural Change in Korea: The Saemaeul Undong.* Seoul: Seoul National University Press.

Willis, Bob. 1989. "Asia's '4 Dragons' Set to Mature in 90s." *The Korea Herald*, 7 December.

Yonhap News Agency. 1989. *Korea Annual 1989.* Seoul: Yonhap News Agency.

Yoo, Jong Hae. 1987. "Interventions and Innovations for Administrative Reforms in Korea: The Saemaeul Undong." *Journal of East and West Studies* 16 (fall/winter): 57-77.

Yu, Chun Kyu. 1988. *Tax Aspects of Foreign Companies Doing Business in Korea.* Seoul: Sekyung Publishing, Inc.

The Politics of Structural Adjustment in South Korea:

Analytical Issues and Comparative Implications

Moon Chung-in

South Korea has experienced two waves of economic success. The first was the timely and effective transition from an import-substitution industrialization to an export-led development strategy in the mid-1960s and the subsequent economic growth. The second was the superb adjustment efforts in coping with an acute economic crisis in the early 1980s. The former has drawn world-wide attention, being touted as a model of Third World development or as an ideal "pathway from the periphery" (Haggard 1990). Despite powerful endorsement by the International Monetary Fund (IMF) and World Bank, however, the latter has not yet been subjected to active scholarly debates (Kincaid 1983; Aghedli and Ruerte 1985).

The article will explore this neglected dimension of South Korea's macroeconomic stabilization and structural adjustment efforts in the first half of the 1980s. The primary concern of this article lies in elucidating the political dynamics of economic adjustment by focusing on its political constraints and consequences. It also aims at generating some comparative implications for developing countries in Asia and the Pacific.

The first section of the article attempts to clarify some analytical

* Originally published in Vol. 31, No. 3 (Autumn 1991).

Moon Chung-in (Mun, Jeong-in) is Dean of the Graduate School of International Studies and Professor of Political Science at Yonsei University. He received his Ph.D. in Political Science from University of Maryland. His publications include *Economic Crisis and Structural Reforms in South Korea: Assessments and Implications* (2000). E-mail: cimoon@yonsei.ac.kr.

issues related to the politics of structural adjustment. The second section traces the origin of the economic crisis in the late 1970s and the early 1980s by delineating the dynamic interplay of external shocks and internal mismanagement. The third presents the empirical dimensions of macroeconomic stabilization and structural adjustment between 1981 and 1985. The final section discusses the political dynamics of the adjustment efforts, and draws some comparative implications of the South Korean experience for other developing countries in the process of implementing structural adjustment.

The Politics of Structural Adjustment: Some Analytical Issues

The concept of structural adjustment is diverse, and its operational definition varies depending on scholarly tradition and institutional affiliation. As early as 1974, in the wake of the first oil shock, the IMF defined structural adjustment as an economic policy measure to overcome "serious payment imbalances relating to structural maladjustments in production and trade where prices and cost distortions have been widespread" (IMF 1975, 88-90). Developing countries' access to the Extend Fund Facility has been tied to the satisfaction of these measures involving traditional policy instruments such as the exchange rate and monetary and fiscal restraint. Following the Third World debt crisis in the late 1970s and early 1980s, however, structural adjustment measures were broadened to include policies on prices, taxes and subsidies, interest rates, and even on wages. In view of this, structural adjustment is an attempt to reverse slow economic growth and to correct an inherently weak balance of payments position which prevents pursuit of an active development policy.

More recently, however, the concept of structural adjustment has been understood in a more comprehensive manner. It is not limited to short-term macroeconomic management and adjustment to cope with external shocks, but is extended to a wide range of policy measures to induce long-term changes in economic structure as well as medium-term changes in incentive structure. Industrial restructuring, financial reform, foreign economic reform, and the overall economic management reform all constitute the important components of structural adjustment measures.

The experience of structural adjustment has differed from country to country depending on the specific context. For advanced industrialized countries, structural adjustment usually implies positive adjustment in which changing comparative advantage dictates the direction of economic structure and market outcomes. For example, the sunset industries facing external market competition are phased out or converted to more competitive sectors through market mechanisms, rather than protected and subsidized (Zysman and Tyson 1984; Porter 1990). Adjustments in the newly industrializing countries (NICs) such as South Korea involve three-tier policy measures: short-term macroeconomic management to cope with external shocks, medium as well as long-term structural rearrangements to the enhance international competitiveness through the readjustment of incentive system, and the overall structural changes of the national economy. In the case of the NICs, as opposed to market-induced structural change of advanced industrialized countries, the state plays a crucial role in initiating and implementing structural adjustment (Moon 1990b; Haggard 1990). Finally, countries in a severe debt crisis such as those of Latin America have been forced to implement primarily short-term macroeconomic management as dictated by the conditionalities of multilateral lending institutions (Foxley 1983).

Despite the diverse experiences of structural adjustment, most developing countries including those in Asia and the Pacific have engaged or have been forced to engage in a broadly defined structural adjustment, which can be characterized as neoconservative reform. Neoconservative reform refers to a form of "structuralism using orthodox instruments" (Foxley 1983, 17). It aims at both short-term adjustment and a radical transformation of the national economy through assertive changes in incentives and economic structure.

Pursuing short-term adjustment and transforming the national economy through neoconservative prescriptions, however, entail formidable political constraints since they inflict substantial social costs and elicit intense political opposition from the affected sectors of society. This is precisely because the reform is usually predicated on a realignment of incentives and benefits among contending social forces. Cutting subsidies, tightly controlling money supply, disciplining labor, readjusting credit allocation, opening up once protected domestic markets and so forth produce a precarious political equation of winners and losers, politicizing the entire process of economic reform.

As Latin American experiences explicitly demonstrate, it is for this reason that pluralist democratic regimes are usually unable to implement consistent and coherent neoconservative reforms effectively, resulting in a stop-and-go implementation. In a similar vein, it has been widely hypothesized that, though dependent on the types of regime and underlying social coalitional bases, strong states based on military authoritarian government are most likely to succeed in implementing reforms (Haggard and Kaufman 1989).

The paradox of the neoconservative reform is that its success does not necessarily guarantee increased political support for the regime. Macroeconomic stabilization aims at eliminating "public bads" (e.g., inflation and balance of payments), but its beneficiaries tend to be free riders refusing to translate their gains into political support for reformers. On the other hand, viewed from the political calculus of regime survival, structural adjustment is also a losing proposition not only because of lagtime effects associated with it, but also because of unwarranted political opposition resulting from the imposition of social costs. These political backlash effects usually deter political leaders from pursuing the reform actively.

For the reasons cited above, structural adjustment cannot be meaningfully understood without making reference to its underlying political dynamics. In most cases, political, not economic, rationality dictates the nature and direction of neoconservative reforms and structural adjustment. Against the backdrop of this observation, I will examine the Korean experience of economic crisis, neoconservative reforms, and the resulting political dynamics in the first half of the 1980s, and will draw some comparative implications for other developing countries in a situation similar to that of South Korea.

External Shocks, Internal Mismanagement and Economic Crisis

After a relatively long period of sustained economic growth, the Korean economy began to falter in 1979. Growth rates averaging 9.9% during 1962-1978 fell to 2.2% in 1979-1981, and inflation soared to 26.4% from an annual average rate of 16.1% in 1962-1978. Real growth in exports fell from an annual average rate of 27.4% during 1962-1978 to 7.5% during 1979-1982. The current account deficit grew from $1.1 billion in 1978 to $4.4 billion in 1981 (World Bank 1980; Economic Planning

Board 1986).

Exogenous shocks contributed to the downturn. The second oil shock was severe, accelerating inflation and balance of payments deficit. Payments for oil imports increased from $2.17 billion in 1978 to $6.34 billion in 1981, accounting for 10.3% of GNP. Equally devastating was the sharp rise in interest rates following the second oil shock. In contrast to the other East Asian NICs, Korea borrowed heavily during the 1970s in order to finance heavy industrialization. LIBOR (London Interbank Offering Rate) rose from 8.7% in 1978 to 16.8% in 1981, increasing Korea's annual interest burden from $1.03 billion in 1978 to $3.65 billion in 1981. Korea also suffered a major crop failure in 1980. Average annual rice production during 1976-1979 was 5.6 million tons. This dropped to 3.5 million tons in 1980, aggravating inflationary pressures (EPB 1982, 5-7).

While exogenous shocks contributed to Korea's difficulties, there is a broad consensus that economic mismanagement over the 1970s was also to blame. From the mid-1970s, Korea pursued a strategy of rapid development of heavy and chemical industries (EPB 1973; Haggard and Moon 1983). Disregarding the inflationary consequences, from 1977 to 1979 Korea allocated 80% of total investment in manufacturing to heavy industry through the state-owned banking sector via so-called "policy loans" (World Bank 1980, 12). Excessive credit expansion created inflationary pressure. It also aggravated labor shortages, especially in high-skill categories. Wage increases outstripped gains in productivity. During 1975-1980, real wages rose by 13.4%, while productivity increased by only 11.2%. The sharp surge in wage rates in the latter part of the 1970s was later blamed for inflation and a weakening of Korea's international competitiveness (EPB 1982, 7).

Moreover, the priority given to the development of the heavy and chemical industry sectors naturally favored *jaebeol* (business conglomerates), which enjoyed heavily subsidized credit, monopoly or oligopoly market positions, extensive protection and, in some sectors, guaranteed sales through government procurement. By the end of the seventies, a handful of the largest *jaebeol* dominated the economy. Total value-added production of the top fifty conglomerates accounted for 43% of GDP in 1978 (Bank of Korea 1984; *Hankook Ilbo* 1981). Industrial concentration elicited intense political debate on the issue of the trade-off between growth and equity. It was even more heated because small- and medium-sized enterprises were victimized as a result of industrial concentration.

Managing the Crisis:
Macroeconomic Stabilization and Structural Adjustment

The appearance of economic difficulties precipitated intense debate within and outside the government on its causes and possible remedies (Michell 1981; KDI 1982a; Haggard and Moon 1986). A number of technocrats articulated the view that the crisis emanated from structural problems stemming from the program of industrial expansion launched by Park Chung-hee. Such a view, however, was tantamount to admitting the economic shortcomings of the Park regime. Initially, the crisis was explained in cyclical terms, with prescriptions focusing on demand management. But as the crisis deepened in late 1978, those proposing a structural analysis gained ground within the government. The 17 April 1979 Stabilization Measure reflected their ascent, admitting to not only problems in macroeconomic policy but in overall industrial strategy and the style of economic policymaking as well. The measure identified three key policy objectives: price stability, structural change, and the establishment of a competitive economic system through a series of liberalizing reform (KDI 1982a).

Before the measure was fully implemented, Korea went through a traumatic political change: the assassination of President Park and the birth of the Fifth Republic. The regime change did not obstruct the reforms but rather facilitated them. Seeking to distance itself from Park's policies, the Chun Doo-hwan regime tuned to the neoconservative monetarists, who had been a minority under the previous regime, and elevated them to positions of importance in the new government (Haggard and Moon 1986, 1990).

Stabilization: Imposing Short-term Costs

The first task under the new regime was price stabilization. In restoring macroeconomic stability, the conventional policy tools of fiscal restraint and monetary control were used, coupled with a freeze on wages.

1) Fiscal Restraint

Fiscal discipline, a central component of the stabilization effort, was stringent. The rate of increase in government expenditure dropped from 21.9% in 1981 to zero in 1984. These figures are quite impressive, when compared with average annual growth rates of government spending of 28.9% during 1962-1969 and 28.1% from 1970-1979 (EPB 1986).

The ability of the government to trim the budget rested on its insulation from political pressures. Korea's fiscal structure is quite rigid, with about 70% of the entire budget "untouchable." A bilateral defense burden-sharing agreement with the U.S. stipulates that Korea allocates at least 6% of its GNP for defense. This normally accounts for over 30% of the budget. Debt service, grants to local governments, educational financing and wages for public servants account for another 40%, leaving 30% of the budget manipulable. Given these rigidities, budget cutting involved severe reductions in expenditures for social and economic development as well as general administration. The most noticeable squeeze came from the general administrative sector in terms of a wage freeze (3% increase in 1982, freeze in 1983, 3% in 1984, and 7% in 1985) and early retirement of public employees (55 age cap). In addition, a massive organizational reform of the government sector was implemented under which redundant and overlapping government agencies were either eliminated or merged (EPB 1983a, 1973b; Jo 1983).

More substantial fiscal cuts were realized in special account items, primarily government subsidies. As other studies have noted, cutting subsidies has generally been a major stumbling block to successful stabilization efforts (Diaz-Alejandro 1981; Dell 1982; Nelson 1984). In Korea, however, a number of subsidies ware targeted. The Grain Management Fund, by which farmers received average annual grain price increases of 20.25% during the 1970s, was cut to 14% in 1981, and was frozen in 1982. In 1983, there was only a 3% increase (EPB 1983b, 48-49; Yoo 1983; Kim 1974). A similar cut was also made in the Fertilizer Account, which subsidized fertilizer prices (Lee Sun 1983). The private sector was not immune to the effects of fiscal discipline. Over 30 public funds established to finance government-sponsored projects were either eliminated or transferred to state-owned financial institutions. The National Investment Fund, which was instrumental in financing the heavy chemical industrial sector, was gradually reduced and transferred to banking institutions, while the Machinery Industry Promotion Fund and the Electronic Industry Promotion Fund were eliminated. Public enterprises, another source of fiscal deficits, were also subject to tighter government scrutiny (EPB 1982).

2) Wage Control

From 1976 through 1979 Korean workers enjoyed rapidly rising real wages. During the stabilization period of 1981-1984, this trend was reversed. Real wages actually fell in 1980 and failed to match labor productivity gains in 1982-84. In 1981, labor productivity increased by 18.1%, while real wages dropped by 1% (*Hankook Ilbo* 1985).

In curbing wage growth, the Korean government relied on various controls as well as directly repressive state intervention aimed at limiting labor's political power. The government first announced an annual wage policy in 1981. Plans for implementing a minimum wage system were to be delayed. However, government action was not limited to checking wage increases. A broader set of actions were aimed at the structure of the labor movement itself and the capacity of the government to intervene to manage labor disputes. Through amendments to the Trade Union Law, the government altered existing union structure, decentralizing the union movement to the company level. A new Labor Dispute Law increased the government's power in the mediation of disputes, subjected collective action to prior government approval, and most interestingly, prohibited the involvement of outside groups—grass-roots church organizations and students, in particular—in labor disputes (Launius 1984; *Monthly Review of Korean Affairs* 1984; Haggard and Moon 1986).

3) Monetary Control

Fiscal restraint was accompanied by tight monetary and credit controls. Korea proved successful in managing money supply growth. During the boom period (1977-1978), money supply (M2) grew at more than 35% a year. But for the first two years of stabilization, those figures were cut to 25% and 27%. During 1983 and 1984, money supply growth dropped to 15.2% and 7.7%, rising again in 1985 to 16.3% (EPB 1986).

The government succeeded in tightening the money supply through credit control, particularly to the public sector during 1980-1981, the rate of increase in credit to the public sector was over 100%, but it was reduced to negative growth in 1983 (-6.7%) and 1984 (-2.0%). This was possible because of a reduction in government borrowing from the Bank of Korea needed to finance fiscal deficits. Credit to the private sector was also controlled, though not as sharply. The annual growth rate of 39.6% in 1980 was cut back to 30% in 1984. Overall, the annual average growth rate of domestic credit was reduced from 41.9% in 1980 before active pursuit of stabilization measures, to 13% in 1984 (Lee Soon-jae 1986, 30-31).

Structural Adjustment Measures

The long-term program of the reformers was not limited to stabilization alone. More fundamental was the effort to realign the state's role in the economy by pursuing both extensive structural reform of the national economy and a more market-oriented style of economic management. Structural adjustment entailed three sets of reforms: industrial restructuring, financial reforms, and liberalization of the domestic market. Each involved a restructuring of the government's political relationship with key social groups.

1) Industrial Restructuring

An important cause of the crisis of 1979-1980 was the industrial policy associated with the heavy industry drive. The availability of concessional policy loans led to excessive and duplicate investment, surplus capacity, and business concentration (Haggard and Moon 1983; KDI 1982). Two principles guided government efforts to restructure the heavy industry sector: "rationalization" and a reduction of industrial concentration (EPB 1983).

The first task was to reorganize six problem sectors, prominently including automobiles and power-generating equipment, in which problems of surplus capacity had emerged as the result of duplicated investment and poor planning. Lines of business were consolidated by mergers, particular products were assigned to specific firms and foreign participation was invited (Haggard and Moon 1983, 182-183). Support was extended to a new range of "strategic" high-technology industries such as semiconductors, computers, telecommunication, aerospace that seemed more suited to Korea's comparative advantage. This industrial restructuring was, however, to be accompanied by a change in style of economic management away from discretionary, sector-specific intervention. While assistance was to be given to the private sector, more emphasis was placed on indirect, non-discretionary supports such as incentives for research and development and manpower training (*Dong-a Ilbo* 1985; *Chosun Ilbo* 1986).

At the same time, the government undertook to reduce the level of concentration in the manufacturing sector by giving greater attention to small- and medium-sized firms. Emphasis on heavy industry had led to a relative neglect of the small- and medium-sized firms that remained central to Korea's exports of light manufactures. These firms had faced the most intense protectionist pressures, but they had also exhibited great flexibility in adjusting and upgrading in the face of market pressures even as credit was channeled to larger companies. Besides, Korean exports of more advanced industrial products—automobiles, ships, heavy machinery, etc.—relied heavily on parts and components supplied by Japan. This reliance decreased value-added and contributed to trade deficits. Furthermore, heavy dependence on Japan, a competitor in many of the same sectors, made Korean manufacturers vulnerable. Far greater opportunities thus appeared to exist for import-substitution in the parts and components industry, sectors in which small size and flexibility constitute an advantage.

Lending priorities were thus readjusted to foster small and medium-sized firms. A Long-Term Plan for the Promotion of Small and Medium-Sized Industries was established, and tax laws were amended to boost the sector by reducing the preferences granted to the *jaebeol*. They were also given special access to bank funds. Commercial banks are required to set aside 35% to 55% of their newly-available bendable funds for small and medium business. The Ministry of Commerce and Trade launched a plan to integrate the small parts and components manufacturers and large firms into closely-knit production complexes in order to enhance linkages and flexibility (*Business Korea* 1984, 28).

To erase the image of the state's discretionary protection of big business, more direct actions were also taken to reduce industrial concentration. In April 1981, the government enacted the Monopoly Regulation and Fair Trade Law. The law covers a wide range of issues including supervision of the leading producers in each sector, regulation of business concentration, and protection of subcontractors. Special emphasis was placed on preventing conglomerate concentration through cross-investment, reciprocal buying and cross-subsidization among *jaebeol* subsidiaries (Lee Jai-ook 1984; Bennett 1985).

2) Financial Reform

Reforming the financial sector involved liberalization, rationalization and internationalization (Cho and Cole 1986; KDI 1982a and 1982b). Liberalization aimed at greater bank autonomy in determination of credit allocation, in part through the privatization of state-owned commercial banks. Policy loans and administrative guidance over bank portfolios have been reduced, though the government still exercises influence over banks through its ability to appoint key personnel. Privatization also had its limits. While the government relinquished its holdings in the five commercial banks in the county, important overseeing and regulatory powers were retained. The new Bank Law limited the largest groups' holdings in the new banks, and their lending practices were carefully monitored and regulated to avoid their capture by the *jaebeol.*

Rationalization involved restructuring the financial sector to allow greater competition. First, the government lifted restrictions limiting competition among different types of financial institutions, resulting in a dramatic upsurge in the non-bank private financial sector (i.e., secondary financial institutions). This sector, which includes investment and insurance companies and direct credit markets for corporate bond and commercial paper, grew rapidly over the early 1980s and is not subjected to the restrictions governing commercial banks. As a result, the large groups have moved aggressively into this area, which was designed to stamp out illicit financial dealings and to absorb curb market funds into legitimate financial institutions.

Another significant measure, though still delayed, was the effort to enforce a "real name" system, which prohibits by law any financial transactions under false names. This measure sought to restore public confidence in the integrity of the financial system in the wake of a series of curb market related financial scandals. Not only would this reform eliminate the dual structure of financial institutions, but it would also increase tax revenues through the effective detection of financial dealings under false names and illicit accumulation of wealth through curb market speculation.

The Korean market was also made more open to the operation of foreign banks, in part due to an increase in American pressure for national treatment. In 1983, a new commercial bank was launched as a joint venture between seventeen Korean banks and the Bank of America, a small move away from the highly protectionist stance the government had previously taken. Initial steps were made toward granting national treatment for foreign banks, which previously faced a number of restrictions on their operations. These included, among others, limitations on local currency operations, lack of access to the central bank's rediscounting facilities and inability to issue negotiable certificates of deposit. These reforms have moved slowly and are the subject of ongoing negotiations with the United States (USTR 1985). In addition, the government has also pursued plans to liberalize and internationalize the capital market. The major features of the plan include allowing investment in the secondary market, allowing corporations to raise funds directly through issues in foreign markets, the mutual listing of stocks between Korea and overseas markets, and a greater volume of dealings between domestic and foreign securities companies (Lee Sang-Myeon 1985, 1-13).

3) Liberalizing the Domestic Market

Import liberalization and the easing of restrictions on foreign investment have formed an important component of the economic reforms. Entering the 1980s, Korea faced a different domestic and international environment, which created strong pressure to liberalize. Internally, protection contributed to monopoly and oligopoly pricing practices in the domestic market, which cut against the goal of price stability. Protection was also seen to erode international competitiveness. Equally important was the growth of protectionist sentiment among the advanced industrial states, and particularly the United States, where trade policy became more aggressive over the seventies (Lee, McLaurin, and Moon 1988, ch. 3). Against this backdrop, the Korean government was forced to liberalize a wide range of farm products and consumer goods manufactured by small and medium-sized firms. In addition, the service sector, including insurance, was subjected to a gradual liberalization. In 1983, a five-year tariff package was passed with the aim of increasing the import liberalization ratio to 88% by 1985 and 95% by 1988 (KDI 1982a, 897-911; *Hanil Monthly* 1984, 5-13).

Korea has also sought to liberalize its policies on foreign direct investment, which have been the most restrictive of the four East Asian NICs (Haggard and Cheng 1987). This has involved two policy thrusts: on the one hand, a commitment to easing entry; on the other, a dismantling of a number of special incentives extended to foreign firms. In 1984, the move was made from a positive list system, under which foreign investment was allowed only in designated industries, to a negative list system, in which all foreign investment is automatically approved unless otherwise specified. In the past, the government exercised tremendous discretion over the entry of foreign firms, seeking to influence corporate behavior with regard to local participation, management and control, local procurement, exports, technology transfer, and intra-corporate fees for services. Since these policies involved significant administrative discretion, the precise impact of the stated goal of liberalization cannot be judged. Restrictions on the repatriation of principal and the remittance of dividends were lifted. To assist the recovery of the heavy and chemical sectors, measures were taken to ease the licensing of technology mainly by limiting the generous tax exemptions extended to foreign firms. These exemptions have been either abolished or scaled back with the aim of equalizing the incentives facing foreign and local forms (MOF 1985).

The underlying theme of the structural adjustment measures has been the transition to an economy in which the private sector and the price system would play a greater role in determining the allocation of resources. It is often forgotten that such a transition demands basic changes in the economic management style of the government. The concept of "indicative" planning was for the first time introduced in the Fifth Five-Year Development Plan, departing from the previous style of direct orchestration of the private sector through the outline of strategic objectives. As argued above, industrial policy began to show a change from discretionary intervention and industrial targeting to nondiscretionary and market-conforming interventions. At the same time, unilateral administrative guidance has been gradually replaced by consultation and consensus between the state and business.

The Politics of Structural Adjustment

The long-term consequences of the structural adjustment measures remain to be seen, but the short-term results of the stabilization were remarkably successful. Austerity measures curbed inflation from 28.7% in 1980 to 2.3% in 1984, while sustaining high growth rates (5.6% in 1982, 9.5% in 1983, and 7.5% in 1984). Balance of payments deficits were also greatly improved from $4.4 billion in 1981 to $1.37 billion in 1984. Exports steadily increased from $20.67 billion in 1981 to $26.35 in 1984, assisted by the continuing strength of the dollar relative to the won. Unemployment eased somewhat from 4.4% in 1981 to 3.9% in 1984.

Success, however, was obtained through considerable social costs, which were rather unevenly spread across different social sectors (Table 1). Fiscal restraint severely victimized farmers by cutting the grain management fund and eliminating the fertilizer account. Import liberalization for farm products, which was hastily implemented under mounting pressures from the U.S., further crippled the farm sector. The reforms also victimized labor. While nominal wages began to grow again by 1982, real wages lagged behind labor productivity, and the labor movement was forced to undergo a restructuring that significantly weakened its political clout.

Even big business was chosen as the prime target. Tight credit control paralyzed the cash flows of big business, while the enactment of the Monopoly Regulation and Fair Trade Law undercut and limited its interest. Forced mergers and the consolidation of the heavy and chemical industries under the name of industrial rationalization made big business atrophic. Nevertheless, it eventually become the primary beneficiary of the reform. Although tight credit control and elimination of policy loans dealt a blow to big business, the banking and financial liberalization created a new niche in which it could gain greater access to credit. The rise and expansion of secondary financial institutions, which were virtually dominated by big business, exemplifies this trend. Furthermore, internationalization of banking and financial markets provided *jaebeol* with additional sources of corporate financing. Because discretionary credit control was the key instrument for controlling the private sector, the decreased dependence of big business on the state in the wake of liberalization has made it less constrained by the state, paving the way for further conglomeration.

However, the reform did not victimize and alienate all sectors of society. The "silent" majority of the middle class (i.e., owners of small- and medium-sized firms, and professional, managerial, and technical workers), which rapidly expanded through the 1960s and 1970s, was an exception. While macroeconomic stabilization was targeted for winning popular support from the broadly defined middle class, structural adjustment was designed in such a way to coopt small- and medium-sized firms. The middle class enjoyed the fruits of stabilization, but small- and medium-sized firms ended up being victims rather than beneficiaries of structural adjustment. Banking liberalization further limited their access to bank credit because banks under the new system were reluctant to give loans to small and medium firms that lacked collateral. The import

Table 1. Structural Adjustment, Policy Cleavages, and Coalitions

Policy	Contents	Favored	Threatened Interests	Outcomes Interests
Macro-economic balance	• fiscal discipline	international lending institutions/ technocrats	farmers/labor/ low-level civil servants	restraint prevailed
	• monetary control	international lending institutions/ MOF/EPB	all sectors of the economy/big business/ruling party	stop and go control, but tight money control
	• wage restraint	business/foreign investors	labor	tight wage control/ 22.7% in '80 to 8.1% in '85
Structural adjustment	• industrial restructuring 1) rationalization	banking industry/ new targeted industries	big business/ industry	in progress
	2) diversification/ deconcentration	select small- and medium-sized firms	big business	monopoly regulation and fair trade law/in progress, but limited adjustment
	• financial reform 1) liberalization/ bank autonomy	banking industry/	big business/ curb market	privatized five commercial banks/ gradual elimination of policy loans
	2) rationalization	big business/ banking financial industry/ technocrats	curb market/ ruling party	rise of secondary financial institutions/ real name deposit system delayed
	3) internationali-zation	big business/ foreign interests	local banking industry/loose coalition of nationalist opposition	preferential treatment of foreign banks/ gradual opening of security market
	• foreign economic reform 1) import liberali-zation	importers/foreign interests	farmers/small- and medium-sized firms/ technocrats(MCI/ MOA/MOH)/ loose coalition of popular sector	liberalization from 68.6% in '80 to 87.7% in '85
	2) liberalizing FDI	local partners/ foreign interests	potential com-petitors/loose coalition of political oppo-sition equality	opening of 480 industrial sectors to FDI with 100% equality

liberalization plan originally designed to protect the interests of small and medium firms produced the reverse result, fostering the importation of goods manufactured by them.

Uneven spread of social costs and unintended consequences of stabilization and structural adjustment highly politicized the process of neo-conservative reform. Nevertheless, the reform was successfully initiated and implemented. How was this possible? The key was a strong state coupled with an authoritarian regime. While the quasi-revolutionary military leadership at the beginning of the reform smoothly facilitated its initiation, the ascent of a new technocratic group and the insulation of economic decision-making from popular pressure through authoritarian controls made its implementation effective. In other words, the successful initiation and implementation of the reform was a product of the unique historical and structural configuration of the political system under the Fifth Republic.

What then were the political consequences of the reform? Has the success of macroeconomic stabilization and structural adjustment brought about political dividends for the reformers? Ironically, the success fostered the collapse of the Chun regime, and opened new venues for democratic transition. The reform succeeded in removing "public bads" (i.e., inflation) and in reestablishing growth which allowed all to benefit. Yet the beneficiaries proved to be free riders. Given the Chun regime's unpopularity stemming from illicit seizure of political power and the Gwangju Incident, political support should have been consolidated through sectoral microrewards.

Stabilization and structural adjustment measures did not produce such rewards but rather undercut them through the reduction of rents to favored groups—preferential credits, protection and so forth. These sectoral rewards were the means through which political coalitions were formed and sustained; removing them posed a problem parallel to the free rider problem in the theory of collective action (Olson 1965, 1982; Bates 1981). While all benefit from the provision of the public goods, there is a tendency for them to be undersupplied. As a result, the pursuit of public goods by spreading the costs of adjustment widely depreciates the political value of the reform. The mismatch of macroperformance and microrewards in the process of the reform fundamentally undermined the foundation of the Chun regime's political support and legitimacy.

Another important political consequence of the reform is the substantial realignment of coalitional dynamics. The reform fostered the dissolution of the Park regime's developmentalist coalition composed of the state, big business, and farmers by both alienating farmers and disciplining big business. By the very nature of the reform, however, the Chun regime failed to develop a new coalition that could replace the old one. The middle class, which the Chun regime considered the backbone of its social coalitional base, turned out to be a free rider. As a result, the Chun regime ended up a naked power without a corresponding social support base, which in turn facilitated its collapse.

Conclusion: Comparative Implications

The Korean experience reveals several interesting comparative implications for other developing countries.

First, structural adjustment is not a narrow concept confined only to industrial restructuring or macroeconomic management. It involves the complex processes of economic adjustment compromising macroeconomic, sector-specific industrial, financial and banking, and trade policies as well as overall economic management style.

Second, structural adjustment cannot be separated from political processes. Since it inflicts uneven social costs on various segments of society, its initiation and implementation are, more often than not, politicized. The Korean experience illustrates that even under tight authoritarian control, structural adjustment efforts invite fierce political opposition and contestation. Likewise, structural adjustment measures, which disregard political consequences, are bound to fail or at least to be disruptive.

Third, the success of structural adjustment often depends on regime type and state structure. Executive dominance, bureaucratic unity and effectiveness, and relative insulation of the economic policy making and implementation accounted for the Korean success. In this sense, state autonomy and strength, if not the authoritarian mode of governance, are a necessary condition for successful structural adjustment. Weak states are very unlikely to initiate and implement coherent, consistent, and effective structural adjustment measures (Moon 1990a).

Fourth, the Korean experience suggests the paradox of the "Faustian bargain," in which short-term political gains are likely to undermine long-term economic ones. The Chun regime actively pursued the neoconservative economic reform in order to enhance its political support. However, the reform and subsequent economic success did not bring about political dividends. On the contrary, they eroded the political support base of the Chun regime. Judging from the Korean experience, structural adjustment must be less attractive for political leaders in countries where ruling regimes are tainted by weak legitimacy and low political support simply because it is politically too risky.

Finally, even strong states do not automatically guarantee the intended outcomes of structural adjustment (Moon 1990a). Furthermore, good policy choices do not necessarily promise good economic performance. Sheer luck, often associated with the boom and bust cycles of international and domestic markets, may be more accountable for economic performance.

All in all, the above discussion implies that the Korean experience cannot be easily transferred or replicated elsewhere in Asia and the Pacific. Indeed, structural adjustment, at least viewed from its underlying political dynamics, is context bound, and it is very difficult to generalize about the determinants of successful adjustments.

REFERENCE

Aghedli, Vijan, and Marquex Ruerte. 1985. *A Case of Successful Adjustment: The Korean Experience during 1980-1984.* Washington, D.C.: International Monetary Fund.

Bates, Robert. 1988. *The Political Economy of Development: The Rational Choice Perspective.* Berkeley: University of California Press.

Burmeister, Larry. 1986. "Warfare, Welfare and State Autonomy: Structural Roots of the South Korean Developmental State." *Pacific Focus: Inha Journal of International Studies* 1: 121-146.

Business Korea. 1984 December.

Cho, Yoon Je, and David Cole. 1986. "The Role of the Financial Sector in Korea's Structural Adjustment." Cambridge: Harvard Institute for International Development.

Dell, Sidney. 1982. "Stabilization: The Political Economy of Overkill." *World Development* 10.

Diaz-Alejnndro, C. F. 1981. "Southern Cone Stabilization Plans." In *Economic Stabilization in Developing Countries,* edited by W. R. Cline and S. Weintraub. Washington, D.C.: Brookings.

Dong-a Ilbo. 1985 September.

Economic Planning Board (EPB). 1986. *Economic Indicator.* Seoul: EPB (in Korean).

_____. 1983a. "National Budget Freeze and Policy Background: Educational Materials." Seoul: EPB (in Korean).

_____. 1983b. *The Fifth Five Year Social and Economic Development Plan Guidelines for Revision.* Seoul: EPB (in Korean).

_____. 1982. "Present Status of Our Economy and Management Policies," Seoul: EPB (in Korean).

_____. 1973. *Heavy and Chemical Plan.* Seoul: EPB.

ESCAP. 1991. *Industrial Reconstructing in Asia and the Pacific.* Bangkok: ESCAP Secretariat.

Foxley, Alejandro. 1983. "Latin American Experiments" in *Neo-conservative Economics.* Berkeley: University of California Press.

Haggard, Stephan. 1990. *Pathway from the Periphery.* Ithaca: Cornell University Press.

_____. 1985. "The Politics of Adjustment." *International Organization* 39: 505-534.

Haggard, Stephan, and Chung-in Moon. 1990 "Institutions and Economic Policy: Theory and a Korean Case Study." *World Politics* XLII No.2: 210-237.

_____. 1986. "Industrial Change and State Power: The Politics of Stabilization and Structural Adjustment in Korea."

_____. 1983. "The South Korean State in the International Economy: Liberal, Dependent, or Mercantile?" In *Antinomies of Interdependence: National Welfare and the International Division of Labor,* edited by John Gerard Ruggie. New York: Columbia University Press.

Haggard, Stephan, and Tun-jen Cheng. 1987. "State Strategies and Local Capital in the Gang of Four." In *The Political Economy of the New Asian Industrialism,* edited by F. Deyo. Ithaca: Cornell University Press.

Haggard, Stephan, and Robert Kaufman. 1787. "The Politics of Stabilization and Structural Adjustment." In *Developing Country Debt and Economic Performance,* edited by Jeffrey Sachs. Chicago: Chicago University Press.

Hanil Monthly. 1984.

Hankook Ilbo. 1985. 25 April.

_____. 1981. 19 September.

International Monetary Fund (IMF). 1977. *Annual Report.*

Kaufman, Robert. 1985. "Democratic and Authoritarian Responses to the Debt Issue: Argentina, Brazil and Mexico." *International Organization* 39: 473-504.

Kim, Mann-Kyu, Kwang-il Baek, and Chung-in Moon. 1987. *South Korea's Trade Lobbying Strategy in the U.S.* Incheon: Inha University Press.

Kincaid, G. R. 1983. "Korea's Major Adjustment Effort." *Finance and Development* (December): 20-23.

Koo, Hagen. 1986. "Social Class Formation and Social Conflict in South Korean Industrialization." Paper presented at the annual meeting of the American Sociological Association, New York.

Korean Development Institute (KDI). 1982a. *Collection of Materials on Economic Stabilization Policies.* Seoul. KDI (in Korean).

_____. 1982b. *Fundamental Tasks of Industrial Policies and Directions for Reform.* Seoul: KDI (in Korean).

Launius, Michael. 1984. "The State and Labor in South Korea." *Bulletin of Concerned Asian Scholars* 16.

Lee, Jai-ook. 1984. "The Fair Trade Law: What Went Wrong?" *Shin Dong-A*, (November): 430-442.

Lee, Manwoo, Ronald McLaurin, and Chung-in Moon. 1988. *Alliance under Tension.* Boulder: Weshiew Press.

Lee, Sang-Myeon. 1985. "The Internationalization of Korea's Financial Markets." *Monthly Bulletin of Exchange Bank* 14.

Lee, Soon-Jae. 1986. "Recent Changes in the Financial Sector in Korea." *Monthly Review of the Foreign Exchange Bank* 14.

Lee, Sun. 1783. "Analysis of the Fertilizer Account Operation" (in Korean). In *Gukga yesan-gwa jeongchaek mokpyo* (National Budget and Policy Objectives), edited by Choe Gwang. Seoul: Korean Development Institute.

Michell, Tony 1981. "What Happens to Economic Growth When Neo-Classical Policy Replaces Keynsian?: The Case of South Korea." *IDS Bulletin* 13: 60-67

Ministry of Finance (MOF). 1985. *Foreign Investment Guide to Korea.* Seoul: MOF.

Monthly Review of Korean Affairs. 1984 June.

Moon, Chung-in. 1990a. "Beyond Statism: Rethinking the Political Economy of Growth in South Korea." *International Studies Notes* 15.1: 24-28.

_____. 1990b. "The Future of the Newly Industrializing Countries: An 'Uncertain Promise'?" In *Transformation in the Global Political Economy,* edited by Dennis Pirates and Christine Sylvester. New York: St. Martin's Press.

Nelson, Joan. 1984. "Politics of Stabilization." In *Adjustment Crisis in the Third World,* edited by E. Feinberg and Valarina Kallab. Washington, D.C.: Overseas Development Council.

O'Donnell, Guillermo. 1973. *Modernization and Bureaucratic Authoritarianism: Studies in South American Politics.* Berkeley: Institute of International Studies. University of California, Berkeley.

Olson, Mancur Jr. 1982. *The Rise and Decline of Nations: Economic Growth, Stagflation, and Social Rigidities.* New Haven: Yale University Press.

_____. 1965. *Theory of Collective Action.* Cambridge: Harvard University Press.

Porter, Michael. 1990. *The Competitive Advantage of Nations.* New York: Free Press.

Seo, Gwan-mo. 1984. *Hyeondae hanguk sahoe-ui gyegeup guseong-gwa gyegeup bunhwa* (Class Formation and Class Differentiation in Contemporary Korean Society). Seoul: Hanul Publishing Co.

Skidmore, T. E. 1977. "The Politics of Economic Stabilization in Postwar Latin America." In *Authoritarianism and Corporatism in Latin America,* edited by James M. Malloy. Pittsburg: University of Pittsburg Press.

United State Trade Representative (USTR). 1975. *Annual Report on National Trade Estimates.* Washington, D.C.: USTR.

Wade, Robert, and Cordon White, eds. 1984. "Developmental States in East Asia: Capitalist and Socialist." *IDS Bulletin* 15.

World Bank. 1980. *Korea: Current Development and Policy Issues.* Washington, D.C.: World Bank.

Yu, Byeong-seo. 1983. "Grain Management Account." In *Gukga yesan-gwa jeongchaek mokpyo* (National Budget and Policy Objectives), edited by Choe Gwang. Seoul: Korean Development Institute.

Zysman, John, and Laura Tyson, eds. 1984. *American Industry in International Competition.* Ithaca: Cornell Univ Press.

Who Benefits from Industrial Restructuring?:
Reflections on the South Korean Experience in the 1980s

Song Ho Keun

Introduction

South Korea's (henceforth, Korea) rapid economic growth has attracted the world's attention and generated a substantial literature in development studies that explores the driving forces behind this economic achievement (Amsden 1990; Deyo 1989; Gereffi and Wyman 1990). A recurrent conclusion is that, in spite of political instability, the Korean state shows an outstanding capacity to implement economic policy and to increase national competitiveness in global markets.

However, it is important to point out that the focus on Korean economic development as a "miracle" hides more than it reveals. Instead of contributing to the improvement of social conditions, state-led capitalism in Korea has intensified social conflict, in many ways, in exchange for successful economic expansion. The Korean state maintained the "growth first and distribution later" principle and exercised strict control over economic planning and policy implementation. Industrial restructuring, carried out from the early 1970s up to the present, reflects the state reliance on the "trickle-down effect" and the sacrifice of political freedom.

* Originally published in Vol. 31, No. 3 (Autumn 1991).

Song Ho Keun (Song, Ho-geun) is Professor of Sociology at Seoul National University. He received his Ph.D. in sociology from Harvard University in 1989. He is mainly interested in the sociology of labor, social policy, theory of sociology, etc. He has authored many books including *Jisik sahoehak* (Sociology of Knowledge) (1990), *Yeollin sijang, dachin jeongchi* (Open Market and Closed Politics) (1994), and *Sijang-gwa bokji jeongchi* (Market and Welfare Politics) (1997). E-mail: hknsong@snu.ac.kr.

Two outcomes of this policy are worth examining in detail. First, the level of social inequality is worse than what the state has publicly admitted. Second, state-led capitalism consolidated the political foundation of Korea's authoritarian regime. The relatively long duration of Korea's authoritarian rule is mainly due to the state capacity to manage the contradiction between accumulation and legitimation (O'Connor 1973). Consequently, the "miracle" designation conceals the deteriorating conditions of Korean society—socioeconomic inequality and political repression. In this respect, the "Korean miracle" has been misunderstood, obscuring the long shadows cast by the rising sun.

In terms of the state-capital relationship, however, economic development undermines the rationale for state intervention in ways which reduce bureaucratic efficiency in economic planning and policy implementation and weaken the relative autonomy of the state. Recent phenomena enable us to assume that private capital pushes the Korean state to be a loyal partner in capital accumulation.

This paper will analyze the social consequences of industrial restructuring, focusing on two social and political crises exacerbated by the Korean economic miracle: inequality and political repression. The focus will be on state policies and their social impact in the process of industrial restructuring over the past two decades. This paper seeks to cast a new light on the "Korean model" for the developing countries in Asia that are attempting to replicate the Korean experience in pursuit of rapid and successful export promotion.

From Market Shaping to Market Conformity: Industrial Restructuring Since the 1970s

Definition of Industrial Restructuring

Although industrial restructuring is an integral part of the development process, there are diverging views on its definition. Broadly defined, industrial restructuring refers to structural changes in the national economy led by a centralized economic institution, such as the government, towards a more advanced stage of development (ESCAP 1990, 4).

Since the second oil shock, the World Bank and IMF, however, have suggested a more specific concept to confine the issues within structural adjustment and stabilization. The World Bank and IMF have placed policy emphasis on the following: reforming of the incentive structure, restructuring of public investment priorities, improving budget and debt management, and reorienting of institutional structures (ESCAP 1990, 6). Although the policy packages provided by the World Bank and IMF have emphasized vigorous state intervention, they have an important message that economic management should rely upon market mechanisms (versus administrative control) and the expanded role of the private sector (versus the public sector) (ESCAP 1990, 6).

This study will use both broad and narrow definitions for a proper understanding of the Korean context. More specifically, this study will adopt the dichotomous distinction of industrial policy suggested by Johnson (1982). Examining the Japanese historical legacy of policy implementation since the Meiji Restoration, Johnson describes two basic components of industrial policy, corresponding to the micro and macro aspects of the economy: first, what the Japanese call "industrial rationalization policy," and second, "industrial structure policy" (Johnson 1982, 27). Simply defined, industrial rationalization is a set of "state policies at the micro level, [and] state intrusion into the detailed operations of individual enterprises with measures intended to improve those operations" (Johnson 1982, 27).[1] Industrial structure policy, on the other hand, "concerns the proportions of agriculture, mining, manufacturing, and services in the nation's total production; and within manufacturing it concerns the percentages of light and heavy and of labor-intensive and knowledge-intensive industries" (Johnson 1982, 28). Simply put, "the heart of the policy is the selection of the strategic industries to be developed or converted to other lines of work" (Johnson 1982, 28).

Policy Implementation for Industrial Restructuring

The industrial restructuring since the early 1970s has had two distinctive phases: heavy chemical industrialization (henceforth, HCI) in the 1970s and industrial structural adjustment for economic stabilization (hence-

---

1. According to the official white paper, Chalmers Johnson classifies industrial rationalization policy into four specific clusters: (1) the rationalization of enterprises, (2) the rationalization of the environments of enterprises, (3) the rationalization of whole industries, and (4) the rationalization of the Industrial structure in order to meet international competitive standards (Johnson 1982, 27).

forth, ISA) in the 1980s. These macro-level policies contributed to economic development through export manufacturing and a rapid transition to technology-intensive production in different ways (Choi 1987).

At the macro-level, HCI and ISA shared the goal of promoting export manufacturing and the rapid transition to technology production. Park Chung-hee's Yusin regime (1972-1979) consolidated the foundation of technology-intensive production, following the arrangement of administrative and financial institutions to facilitate the export of manufactured consumer goods, such as textiles, during the 1960s. Above all, the Yusin regime set the expansion of the employment base and the production capacity of industrial sectors, and the enrichment of technology and knowledge-intensive production within manufacturing as its primary goals. Facing the second oil shock and the decline of national competitiveness in world markets, Chun Doo-hwan's regime (1980-1987) had to shift the basis of production to ISA in order to further advance Korea's industrial goals.

However, at the micro-level, there were major differences in policy content and orientation between the two regimes, which are most evident in export control (Bhagwati 1978; Krueger 1978). Simply put, the Yusin regime heavily favored the strategic and heavy industries, and large-scale firms owned by big conglomerates in the allocation of state resources and benefits. In contrast, the Chun regime, which assumed power through the military coup, adopted economic policies for industrial structural adjustment, contrived in the late Yusin regime. The Chun regime reemployed economic bureaucrats of the previous regime and ordered them to carry out the blueprint which they called the "Economic Stabilization Policy" (*gyeongje anjeonghwa sichaek*). The basis of the policy was readjustment and deregulation.

In short, industrial restructuring during the two authoritarian regimes, between 1972 and 1987, in Korea was vigorously carried out in order to successfully achieve export promotion and technology-intensive manufacturing in the two different phases: HCI and ISA. The HCI was based on a market-shaping policy in which the state attempted to reduce the reliance of the national economy on market mechanisms to a degree which would facilitate heavy chemical industrialization. The HCI became firmly established even though it resulted in hyperinflation and the erosion of national competitiveness. On the contrary, the ISA adopted a market-conforming approach with which the state attempted to resume reliance on market mechanisms by readjustment and deregulation. It can be argued that these two measures were effective in strengthening export promotion based on technology-intensive production in Korea. However, industrial restructuring brought about a significant change in state-led capitalism: private capital gained more control of the national economy, forcing the state to be more supportive of its class interests. As a result, the market-conforming methods of state intervention ran counter to equality, and the structural dependence of the state on capital delayed the transition to democracy.

The Limited Autonomy of the State: Stabilization Policy and Monopolization

O'Connor explains that the state in capitalist society is faced with the contradiction between accumulation and legitimation (O'Connor 1973). He argues that, in order to efficiently resolve the contradiction, the state attempts to increase interrelationships with private capital. In this sense, the economic recession of 1980 drove the state to increase its dependence on private capital, which had begun to express its dissatisfaction with excessive state intervention. Concomitantly, the stabilization policy of the ISA project was, by its very nature, to increase the market mechanisms which functioned to strengthen the voice of private capital vis-à-vis the state. The stabilization policy served to consolidate capitalist influence in Korea's political and economic arenas throughout the 1980s.

Stabilization contained a few important policy measures: revision of export control, privatization of the banking system, and liberalization. First, the state reduced export incentives in various ways, attributing the economic bottleneck of the late 1970s to the extreme disequilibrium caused by the state's strategy of nurturing heavy chemical industries. Second, the state promoted privatization of commercial banks through selling the state-held stocks to the capitalists. The state decided that direct control of the banking system was no longer efficient for the rapid shift from a state-led economy to a capital-led economy. Third, the state carried out liberalization rapidly due to international pressure, mainly from the United States. Since liberalization permitted foreign manufacturers to move into the domestic markets, it generated a feeling of crisis among local capitalists.

The state implemented many additional measures to stabilize the distorted economic structure and to strengthen the autonomy of private capital. The stabilization policy concentrated on three objectives: (1) to overcome stagnation, which the Chun regime had inherited from the HCI, (2) to "rationalize" declining industries, and (3) to promote high-tech industries as the main exporters.

There are conflicting views about actions taken by the state and their outcomes. It has been argued that stabilization for industrial restructuring in the 1980s was based on a mixed strategy of state-led capitalism and market-conforming methods, with the state remaining as the main actor in economic development (Kim Hyeong-guk 1991). A radical study contends that the state intended to strengthen the foundation of authoritarianism and paved the way for a "fascist state" through vigorous industrial restructuring. It placed emphasis on the conservative alliance between state and capital which is extremely resistant to challenge from the working class (Kim Gyun 1991).

This paper is more closely aligned with the first assessment, but recognizes its criticisms. First, the stabilization policy of the 1980s served to significantly weaken the rationale for state intervention, even though it was initiated and carried out by the state. It resulted in the penetration of private capital into the arena of economic planning and implementation, which had been exclusively occupied by the state. Second, industrial restructuring was successful, but contributed to the increasing political and economic influence of monopoly capital. In the economic arena, monopolization proceeded at an unprecedented rate, generating a multifaceted disparity and segmentation of production and labor markets. In the political arena, monopoly capital penetrated into the policy-making process of the state through the conservative alliance between state and capital. Simply put, privatization served to promote monopolization in every field. It can be stated that the state intentionally withdrew interventionist measures for development, confining its function to regulation – regulation for improving industrial environment and infrastructure for private capital. However, social problems arose because the regulation did not work for the economic well-being and political freedom of most people in the society.

Market Conformity against Equality: Social Consequences

It has been argued that the both sets of economic policy served the rapid growth of monopoly capital; while the first policy provided enormous opportunities and an institutional basis for private capital, the second permitted private capital to extend its market power. If there is no strong state regulation of capitalist interests in expansion, monopolization inevitably grows at the expense of distribution. In contrast to what classical economists assert as the advantage of market competition, as reflected in the recommendations of the World Bank and IMF, the politics of stabilization frequently leads to inequality, particularly in an authoritarian society where the policy-making process cannot be affected by civil interest groups. In this respect, it can be stated that "the politics of market conformity against equality" is the heart of the Korean experience. Below I will describe how equality is undermined: industrial concentration, income distribution, labor market policy, housing policy, environmental degradation, and social welfare.

Industrial Concentration: Intra-Sector Disparity

Industrial restructuring had two effects on the national economy which are seemingly contradictory. Between sectors, it pulled up the productivity of other economic sectors, such as the agricultural and service sectors, through maximizing the trickle-down effect. Within the manufacturing industry, it enlarged the disparity between traditional and modern industries, on the one hand, and small and large-scale firms, on the other.

When we focus on the overall effects of industrial restructuring on the national economy, it contributed to the reduction of economic disparity among primary, secondary, and tertiary sectors. In other words, Korea has been successful in reducing the inter-sector disparity. To explain the degree of equality between sectors, Seeghaas suggests a "homogeneity score" which is calculated by adding up the differences of ratios between labor force distribution and GDP contribution (Seeghaas 1982). The smaller the score, the higher the degree of homogenization and, thus, "development with equality." Korea lessened the inter-sector disparity from a score of 58 to 30 in its thirty years of export-led growth. Nevertheless, Korea was unable to lower its disparity level to that of Japan or Taiwan.

However, it should be pointed out that the relative success in lowering inter-sector disparity was obtained at the expense of intra-sector disparity, particularly within manufacturing. As a result, Korea began to surpass Japan's level of industrial concentration at the end of the 1970s.

Table 1 displays various indices regarding industrial concentration. A few points are worth mentioning. The number of large firms with over 500 workers peaked in 1978 at 643, with an employment share of 44% of the total number of workers in the manufacturing sector. In spite of the annual fluctuations in the number of firms and employment share, the economic importance of large firms is considerable: they have accounted for over half of total production since 1973. The concentration ratio is remarkable, particularly in machinery and basic metal industries. In these industries, the five largest enterprises share 60% to 70% of total production (CR5 in Table 1). In all industries, 50% to 60% of total production is attributed to the three largest conglomerates (CR3 in Table 1), and over 30% of total production is attributed to the fifty largest firms (sixth row in Table 1). These figures indicate that industrial restructuring has markedly heightened industrial concentration.

In sum, industrial restructuring sought to strengthen technology-intensive manufacturing in two stages. First, by consolidating the industrial foundation of strategic industries assigned mostly to big conglomerates, monopoly capital was fully nurtured with state protection in this period. Second, excessive state intervention was mitigated and reliance on market mechanisms increased. The government's shift to market-conforming methods meant an abatement of monopoly capital regulation, so that monopoly capital prospered without barriers in the 1980s. Although the

Table 1. Industrial Concentration (%)

Category	1963	1973	1978	1983
1. No. of Large Firms*	72	402	643	574
2. Ratio of Workers Employed in Large Firms	22	43.7	43.9	37.3
3. Share of Production by Large Firms	27.8	54.1	56.6	56.4
4. CR5 Machinery Basic Metal	30.9	70.1	69.6	61.2
5. CR3 All Industries		58.5	57.0	62.0
6. Share of Production by Largest Firms		32.9	35.0	36.6

Source: Kim (1989), p. 189.
*Large firms which employ over 500 workers.

two stages for industrial restructuring contain quite different policy components, they both strengthened monopoly capital and, thus, increased industrial concentration in Korea.

Income Distribution

Korea has been praised for "development with equality" such that economic growth has improved income distribution between different social groups. It is widely accepted that, by relying on foreign loans, Korea sustained low-income inequality during its high-speed growth. Korea is thus an exception to the thesis of "development with inequality." Table 2 shows the trend of income inequality for select years between 1965 and 1988. First, the Gini coefficient, which is frequently used as an indicator of inequality, was 0.344 in 1965, and remained below 0.4 throughout the period until 1988. A close look indicates that income inequality consistently increased up to the mid-1980s, but went down slightly in the second half of the 1980s. Second, in contrast to the decrease of inequality, the income ratio between the richest 20% and the poorest 40% slightly deteriorated (the third row in Table 2). Nevertheless, it is not incorrect to state that a Gini coefficient in the range of 0.3 to 0.4 indicates a level of income inequality relatively low by international standards.

However, it should be noted that an assessment based on the Gini coefficient hides more than it reveals when income data are not reliable. Although Korea's income statistics are comparatively abundant and, more often than not, useful, income data only contain regular income after tax, ignoring unearned income which is a practical source of the luxurious life of the upper class. The importance of unearned income particularly increases when rapid economic growth offers enormous opportunities for capital accumulation through speculation in real estate.

Thus, it is not surprising that when property such as landownership and financial assets are factored into the inequality measure, the story changes dramatically. While income inequality is relatively low, as shown in Table 3, landownership and financial assets are unevenly distributed and they boost the Gini coefficient to well above 0.5. When inequality was measured by the distribution of financial assets, for instance, the Gini coefficient was 0.561 in 1988. Moreover, a recent survey of landownership in 1988 reports that over 60% of property in the six largest cities was monopolized by the richest 5% of all households (see Table 3). Consequently, the traditional index of social stratification, such as occupation and schooling, is gradually losing its theoretical and empirical relevance in the Korean context as ownership of housing and land plays an increasingly critical role in the reproduction of the social class system.

In contrast to the positive appraisal by foreign observers, social discontent arising from the uneven distribution of landownership and financial assets has become intense. More often than not, anxiety from the skyrocketing prices of housing, particularly of condominiums and private apartments, can easily explode and turn into an extreme distrust of the government, thus precipitating political instability. In order to ease public discontent with inequality, the government recently provided a series of distributive policies in "The Revision of the Sixth Five-Year Economic Development Plan" (EPB 1988). However, implementation of these progressive ideas was blocked by the National Assembly. The plan also provoked strong resistance by the ruling class and, thus, finally, the state's attempt to improve distribution failed. In sum, insofar as inequality is concerned, industrial restructuring frustrated the long-cherished vision for development with equality.

Table 2. Income Distribution (%)

Category	1965	1970	1975	1980	1985	1988
Highest 20%	41.8	41.6	45.3	45.4	42.7	42.2
Lowest 40%	19.3	19.6	19.9	16.1	18.9	19.7
Ratio*		1.61	1.93	1.89	1.97	1.85
Gini	.344	.332	.391	.389	.345	.336

Source: Economic Planning Board and KDI.
* Highest 27%/ lowest 40%

Table 3. Concentration of Landownership in the Six Largest Cities

Category	All	Seoul	Busan	Daegu	Incheon	Gwangju	Daejeon
Highest 5%	65.2	57.7	72.3	72.6	64.2	55.7	65.1
Highest 10%	76.9	65.9	81.4	82.4	77.8	69.4	76.4

Source: Korea Research Institute for Human Settlement (1989).

Labor-Market Policy

The emergence of private capital as a primary actor in the labor market is another important outcome of industrial restructuring. For years of high-speed growth under the authoritarian regime, the state played a crucial role in determining the structure of labor markets in ways which suppressed the functions of labor-market institutions in order to increase market competition (Song 1989). This means that the state practiced repressive methods to weaken institutional protection, particularly for production workers. As a result, workers, skilled and unskilled, were highly vulnerable to a wage-competition market (Thurow 1975). The situation of industrial workers in Korea is "equitable" in the sense that most industrial workers belong to a labor market without institutional forces, in which the market-pricing mechanism is predominant.

From a comparative point of view, there are four kinds of institutional forces in labor markets: minimum wage laws, labor unions, public welfare policies, and the firm's internal labor market (Fields 1982; Fields and Wan, Jr. 1986). It should be noted that these four institutional forces were totally absent from Korea's working-class labor market. The absence of institutional protection is commonly associated with authoritarian politics, which attempt to atomize individual workers while undermining their organization as an interest group. As stabilization proceeded, however, many important changes occurred. For the period 1972-1987, labor unions were not permitted to conduct collective bargaining. Organized labor now participates in negotiations, however, discussing issues related to working conditions. Minimum wage laws were enacted in 1988 and have been applied to all firms. Health insurance was introduced in 1976 and extended to all workers in 1988. And finally, large firms have rearranged their own administrative rules and payment schemes.

The state provides basic institutional protection for workers. This does not mean that the state became a vigorous actor in the market transactions of labor, but rather that the state withdrew its repressive control and permitted private enterprises to decide company rules on their own. Consequently, a firm's internal labor market was formulated at the enterprise level. Workers, who had been regulated by similar rules in homogeneous markets beyond firm boundaries, were atomized by structural factors such as industry, occupation, and size of firm. Wage schemes and promotion ladders diversified significantly following the state retreat from the forefront of market regulation. Instead, private capital, i.e., employers, emerged as a primary determiner of working conditions. The end result was the segmentation of the labor market.

Korea: A Welfare Laggard

Although the state made an effort to introduce public welfare programs in the late 1980s, Korea must be considered a welfare laggard, in light of the way in which the state implemented the politics of industrial restructuring against distribution. As described above, the absence of institutional protection in labor markets reinforced market competition among workers. The state prevented any labor market institution from intervening in the determination of working conditions. In this sense, there existed a close affinity between authoritarian rules and the market-conforming methods of state intervention.

Borrowing Marshall's concept of social rights, Esping-Anderson defines the welfare system as the degree of "de-commodification" (Esping-Anderson 1990). He argues that the most basic criterion for social rights must be the degree to which they permit people to meet their living standards independent of pure market forces. The concept refers to the degree to which individuals, or families, can uphold a socially acceptable standard of living independently of market participation. In these terms, the Korean state is not a "welfare state" for it openly exposes people to market mechanisms without any institutional protection.

There are two reasons for the delay of welfare programs in Korea. First, the state is adverse to welfare spending, and instead places emphasis on mobilizing economic resources and accumulated capital to encourage strategic industries. The state has relied on "trickle-down" economics to ultimately contribute to the improvement of living standards. Second, the state urged capitalists to take charge of providing welfare services within their own companies, a practice which is deep-rooted in and peculiar to East Asian newly industrializing economies (NIEs). In effect, company welfare programs are predominant in Korea, providing most workers with limited fringe benefits such as housing support. However, these programs only benefit managerial workers; production-line workers are entirely excluded. Compared to Japan, Korea's company welfare programs affect only the upper tier of the labor-market pyramid. It is correct to state that company welfare programs function to reinforce the inequality-increasing effect.

This phenomenon is in agreement with the results of a survey conducted by the Ministry of Labor in 1991 which found that a large gap in social insurance benefits exists between the social classes. The report surprisingly states that while the richest 20% received 7,000 won (about $10) per month, the poorest 20% only received 800 won (about $1) in 1990. This amounts to 0.4% of average monthly earnings for the richest 20% and 0.2% for the poorest 20% (Ministry of Labor 1991), demonstrating a case in which public welfare reinforces inequality rather than reduces it. The principle of the more to the rich, the less to the poor is a basic element of the social welfare politics in Korea.

The Failure of the Housing Policy: The Leader of Inflation

The housing problem in Korea is inseparable from the two most severe social problems—inflation and speculation. In theory, economic development triggers inflation everywhere, generating numerous opportunities for accumulating wealth. Where illegal opportunities and corruption prevail, social discontent grows under the lack of state regulation and, more often than not, the lack of political legitimacy of the authoritarian regime. Considered against the government's goal of making a rapid transition to technology-intensive production, industrial restructuring has been successful. From the societal point of view, however, it has been a great failure. Economic growth should be supported by a sound work ethic and a system of positive social values.

In order to placate the lower-class frustration with the housing problem, the Rho Tae-woo regime promised to curb the soaring price of private housing by increasing the supply of private apartments. The Rho government proclaimed its intention of building two million apartment units by 1992. The government also specified rules for purchasing private housing, which large construction companies were assigned to build in major cities. This supply-side policy paralleled the market-conforming method of state intervention in the economic arena. The state was convinced that expanding the supply would control the cost of private housing. This classical market assumption did not work, however. Prices soared and the rich monopolized the housing market, while the lower classes were gradually alienated from their long-cherished dream of owning their own homes. The lower classes have continually suffered from the skyrocketing prices of private housing, rent, and land. Table 4 shows the increase rate of land and housing prices, in comparison with

Table 4. The Increase Rate of Land and Housing Prices,
GNP Growth and Inflation (%)

Category	1975 (A)	1980	1985	1987 (B)	B/A
Land	100.0	328.1	533.5	656.5	6.5
Housing	100.0	355.3	397.0	400.8	4.0
GNP	100.0	174.4	210.8	275.4	2.8
Inflation	100.0	224.3	289.0	363.0	3.6

Source: Economic Planning Board (1990).

Table 5. The Population of Home Owners by Major Cities (%)

City	Seoul	Busan	Daegu	Incheon	Gwangju	Daejeon
	58.7	55.4	53.6	59.8	52.4	55.3

Source: Korean Research Institute for Human Settlements, *A Plan for Introduction of Public Conception of Land* (1989).

GNP growth and inflation. Table 5 indicates the population of home-owners in the major cities.

Table 4 and Table 5 support the above description. First, land prices increased six fold and housing prices quadrupled for the 1975-1987 period of industrial restructuring. Inflation increased by 3.7 times but GNP grew by only 2.8 times in the same period. This means that people earning fixed salaries were unable to buy houses or land. Conversely, the rich who could already afford housing became more affluent through speculation. Second, the population of homeowners amounted to only 50% to 60% in major cities in Korea. In this respect, one can argue that the increased housing supply served to stabilize the soaring price of private houses in the long run. Reality tuned out to be quite the opposite of the classical market assumptions.

The Absence of Environmental Protection: The Growing Threat of Pollution

Where rapid industrialization occurs without corrective measures and policies to minimize environmental degradation, destruction of the environment not only threatens everyday life in both rural and urban areas but also undermines the national effort for economic development. Korea is a good example of economic development without policy measures for environmental protection. It was not until 1988 that the government reorganized the Ministry of Environment, specifying administrative regulations in detail.

In Korea, environmental destruction particularly accelerated during the HCI of the 1970s when petrochemical, which release toxic gases, were imported from Japan and the United States. It is well known that advanced capitalist countries are reluctant to operate toxic industries and have made efforts to export them to less-developed countries with cheap labor. The 1984 Bhopal tragedy in India exemplifies how underdeveloped countries were forced to experience industrial catastrophies. There is no doubt that the accident at Chernobyl in the Soviet Union was the worst environmental disaster the modern world has ever experienced. Unfortunately, toxic industries are found in every industrial region of Korea. The problem worsens when these toxic industries operate without proper environmental protection infrastructure. Three kinds of environmental pollution have caught public national attention recently: pollution of public water supplies, coastal resources, and the atmosphere.

In March 1991, the entire nation was horrified by the public disclosure that an electronic firm had secretly dumped a large amount of untreated industrial waste containing toxic chemicals into the Nakdonggang river. The second and third largest cities in Korea, Busan and Daegu, are wholly dependent on this river for their water supply. The results were fatal: miscarriages, disease, ecological destruction, and lack of clean water. The second issue is coastal pollution caused by land reclamation: water drainage from the reclaimed land increased salinity and piled heaps of eroded earth along coastal areas which devastated marine resources and ruined the economies of fishing villages. It is tragic that many fishing villages and harbors are now vacant, populated only by abandoned boats. The third issue is the atmospheric pollution in industrial cities where the air is almost unbreathable and can cause headaches and vomiting. Big cities like Incheon, Seoul, and Busan are notorious for their air pollution. In May of this year, a couple of workers died after breathing in toxic fumes at their workplace, Wonjin Rayon, a manufacturer of textiles. This accident provoked outcries of managerial cruelty and, eventually, of the lack of government regulation of private enterprises. Concerns about the environment have been growing nation-wide.

However, a problem arises from the lack of government regulation of private capital. State regulation is rapidly declining as private capital expands its power in the economic and political arenas. Korea exemplifies a case wherein all resources are mobilized to accelerate economic growth at the expense of other societal concerns and values. Policy makers and capitalists valued the expansion of production capacity over environmental protection. Such safeguarding measures are expensive, thus resulting in a reduction of profits. The alliance between the state and capitalists buttresses the interest of the ruling class in profit maximization, and this political linkage encourages bureaucrats to weaken regulation of private capital. Corruption blocks the implementation of corrective measures. Consequently, environmental pollution grows and poses a serious threat to the entire nation.

Frustrated Democratization: Political Repression

It is well known that Korea's high-speed growth has been backed by authoritarian politics. In this respect, the Korean case seems to counter Lipset's optimistic prediction that economic development improves the opportunity for democracy (Lipset 1961). Although the public protests of 1987 were a watershed for democratization in Korea, the state successfully managed the crisis by using an accommodationist strategy which functioned to placate the public and effectively weakened workers' radicalism.

There are many factors explaining why Koreans failed to overthrow the authoritarian regime during the period of "political *abertura*," but the most important are the political cleavages which had developed between all social groups during the two authoritarian regimes. Voters were divided into many factions by primary interests based on regional ties, which also led to the division of the political opposition. These primary interests superseded secondary interests such as generation and class divisions. In addition, the ruling party made use of anticommunist and anti-labor ideologies in order to mobilize support from the middle class, which showed its strong preference for political and economic stability. The Rho government quickly mended institutional cleavages to put an end to the political *abertura*, and finally, turned again to authoritarian rules. While the previous two authoritarian regimes were hard, Rho's regime was soft, in that political opposition was permitted, but only along a limited range. However, the Rho government firmly believed that labor repression is required to achieve rapid economic growth. In the sphere of industrial relations, there is no difference between the present and past regimes.

A Will to Work?

It is well known that Korean workers are hard-working and productive. As an explanation, foreign scholars have focused on the application of Confucian values to inspire workers to regard firms as a family in order to improve social harmony and team cooperation. Vogel emphasizes in his research on the cultural background of the Japanese "miracle," that a familial ideology functions to encourage workers to consider the company's profits as more valuable than individual interest (Dore 1973; Vogel 1979). Korea, however, differs from Japan in many respects: first, employers do behave like a household head but are reluctant to show a paternal benevolence to employees, and second, employers enforce excessive work without due compensation. From the workers' point of view, it is widely perceived that they are forced to work like "animals" without being able to exercise their rights, and company welfare programs remain perfunctory. In truth, the state mobilizes the ideology of industrial paternalism to legitimize "the system of low-wage and long-hours worked." This system has been mandated by the state strategy of "growth first and distribution later." In this sense, Korea's industrial relations are characterized not by industrial paternalism but by "authoritarian patriarchism" (Song 1991). As a result, workers were discouraged and the working spirit rapidly degenerated in factories and firms.

Korea's System of Labor Repression: Market Mechanism Versus Corporate Mechanism

Since authoritarian labor control is a feature common to East Asian NIEs, it has been argued often that there is a structural affinity between export-promotion strategy and labor repression (Deyo 1989; Deyo, Haggard, and Koo 1987; Gereffi and Wyman 1990). This argument is more true of Korea, which completed a radical turn to authoritarian repression with the acceleration of industrialization in 1972. The state repression worked so efficiently that organized labor was almost totally silenced on the subject of workers' rights. However, the labor uprising of 1987 was a turning point for working-class politics in Korea. The state withdrew its instruments of repression, and capitalists, hiding behind the state, began to implement organizational and managerial reforms to placate the workers. In many respects, however, the system of labor repression has yet to change significantly.

From a comparative perspective, there are two patterns of labor repression in accordance with the nature and power structure of the authoritarian regime: market mechanisms and corporative mechanisms (Valenzuela 1988). The market mechanism suppresses workers by enforcing atomization of individuals and the exclusion of organized labor from political participation. This pattern is largely prevalent in East Asian NIEs despite some variation. Korea's labor system can be categorized as repression through the market mechanism. In contrast, the corporative mechanism suppresses workers by encouraging unionization and then incorporating organized labor into the political arena. In this pattern, the state coopts and preempts important sectors of the working class by providing state subsidies and welfare benefits. Associational activity is permitted, a system of "inducements and constraints" activates the "give-and-take politics" in this pattern (Collier 1980). Most Latin American NIEs belong to this pattern of labor repression, with some variations.

The relative success of industrial restructuring in the past two decades has been achieved through the sacrifice of workers' rights and freedom. Whether the state concedes to worker demands for "democracy in the workplace" ultimately hinges on the transition to democratization. In this respect, the mass labor uprising of 1987 demonstrated the limitations of labor repression based on market mechanism. However, how far the working class succeeded in pushing the state toward democratization and how far the state perceived the demands of the working class as a political menace are questions still open to discussion. The state has expanded its political base in search of a way to return to the old machine of labor repression since the launch of "the politics of security" (*gongan jeongguk*) in late 1988. However, it is clear that the labor dispute of 1987 was a watershed in the restructuring of industrial relations in Korea (Song 1991).

Conclusion: Reflections on the Korean Experience

This discussion has emphasized the social and political consequences of industrial restructuring in Korea. Korea has been praised by foreign scholars for the successful implementation of policies for industrial structural adjustment. However, this appraisal, which means to draw lessons for adaptation to other national contexts, tends to exaggerate what Korea has achieved and ignore what Korea has sacrificed in its pursuit of economic success.

There have been two approaches to the Korean "miracle." One emphasizes state-led capitalism, in which a strong state is fully equipped with the capacity to implement policies for economic growth. Charismatic leadership empowers highly-educated technocrats and the economic machine, like the Economic Planning Board, to pursue its goal. However, state-led capitalism declined dramatically, and the interventionist state role is now changing from developmental functions to regulatory functions. Though this change is not yet complete, the influence of private enterprises on the national economy is growing remarkably. It indicates that the private sector will emerge as a major driving force in the near future.

The other approach focuses on cultural legacies such as Confucian values including familial ideology and work ethics. MacFarquhar argues that there is a selective affinity between Confucianism and modernization, displaying merits and virtues in the modern version of Confucianism he terms "post-Confucianism" (MacFarquhar 1980; Friedman 1988). Unlike Japan, however, it is hard to deny that industrial paternalism is merely a managerial strategy of an authoritarian Korea. Workers are not inspired to work hard. Employers charge that workers have become lazy. This assertion, however, is unfair, and distorts what workers have endured so far. Many serious conflicts and violent disputes have broken out. Workers have abandoned enterprise consciousness and have turned to class consciousness. This cultural approach is unable to explain why workers become violent.

This paper has focused its analysis on the darker side of the Korean development, demonstrating that industrial restructuring through the HCI and the ISA has functioned contrary to a "development with equality." The politics for industrial restructuring brought about significant changes. First, state-led capitalism was eclipsed by the growing influence of private capital, and the state changed its role from vigorous intervention to institutional regulation for the consolidation of infrastructure. Second, private capital replaced the state as a primary actor in the forefront of economic development. Monopolization proceeded so rapidly that it strengthened the segmentation of production and labor markets. Third, the increasing reliance on market mechanisms supports growth of monopoly capital but impairs the government capacity to implement policies for equality. Furthermore, the state now intends to be no more than an onlooker to the increasing social discontent resulting from widening inequality.

Who benefits from, and what are the advantages and drawbacks of, industrial restructuring? Undoubtedly, it contributed to improving the overall standard of living. However, the allocation of benefits differs according to social class: the middle and upper classes are the beneficiaries, and the lower classes including peasants, the urban poor, and the working class is entirely excluded. Moreover, the lower classes have suffered from the soaring prices of housing, land, and inflation. As industrial restructuring reinforced the relative deprivation of the lower social strata, social discontent grew rapidly and class conflicts deepened. Unfortunately, however, the Korean state relied on repressive methods to weaken political challenge from below.

REFERENCES

Amsden, Alice. 1990. *Next Asia's Giant.* Oxford: Oxford University Press.
Bhagwati, Jagdish. 1978. *Anatomy and Consequences of Exchange Control Regimes.* Cambridge: Ballinger Publishing Company.
Choi, Byung-Sun. 1987. "Institutionalizing a Liberal Economic Order in Korea: The Strategic Management of Economic Change," Ph.D. diss., Harvard University.
Collier, Ruth. 1980. "Inducement Versus Constraints: Disaggregating Corporation." Institute of Industrial Relations. Berkeley: University of California Press.
Deyo, Frederic C. 1989. *Beneath The Miracle.* Berkeley: University of California Press.
Deyo, Frederic C., Stephan Haggard, and Hagen Koo. 1987. "Labor in the Political Economy of East Asian Industrialization." *Bulletin of Concerned Asian Scholars* 19.2.

Dore, Ronald. 1973. *British Factory—Japanese Factory.* Berkeley: University of California Press.

ESCAP. 1990. "Challenges and Opportunities of Restructuring the Developing Escap Economies in the 1990s, with Special Reference to Regional Economic Cooperation."

Esping-Anderson, Gosta. 1990. *The Three World of Welfare Capitalism.* Princeton: Princeton University Press.

Fields, Gary. 1982. *The Labor Market and Export-led Growth in Korea, Taiwan, Hong Kong, and Singapore.* Seoul: Korea Development Institute.

Fields, Gary, and Henry Wan, Jr. 1986. "Wage-Setting Institutions and Economic Growth." Mimeo. Cornell University.

Friedman, David. 1988. *The Misunderstood Miracle: Industrial Development and Political Change in Japan.* Ithaca: Cornell University Press.

Gereffi, Gary, and Donald Wyman. 1990. *Manufacturing Miracles.* Princeton: Princeton University Press.

Haggard, Stephan. 1986. "The Newly Industrializing Countries in the International System." *World Politics* 38 (January).

Johnson, Chalmers. 1982. *MITI and Japanese Miracle.* Stanford: Stanford University Press.

Kim, Hyeong-gi. 1989. *Hanguk-ui dokjeom jabon-gwa imnodong* (Monopoly Capital and Labor in Korea). Seoul: Kkachi Publishing Co.

Kim, Hyeong-guk. 1991. "Interaction between Government Strategy and Private Enterprises in Industrial Structural Adjustment." In *Hanguk jeongchi gyeongje ron* (A Study of Korea's Political Economy), edited by An Cheong-si. Seoul: Bobmun sa.

Kim, Gyun. 1991. "Industrial Restructuring and Capitalism in the 1980s in Korea." In *Hanguk jabonjuui-ui ihae* (The Understanding of Korea's Capitalism), edited by Korean Association for Social and Economic Studies. Seoul: Hanul Publishing Co.

Krueger, Ann O., et al. 1978. *Liberalization Attempts and Consequences.* Cambridge: Ballinger Publishing Company.

Lipset, S. M. 1961. *Political Man: The Social Basis of Politics.* Baltimore: The Johns Hopkins University Press.

MacFarquhar, R. 1980. "The Post-Confucian Challenge." *The Economist.*

O'Connor, James. 1973. *The Fiscal Crisis of the State.* New York: St. Martin's Press.

Seeghaas, Dieter. 1982. *Von Europa Lernen.* Sulukamp.

Song, Ho Geun. 1989. "State and the Working-Class Labor Market in South Korea, 1961-1987." Ph.D. diss., Harvard University.

————. 1991. *Working-Class Politics and Market in South Korea.* Seoul: Nanam Publishing House.

Thurow, Lester. 1975. *Generating Inequality.* New York: Basic Books.

Valenzuella, Samuel. 1988. "Labor Movements in Transition to Democracy: A Framework for Analysis." Paper presented at the Conference on Labor Movement and Redemocratization, Kellogg Institute, University of Notre Dame.

Vogel, Ezra. 1979. *Japan as Number One*. New York: Harbor Torch Books.

Statistical Books

Economic Planning Board (EPB). 1988. *Social Indicator in Korea 1988*. Seoul: EPB.

_____. 1990. *Social Indicator in Korea 1990*. Seoul: EPB.

_____. *Economically Active Population Survey*, annual.

Ministry of Labor. 1980. *Yearbook of Labor Statistics 1980*. Seoul: Ministry of Labor.

_____. 1988. *Yearbook of Labor Statistics 1988*. Seoul: Ministry of Labor.

_____. 1991. *Yearbook of Labor Statistics 1991*. Seoul: Ministry of Labor.

Ministry of Science and Technology. 1988. *Yearbook of Technology and Science*. Seoul: Ministry of Science and Technology.

World Bank. 1990. *World Development Report 1990*. Washington, D.C.: World Bank.

Economic Development and Democracy:
Korea as a New Model?

Han Sang-Jin

Introduction

The social sciences have drawn much attention to the relations between economic development and democracy since 1959 when Seymour Martin Lipset formulated his theory of modernization. His contention that economic development serves as the basis for political democracy was then seriously challenged by dependency theory and O'Donnell's (1973) theory of bureaucratic authoritarianism–both largely reflecting the experiences of Latin American military regimes. Yet, as democratic changes around the world gained new momentum in the middle of the 1970s, beginning in Southern Europe and then appearing in Asia, researchers began to reinvestigate the linkages between political authoritarianism and economic growth in depth, with heightened interest in the political consequences of economic development and the possible economic consequences of democratization itself.

Given the complexity involved in these relationships and the immense difficulties of many countries (especially the former socialist countries) in carrying out the dual tasks of democratization and economic reform simultaneously, more and more observers now tend to view East Asia (Korea, Taiwan, Thailand) after Southern Europe (Spain, Portugal,

* Originally published in Vol. 35, No. 2 (Summer 1995).

Han Sang-Jin (Han, Sang-jin) is Professor of Sociology at Seoul National University. He received his Ph.D. with a dissertation entitled "Discourse Method and Social Theory" from Southern Illinois University at Carbondale in 1979. He has authored a number of books including *Habermas and the Korean Debate* (1998). E-mail: hansjin@snu.ac.kr.

Greece) as a model of successful transition in both aspects. If we take a perspective of historical comparison, there seems to be good reason for this judgment. As Przeworski (1991, 171) has already pointed out, it is "exceedingly rare," if not impossible, that a given country under strong authoritarian rule is able to accomplish both sustained economic development and democracy.

This brings us to the specificities involved in the East Asian experience of historical transition. Is there an East Asian model of democracy which is unique *sui generis*? Or, to put it more generally, is there any distinctively East Asian pattern of (democratic) transition which may serve as a model for other countries undergoing historical transformation? In view of the fact that the economic performances of Japan, Korea and China, for example, have been more successful than their conventional counterparts, that is, the U.S., the newly industrializing countries (NICs) on other continents and former socialist countries, one may find these questions tempting, at least in appearance. Until recently, however, it was not clear whether East Asian countries could really serve as a model because one crucial factor seemed to be lacking—democracy.

Samuel Huntington and Bruce Cumings on East Asia

Samuel Huntington's (1991, 12-34) argument is a case in point. He once observed that "the interaction of economic progress and Asian culture appears to have generated a distinctively East Asian variety of democratic institutions." The model of this development is Japan. Huntington's concept of Asian democracy is strictly procedural. As a system of "equitable and open competition for votes between political parties without government harassment or restriction of opposition groups," the East Asian model is different from the Western political system in that the former involves only "competition for power but not alternation in power." All parties are allowed to participate in elections, but participation in office is possible only for those in the mainstream party. Huntington insists, "this type of political system offers democracy without turnover. It represents an adaptation of Western democratic practices to serve not Western values of competition and change, but Asian values of consensus and stability."

Huntington draws a sharp line here between Western and Asian cultures, treating Japan as a representative of a distinctively Asian variation of democracy. It is well known that the uninterrupted dominance of the Liberal Democratic Party has contributed greatly to Japan's political stability and economic development during the last several decades. Huntington does not criticize this one-party domination but rather highlights its distinctiveness. From the Western viewpoint, however, Japanese politics until recently might seem far less attractive than presented by Huntington, since there has been no horizontal transfer of political power. The level of public frustration also has also been high because Japanese politics involved systematic corruption. Indeed, one may say that Japanese capitalism looks attractive, but not Japanese politics.

Bruce Cumings's argument (1989) is another example of critical reflection. He writes that the Korean path of democratic transition was likely to be abortive because of the coercive capacity of the Korean bureaucratic authoritarian regime, which is "beyond the imagination of any South American state or leaders." The Korean state is, according to him, "comparable to the 1930s Japanese model with its militarist and quasi-fascist baggage." Consequently, neither the political parties, the bourgeoisie, nor the labor unions has enjoyed any sense of autonomy. On the contrary, the political parties remained fragile, the bourgeoisie weak and the labor unions excluded. He concludes that:

> The bureaucratic-authoritarian capacity is for now mostly latent, but capable of imminent mobilization; as such it rests like a dead hand on the business of democratization, always retarding progress and unnervingly ready to terminate unacceptable outcome. That the structures are so much stronger in Korea than in Latin America merely means that the abertura is more inherently abortive (Cumings 1989, 27).

Yet Korea is well known for its rapid economic development. It has transformed itself from a typically agrarian society into a modern industrial one within the span of a single generation. This speed of industrialization is unprecedented. At the same time, however, as Cumings succinctly points out, the legacy of repressive authoritarianism is particularly strong in Korea. The state fostered economic growth vigorously while preventing the workers from political participation and fair consumption. This exclusionary aspect of bureaucratic authoritarianism was so extensive during the 1970s that it outpaced the level of repression experienced by our colleagues in São Paulo and Buenos Aires. Indeed Korean economic development looks attractive, but not Korean politics.

Lee Kuan Yew and Kim Dae-jung

This sort of ambivalence prevails not only among intellectuals but also among foreign observers. But what if the political terrain of East Asia is in the process of fundamental change? Huntington (1991) once noticed that "the Japanese model of dominant-party democracy has spread else-where in East Asia." He had in mind first Korea, where the ruling party and two of the three opposition parties merged into a grand conserva-tive party, and second Taiwan, where the Guomindang initiated liberal-ization from above and seemed likely to remain the dominant party in the future. Since then, however, the scope of change in East Asia has greatly exceeded expectation. As we all know, the dominance of Japan's Liberal Democratic Party has been badly shaken, effecting the first polit-ical turnover since the middle of the 1950s. Likewise, in Korea, where the chance for democracy seemed slim, at least according to Cumings, democratic transition has unfolded rather successfully, finally giving birth to a civilian government after 32 years of military rule.

These episodes are significant by themselves, probably signaling more fundamental changes occurring in East Asian politics. One may question legitimately, therefore, whether it is still meaningful to view Asians as preoccupied with collectivity and order in contrast to such Western val-ues as individualism and competition. Furthermore, continuing to speak of an East Asian variety of democracy in apologetic tones appears highly problematic.

Yet there is one notable exception: Lee Kuan Yew who retired in 1990 after 39 years as prime minister of Singapore. Backed by his successful career and the economic prosperity of Singapore, Lee Kuan Yew now speaks of a distinctively East Asian model of politics, arguing that West-ern-style democracy is not applicable to East Asia. His argument is based on the cultural differences between East and West and their sociopolitical implications (Lee 1993). He seemed originally interested in justifying his autocratic regime by Confucianism and then expanded his lexicon to include "Asian Democracy" and Asian human rights, eventu-ally, moving on to defend an essential "Asian-ness" which no longer embraced democracy but turned out to be nothing more than authori-tarianism.

Two points must be stressed in this regard. First, although Lee has vigorously argued the fundamental difference of Asia from the West, saying that "no society is able to cast aside its basic way of doing things, and go and adopt a completely new style" (Lee 1993, 582), he seems to have employed the East-West cultural dichotomy prevalent in Western thought. Focusing on the binary oppositions deeply anchored in Western philosophy's dualist metaphysics, one critic has claimed that the East-West split "has mutated into a new symbolic geography with the East now being Asia, with the East-West struggle being between Asia and Europe-North America" (Callahan 1994, 3). Furthermore, one may argue that there are striking similarities between Lee Kuan Yew's defense of Asian-ness and Samuel Huntington's "clash of civilizations" insofar as both rely on the same essentialist concept of culture. An epistemological critique suggests that Lee's concept of Asia is nothing but a duplication of Western metaphysics. In other words, one may question whether Lee's image of Asia as opposed to the West really represents the depth and the flexibility of an "Asian" way of thinking.

Second, a more serious and substantive critique has been raised recently by Kim Dae-jung (Kim Dae Jung 1994) in direct response to Lee Kuan Yew. Confronting Lee's objection to "foisting an alien system indiscriminately on societies in which it will not work" (Zakaria 1994, 110), Kim carefully examines whether democracy is such an alien system to Asian cultures. Kim's (1994, 191) conclusion differs from Lee's decisively: "A thorough analysis makes it clear that Asia has a rich heritage of democracy-oriented philosophies and traditions. Asia has already made great strides toward democratization and possesses the necessary conditions to develop democracy even beyond the level of the West." The biggest obstacle to democracy in Asia is, according to Kim, "not the cultural heritage but the resistance of authoritarian rulers and their apologists" (Kim 1994, 174).

Kim's observation of the relations between economic development and democracy is particularly interesting. He argues that democracy will be ever more indispensable in Asia where economies are now moving from a capital- and labor-intensive industrial phase into an information- and technology-intensive one. Indispensable for and required of this transition is, he insists, the freedom of information and creative discourse. With this argument, Kim shows us why Lee Kuan Yew's attempt to combine a free market economy and political authoritarianism must be seen as dubious.

Economic Consequences of Political Authoritarianism

One of the commonalities of East Asian development is that political authoritarianism, whether it is "soft" (like Japan, cf. Johnson 1975; Curtis 1988) or "hard" (like Korea and Taiwan, cf. Cheng and Haggard 1992), has been consistently successful in promoting and managing economic growth. This state-led authoritarian capitalist development can be taken, therefore, as the starting point of analysis.

Originating from this elective affinity between political authoritarianism and socioeconomic modernization, there have appeared ambiguities typical of East Asia. On the one hand, as a consequence of this economic transformation, social structures began to change very rapidly. This is well documented in the changes in the structures of employment, industrial sectors, social classes, etc. and also in the rate of urbanization, education and so on. These changes have the potential to strengthen civil society, providing more favorable conditions for democracy. On the other hand, due to the overwhelming dominance of the state in economic development, the legacy of the authoritarian state apparatus remains largely intact, not only in the transitional but also in the post-transitional period.

As will be demonstrated below, this constrained pattern of change has distanced democracy in Asia from progressive ideas of substantive democracy. Democracy remains largely confined to procedural democracy at the political level, falling short of economic and social democracy and political participation. What ensues may be termed "bourgeois hegemony" or "middle class democracy" (Murakami 1984; Koppel 1994). We need to keep this in mind if we want to grasp what is going on in real terms.

Let me briefly substantiate each of these points with reference to Korea. The first issue is why and how the bureaucratic authoritarian (hereafter BA) state was capable of steering economic development successfully. An answer to this seems to lie at least partially in the cohesion of power elites linking the military and the technocrats as each performed its own role in divided cooperation. The Economic Planning Board (EPB) was the power base of the technocrats while the security and information agencies were that of the military. These two dominant segments of BA were united with the belief that national wealth and military power ought to be increased through industrialization. This internal cohesion made it possible for the state apparatus to pursue economic policies consistently, at least until the middle of the 1980s. This cohesion, in turn, was made possible by the strong leadership of President Park Chung-hee, in whose hands political power was excessively concentrated. Another equally important condition was the segregation mechanism by which the civil dissidents were effectively shut out of the decision-making processes (Han 1988).

It is useful here to focus on the specific selectivity built into the state economic apparatus. Rather than relying on a sort of compromise between government and enterprise, the state decided to induce, almost forcefully, the enterprises to comply with the goal it had established. The state used various means to this end. It measured the extent to which each enterprise contributed to the export goal set by the state and favored the more competitive enterprises with more subsidies.

A good example of this forceful and preferential treatment was the heavy and chemical industrialization policy pursued during the 1970s (Han 1988). Despite the first oil shock, the Korean government poured enormous national resources into building and expanding the steel, machine, chemical, shipbuilding, and non-ferrous metal industries. The underlying motives are not difficult to understand. These industries were declared to be fundamental for industrial expansion and the basis for national defense. An interesting point to note in this regard is that there was no demand at all for this policy from domestic enterprises. On the contrary, the state acted independently in forcing the enterprises to move in a predetermined direction. By doing so, the Korean BA not only facilitated economic growth but also solidified the capitalist class, the middle class, and the skilled working class.

Included in this inducement scheme were financial, banking, and tax benefits. The secret lay in the state control of the pipelines of capital supply over the private sectors (Woo 1991). Since direct investment by multinational corporations was very low and private enterprises were limited in mobilizing their own domestic capital, the Korean bourgeoisie had no choice but to depend on the financial and banking capital supplied by the state. The state was in a position to apportion enormous amounts of foreign loan capital, special funds, and other programs designed to promote the export sectors, particularly the heavy and chemical industries. The state also used such devices as policy loans, industrial subsidies and other legally stipulated means by which it reduced or exempted duties, alleviated customs, and deferred debt redemption.

The prevailing image of the state has been that it ought to stand above the private sectors. Deeply anchored in the Confucian norm of public service, this self-understanding has had enormous implications for the influence of state policy over economic enterprises, including large conglomerates. To be sure, the state played a large role in creating these business groups. Though creator of the bourgeois class, the state has never treated it as an equal partner. On the contrary, it has wanted to operate over and above the private sectors, trying to discipline them, albeit not in the traditional way, but in a capitalist way. It is not correct, therefore, to describe the relations between government and economic enterprises as symbiotic as is often done with Japanese capitalism. Rather, the concept of a "disciplinary" regime (Amsden 1989) is more applicable to the Korean case. The state disciplined not only the workers but also the capitalists.

These descriptions involve idealizations, of course. The recent experiences of bureaucratic pathologies clearly show that the degree of state autonomy and elite cohesion has seriously deteriorated during the last several years. Furthermore, the Korean BA has long suffered from the systematic exclusion of the public and the consequent lack of political legitimacy. This exclusion has triggered the breakdown of political trust, the proliferation and intensification of social conflicts, and the widening gap between the rich and the poor. Furthermore, corruption stemming from the fusion of state power and business has become widespread. The excessive concentration of wealth in a handful of business conglomerates has also continued to be a serious social issue.

Thus, it is important to take into account the contradictions inherent within the Korean BA. The BA regime was highly successful in accelerating economic growth, but it could not maintain this growth because of its built-in contradictions. Even the idea of a disciplinary regime is now problematic. Originating in the Japanese militarism before World War II (Cumings 1989), state discipline could be effective only insofar as the still growing enterprises needed support from the state. Once the economy became self-maintaining, the state's disciplinary stance became a source of strain, not a mutually accepted parameter of interaction. Since then, we have witnessed discontent surfacing among the business conglomerates, not to mention the widespread labor conflicts. The former head of the Hyundai Group Chung Ju-yung's bid for the presidency in the 1992 election points to this discontent.

Political Consequences of Economic Development

One of the salient features of contemporary social sciences in general and political sociology in particular is the enormous amount of attention paid to the transition from authoritarianism to varieties of democracy. A great deal of literature has been produced dealing with the experiences of Southern Europe, Eastern Europe and Latin America. Meanwhile, significant political changes have also taken place in East Asia, as I have described above. Seen comparatively, the East Asian transition is notable because its economic success, rather than the failure of political authoritarianism, has contributed significantly to political liberalization and democratic transition. How can we then best understand the common characteristics of these East Asian transitions?

I would like to advance the thesis that, as civil society has become strengthened in the process of socioeconomic modernization, the disjuncture between institutionalized politics (mostly the state, but including the political parties) and civil society has become increasingly serious and, as such, has provided the major impetus for change (Han 1994a). Civil society is here understood in its dual aspects: that is, the public sphere in which themes and identities are formed and dispersed, constituting the moral and discursive basis of social formations; and social movements which attempt to aggregate, articulate and channel interests of concerned social groups into the political, administrative, and economic processes of decision-making (Habermas 1992; Cohen and Arato 1992). I shall illustrate three conspicuous reasons for this discrepancy.

First, alongside the state-led authoritarian industrialization, the middle classes and skilled workforce in each country have greatly expanded and acquired a political voice. More often than not, they were placed in a position of ambivalence since they were economically empowered but politically excluded. Their frustration increased with time because the channels of political participation remained largely restricted or closed (Han 1989).

In Korea, for example, disillusionment over the regimented television broadcasting, especially the Nine O'clock (Evening) News was particularly grave in the middle of the 1980s. The gap between institutionalized politics and civil society grew, resulting in the political activism of the middle class, the student movement, and the workers strikes. University professors, literati, clergy, and other intellectuals made statements of protest demanding democratization with the belief that this would reduce unnecessary social costs. Together, these acts had a widespread impact on society.

A precipitating factor in the transition to democracy was an incidence of police torture which resulted in the death of a Seoul National University student in early 1987, and the subsequent cover-up by the police. The middle class and civil society were enraged by this incident and loudly demanded a full disclosure. The media took advantage of it to increase their autonomy from state control, joining the historical waves of liberalization and democratization. These diverse efforts culminated in the June Uprising in 1987, a breakthrough in the democratic transition.

Second, corruption has become deeply embedded in institutionalized politics as a by-product of state-led industrialization. Corruption is not unique to East Asia; it is also a serious problem elsewhere. What is specific to East Asia, however, is the influence of the Confucian ethic of the public servant. Because of this cultural tradition, the response of East Asian civil societies to systemic corruption of the political system and bureaucracy seems to have been accompanied by a bitter sense of injustice and betrayal less deeply felt on other continents. Yet it must be stressed that the level and scope of corruption may vary depending on the country. The government bureaucrats in Japan and Taiwan, for example, have been less implicated in corruption than the politicians, whereas in Korea and China they are considered equally corrupt. Consequently, public distrust focused on different targets in each country. On the whole, however, corruption has been an important reason why an increasing number of citizens have become frustrated over institutional politics (Reed 1994; Iwai 1994).

Third, in the post-transitional period, the idea of political representation, representational institutions, and elites have been losing public trust. Despite elections regularly held on the basis of universal franchise, the public increasingly regards politics as the game of politicians maneuvered by factional bosses behind a curtain. The elected officials are seen not as representing and articulating the interests of the citizens but, on the contrary, as acting on the assumption that the mandate of the people is simply handed over to them (in O'Donnell's terms "delegative democracy"). In this context, the feeling of "anti-politics" and the lack of political party identification is rapidly spreading through civil society, especially among younger generations. This can be easily confirmed in numerous national surveys in Japan and Korea, for example.

The political consequences of economic development are here unmistakable. Democratic transition in East Asia can best be understood from a perspective which focuses on the cleavage between institutionalized politics and civil society. In Korea, for example, the prime mover toward democratization has been neither the working class, as elsewhere, nor the political parties and elites. On the contrary, the momentum for change has come by and large from civil society within which the challenges from the middle class are of crucial significance. This means, however, that the democratic reforms in East Asia may be considerably undermined or even eliminated if the middle class is transformed into a conservative force (Bunbongkarn 1994; Koppel 1994).

It is in this context that we need to examine Adam Przeworski's (1991, 96) sharp criticisms of the methodology of macro-historical comparative sociology. He recognizes that "objective conditions do delimit the possibilities inherent in a given historical situation," but argues that these conditions cannot be directly translated into determinants, which must be grasped instead within the local context in which social forces and institutions are enmeshed in their specific relationships.

With this reasonable perspective, however, what he actually does is to emphasize the modes of elite's interaction. Vital for democracy, according to him, is the channeling of social movements into institutional politics. If autonomous movements emerge in civil society, yet find no institution where they can present and negotiate their interests, he argues, "the only place where the newly organized groups can eventually struggle for their values and interests is the street" (Przeworski 1991, 59). For this reason, Przeworski primarily draws attention to institutionalized politics, defending the position that "successful transition can be brought about only as a result of negotiation."

Przeworski's argument sensitizes us to the importance of the institutional capability of mediation and negotiation between interests. Nevertheless, he seems to retreat to elite theory in the end. He declared that democracy can last only when two conditions are met, that is, "a fair chance to compete within the institutional framework and to generate substantive outcomes" (1991, x). Yet his game-theory approach seems incapable of grasping the dynamism of civil society as a source of the driving energy for substantive social justice. In other words, it is too limiting to discuss democratic reform while heavily relying on those political forces which have already been clustered around political institutions. The major forces of change still seem to lie outside, not inside, institutionalized politics. If the outside energy dries up or disappears, it seems very unlikely that any political leader or faction will take the initiative to pursue serious and consistent structural reform.

All these issues boil down to the question of whether or not–and if so, to what extent–civil society in East Asia will be able to nurture the potential for democracy in social movements and the public sphere. An alarming portent of the future is that the mass media, particularly the press, have become so powerful and conservative in the post-transitional situation that they are almost reigning over civil society (Han 1995). A key question, then, is whether there is any social force with the capacity to pursue hegemony in a way that goes beyond the shortsightedness associated with the middle class. We may say that democracy in Japan, for example, depends on the further diversification of "the new middle mass" (Murakami 1984) as much as democracy in Korea has been shaped by the development of the "middling grassroots" (Han 1994b). According to a recent hypothesis, the new Japanese middle mass has been further diversified into the new Japan-oriented and the new citizen-oriented groupings (Shoji 1994). This is a social basis for recent political changes in Japan. Likewise, the middling grassroots in Korea, historically formed out of the shared experiences of student activism and popular movements during the last thirty years may provide an insight into why the democratic transition in Korea signifies the empowerment of the middling grassroots, though in a limited way, and how the limitations of the present civilian government can be overcome in the future.

Economic Consequences of Democratization

The extent to which political democracy affects economic policy cannot be answered in general terms. It can make significant differences in some cases, but not in others. To a certain extent, this may depend on whether reform moves into the socioeconomic domains or remains confined to the political one, giving a free hand to bourgeoisie.

In many Asian countries, democratization falls short of substantive reforms. The popular expectation of distributive justice and equal participation in all major institutions is often frustrated, even though the overall economic situation may look much better in East Asia than elsewhere.

In Korea, where the bourgeoisie has not achieved hegemony and the labor integration function of the capitalist enterprises remains poorly developed (Eckert 1990), democratic reform means several things. Although it appears to stimulate restructuring politics and promote economic and social democracy, research shows that the economic consequences are moving the opposite direction.

The recent strike of the Seoul subway workers in June 1994 is a case in point. Having failed in wage negotiations with the subway management, the labor union decided to go on a legitimate sit-in. The space for negotiations remained open and there was much contact between both sides. However, the government, anticipating the side effects that might occur if the strike was actually made, suddenly sent in the combat police who forcibly removed the workers staging the sit-in. Shocked, the labor union responded by launching an illegal strike immediately, without waiting for the end of the cooling-off period during arbitration. The government refused to accept that it was at fault, and extensively publicized the illegality of the strike. The citizens not only suffered everyday inconveniences, but also felt uneasy about the worsening of domestic conflicts in the international context of strain over the North Korean nuclear issue. In a head-on confrontation between state power and the labor unions, the public could in no way take the side of the latter. Public opinion overwhelmingly demanded the prohibition of the illegal strike. With such public support, the government broke up the subway strike, effectively cutting off solidarity strikes by other unions.

In contrast, the power of the business conglomerates has increased under the civilian government. This trend is clearly related to the policy of internationalization and globalization which favors internationally competitive economic sectors. Here we can see the irony in the difference between the past authoritarian regimes and the present civilian government. The past regimes used various measures to discipline the business groups in an attempt to regulate the concentration of economic power. The situation has changed, however, with the civilian government, which not only exempted business groups from the burden of political contributions but also increasingly depended on them in its pursuit of a globalization policy. Thus the business conglomerates are now finding themselves in a position where they can speak out with far more confidence than under any of the past authoritarian regimes.

For example, the government has not only relaxed the provisions regulating the business conglomerates but has also aggressively encouraged them to participate in such high-income areas as the privatization of the former government-run corporations and the formation of infrastructures such as highways and ports. It has loosened the policy measure designed to prevent capital concentration in a few conglomerates while limiting the bank loans to them and curbing non-business-use real estate transactions. Consequently, economic concentration has accelerated. The total sales of the 30 largest business conglomerates amounted to 78.8% of the GNP in 1992, but this figure increased visibly to 80.4% in 1993 and 82.2% in 1994. In particular, the total sales of the five largest conglomerates–including Hyundai, Samsung, Daewoo, Lucky Goldstar, and Sunkyung–amounted to 53.3% of the GNP in 1993 and increased to 54.1% in 1994 (*Maeil Business Newspaper*, 1 April 1995). Such a high proportion is, indeed, impressive and possibly unique.

There is consequently a growing asymmetry between capital and labor in terms of available power resources. Industrial workers, whose numbers have increased dramatically during the last 30 years, still remain very weak in organized strength compared with the business conglomerates. More often than not, the labor union patronized by the management provides the cause of the labor-labor disputes. Once a labor union patronized by the management is registered, it is illegal for the workers to organize another union because only one union is allowed in each establishment. Since the intervention of a third party is prohibited, even the solidarity between labor unions is hard to achieve and is subject to surveillance and punishment by the state power. The labor unions remain isolated from political activity while the workers' demands for participation in management are rejected.

We are left with question why the imbalance of power between Korean labor and capital has developed to such an extreme. One plausible answer is that as a consequence of democratization, the power of the business conglomerates has been so greatly expanded that they are now attempting to circumscribe state power and define their own parameters of activity (Rueschemeyer and Stephens 1992).

Conclusion

This paper began with the issue of whether there is any distinctively East Asian model of democracy or democratic transition and demonstrated that neither Huntington's nor Lee Kuan Yew's answer is sufficient. The one dominant-party model of democracy seems to have lost credibility, as have the Confucian authoritarian politics in Singapore. On the contrary, I have argued that it is more useful and appropriate to read Asian philosophies and traditions in a way suggested by Kim Dae-jung. Both Bruce Cumings and Adam Przeworski also make the strong points that since many East Asian countries are still living under the legacy of the past authoritarian regime and, consequently, our capacity for institution-building seems to lag behind our capacity for movement. We should keep this in mind if we are not to fall into a naive optimism.

How to assess the strengths and limitations of democracy in East Asia is still an open question. Recently, a foreign expert observed that democratization in Korea, for example, "is likely to be slower than some Koreans might wish and may be too fast for some of the more traditionally minded" (Steinberg 1995, 42). He displayed slightly more optimism when he said that "the forces of pluralism are likely to prevail over time. As a Korean observer, however, I remain a bit more cautious since democratic consolidation, as the main agenda nowadays, requires something quite more than what we have achieved in the processes of democratic transition."

Having said this, however, it seems useful to explore the value of the Korean model of state-led authoritarian economic development. This model can be considered if, and only if, for some historical and sociopolitical reasons, a given country has to postpone political freedom for the alleged purpose of accelerating economic growth as rapidly as possible. BA with successful economic achievement is then far better than BA with a crumbling economy. The evolution of Chinese politics and market economy may be examined from this perspective (Nolan 1990). Likewise, it can be understood why the former socialist countries, surrounded by the immense difficulties of double transformations in their political and economic arenas, are interested in exploring the lessons of the Korean experience for possible borrowing.

Overall, the East Asian experiences may look attractive in the sense that these countries have achieved sustained economic development for several decades. They may look even more attractive since procedural democracy has been institutionalized in Korea and Taiwan, following Japan. Crucial for democratic consolidation, however, is the capacity of civil society to be the basis of democratic institutions, in which cultural identities and diversity are nurtured and developed. In this respect, the potential of East Asia cannot be ignored. The rich cultural traditions, whether they be Confucianism, Buddhism or anything else, need to be creatively interpreted and reinvented to formulate a globally-oriented civil solidarity. Those cultural activities will be of particular importance in the turn to the postmodern. It is in this sense that we can expect new visions for civilization to come from East Asia. It is indeed exciting to think about this possibility, and will remain as much so in the future as it is now.

BIBLIOGRAPHY

Amsden, Alice. 1989. *Asia's Next Giant: South Korea and Late Industrialization.* Oxford: Oxford University Press.

Bunbongkarn, Suchit. 1994. "Democratization in Thailand: The Role of Economic Development and Political Liberalization." IPSA Asian Conference Paper.

Callahan, William. 1994. "Rescripting East/West Relations: Rethinking Asian Democracy." IPSA Asian Conference Paper.

Cheng, Tun-Jen, and Stephan Haggard, eds. 1992. *Political Change in Taiwan.* Boulder: Lynne Rienner Publishers.

Cohen, Jean, and Andrew Arato. 1992. *Political Theory and Civil Society.* Boston: MIT Press.

Cumings, Bruce. 1989. "The Abortive Abertura: South Korea in the Light of Latin American Experience." *New Left Review* 173: 5-32.

Curtis, Gerald. 1989. *The Japanese Way of Politics.* New York: Columbia University Press.

Eckert, Carter. 1997. "The South Korean Bourgeoisie: A Class in Search of Hegemony." *Journal of Korean Studies* 7: 15-148.

Habermas, Jürgen. 1992. *Geltung und Faktizitaet.* Frankfurt am Main: Suhrkamp.

Han, Sang-Jin. 1989. *Bureaucratic Authoritarianism in Korea.* Seoul: Moonji-sa.

_____. 1994a. "From Bureaucratic Authoritarianism to Civil Society." Paper presented at the IPSA World Congress, Bielefeld, Germany.

_____. 1994b. "What is New about the Korean Democratization: The Empowerment of the Middling Grassroots and their Future." Paper presented at the IPSA World Congress, Berlin, Germany.

_____. 1995. "Media and Mediations: The Public Sphere in Korea's Democratic Transition." Paper presented at Georgetown Conference, Washington D.C., USA.

Huntington, Samuel. 1991. "Democracy's Third Wave." *Journal of Democracy* 2.2: 12-34.

Iwai, Tomoski. 1994. "Political Reform in Contemporary Japan." IPSA World

Congress Paper.

Johnson, Chalmers. 1975. "Japan: Who Governs?" *Journal of Japanese Studies* 2.1: 1-28.

——. 1989. "South Korean Democratization and the Role of Economic Development." *Pacific Review* 2.1: 1-10.

Kim, Dae Jung. 1994. "Is Culture Destiny? The Myth of Asia's Anti-Democratic Values." *Foreign Affairs* (November/December): 189-194.

Koo, Hagen. 1990. "From Farm to Factory: Proletarianization in Korea." *American Sociological Review* 55: 669-681.

——. 1991. "Middle Classes, Democratization and Class Formation: The Case of South Korea." *Theory and Society* (Summer).

Koppel, Bruce. 1994. "Perspectives on Democratization in Southeast Asia." ASA Conference Paper.

Lee, Kwan Yew. 1993. *Selections from 40 Years of Political Writings.* Singapore: Lianhe Zaobao Press.

Lipset, Seymour Martin. 1959. "Some Social Requisites of Democracy: Economic Development and Political Legitimacy." *American Political Science Review* 53.

Murakami, Yasusuke. 1984. *The Age of the New Middle Masses.* Tokyo: Chuo Koron Sha.

Nolan, Peter. 1990. "China's New Development Path: Toward Capitalist Markets, Market Socialism or Bureaucratic Muddle?" In *The Chinese Economy and Its Future*, edited by P. Nolan & D. Fureng. Cambridge: Polity Press.

O'Donnell, Guillermo. 1973. *Modernization and Bureaucratic Authoritarianism.* Berkeley: University of California Press.

Przeworski, Adam. 1991. *Democracy and the Market: Political and Economic Reforms in Eastern Europe and Latin America.* London: Cambridge University Press.

Reed, Steven. 1994. "The Response of the Japanese Electorate to Scandal." IPSA World Congress Paper.

Rueschemeyer, D. and E. Stephens. 1992. *Capitalist Development and Democracy.* Chicago: University of Chicago Press.

Shoji, Kokichi. 1994. "Small Change Makes Big Change: Changing Japanese Life-Style and the Political Change." ASA Conference Paper.

Steinberg, David. 1995. "The Republic of Korea: Pluralizing Politics." In *Politics in Developing Countries: Comparing Experience with Democracy*, edited by Larry Diamond and Juan J. Linz. Boulder: Lynne Rienner Publishers.

Woo, Jung-en. 1991. *Race to the Swift: State and Finance in Korean Industrialization.* New York: Columbia University Press.

Zakaria, Fareed. 1994. "A Conversation with Lee Kuan Yew." *Foreign Affairs* (March/April): 109-126.

PART III

THE 1997 FINANCIAL CRISIS AND ECONOMIC RESTRUCTURING

Korea's 1997 Currency Crisis:
Causes and Implications

Jwa Sung-Hee & Huh Chan Guk

I. Introduction

By the mid-1990s, the Korean economy appeared to have leveled off, having reached a plateau of a high single-digit growth rate. As the world's 11th largest economy, Korea's newly found stature was officially acknowledged in 1996 when it became a member of the OECD. At the beginning of 1992, general inflation, measured in terms of the GDP deflator, stabilized at close to 5%. There was no real concern over the financial condition of the government as it had generally maintained a balanced budget over the years. A current account deficit persisted but did not seem to be a cause for alarm. In fact, in the previous ten years, it had never risen beyond 5% of the GDP. These indicators were all

* Originally published in Vol. 38, No. 2 (Summer 1998).

Jwa Sung-Hee (Jwa, Seung-hui) is President of the Korea Economic Research Institute. He received his Ph.D. in Economics from University of California at Los Angeles in 1983. He has authored many books, including *Jinhwaronjeok jaebeol ron* (An Evolutionary Theory of the *Jaebeol*) (1998), *A New Paradigm for Korea's Economic Development: From Government Control to Market Economy* (Palgrave 2001), and *The Evolution of Large Corporations in Korea: A New-institutional Economics Perspective of the Chaebol* (Edgar Elgar, forthcoming). E-mail: shj@keri.org.

Huh Chan Guk (Heo, Chan-guk) is Director of Macroeconomic Studies at the Korean Economic Research Institute. The theme of his doctoral dissertation was "Money, Monetary Policy and Behavior of Nominal Variables in Real Business Cycles" (Ph.D in Economics, University of California at Santa Barbara, 1989). He has authored "Risk and Returns of Financial-Industrial Interaction: The Korean Experience" (co-authored) (1998) and "Expectations, Credibility, and Disinflation in a Small Macroeconomic Model" (1998), etc. E-mail: chan.huh@keri.org.

drawn from key Korean macroeconomic data until the end of 1996.

Throughout the early 1990s, many had viewed Korea's experience of state-led economic growth as a development model success story in which the government could play a more important role in making resource allocation decisions vis-à-vis markets. However, the situation started to deteriorate rapidly in 1997. The speed with which foreign exchange liquidity problems reached crisis proportions caught many of us by surprise. Beneath the placid surface, some potentially serious structural imbalances had been building up over time. The lack of a self-regulating price mechanism was a fundamental cause of some of these problems. Lack of competition in goods markets gave rise to inefficiency in the corporate sector. Scarce bank credit was used as a key inducement and was made available inexpensively to businesses entering industries targeted by government policy. A weak banking sector resulted. Prudent regulations took a backseat to the financing of industrialization. One immediate consequence was lending concentration; another was a heavy reliance on cheap foreign short-term capital. Even allowing for overreactions by foreign investors, the ground was fertile for the liquidity problem to bloom into a full-blown crisis.

The objective of this article is to provide a systematic account and analysis of the recent development in and outside Korea rather than to merely compare data against a particular theoretical model. In our judgment, any shortcomings that arise from not using a specific frame of reference are adequately compensated for by the benefits of offering general descriptions and analyses of the key factors underlying the evolution of the recent crisis.

We provide an overview of the key structural as well as cyclical issues using anecdotes, descriptive statistics, and a time series Vector Error Correction Model (VECM) of nominal wages, labor productivity, and inflation. In particular, we contend that Korea's strong-won foreign exchange policy deserves a large portion of the blame. In addition, we examine cyclical and short-term Korean macroeconomic and external developments in 1996 and 1997.

Our use of the VECM model is for a purely descriptive purpose, and in this way, our work differs from some recent work by Korean authors. For example, Yi and Yi (1998) employ a stylized model of key macro variables to ask whether the foreign exchange crisis could have been predicted based on a set of macro variables and external conditions. In our view, a stylized macro model is not rich enough to incorporate the various structural imbalances that contributed to the breakout of the 1997 crisis. To the extent that the problems are microeconomic in nature, a model that focuses on macroeconomic variables is unlikely to be adequate.

As for the primary immediate causes of the crisis, it is our opinion that the collection of measures taken by the Korean government in 1997 triggered the blowout rather than any one particular policy measure implemented during the second half of the year. Some Korean authors have focused on finding the key catalyst event for the crisis in late 1997. For example, Bak and Yi (1998) point to the Korean government's blanket guarantee of deposits and interest on all deposits at all financial institutions including technically insolvent ones in October of 1997. Some point to the effective nationalization of the failed Kia Motors and the subsequent downgrading of the credit ratings of the Korea Development Bank's papers by Moody's. The KDB papers, carrying the *de facto* sovereign rating of Korea, were traded in international capital markets.

But our view is that under the circumstances faced by the Korean economy, nothing short of a complete removal of the exchange rate band sometime in early 1997 could have made a difference. The crucial factors were the structural background, the Korean government's insistence on the strong-won policy until early 1997, and the breakout of the ASEAN crisis in the summer of 1997.

Aside from reasons related to the rapid movement of the international capital flow, both structural as well as cyclical causes for the recent crisis also exist. Understanding these factors and how they contributed to the crisis will be invaluable to both policymakers and academics here and abroad. The next crisis will almost certainly be of a different variety. Nonetheless, a clear understanding of this one can only help us in preparing for the next one.

The rest of the paper is organized as follows: Section II provides a brief sketch of what happened in Korean financial markets in the latter part of 1997. In Section III, we present an overview of key structural issues. Section IV examines more cyclical and short-term Korean macroeconomic and external developments in 1996 and 1997. In Section V, we employ a time series Vector Error Correction Model (VECM) of nominal wage, labor productivity, and inflation to add some quantitative content to the question of the effect of the strong exchange rate on inflation. In Sections VI and VII we offer some assessments of the post-IMF intervention period and the dilemma facing Korean policymakers. Section VIII presents our conclusions.

II. A Quick Glance at the Crisis

This section sketches the key events in Korean financial markets during the latter part of 1997. The single most important development in the period leading up to Korea's financial crisis was the currency crisis among the ASEAN countries in mid-1997. The focus of the international capital market naturally shifted towards what was seen as the next set of vulnerable economies, i.e., the four first-generation tigers (Hong Kong, Singapore, Taiwan, and Korea) which had potential exchange rate misalignments. Beginning in August 1997, international investors started to probe these countries for "quick profit" opportunities. Already beset by a series of bankruptcies of large firms that started early in the year, Korea appeared particularly susceptible to trouble.

The uneasiness felt by international investors over the Korean situation manifested itself in several ways. After hovering near 750 in June and July, the KOPIX (stock price index) started to fall rapidly in September. It reached a nadir of 350.7 on December 12. This falling trend more or less reflected a large-scale exit by foreign investors. Foreign investment in the Korean equity market shrank rapidly by about $1 billion in November alone.

Beginning in November, Korean banks began to face severe difficulties in rolling over their short-term foreign borrowings. The roll-over rate fell from about 80% in October to close to 50% in November, then to about 30% in December. Korean banks faced the worst in December when only about 30% of their foreign counterparts agree to extend credit on an on going basis. The extension of short-term credit to Korean financial institutions fell to about $46 billion from the 1996 level of $65 billion. It fell even further to $29 billion in December 1998. Such a constriction of foreign credit accompanied an accelerated downgrading of Korea's credit rating, as shown in Table 1.

Table 1. Rapid Deterioration in Credit Ratings

	Oct. 23 '97	Nov. 25 '97	Dec. 11 '97	Dec. 23 '97	Feb. 17 '98
Standard and Poor's	AA⁻	A⁻	BBB⁻	B⁺	BB⁺

The exchange value of the Korean won started to fall precipitously in late 1997. The dollar/won rate fell by 11.4% and 44% in November and December, respectively. Concurrently, the daily exchange band within which the exchange rate was allowed to fluctuate was widened from 2.25% to 10% in the second half of November. This band was abandoned altogether in mid-December. Foreign exchange authorities started to intervene in the foreign exchange market from early 1997 to prevent a rapid fall in the exchange rate, expending a substantial amount of foreign exchange reserves. The usable reserve level fell below $10 billion by late November (Table 2).

Table 2. Shortage of Foreign Exchange Reserves

(Unit: $ billion)

	Jan. '97	Sep. '97	Nov. '97	Dec. '97	Jan. '98	Mar. '98
Total reserves	31	30.4	24.4	20.4	23.5	29.7
Held at overseas branches	(3.8)	(8.0)	(16.9)	(11.3)	(11)	5.6
Usable amount	27	22.4	7.3	8.9	12.4	24.1

Together, these developments raised the real prospect of a debt moratorium to both domestic as well as international observers. Such a perception added to the urgency of foreign and domestic investors in their stampede to exit from won holdings. To avert a crisis, the Korean government made a request for IMF financial aid on November 21. The IMF intervened and extended the first installment of its financial commitment, a $10 billion emergency loan, on 24 December 1997.

III. Structural and Long-term Factors

Unfortunately, there were a number of long-term structural problems that provided fertile ground for the seeds of the recent crisis. Bolstered by the success of a government-led growth strategy starting in the 1960s, key economic players—government, businesses, academia—took active government intervention to be most suitable path for Korea. A similar experience in Japan during the rapid growth period also provided a useful benchmark. As in many other areas, both the foreign exchange supply and demand (quantity) as well as the exchange rate (price) were heavily regulated. The obvious and direct legacy of such a history has been the lack of a self-correcting price mechanism. Key factors will be reviewed in turn.

First, Korea relied on foreign borrowing by the government or banks rather than foreign direct investment (FDI) for its industrialization. Foreign borrowing has been necessary as growth in investment almost always outpaced domestic saving. For some reason, little emphasis was placed on inward foreign direct investment. Table 3 and Figure 1 show some relevant data that indicate the extent to which Korea relied on foreign direct investment in relation to other sources to finance the industrialization effort. Table 3 shows, in terms of both absolute size as well as the proportion to gross domestic capital formation, that, the FDI has actually been quite modest. This has been the case even when compared to other Asian economies at different stages of development. For example, in proportion to the overall size of capital formation, FDI measured up to about 1% or less for six consecutive years after 1990. In Indonesia, which ranked just above Korea in terms of reliance on foreign direct investment, FDI made up 2.8 to 8.5% of overall capital formation. In comparison, the ratio ranged from 12.1 to 26% in Malaysia. FDI in Korea was similarly minimal in the 1980s. According to Figure 1, Korea's outward direct investment overtook inward investment in the 1988-1989 period. Figure 1 also shows that FDI has been dwarfed by external debt in Korea. The right-hand scale, which measures the external debt, is about 30 times the left-hand scale that measures FDI.

At the same time, tight control has been imposed on corporate borrowing from abroad.[1] This placed excess demand on bank funds, which

---

1. It is interesting to note that blocking the Korean corporate sector from borrowing directly from international financial institutions had a distinct drawback that has been overlooked. Typically, large international financial institutions have to justify their lending decisions based on an objective analysis of creditworthiness. This means asking many questions about the prospective projects, general level of financial obligations, profitability of the project to be funded, etc. In comparison, Korean businesses did not have to answer many of these questions when they dealt with Korean banks. Thus, the policy that blocked corporate sector's direct foreign borrowing might have had more adverse consequences than benefits envisioned when the restriction was initially put into place.

*Table 3. Ratio of FDI Flows to Gross Fixed Capital Formation
in the Asian Countries Most Affected by the Financial Crisis, 1990-1996*

(Unit: %)

Country	1990	1991	1992	1993	1994	1995	1996
Indonesia	2.8	3.6	3.9	4.3	3.8	6.7	8.5
Republic of Korea	0.8	1.0	0.6	0.5	0.6	1.1	1.3
Malaysia	16.8	23.8	26.0	22.5	15.9	12.1	13.2
Philippines	5.2	6.0	2.1	9.6	10.5	9.0	7.3
Thailand	7.1	4.9	4.8	3.6	2.3	2.8	3.2
Memorandum:							
South, East and South-East Asia	4.0	3.9	4.5	6.5	7.3	7.3	8.2

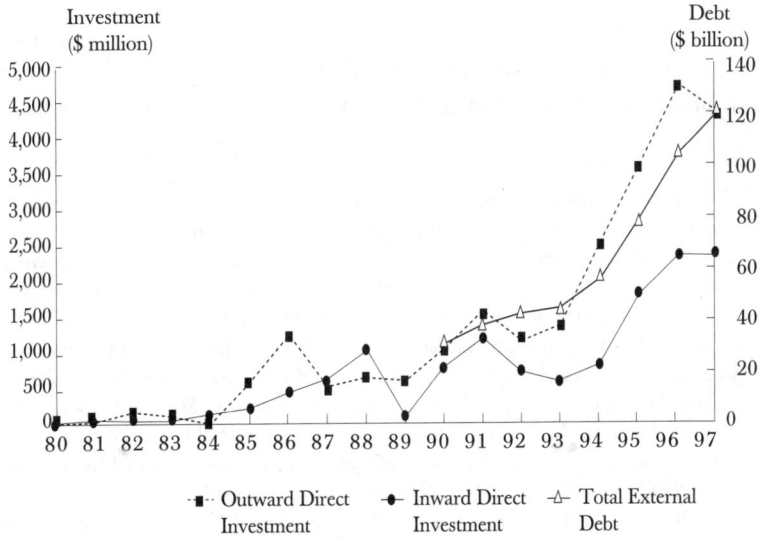

Figure 1. Outward direct investment (left scale), inward direct
investment (left scale), total external debt (right scale)

in turn pushed banks to borrow from abroad. Also, since the early 1990s, the Korean government has adopted policies that discourage long-term borrowing, leaving banks no alternative other than to rely heavily on short-term foreign borrowing.[2] These circumstances led to the accumulation of a large stock of foreign debt and a vulnerable foreign liability structure.

Second, the strong industrial policy pursued by the government for several decades has left clear marks on the Korean industrial organization. Using easy credit as the main inducement, the Korean government encouraged businesses to participate in sectors it favored. The push for heavy and chemical industries up to the early 1980s is the most well-known example. This policy regime has fostered the growth of large corporations engaged in many lines of business. It paid to get into industrial areas favored by the government regardless of the immediate difficulties, such as a lack of know-how or related experience. Such a policy led to a monopolistic or oligopolistic market structure. The resulting industrial organization structure tended to reduce competition among businesses in the product market which in turn fostered inefficiency in many Korean firms.[3]

Third, a key consequence of the government's close involvement in directing bank credit has been a weak Korean banking sector. Other than banks, businesses had few alternative domestic funding sources

---

2. For example, financial institutions needed to clear a much higher level of bureaucratic permission to raise long-term funds opposed to raising short-term funds.

3. It is difficult to quantitatively capture this conjecture in a succinct way. However, one could use indicators of firm concentration in a particular industry as a proxy for the degree of competition. One such measure is the so-called "concentration ratio of k," denoted as CR, which measures the share held by k largest firms in a particular product market. For example, CR4 for the soft drink market measures the share of the four largest firms in the soft drink market. According to Shepherd (1982), about 76% of GNP in the U.S. was produced by industries with CR4 of less than 40% until 1980. In comparison, only about 44% of Korea's GDP were produced by industries with the CR3 of less than 40% (Hwang 1998). According to another study on Korea's market concentration, over 87% of markets for manufactured products exhibited the CR3 over 50% in 1980, but the ratio slightly declined to 76% in 1994 (Kim and Yi 1997). There are different views regarding the relationship between market structure and economic efficiency. The fact that only a small number of firms are present in a particular market does not necessarily lead to economic concentration in which few dominant firms exhibit rent-seeking behavior. For a more detailed discussion of this issue in Korean setting, see Hwang (1998).

such as equity and bond markets. Nonetheless, the impetus to expand has remained strong, and hence, they turned to banks for funds. The Korean government-controlled interest rates charged by banks were kept artificially low until a few years ago, making bank funds even more attractive. Consequently, the demand for bank funds has been very strong since the early development period. In addition, a double-digit inflation rate was not uncommon during the past three decades.[4] Taken together, these conditions gave rise to high domestic interest rates and a high reliance on bank funds by Korean businesses.

Another manifestation of the imbalance between banks and non-financial industries is the comparative positions of each type of business in its respective global market. In 1997, 13 Korean firms including two insurance companies made the *Fortune* 500 list of the world's largest firms. On the other hand, the top Korean bank was ranked in 136th place overall in terms of strength in *The Banker*'s list of 1,000 largest banks in the same year. This bank's global ranking in terms of asset size was 186th. As a consequence of such disproportionate growth in the banking and non-banking sectors, it is quite conceivable for an average industrial project to become too large for the bank's capital. Under such conditions, banks become more vulnerable to the potential business failure of a non-banking sector. Some authors attribute the currency crisis to this weakness in the banking system.[5]

Fourth, the industry-bank nexus discussed above also might have been the key factor behind the high leverage ratio seen in the Korean corporate sector. When there is a plentiful provision of bank funds at concessionary interest rates for those setting foot into the industries targeted by government policies, it is rational to load up on as much cheap credit as possible. This directly translates into expanding the overall size of business operations above and beyond the level that might be justified by the prevailing cost of funds in an open market. Such an environment might have determined the initial conditions of the corporate financial structure, conditions which have persisted ever since. The resulting pat-

---

4. Inflation reduces the real value of the debt burden on the debtor. The Korean corporate sector benefited from high inflation in the past since a high leverage ratio has been common to most large businesses.

5. For a comprehensive discussion of international comparisons, see Kaminsky and Reinhart (1996). For further discussion of the Korean banking sector, see Jwa and Huh (1998).

tern of corporate financing would require an ongoing supply of funds with low costs to sustain. By pursuing one industrial policy after another (eg. heavy and chemical industries in the 1970s and "high-tech" industries in the 1990s), the government has continued to provide new sources of subsidy. However, the more direct forms of government subsidy have been gradually phased out, thus increasing the financing burdens on the Korean corporate sector. In some senses, the series of bankruptcies in early 1997 may have been taken as a strong signal that the state was ready to withdraw from the close industry-state relationship of the past. This might have set off the alarm to investors regarding the viability and sustainability of many firms, which in turn provided yet another reason to depart from the Korean equity market.

Fifth, we turn to labor market issues. Rapid industrialization and a broadening in the scope of economic activity led to a high demand for labor which naturally resulted in a general shortage of labor. The wage level came under heavy pressure. This was particularly noticeable in the late 1980s when organized labor gained power in the wake of the Korean government's abandonment of its long-standing anti-labor union posture. This step was taken as part of a comprehensive liberalization of democratic political activities. Upward wage pressures continued to increase in the early 1990s. On average, the overall wage level rose by 12.8% over the 1992-1996 period, while the average consumer price index (CPI) inflation rate was 5.3%. These figures imply an average real wage growth rate of 7 to 8%. It is difficult to believe that there were efficiency-induced productivity spurts of that magnitude per year in the same period. It turns out that a rapid accumulation of capital during the same period could account for a good part of the increase in labor productivity.

In addition, the growing influence of unions added to a rigid labor market. In 1987, the number of labor strikes surged to 3,749 after averaging less than 300 until then. The increasing influence and militancy of unions made the layoffs of workers more difficult. The continuing practice of lifetime employment also contributed to the problem of low job mobility. Combined, these factors gave rise to high labor costs (see Table 4 for an international comparison).[6, 7]

---

6. There is a strong positive correlation between the size of firms (in terms of number of workers) and the degree of union formation. For example, for firms with 100 to 999 workers, the union organization rate which measures the proportion of work-

Table 4. International Comparison of Factor Costs

				(Unit: %)
Wage (manufacturing '87–'94)	3.0	1.2	5.4	16.2
Land (factory, $/m², '95)	5-10	195.6	48.4	226.8
Borrowing rate of interests ('95)	8.5	4.3	6.2	11.7

Sixth, while there have been sporadic attempts to address the problems mentioned so far, especially since the early 1990s, they have all failed. Persistently high domestic costs started to erode the competitiveness of Korean exports. Some observers also point to a lack of new product lines to overcome cost disadvantages as another factor for the loss of competitiveness. One way that businesses responded to the declining competitiveness was to relocate manufacturing facilities to low-wage Southeast Asian countries, as well as to China. Many firms in the light manufacturing sectors reacted this way. The rapid rise in outward FDI shown in Figure 1 appears to reflect such a movement by light manufacturing firms. An increase in exports to Southeast Asian countries was another manifestation of the weakening of export competitiveness. For example, the proportion of exports to Asian countries to the total Korean exports rose from 10.2% in 1991 to 15.5% in 1996. While this could be interpreted as a diversification in the destinations of exports, the fact that the total exports to the U.S. (and other advanced countries) has

---

places with organized unions is about 30%. The unionization rate jumps to 76% for firms with more than 15,000 workers in 1993. Unions at large firms in general tend to be more militant. One interesting explanation focuses on Korean industrial organization. As mentioned earlier, large firms faced an inelastic demand in the goods market due to a monopolistic or oligopolistic industrial structure. This, in turn, increased the margin for rent-sharing behavior on the part of the employees. There is also some evidence suggesting a presence of a "large" firm premium. In the late 1980s, wage increases were more rapid for employees of large firms compared to wages for employees of smaller firms (Kim and Yi 1997).

7. An interesting survey on worker overhang was conducted by the Korea Employers Federation in 1997 using a sample of 233 firms with over 100 employees. 37.5% of responding firms with 1,000 or more workers said that they have too many workers. Respondents pointed to mid- to upper-level management rank as the most saturated. About 80% of firms respondeding that they have too many workers also indicated that they need to reduce employment by 5-15% to achieve the appropriate level (KEF 1997).

declined suggests a less favorable interpretation. The net effect was a deterioration in international competitiveness and terms of trade. Subsequently, current account deficits started to grow.[8]

Seventh, more directly related to the recent crisis was the foreign exchange rate policy. Since the early 1990s, the Korean foreign exchange authorities have pursued a strong-won policy. The two main reasons for this stance were to achieve domestic price stability and to encourage a shift in the composition of exports to more high value-added items by removing the simple price advantage due to a weak won.[9] Both goals were reasonable in that they aimed at addressing some of the problems explained earlier. However, with the benefit of 20-20 hindsight, the standpoint of policymakers turned out to have been too rigid. Unfortunately, market pressures for the won depreciation were partly deflected by increases in capital inflow that followed capital flow liberalization measures taken since the early 1990s. Table 5 shows our estimates of an equilibrium won/$ exchange rate and the extent of the won overvaluation.

Another key factor that contributed to the foreign exchange policy complacency was the strengthening trend in the yen/dollar exchange rate following the 1985 Plaza Accord. After rising from 239 yen per dollar in 1985 to 168 yen per dollar in 1986, the yen continued to strengthen against the dollar and reached a peak of 284 in the second quarter of 1995. Such a strong yen enhanced the price competitiveness of Korean exports competing against goods made in Japan. Many firms in heavy and chemical industries as well as semiconductor manufacturers enjoyed a period of robust export growth. Largely aided by the strong yen, Korea experienced a current account surplus for four years running starting in 1986.

---

8. A factor that might have negatively affected the profitability of businesses is the high cost of the transportation and distribution of goods. Surface road transportation made up some 50 to 70% of the total physical distribution in a typical year in the early 1990s. By some estimates, the distribution cost in Korea was about 15% of the Korean GDP in 1993, compared to 10% in the U.S. Basically, poor and congested road conditions due to little investment in social infrastructures over a prolonged period and increased traffic appear to have raised distribution costs in Korea.

9. Some policymakers viewed this as a very important issue for improving Korea's competitiveness in the long term.

Table 5. Real Effective Exchange Rate

	Actual Rate (A)	Real Effective Rate	PPP-based Equilibrium Rate (B)	A-B
1986.12	864.49	104.32	828.68	35.81
1987.12	794.74	104.19	762.78	31.96
1988.12	685.03	88.03	778.18	-93.15
1989.12	675.17	81.90	824.38	-149.21
1990.12	715.75	87.29	820.01	-104.26
1991.12	757.28	87.63	864.20	-106.92
1992.12	788.62	88.67	889.34	-100.72
1993.12	809.40	89.78	901.56	-92.16
1994.12	791.86	87.52	904.78	-112.92
1995.12	771.08	83.74	920.77	-149.69
1996.12	839.02	86.46	970.46	-131.44
1997.03	896.20	88.92	1007.82	-111.62
1997.06	889.49	89.62	992.47	-102.98
1997.11	1035.22	96.76	1069.84	-34.62
1997.12	1494.04	134.77	1108.56	385.48
1998.01	1707.3	149.10	1145.01	562.28
1998.03	1489.26	133.14	1118.59	370.67
1998.05	1399.05	119.30	1172.69	226.36

Notes: The real effective exchange rate index (REERI) is obtained with the formula below, where i means i'th country among Korea's 16 major trading partners, St is the foreign currency price in terms of Korean won at period t, and Pt means the price level at t and superscript k means Korea's variable. Korea's 16 major trading partners include Australia, Canada, Taiwan, France, Germany, Hong Kong, Indonesia, Italy, Japan, Malaysia, Netherlands, Singapore, Thailand, United States, United Kingdom, and China.

REEI $= \Sigma [((Sit/Si0) \times ((Pit/Pi0))/(Pkt/Pk0)] \times 100$

Source: Korean Economic Research Institute.

IV. Cyclical and Short-term Macroeconomic and External Factors

In addition to the structural issues discussed above, there was a set of medium- and short-term cyclical policy developments building up to the recent crisis. Starting with the cyclical factors, the most recent cyclical peak in output growth was reached in late 1995. However, in some senses, the Korean economy has not really recovered from the extended slowdown that started in 1987. There were identifiable sources for the two subsequent upturns seen in 1989 and 1993 (Figure 2). The first one could be attributed to the stimulative government policy drive to add two million new housing units, which was a key campaign commitment.[10] For example, the construction sector's real output grew at the rate of about 15% for a five-year period starting in 1987. In comparison, it had averaged about 5% in the previous three years.

The second upturn can be explained mostly by a steady pickup in semiconductor exports. Aiding the 1993 upturn was the Japanese yen's appreciation that lasted until 1995. Also, due to healthy economic conditions in many G-7 countries, especially in the U.S., demands for imports were strong.

In late 1995, macroeconomic conditions started to deteriorate once again due to the ever-worsening terms of trade (see Table 6). Conditions in the external sector turned unfavorable and the current account bal-

Figure 2. Real GDP growth rate (four quarter moving average)

---

10. Though the Korean government did not expend any of its budget on building housing units, policy measures were taken to facilitate such goals. For example, land for new construction projects was readily made available. As a result, several new medium-size satellite cities that house about half a million each were constructed around the Seoul metropolitan area.

Table 6. Terms of Trade

	Unit Value of Export	Unit Value of Import	Terms of Trade
'95	100.0	100.0	100.0
'96	86.6	98.8	87.7
'97 1/4	77.8	98.6	78.9
2/4	76.3	93.5	81.6
3/4	75.1	97.1	77.3
4/4	69.0	96.7	71.3
'97	74.5	96.5	77.2

*base year 1995=100.0.
Source: Bank of Korea and Korea Economic Research Institute.

ances started to deteriorate. Although the situation was not as serious as in the ASEAN countries, the Chinese yuan's devaluation in 1993-1994 was also a negative factor for Korea's exports. The yen started to depreciate against the U.S. dollar in 1995, eroding the competitiveness of Korean exports. In addition, starting in 1996, the price of semiconductors that made up almost a quarter of the total Korean exports started to fall dramatically. For example, the price of a 16 DRAM chip fell from $50.6 in 1995 to $3 in February 1998. Also, during the period leading up to 1997, imports of both consumption as well as capital goods increased rapidly. This was a by-product of the strong-won policy which made imports inexpensive. Consequently, the current account deficit widened to 4.9% of the GDP in 1996 from 1.4% in 1995.

As shown in Table 7, the pace of short-term capital inflow has noticeably quickened in 1994. After remaining below 45% until 1994, the proportion of short-term debts started to increase and exceeded 60% of the total external debts by 1997. Such a shortening of the average debt maturity made the Korean economy's debt structure vulnerable to distresses associated with the rapid movements of foreign capital.

Moreover, Korean businesses continued to rely heavily on debt financing. For example, the average leverage ratio for the 30 largest businesses in 1996 was 387%. Thus, the resulting heavy debt service burden not only depressed profitability but also exposed the corporate sector to potentially serious cash-flow problems. Sluggish export growth after 1995 started to put a damper on the profitability of firms as shown in Table 8.

Table 7. Details of Korea's Total External Liabilities

(Unit: $ billion)

	End of 1996	End of Nov. '97	End of Dec. '97	End of Apr. '98
Long-term debts	57.5	72.9	86.0	113.3
Short-term debts	100.0	88.9	68.4	41.9
Total	157.5	161.8	154.4	155.2

Notes: The difference between the total debts between the IMF standard and World Bank standard is $33.6 billion in Dec. 1997. The IMF standards includes the offshore financing of the head office ($17.8 bil.) and overseas branches ($15.8 bil.) of domestic financial institutions, which has been employed in overseas limitedly.
Source: Ministry of Finance and Economy.

Table 8. Listed Firms' Profits in First Half of Recent Years

(Unit: billion won, %)

	1995	1996	1997
Salves (Y-over-Y change)	25.46	18.60	14.22
Net profit (Y-over-Y change)	42.05	−40.22	−28.45

Starting in early 1997, there was a string of failures of some well-known businesses. The Hanbo Group topped the list with its sudden demise in January 1997, and then Sammi Steel failed in March 1997, with the Kia Group following in September 1997. These events heightened concerns about the short-term prospects for the Korean corporate sector in general. Banks' exposure to the failed firms through lending concentration led to a rapid deterioration in the soundness of the banking sector (Jwa and Huh 1998). According to official statistics, the proportion of Korean banks' non-performing loans to total loans rose from 3.9% at the end of 1996 to 6.6% by September 1997. For the two banks that were most severely affected, the non-performing loan ratios rose from 6.7% and 9.3% at the end of 1996 to 17% and 15% by September 1997 respectively.

Such deteriorating conditions among the Korean banks were obviously a real cause for concern in international capital markets. One immediate effect was the cutback in credit extensions to overseas branches of Korean banks by international financial institutions. This in turn forced the Korean foreign exchange authorities to use official foreign exchange reserves to ease financing difficulties experienced by the overseas branches of Korean banks (see Table 2). Cutbacks in credit extensions continued towards the end of 1997. This was a special factor that served to exacerbate the currency crisis towards the end of 1997.

Roughly concurrent with these domestic developments, foreign exchange market instabilities in the ASEAN countries developed into a full-blown currency crisis. Some spillover, if not a full contagion, of the crises in the ASEAN countries to Korea was inevitable. Doubts about the sustainability of the exchange rate regime did indeed rise, and capital outflow from the region followed. Such an environment induced both a perceived and a real foreign exchange crisis.[11]

Pressures on the won exchange rate continued from the beginning of 1997. One clear indication of a potential misalignment was the growing gap between the rates in the on-shore market and the off-shore forward market. At times, the off-shore won/dollar exchange rate exceeded the on-shore rate by close to 30%. However, the foreign exchange authorities resisted these pressures with vigor. The Korean foreign exchange authorities appeared to have successfully resisted the devaluation pressure by late spring of 1997.

Nevertheless, the downward pressures intensified with the outbreak of the ASEAN crisis in July. Korean foreign exchange authorities continued to expend foreign exchange reserves to defend and/or slow down the depreciation of the won. Their efforts were decidedly unsuccessful and a rapid depletion of foreign exchange reserves resulted, as shown in Table 2. The pace of capital outflow quickened, and the downward pressures on the won became inescapable due to dwindling foreign exchange reserves. The prospect of the failure to meet external obligations became real. The IMF intervention took place as this realization started to spread widely.

---

11. See Choe (1998) for a comprehensive overview of the external developments in the period leading up to Korea's crisis.

V. Quantitative Analysis of the Role of the Strong Exchange Rate

Here, we attempt to add more quantitative content to the key issue of the strong exchange value of the Korean won. Our approach is to estimate a time series model of nominal wage, labor productivity, and inflation in the general price level using data since the 1970s as a benchmark. Once we establish the baseline model, we can then examine the question of how unusual the behavior of those variables in the recent period has been. We also gauge whether or not some of the factors discussed in the previous section could account for the unusual behavior in those variables included in the model.

The baseline model consists of the nominal total compensation (nominal wage), output per hour (labor productivity), and the consumer price index (inflation). The setup is motivated by a well-founded hunch that real wage and labor productivity move together, that is, that they have a cointegrating relationship over the long term.[12] Based on this, the real wage could be separated into two components: the nominal wage and the price level. Hence, they make up the three variable system of the Vector Error Correction Model. Table 9 shows the estimation results of the baseline model using data from the two sample periods of 1975Q1-1987Q4, and 1975Q1-1996Q4.[13]

Table 9 shows that the model does much better in explaining inflation in the CPI and nominal wages than in explaining productivity. This is intuitive because one can expect a closer correlation between wages and inflation than between either one with productivity. Hence, it is reasonable to expect a simple model of the three variables to exhibit the pattern as seen in Table 9.

It is interesting to note that the error correction term significantly

---

12. We follow the reasoning and application of a VECM model to U.S. data by Huh and Trehan (1995). The data used were: total compensation (including benefits), total output divided by total hours, and the consumer price index for nominal wages, productivity, and prices, respectively. Series were logged first then adjusted by multiplying by constant numbers to scale them to be comparable to each other. Growth rates were calculated by first differencing each series.

13. The first sample period was chosen based on the discussion given in the previous section regarding the late 1980s. Namely, there was a clearly identifiable shift in the social and political environment in Korea.

Table 9. Vector Error Correction Model
of Nominal Wage, Consumer Price Index, and Output per Hour

Variables	(Sample 1975:1 – 1987:4)			(Sample 1975:1 – 1996:4)		
	ΔCPH	ΔPDF	ΔOPH	ΔCPH	ΔPDF	ΔOPH
Constant	0.04 (1.55)	**0.028** **(1.96)**	**0.03** **(2.34)**	**0.07** **(4.92)**	–0.00 (–0.09)	0.01 (1.70)
ΔCPH t–1	**–0.71*** **(–2.19)**	**–0.49** **(–2.62)**	–0.12 (–0.79)	**–0.40** **(–3.06)**	0.66 (0.85)	0.13 (1.96)
ΔCPH t–2	–0.03 (–0.10)	–0.28 (–1.42)	0.04 (0.25)	–0.10 (–0.67)	0.15 (1.59)	**0.14** **(1.86)**
ΔCPH t–3	**0.48** **(1.70)**	–0.26 (–1.65)	0.11 (0.84)	0.14 (0.97)	0.06 (0.65)	0.11 (1.48)
ΔCPH t–4	0.11 (0.50)	0.08 (0.66)	0.05 (0.50)	0.13 (1.07)	0.12 (1.60)	0.09 (1.38)
ΔPDF t–1	**–0.45** **(–1.71)**	–0.00 (–0.05)	–0.06 (–0.54)	–0.15 (–0.79)	0.15 (1.31)	0.02 (0.20)
ΔPDF t–2	**0.52** **(1.97)**	0.21 (1.38)	0.08 (0.64)	**0.51** **(2.64)**	**0.39** **(3.32)**	0.09 (0.95)
ΔPDF t–3	–0.00 (–0.00)	**0.32** **(2.12)**	0.08 (0.64)	–0.11 (–0.55)	0.20 (1.73)	0.05 (0.47)
ΔPDF t–4	0.16 (0.61)	0.18 (1.19)	0.03 (0.25)	0.20 (1.14)	–0.08 (–0.72)	–0.05 (–0.51)
ΔOPH t–1	0.22 (0.47)	**0.61** **(2.22)**	**–0.48** **(–2.13)**	–0.34 (–1.15)	0.03 (0.17)	**–0.51** **(–3.43)**
ΔOPH t–2	0.11 (0.20)	0.38 (1.23)	–0.24 (–0.96)	**–0.55** **(–1.70)**	–0.05 (–0.26)	–0.25 (–1.58)
ΔOPH t–3	–0.05 (–0.11)	0.21 (0.73)	–0.23 (–1.00)	**–0.59** **(–1.87)**	–0.12 (–0.63)	–0.22 (–1.44)
ΔOPH t–4	–0.34 (–0.85)	0.11 (0.47)	**0.02** **(2.34)**	**–0.79** **(–2.87)**	–0.02 (–0.12)	–0.10 (–0.77)
EC (–1)	0.18 (0.95)	**0.41** **(3.59)**	0.15 (1.63)	**–0.09** **(–3.74)**	–0.02 (–1.06)	–0.01 (–0.56)
R^2/adj.R^2	0.44 (0.22)	0.73 (0.63)	0.39 (0.15)	0.42 /0.31	0.59 /0.52	0.22 /0.07
S.E.E	0.05	0.03	0.02	0.04	0.03	0.02

ΔCPH : Growth rate in compensation for an hour
ΔPDF : Growth rate in consumer price index
ΔOPH : Growth rate in output per hour
EC (–1) : Error Correction Term
– EC (1975:1 1987:4) = CPH – 0.380449PDF – 1.239144OPH+0.003717
– EC (1975:1 1996:4) = CPH+1.312306PDF – 5.030434OPH – 0.731934
* Numbers in parentheses are t-statistics. Significant cases (5% or less) are given in bold.

enters first in the inflation equation for the first sample period, then in the wage equation in the second case. Such a shift suggests that the relationship between the nominal wage and the price index variables might have shifted since 1987. In terms of short-term dynamics, there is generally more interaction between the nominal wage and the CPI inflation than between either of the two and productivity.

Our intention is to use the model as a frame of reference to learn about potential misalignments in the Korean economy in the late 1980s as well as in the 1990s.

One way to capture unusual data patterns is to compare the model's forecast to actual data. For these, we use the model estimated from the 1975Q1-1996Q4 sample period to forecast one to four quarters ahead until 1996Q4. The top panel of Table 10 provides the forecast accuracy statistics for the model's inflation forecast. One clear pattern is that the model overpredicted the actual inflation. Since a forecast error is measured as actual minus forecast, minus signs on mean errors suggest this

Table 10. Forecast Accuracy Statistics
for One to Six Quarter Ahead Inflation (1988Q1 – 1996Q4)

Base Line Model

	Mean Errors	Mean Absolute Errors	Root Mean Square	Number of Observations
1 quarter ahead	−0.075	0.077	0.089	36
2 quarter ahead	−0.078	0.081	0.914	35
3 quarter ahead	−0.108	0.110	0.124	34
4 quarter ahead	−0.115	0.115	0.128	33
6 quarter ahead	−0.147	0.147	0.162	31

Model with Exchange Rate Variable

	Mean Errors	Mean Absolute Errors	Root Mean Square	Number of Observations
1 quarter ahead	−0.038	0.055	0.066	36
2 quarter ahead	−0.020	0.051	0.059	35
3 quarter ahead	−0.028	0.059	0.068	34
4 quarter ahead	−0.009	0.062	0.070	33
6 quarter ahead	0.002	0.063	0.072	31

point. This is not surprising given the rapid rise in nominal wages in the forecast period.

Also noticeable is the fact that mean errors and mean absolute errors have same magnitudes with the opposite sign. This is a clear indication of the model's overpredicting bias.

One conjecture from the above discussion is that the strong-won exchange rate has helped to keep inflation low despite the strong growth in wages. This can be examined by gauging the impact of adding an exchange rate variable in the model. The bottom panel of Table 10 compares the forecast accuracy measures from the model that includes the exchange rate variable. The variable used for this exercise is the difference between the actual won/dollar exchange rate and a purchasing power parity-based equilibrium exchange rate. Both are shown in Table 5. When they are compared to those shown in the top panel, the first striking contrast is that the mean errors are drastically smaller in the case with the exchange rate. For example, for the 6-quarter ahead forecast, the forecast error of the model with the exchange rate is about one-seventieth of that for the baseline case. Adding the exchange rate variable clearly reduces the model's tendency to over predict actual inflation. Furthermore, all forecast accuracy measures improve substantially. That is, the robust inflation record since the late 1980s can be explained by the strong exchange rate value of the Korean won.

VI. After the Crisis: Prognosis

The IMF stepped in with a "to do" list that prescribed a tightening of domestic credit conditions as well as stringent fiscal austerity. While a tight credit (monetary) policy is necessary for exchange market stability, it is not clear if it is indeed needed beyond the immediate period following the crisis. As discussed in the previous section, the current crisis had more to do with a collapse of international lenders' confidence in the Korean economy than with a balance of payment imbalance accompanied by a soaring domestic aggregate demand and rise in imports. Hence, a tight monetary and fiscal policy prescription might be desirable only to the extent that they help to calm the frayed nerves of foreign investors. The IMF's policy prescriptions can be better understood from the perspective of a creditor who is lending a sizable part of his scarce capital to a troubled debtor: the IMF has to make sure that it can recoup the financial resources committed to Korea on an emergency basis. To do that, one starts with the most conservative set of policy prescriptions implemented successfully many times before. Perhaps the past successes of this strategy figured more importantly to the decisionmakers than the feeling that the Korean crisis may have needed a different medicine from the one applied to the economies of various Latin American countries.

Various foreign exchange indicators suggest that the short-term external liquidity crunch is more or less over for the moment. The won/dollar exchange rate has remained stable around 1,400 won per dollar for several months (Table 5). Official foreign exchange reserves stood at $34.4 billion at the end of May. The total external debt is still quite large but with the successful completion of the debt renegotiation early this year, the average maturity of debt has been extended and Korean financial institutions are reporting little trouble in obtaining the roll-over of their foreign borrowing. Despite the apparent stability of the foreign exchange market, the Korean economy is still not out of the woods.

At present, the Korean economy is entering into uncharted territory. In particular, it has to implement many reform measures that were previously unthinkable in both the corporate and banking sectors. These are challenging tasks in ordinary times. However, the severity of the problem intensifies due to the fact that these are to be carried out in the face of an unprecedented and still rising unemployment rate.

A significant contraction in domestic aggregate demand appears to be underway. The unemployment rate has risen from the 1997 fourth quarter level of 2.8% to 5.3% in March of 1998. The consensus forecast is that this will rise in the immediate future as the structural adjustment of closing down some operations by banks and businesses begins in earnest. In the first quarter, industrial production and shipments each fell by close to 8%. A five percent contraction in inventories in the same period suggests that the reductions in industrial production and shipment are not temporary stock adjustments. Indicators for domestic investment this year are also plunging. The industrial production and orders for machinery respectively fell by 10 and 51% (year-over-year) in March. Both construction orders and building permit issuances fell by 20% in March. Most indicators for consumption, such as sales at both retail and wholesale levels, also fell by large amounts in the first quarter. The account balance exhibited a surplus of $107 billion in the first quarter. Both a moderate increase in exports (8.7%, on a year-over-year basis), and a sharp reduction in imports (−35.4%, on a year-over-year basis) have contributed to this surplus. However, continued cutbacks in imports do not bode well for a continued growth in exports. That is because raw materials for exports typically make up a good portion of imports. Thus, cutbacks in imports of raw material will lead to a lower export growth down the road.

The seriousness of this current situation is not helped by the fact that key Korean economic policy decisions have to be made jointly with the IMF. Beggars cannot be choosers. However, a strong case can be made to the IMF partner if Korean policymakers come to the conclusion that different policy priorities and prescriptions are needed to preserve the long-term viability of the Korean economy. Viewed from this perspective, it might be more desirable to think about how to tackle the problem at its roots.

The first priority should be to lower interest rates. In the absence of a large-scale debt write-off or a debt/equity swap that can drastically reduce the debt servicing burden borne by the Korean corporate sector, the current level of interest rates is not tenable. Second, the Korean government should be given room to use fiscal policy more flexibly. It is a general practice in advanced economies to make a clear distinction between cyclical and structural government deficits. For example, the Maastricht criteria for an acceptable level of budget deficit for the countries joining the European Monetary Union (EMU) was delineated in terms of the structural deficit. Hence, given current economic conditions in Korea, now is the time to rely on a deficit-financed fiscal policy.

VII. After the Crisis: Policy Dilemma

The basic dilemma is as follows: on the one hand, as discussed above, the crux of the structural problems underlying the current difficulties is that the Korean government has played an active role in all facets of economic life, leaving various market institutions weak. For too long, the government relied on its ability to direct or persuade banks and businesses. Hence, phasing the government out of its center stage role has to be the top priority. For example, it was the government which made long-term foreign borrowing more difficult, thus directly forcing Korean banks and businesses to rely mostly on short-term borrowing. This makes one wonder whether this kind of concentration on short-term debt might have resulted had the government completely refrained from attempting to control the external debt maturity structure.

On the other hand, however, current economic conditions might deteriorate too much, leading to a general breakdown of the economic and social order. In addition, there is a need for a responsible "monitor" who can ensure the implementation of genuine reform measures. The government might be the only player that can step in to moderate the speed as well as the magnitude of the economy's fall. These two considerations call for an active role to be played by the government. For example, the government has to decide how to address the banking sector's severe loan problems. Without substantive resolutions of the issue, putting troubled banks on the selling block will not attract any takers.

Deciding what to do and what not to do under these circumstances is not an easy task. At the same time, making a list of priorities is paramount. The highest priorities should be given to the following two issues: First, how to address the rising unemployment rate which, according to some forecasts, is expected to reach 10% or higher later this year. Koreans have not experienced such large-scale unemployment for over three decades. The fact that a good number of the disappearing jobs will be permanently cut adds to the insecurities and uncertainties already felt by workers. Enhancing labor market flexibility has been high on the wish list of many economists who study the Korean economy. So the current round of labor market turmoil could be the catalyst for a more flexible labor market in the future. At the same time, however, the severity of the unemployment problem could be so extreme that it could overtake all other economic issues.[14]

Second, the rehabilitation of the Korean banking sector needs to be treated as an urgent policy issue. The adverse impact of financial disintermediation is seriously worsening the degree of contraction in economic activity lately. The problem of how to dispose of the non-performing assets in the banks' books should command the immediate

---

14. It is imperative that the government establishes a minimum social safety net for the unemployed very soon. Otherwise, the growing size of the unemployment problem as well as attendant social unrest could well derail any effort to take a long-term view and address structural problems in a systematic fashion. Two general approaches are possible. One is the government taking the leading role in addressing the problem. The other is to delay structural adjustments in various private sectors of the economy to blunt the contractionary momentum. In our view, the imputed social costs over the long term would be minimized if the government takes the lead and raises financial resources to provide the necessary income support to the affected workers.

attention of policymakers since it is a problem that will only worsen. Only prompt and decisive corrective actions can restore domestic as well as international investors' confidence in the viability of the Korean banking sector and the government's ability to deal with difficult reforms.

VIII. Conclusion

Most macroeconomic indicators did not betray any signs that things were seriously wrong until the end of 1997. However, the situation started to deteriorate very rapidly indeed. Foreign exchange liquidity problems reached crisis proportions within several months. Among the probable causes, an element of overreaction on the part of foreign investors definitely existed. However, regardless of such a *modus operandi* of foreign capital, we need to put effort into implementing the structural reforms that are beneficial to the Korean economy in the long run. The recent experience has heightened awareness of the need to reform various segments of the Korean economy.

However, the cyclical and short-term economic conditions are deteriorating very rapidly. If the economic contraction is prolonged, the Korean government might not be able to implement the much needed reform measures due to mounting social and economic problems. Thus, from the standpoint of ensuring the successful implementation of structural reforms, efforts should be made to arrest the fall of the Korean economy.

Once the current crisis passes without inflicting too severe structural damage, one beneficial legacy will be the increased awareness among businesses, government, the press and the general public of the need to improve efficiency in all areas. Indeed, since the implementation of the IMF regime, Korea has undergone significant institutional transformations that would never have been enacted in the absence of such developments.

REFERENCES

Bak, Dae-gyun, and Yi Chang-yeong. 1998. "Hanguk-ui oehwan wigi: jeon-gae gwajeong-gwa gyohun" (Korea's Currency Crisis: Developments and Lessons). Mimeo.

Choe, Du-yeol. 1998. "Uri nara tonghwa wigi-ui balsaeng wonin: oebu hwan-gyeong-eul jungsim-euro" (The Causes of Korea's Currency Crisis: With Emphasis on External Environment). Working paper. Korea Economic Research Institute.

Huh, C., and B. Trehan. 1995. "Modeling the Time-Series Behavior of the Aggregate Wage Rate." *Economic Review* (Federal Reserve Bank of San Francisco) 1: 1-13.

Hwang, In-hak. 1998. "Sijang gujo-wa gyeongje hyoyul" (Market Structure and Economic Efficiency). Working paper. Korea Economic Research Institute.

Jwa, Sung-Hee, and C. Huh. 1998. "Risk and Returns of Financial-Industrial Interactions: The Korean Experience." Working paper. Korea Economic Research Institute.

Kaminsky, G., and C. Reinhart. 1996. "The Twin Crises: The Causes of Banking and Balance of Payments Problems." International Finance Discussion Paper, no. 544. Board of Governors of the Federal Reserve System.

Kim, Dae-il, and Yi Ju-ho. 1997. "Nosa gwan-gye gaehyeok-gwa nodong sijang byeonhwa" (Labor-Management Reforms and Changes in Korean Labor Market). *KDI Journal of Economic Policy* III: 5-60.

Korea Employers Federation (KEF), ed. 1997. *Gieop nae yuhyu illyeok mit myeongye toejik jedo-ui hyeonhwang-gwa gwaje* (The Status and Tasks of Redundancy and Early Retirement System in Firms).

Shepherd, W. G. 1982. "Causes of Increased Competition in the U.S. Economy, 1939-1980." *Review of Economics and Statistics* 64: 613-626.

Yi, Yeong-seop, and Yi Jong-uk. 1998. "Hanguk-ui oehwan wigi yecheuk ga-neung haenneun-ga?" (Was Korea's Currency Crisis Predictable?). Mimeo.

"The Global 500 List." *Fortune*, August 1997.

"The Top 1000 Banks." *The Banker*, July 1997.

Corporate Restructuring in Korea:
Experience and Lessons

Lee Jae-Woo

Introduction

The Korean bailout experience is unprecedented in many respects. Korea, once a forerunner among the newly industrializing countries (NICs), unexpectedly needed to be rescued by an IMF bailout fund and after a year and a half of painful struggle, has recently experienced an economic turnaround. The story of the Korean economy's record-breaking growth and its near collapse inevitably brings up innumerable questions on issues such as the efficacy of Korea's development strategy, or more generally, that of all Asian countries.[1]

So far, a number of speculative arguments have been raised among scholars and policymakers concerning the causes of this economic crisis. It is interesting to note that most emphasis has been placed on government-led growth characterized by industrial policies, nonmarket resource (especially finance) allocations, and the excessive debt financing practices of the corporate sector associated with irresponsible lenders. A deci-

---

* Originally published in Vol. 39, No. 3 (Autumn 1999).

Lee Jae-Woo (Yi, Jae-u) is Professor in the Economics Department of Dong-Eui University. Since receiving a Ph.D. in Economics at Texas A&M University in 1990, he has been engaged in studies on Korean *jaebeol*, economic institutions, and economics of law (particularly, antitrust economics). He has published a number of books including *Gieop gyeolhap-gwa gongjeong georae jeongchaek* (M&A and Antitrust Policy in Korea) (1999).

1. See Jwa (1998) and Yoo (1999) for good reviews on competing hypotheses on why the Korean economy collapsed. They summarize tentative hypotheses on the Korean economic crisis from domestic scholars and foreign economic specialists. E-mail: jaewoo@hyomin.dongeui.ac.kr.

sive conclusion about the validity of these arguments has yet to be reached.

The bailout fund for Korea is the first of its type among the NICs, for which the IMF had no experience. Therefore, the IMF's recommendations for Korea, both micro and macro level, continue to be critically evaluated for their effectiveness. This is because Korea's economic environment is significantly different from those of Latin American countries such as Chile and Brazil. The traditional belt-tightening and high interest policies—perhaps reasonable in debt-ridden countries—might not be appropriate for Korea, which is suffering from a high level of private sector debt. Routine policy recommendations by international agencies such as the IMF and the World Bank might produce many side effects, "over-killing" the economy and its corporate players. These "traditional" approaches are arguably not always the best and should be tailored to fit each country's institutional and societal needs.

Korea, once a model for developing economies, is struggling to recover and is experiencing inevitable discontinuities in every field. To paraphrase North (1990), the "relative price" system of the whole society is being fundamentally shifted, which in turn severely impacts all institutions, organizations, and economic players.

To initiate corporate restructuring, the government has launched a rather aggressive corporate reform package backed by the IMF and other international agencies (see Table 1). Some noteworthy measures include the prohibition of cross-guarantees and the introduction of consolidated financial statements. While it is undeniable that the government has made much progress in reforming the corporate (especially the *jaebeol*) governance structure in this area, nevertheless, the government has adopted some highly interventionist policies. For example, formally or informally, it has pushed forward business swaps among *jaebeol* and has advocated the 200% debt-to-equity ratio policy. This policy produced many negative side effects such as the infringement of the property rights of private businesses and rent-seeking behavior on the part of stakeholders, ultimately resulting in increased transaction costs.

Some fundamental issues need to be mentioned in order to precisely evaluate the current corporate restructuring process. To abide by its principle of the "parallel development of democracy and market economy," the Kim Dae-jung administration should have implemented corporate reform in a more institutionalized form. Unfortunately, restructuring so far has depended on the government's hand rather than market

Table 1. Diary of Corporate Restructuring after the IMF Bailout

Date	Contents
13 Jan. 1998	President-elect Kim Dae-jung requests corporate restructuring from the leaders of the nations four largest conglomerates.
14 April 1998	The procedure to force out nonviable big corporations announced.
7 May 1998	The Office of Bank Supervision asks major commercial banks to create a joint committee to sort out nonviable companies among their customers.
18 June 1998	A list of 55 nonviable companies including 20 companies from the five largest conglomerates is announced.
4 July 1998	The government and leaders of the Federation of Korean Industries, an association of large companies, decide to pursue the reform process including business swaps, the so-called "big deals."
28 July 1998	28 companies belonging to ten conglomerates, ranked between 6th and 64th, are put into the workout program
Aug. 1998	Banks ask the five largest conglomerates to amend their financial restructuring plans, which the government thought insufficient.
3 Sep. 1998	Urged by the government, the five largest conglomerates announce that they will implement "big deals" and mergers across seven industries.

forces. There is much more work to be done in order to build up a new system of corporate institutions to better fit the changing corporate environment. In this respect, we may say that the restructuring process is not yet finished and only partially successful. To put an end to the current crisis and return to pre-crisis growth levels, we should be careful not to become complacent. To avoid a second crisis, the corporate sector has no choice but to restructure itself; otherwise it risks another collapse.

For the above reasons, Korea's economic rehabilitation and recovery process is attracting much attention from economists and policymakers around the world. So far, however, there have been few studies on Korea's corporate restructuring policies and corporate responses. This paper attempts to draw a comprehensive picture of what went on in Korea during the crisis. Efforts from both the state and the private sector will be analyzed, paying special attention to the restructuring process of the *jaebeol*. In addition, the ongoing corporate sector restructuring process and policies at stake will be critically reviewed. The *jaebeol* will be the main subject of the analysis. Considering their importance and the externalities they bring to the national economy, their restructuring process and related policies must be studied more carefully.

Reasons for the Corporate Crisis: Micro-micro, Micro, and Macro Perspectives

Many have argued that the ultimate cause of the Korean crisis was over-investment and overdiversification, both aggravated by overindebtedness. Corporate investment is not always value-enhancing; it can be value-destroying if revenues do not exceed opportunity costs. Unfortunately, most Korean business groups were consistently making non-performing investments. According to a report issued by the Korean Stock Exchange (1998), a large percentage of Korean companies has experienced extremely low or even negative (–) economic value added (EVA), indicating that a significant deviation did not occur from an optimal level of diversifying investment. It shows that the accumulated economic value added of 570 non-financial listed companies was minus (–) 1.9 trillion won from 1992 to 1996, a figure indicating value destruction.

A number of possible causes for overinvestment are well summarized in Markides (1996) and Hoskisson and Hitt (1994). Although many

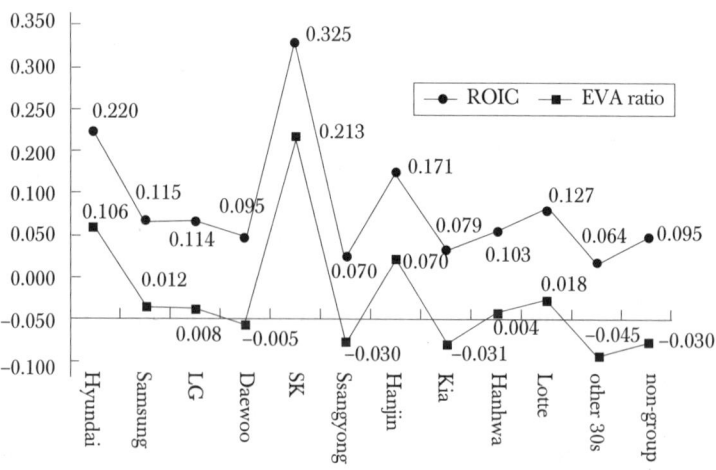

Source: Korea Stock Exchange (1998).

Figure 1. ROIC and EVA of the 30 largest *Jaebeol*

alternative explanations for overinvestment in diversification exist, they are grouped into several main arguments: agency reasons (Jensen and Meckling 1976), the hubris hypothesis, a shift in the optimal (diversification) level (Williamson 1996) and the failure of the market in corporate control. What implications do these theories have regarding Korean *jaebeol* diversification strategy? To answer this question, the chronic overexpansion of the corporate sector must be explained from micro-micro, micro, and macro perspectives.

Micro-micro Perspective

The governance structure of the *jaebeol* did not develop enough to match the pace of Korea's economic growth. The so-called "micromicro" issue of economics for *jaebeol*, to use Williamson's (1996) terminology, is that the governance structure deeply determines the process of strategic decision-making such as entry and exit. Many critics argue that the entrepreneur-manager system of Korean conglomerates, which enables managers to make speedy and flexible decisions favoring highrisk investment, became obsolete and even a source of structural invest-

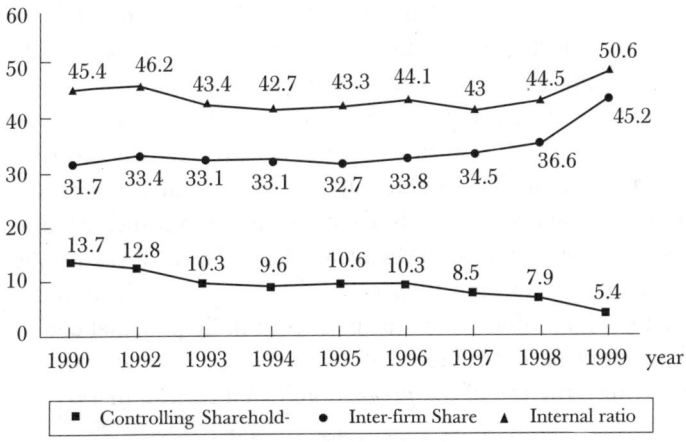

Note: ratios are the averages of the 30 largest *jaebeol*.
Source: Fair Trade Commission.

Figure 2. Yearly trend of owners and internal shares of equity

ment failures.[2]

The equity shares of *jaebeol* chairmen and their families are decreasing as they need to attract external funds from the stock market. They maintain control rights with the help of inter-firm equity investment. Even though they keep control, they need to pay attention to noncontrolling and minority shareholders; if they fail to do so, outside investors will stop cooperating with them.

The current internal management system of the *jaebeol* depends predominantly on the controlling shareholder (or owner). As a result, the board of directors and supervisors inside the company do not monitor the controlling shareholder. It is firmly believed that any board member who dares to oppose the controlling shareholder will lose board membership.

There also exists what is called the "never-fail" myth among the owner-managers of the *jaebeol*. When a project is deemed non-performing, management is often unwilling to abandon it, even halfway before its completion. Since all investments or projects cannot be successful, not admitting failures and postponing the early termination of nonviable projects can have a snowball effect on losses incurred.

Micro Perspective

Micro reasons for overinvestment can also be easily found. For example, oligopoly structures in Korea, dominated mainly by *jaebeol* subsidiaries, might be another crucial factor in explaining overcapacity and overinvestment. Leading companies in major industries, which are export-oriented and exposed to keen competition with international rival companies, cannot help but initiate such large-scale investment. Scale itself determines competitiveness in fixed-cost industries such as automobiles, semiconductors, and petro-chemicals. In addition, firms in oligopolistic markets tend to expand their capacity investments above the cost-minimizing level in order to lead the market or bully potential entrants.[3]

This strategic overinvestment tendency has been exacerbated by the underlying structure of the *jaebeol*-dominated Korean market.

---

2. Jang (1999) and other critics of the *jaebeol* emphasize governance failure as the most serious cause of the economic crisis.
3. Mankiw and Whinston (1986) and classical prisoners' dilemma are examples of capacity games in oligopolistic markets.

Moreover, the infamous "too-big-to-fail" legacy of the largest enterprises is another key factor behind overcapacity.[4] In general, when overinvestment occurs, it can be adjusted through market mechanisms, or through the bankruptcy of nonviable companies and industrial rearrangements such as M&As. However, the government could not let nonviable big enterprises, including *jaebeol,* go bankrupt for several reasons, and thus, eventually resuscitated them with rescue funds and preferential treatment. As a result, they often lost restructuring opportunities which otherwise might have been smoothly guided by market principles. This practice typically causes "moral hazard" for *jaebeol* owners. They are able to expand their businesses to an excessive level without taking a corresponding risk burden.

The strong industrial policy also helps to explain the chronic diversification of *jaebeol.* In the past, the government has exercised the right (through licensing) to choose who could do business, and has controlled new entries formally or informally. Very often, entries have been granted on a stop-and-go basis. To take the preemptive or "first move" advantage during the temporary "go" period, companies simultaneously rushed for new investments, if available, thereby creating an excess supply.

In particular, banks and other financial institutions have been accused of behavior causing moral hazard. They have been effectively addicted to heavy lending which has been guided and even coordinated by the government. They lacked the requisite ability to conduct credit and project analyses and failed to develop such skills. They have contributed to solidifying the "too-big-to-fail" mentality by increasing, rather than withdrawing, loans to nonviable large clients to cover up their loss records. It is for this reason that financial sector restructuring must precede corporate restructuring. Without first correcting the "reckless lending" practices of the financial sector, there is less hope for curing the *jaebeol* habit of "reckless borrowing" and overexpansion.

Macro Perspective

From a macro-level perspective, governmental intervention in the foreign exchange market led to a number of serious market distortions, as explained in Jwa and Huh (1998). For several years before the IMF res-

---

4. See Koo (1998) and Yoo (1999) for the TBTF legacy and its implications for Korean *jaebeol.*

cue, the economy had recorded a series of trade deficits; despite the worsening deficit, the government maintained a cheap-dollar policy.

The government probably believed that at a highly overvalued won, companies could not but restructure themselves to enhance their international competitiveness. But this belief in the effectiveness of "Spartan" policies did not materialize and failed to induce companies to make fundamental changes. Rather, the overvalued won eventually further lowered the export competitiveness of Korean companies.

With such a low dollar, feasibility studies of large-scale projects, mainly debt-financed, were largely erroneous. During this period, most of the leading *jaebeol* were competing against each other for overseas investments, particularly in the transition economies of Eastern Europe.

Profitable projects at an artificial exchange rate, backed up by governmental intervention, turned into nonprofitable ones at market exchange rates. The inconsistent exchange rate policy created nationwide bubbles of investment by companies and also increased consumption by consumers.

Jaebeol, National Economy, and Some Political Hurdles

Before discussing questions of corporate restructuring, we need to pay attention to the issue of the economic concentration of the *jaebeol.* As of 1997, the big five—Hyundai, Samsung, Daewoo, LG, and SK groups—accounted for 28.9% of total assets held by *jaebeol,* 32.4% of turnover, and 8.5% of value added. If the figures are extended to the big thirty, the concentration ratios reach, 46.6%, 46.6%, and 13.0% respectively.[5]

It is undeniable that the *jaebeol's* power in the national economy is enormous. In principle, however, size per se should not be penalized. It is often argued that the absolute size of Korean business groups is quite small when compared with major international companies. For example, the total market value of all listed Korean companies including the *jaebeol* is but one-fifth that of Microsoft.[6]

---

5. See KERI (1999) for the details of economic concentration statistics.
6. There are many large U.S. companies such as Microsoft and GE whose market value is greater than the total of all listed Korean companies. For example, as of 14 August 1998, the market value of Microsoft reached $261.1 billion, and this figure was five times the total market value of all listed Korean companies at that time.

Table 2. Economic Concentration of Jaebeol

(%)

		80-90	1991	1992	1993	1994	1995	1996	1997
Assets	Big 5	21.3	24.6	24.9	24.4	23.9	26.9	27.2	28.9
	Big 30	42.5	45.0	46.1	44.9	43.6	47.3	47.1	46.6
Turnover	Big 5	24.4	27.5	28.9	28.0	28.5	31.7	32.4	32.4
	Big 30	44.0	42.8	45.0	43.1	43.6	47.8	48.4	46.6
Employment	Big 5	2.01	2.59	2.46	2.47	2.56	2.73	2.71	N/A
	Big 30	3.85	4.83	4.34	4.35	4.61	4.68	4.62	

Sources: Hwang (1999) and KERI (1999).

In addition to size-phobia, other factors contribute to the formation of anti-*jaebeol* sentiment among the general public. Serious accusations point at the hand-in-hand relationship between the government and the business world, the allegedly unfair and discriminatory support for big business, and the illegal exercise of monopoly power.

The deep-rooted disenchantment with the *jaebeol* has now become a political constraint that the Korean government must take into consideration when making economic policies. Sometimes, economically irrational but politically favorable policies are adopted, yielding less than optimal outcomes.[7] During restructuring operations, economic rationale has without exception given way to political considerations. Eager to see favorable outcomes from restructuring efforts, the government has excessively meddled with market mechanisms. We have witnessed the so-called "swap deals" in major industries, a strategy resembling the excessive prescription of drugs for reluctant patients—in this case, the *jaebeol.*

The policies of core business specialization and capital restructuring seem to be what the economy needs; however, the government has gone too far in implementing them. For example, the government has set a deadline, namely the end of 1999, for companies to lower their debt-to-equity ratio to below 200%, which applies to all *jaebeol* without excep-

---

7. For example, Korean antitrust laws have a number of seemingly irrational clauses not found in advanced nations' antitrust laws. They regulate aggregate concentration more strongly than market concentration.

tion. If they fail to do so, they risk being peralized in various ways such as the withdrawal of existing loans or the refusal from their main banks to provide new loans.

Debt Restructuring and the Need for Recapitalization

Many believe that the 1997 crisis came without any warning. However, several indicators signaled the coming disaster during the several years before the onset of the IMF crisis. In particular, the profitability of businesses went from bad to worse, while the debt burden of companies continued to increase.

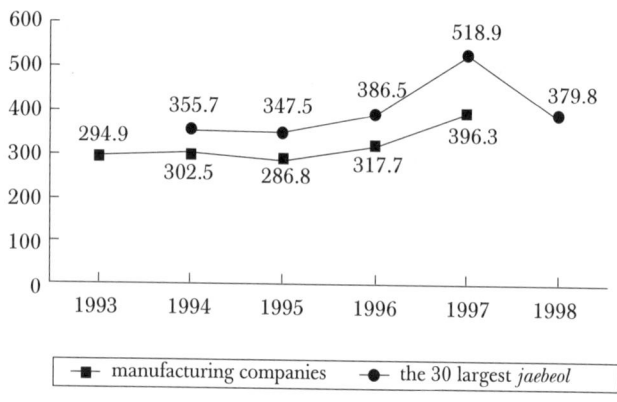

Sources: Bank of Korea; Fair Trade Commission.

Figure 3. Debt-to-equity ratio of manufacturing companies
and the 30 largest *jaebeol*

Bankruptcy among small and medium enterprises kept rising, following the successive collapses of *jaebeol* such as Kia and Hanbo. The situation worsened during 1998, and some conglomerates went into bankruptcy while others balanced on the edge. Among the top 30 business groups, 10 groups, including Donga and Halla, defaulted or technically defaulted (i.e. went under syndicated loan, or into workout, court settlement, or court receivership). Debt-to-equity ratios and year-to-date changes can explain the worsening capital structure of business groups, and due to the won devaluation and soaring interest rates, these figures peaked in 1998.

In particular, the big five groups have undergone the same financial struggle. However, due to relatively better credit, they could issue bonds in the market and build reserves to survive such catastrophically high interest rates. They eventually managed to survive but with much higher debt—an empty victory. Now it is high time for the *jaebeol* to restructure themselves. If they cannot, or will not, then they will remain debt-ridden, vulnerable to shocks, and might face a second crisis in the near future.

General Corporate Restructuring Policies

Korean companies are undertaking restructuring in important areas, namely capital restructuring, business restructuring, and governance restructuring. As already mentioned, the restructuring of the corporate sector has been stimulated by financial distress, but restructuring in capital structures inevitably impacts the corporate governance structure directly, and the business structure indirectly.

For example, the currently popular debt/equity swaps alter the governance structure of companies since debts are converted into equity and debt holders necessarily turn into equity holders. In Korea, banks, the one-time creditors, have now become major shareholders and exercise control rights over companies.

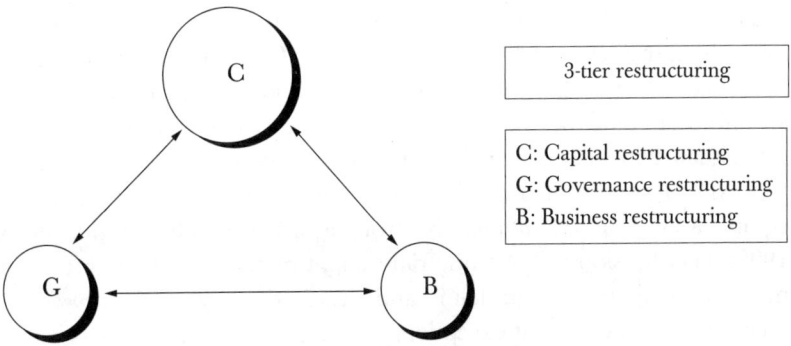

Figure 4. The 3-tier restructuring scheme

This interaction provides a clue as to how corporate restructuring can be planned and implemented. Capital, business, and governance restructuring must be incorporated in an organic way into an integrated reform package. In this respect, to be successful, corporate restructuring policies must be carefully designed with consideration of these interrelationships.

Capital Restructuring

A number of policies have been newly introduced to lower the debts accumulated by the *jaebeol* and to set up a stronger market discipline in capital markets. Not only is issuance of new inter-subsidiary debt guarantees prohibited, but also existing ones must be cleared completely by the end of 1999. The original deadline was after 2000, but after negotiations with the IMF, the date was set earlier to push for a swift restructuring of companies.

The debt guarantee is not a formal statute, but rather a spontaneously formed private practice to overcome the asymmetric information flows between banks and companies. Despite such a positive function, the practice actually served to allocate money predominantly to the *jaebeol* during the period when the "too-big-to-fail" mentality prevailed. Within the current recession, however, debt guarantees are considered to create a system risk for the group as a whole, in which one unit's failure might quickly spread to others. Hence, efforts to untangle the financial interlocking of subsidiaries will contribute to correcting the imperfections in capital markets and reducing risks to society. But, in the long run, a clear principle must be established so that excessive debt guarantees will be managed through the capital market, not through governmental regulation.

The government also recommended that financial institutions sign financial agreements with their partner *jaebeol* and carefully monitor the fulfillment of such agreements. The recommendation has developed into an informal guideline, and as a result, all the *jaebeol* with total loans of more than 250 billion won have to submit restructuring plans. In the process, an important but informal deadline has been set–the debt-to-equity ratio of the *jaebeol* must be brought to below 200% by the end of 1999. The decision to lower the ratio might be appropriate, but it is still not clear whether the guideline and deadline apply to all *jaebeol* and their subsidiaries without exception.

According to the well-known Modigliani-Miller theorem (hereafter M-

M theorem), the optimal capital structure of a firm is determined according to conditions surrounding the firm such as capital market, tax system, and other institutional factors.[8] The upshot of the M-M theorem is that the optimal level of debt-to-equity ratio must be determined differently from industry to industry and even from country to country. Stone (1998) indicates that country-specific legal and institutional environments can cause inter-country diversity in corporate debt structures. Similarly, Williamson (1996) argues that the difference in transaction costs between debt and equity financing explains varying capital structures across projects.[9]

Moreover, the problem of bargaining power erosion has been raised in the negotiation process. Restructuring is also a market activity. Pressed to meet the government's deadline, domestic firms for sale must participate in the restructuring market at the same time. The oversupply of products in M&A markets creates a "fire sale" as domestic firms are sold below their value. It is creating bottlenecks through which firms might have difficulty getting out of financial distress and experience a severe weakening of their bargaining position at the negotiating table. Accordingly, it can be expected that as the deadline draws near, foreign buyers will rush to South Korea to collect jewels at near junk prices.

In correcting the reckless borrowing behavior of companies, banks and other financial institutions should step up their disciplining roles. In this respect, the policy of having financial institutions monitor and supervise the corporate sector's restructuring process is desirable, but that of indiscriminately enforcing the 200% guideline is not. The rigid 200% ratio will force firms into a corner solution, that is, a sub-optimal capital structure. Alternatively, debt ratios in bank-corporate agreements need to take into account different conditions between *jaebeol* and

---

8. Refer to the original paper by Modigliani and Miller (1958) for details on the optimal capital structure. Their main proposition is that the debt-to-equity ratio is independent of the optimality of the capital structure of a firm in efficient capital markets and with no governmental intervention like tax. Ironically, however, the real value of the argument is that the optimal debt-to-equity ratio can be determined differently when the strict conditions are not satisfied in real markets as we observe.

9. Williamson (1996) argues that (1) debt has tax advantages over equity, (2) debt can be used as a signal of differential business prospects, (3) debt can be used by entrepreneurs with limited resources who are faced with new investment opportunities and do not want to dilute their equity position, and (4) debt can be used as an incentive bonding device.

between industries. This program for debt restructuring can be supported by theories on optimal capital structure, including the M-M theorem.

It is uncertain whether the government will retain the guideline after 2000. If it does, corporate freedom would be severely restricted in its degree of financial leveraging. If it does not, a question might arise as to why the guideline was so strictly kept until 1999.

Corporate Governance Restructuring

Governance structure truly matters and some of the reasons can be seen in the following remarks by Goold, Campbell, and Alexander (1994):

> Enterprises are composed of a wide range of stakeholders, and thus affect their interests. If the interests of any of the stakeholder groups are consistently ignored, the enterprise will become unviable. For example, if customers are consistently given a poor deal relative to the alternatives available to them, they will stop buying from the enterprise. If employees are consistently given a poor deal, they will stop working for the enterprise. Similarly, other stakeholders whose needs are consistently ignored will remove their support. There is a minimum requirement for each group to sustain its involvement of a surplus over and above these minimum requirements.

How is the governance structure of Korean enterprises (particularly *jaebeol*) different from a traditional one? A little modification of the basic Berle-Means model could reflect the unique features of Korean enterprises' governance structure, as in Figure 5. In particular, the government has indirectly intervened in industrial governance, by controlling credit rationing from financial institutions. In this sense, the government deserves to become a major stakeholder in the governance structure.

Another distinguishing feature is the *jaebeol*'s ownership and control pattern. The industrial conglomerates are controlled by their large shareholders. The so-called "owners" can exercise power to change management by appointing the board of directors, and to make important decisions for their subsidiaries at will. Many critics, however, argue that this potent exercise of control rights does not balance with their disproportionately low ownership position. Both internal discipline, such as the board of directors and institutional investors, and external discipline, such as hostile takeovers, have failed to monitor or supervise owners'

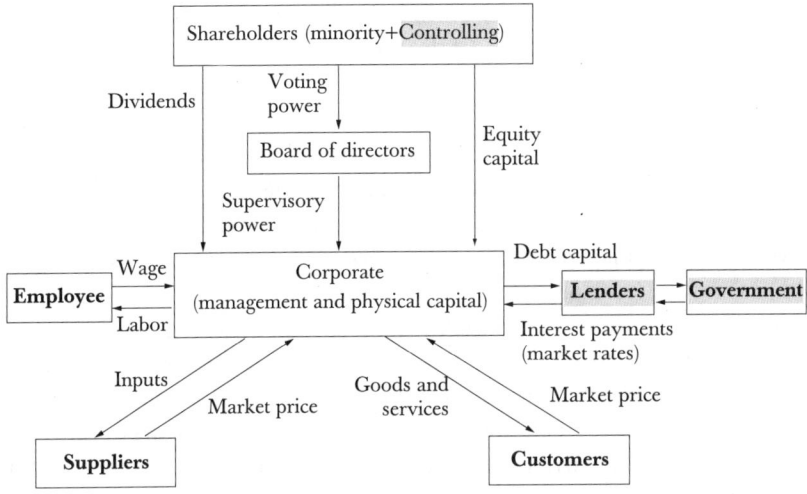

* Shaded areas indicate the tripartite relationship between *jaebeol*, banks, and the government.

Figure 5. *Jaebeol's* corporate governance:
an extension of the Berle-Means model

moral hazard behavior (McKinsey 1998). The excessive business diversification and subsidiary empire building are the results of the controlling family's expansionist strategy, not at its own cost but at the cost of all shareholders.

To reinstitute market discipline, the government launched a number of governance reform measures in 1998. First, the 30 largest business groups must now release consolidated financial statements. This financial report, also recommended by the IMF, will first be issued in 1999. In the past, a *jaebeol* reported several combined financial statements. Each statement was written for a specific subsidiary group with interlocking shares, and accordingly, outside investors had much difficulty in assessing the complete financial status of *jaebeol.*

Second, small shareholders can claim their rights more easily. The minimum number of shares necessary to undertake derivative suits, to call for the dismissal of board members, and to see the accounting books have been lowered significantly. A cumulative voting system has been recently introduced in corporate law. This system could enable small shareholders to put a representative board member in management.

Another crucial policy under consideration is the introduction of share-holder class actions. If legalized, it would greatly impact the behavior of board members and CEOs. If management acted illegally, it could be sued by any shareholder. More importantly, if management lost the suit, then it would have to compensate all shareholders for its wrongdoing.

Third, hostile M&As are considered strong market discipline for man-agement. If its management performs poorly, a company could be taken over, and its management would be ostracized. In the pre-crisis era, hos-tile takeovers were prohibited. Under the old corporate law, if anyone wanted to buy more shares than the legal limit, 10% of total shares, he or she first had to obtain an authorization from the current manage-ment's board of directors. This limit has now been completely lifted. Foreign investors are able to buy up to 1/3 of the total shares of a com-pany without the current management's agreement. The procedure of authorization by the Ministry of Finance for large-scale foreign direct investment has also been lifted. Institutional investors, who have kept silent on management issues, can exercise their voting rights to represent small shareholders' rights in proxy takeover contests.

All these changes in the governance structure will act positively to rec-tify the controlling shareholder's dominance over corporate governance in Korea. In particular, it is the first time that a reform of governance structure has been undertaken so seriously by the government. In the past, *jaebeol* policies centered mainly on financial and business restruc-turing. When *jaebeol* businesses were in financial trouble, in many cases, the government responded with industrial rationalization (and readjust-ments) and company ownership change by force. It was not an institu-tional reform through incentives but an artificial, ad hoc type of reform. In this respect, the current focus on governance structure deserves praise, and a series of revisions of corporate law is a good example of institutional reform.

Business Restructuring

No subject concerning the *jaebeol* attracts more interest but less conclu-sive assessments than the issue of *jaebeol* diversification. The *jaebeol* are allegedly overdiversified, even described as having "octopus-like" expan-sionist strategies. Are the leading conglomerates really so thinly spread over an unreasonably large number of businesses? In terms of sub-sidiary numbers, the answer is "yes." The number has consistently been increasing in the 1990s, indicating the *jaebeol*'s intention to branch out into new businesses.

In terms of diversification measures, however, the answer may be more equivocal. Despite the number of subsidiaries in the double digits, the real measure of diversification has not increased significantly. We computed various measures of diversification of the big five groups, the Bery index (B), the Herfindahl index (H), and the number equivalent (1/H). These indices illustrate that diversification is not as high as is shown by the increasing number of subsidiaries. In particular, the inverse of the Herfindahl index as the number of subsidiaries with equal size is about five. It is equivalent to saying that each *jaebeol* runs about five equal-sized companies. In terms of business area, the figure further decreases, indicating that the average *jaebeol* runs three or more businesses.

Table 3. Diversification Measure

	CR3	H	Bery (=1-H)	1/H
Big 5	0.654	0.207	0.793	5.308
Big 10	0.714	0.241	0.759	4.731
Big 30	0.719	0.236	0.764	4.792

Note: Generally, the Herfindahl Index H $(=\Sigma Si^2)$ is used to measure market concentration, but here it measures the degree of the *jaebeol*'s business focus. *Si* denotes the share of a subsidiary firm *i*' sales to group sales excluding financial subsidiaries in 1997.
Source: KERI (1999).

Nonetheless, these figures do not mean that the family-controlled *jaebeol* have invested at an optimal level. There is always an optimal diversification level that maximizes firm (or group) value and beyond which the firm suffers from profit loss and destroys shareholder value. Many studies show that, over the past several years, Korean companies (and *jaebeol*) have recorded a very low (even negative) rate of return on investment or assets.

These are all indicators that Korean companies will need to reshape and reconstitute their businesses. They will have to focus on core businesses and shed their non-profitable and non-core units. To restructure themselves, they must depend on diverse types of restructuring schemes, such as divestiture, equity carve-outs, spin-offs (split-offs and split-ups),

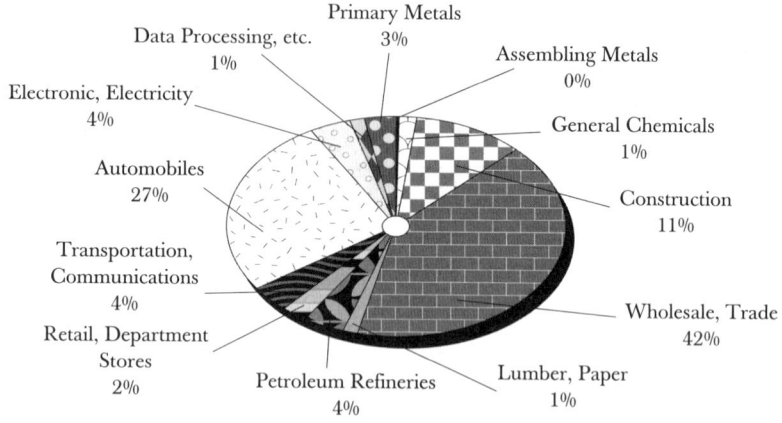

Note: Subsidiary sales distribution across industry.
Source: KERI (1999).

Figure 6. Business portfolio of the Hyundai Group, 1997

business swaps, and strategic partnerships.

However, it is very often argued that many hurdles prevent such restructuring programs from being aggressively implemented. For example, heavy taxes in capital gains, acquisition, and registration tend to increase the transaction cost of restructuring, reducing the chances for market exchange. Having recognized the obstacles, the government has created measures such as temporary tax reductions or exemption. It has turned out, however, that a tax incentive is not sufficient to revitalize restructuring markets, since it is not an exemption but in most cases, a deferment of payment. More aggressive tax cuts should be considered to boost the restructuring market.

In addition, the Labor Act has been changed to expedite the restructuring process. The most serious obstacle for foreign direct investment was the prohibition of worker layoffs. Due to legal revisions, layoffs have now become much easier than before. The Labor Act dictates that, with proper economic reasons, management may layoff employees. Nonetheless this clause does not fully work, creating some gaps between legal provisions and their enforcement. We should carefully monitor whether this gap can be narrowed.

Another government action for business restructuring is the revision of the so-called "three laws concerning the management of nonviable companies" (Law of Court Settlement, Law of Bankruptcy, and Law of Corporate Readjustment). In particular, the Law of Court Settlement has been recently revised so that it is more difficult for the current management of a big company to keep control of its subsidiaries. Big companies are more exposed to the dangers of bankruptcy than in the past. Despite such revisions, few cases have been filed for these legal processes of readjustment, and the situation remains much as before. Instead, informal procedures such as workout programs are more popular. The corporate value recovery program, which was originally applied to corporate restructuring in the United Kingdom, is biased toward the recovery of firms rather than their closure.[10]

In fact, without effective shutdown of the least efficient factories and least competitive companies, market adjustments cannot really take place. In this respect, the workout program has a serious limitation: if it fails, workout companies will be left with a higher amount of debt. The requirements for workouts, then, should be more stringent on companies, and workouts also should be followed by strong self-rescue efforts on the part of companies.

More important than any other policy is the proper working of normal corporate closure procedures, such as bankruptcies and court settlements. So far, there has only been a few closures of failing firms. In this sense, the principle of "no closure, no market clearance" should be upheld.

Policy Case Studies

Big Deal Operations

"Big deals," or more precisely, business swaps, are taking place in eight major industries including the semiconductor and automobile industries. These operations are actually related to the five largest *jaebeol*. While it is true that the deals are showing some results, they are still severely crit-

---

10. See Stone (1998) for the details of the London Approach and other debt restructuring experiences in other countries.

Table 4. Big Deals in Progress

	Before Big Deals	After Big Deals
Semiconductors	• Samsung Electronics Co. • Hyundai Electronics Ind. • LG Semicon Co.	• Samsung Electronics Co. • Hyundai and LG merged into one company (Equity share-out to be discussed later).
Petrochemicals	• Daisan Complex • Samsung General Chemical Co. • Hyundai Petrochemical Co.	• Samsung and Hyundai merged into one company (introduced foreign capital). • SK, LG may merge into Yeocheon Complex.
Aircraft-parts	• Samsung Aerospace Industries Co. • Daewoo Heavy Industries Co. • Hyundai Space & Aircraft Co.	• Form a new, joint company and introduce foreign capital
Rolling stock	• Hyundai Precision & Ind. Co. • Daewoo Heavy Industries Co. • Hanjin Heavy Industries Co.	
Power-generation equipment	• Korea Heavy Industries & Construction Co. (HANJUNG) • Samsung Heavy Industries Co. • Hyundai Heavy Industries Co.	• Unified into one company • HANJUNG takes over Samsung's business.
Ship-engines	• Samsung Heavy Industries Co. • Hyundai Heavy Industries Co. • HANJUNG	• HANJUNG takes over Samsung's business. • Two company systems of HANJUNG and Hyundai
Oil refining	• Hanwha Energy Co.	• Acquired by Hyundai Oil Co.
Autos	• Hyundai Motors, Kia Motors, Daewoo Motors, and Samsung Motors	• Daewoo Motors will take over Samsung Motors. • Hyundai Motor Co. took over Kia Motor Co.

Source: Federation of Korean Industries, December 1998.

icized on account of the governmental intervention behind the scenes. Despite the government's denial of any involvement, it has become common knowledge that "big brother" did meddle and push for these private deals. The government's strong inclination for large-scale swap deals is deeply rooted in traditional industrial policy such as business specialization policy. Above all, it has become clear that such strong industrial policies and nonmarket resource allocation by the government are the very causes of the national crisis. Ironically, this kind of industrial restructuring has been undertaken repeatedly.

A number of problems can be raised concerning the "big deal" operations. First, forced swap deals severely infringe on the property rights of the companies participating in the deal. It is not a purely voluntary trade, as the government is pushing behind the scenes for the early completion of these deals. Generally speaking, trades always take place whenever the benefits from exchange exceed the costs. If voluntary exchanges do not occur, it implies that the transaction benefits are too low, or that their transaction costs are too high. In this respect, all things being equal, the big deals are highly likely to lead to total loss on both sides, or at least to the losses of one party in the deal.

Second, swap deals are fundamentally related to the old government-coordinated business specialization policy. The government does not have relevant information on the optimal level of specialization or diversification, nor is it in a position to direct private companies to reduce the number of their businesses to less than four or five subsidiaries.

Over the last 30 years, diverse types of industrial rationalization have been carried out under the government-led coordination (see Table 5). For example, company rationalization (1969-1971), industrial rationalization (1972), heavy industry investment adjustment (late 1970s and early 1980s), and the policies of core businesses (1990s) all targeted the specialization of businesses. The policy measures adopted in the current industrial readjustment programs appear to be almost identical to those of the previous programs in the 1969-1990 period. Ironically, many of the industries affected by the swap deals are the very industries that were subject to the old rationalization policies. The automobile and heavy industries are regular subjects for large-scale restructuring.

Third, the side effects from governmental intervention can be more serious in the long run. Bureaucrats now have a legitimate right to screen new entries in major industries at issue, and thus will make industrial policy more rigid in the future.

Table 5. Major Cases of Industrial Restructuring and Rationalization in Korea

Policy cases	Contents
Company rationalization measures (1969-1971)	• Implemented in 3 phases – 1st phase: readjustment of about 30 companies in the fields of PVC, auto-making, steel, and chemical fibers. – 2nd phase: denomination and adjustment of 56 insolvent companies – 3rd phase: denomination and adjustment of 26 insolvent companies
Industrial rationalization measures (a part of the 3 August 1972 measures)	• Carried out on 3 August 1972 to ease the financial distress of companies caused by the severe won devaluation and stringent monetary policy that had been implemented following IMF recommendations • Designated 61 industries for industrial rationalization – 30 heavy industries including the steel, nonferrous metals, shipbuilding, and electronics industries – PVC, fertilizer, and petrochemicals • Financial and tax support given to industries that undertook capacity adjustment, business specialization, subcontract system improvement, M&As, financial re-capitalization, and R&D – Financial support by the industry rationalization fund – Exemption of corporate tax and acquisition tax in M&A, and depreciation rate increase – Fiscal subsidy to capacity investment
Investment adjustment of heavy industries (late 1970s and early 1980s)	• Downsizing and readjustment of the overcapacity of heavy industries, caused by the policy of heavy industry development through the 1970s • Support for investment readjustment through M&A and production specialization – Government support through bailout funds • Interest rates lowered in 1982 to ease the financial costs to firms
Core business policy (early 1990s)	• Indirect inducement policy aimed at reducing the level of *jaebeol* business diversification • Bank credit limits lifted and other preferential treatments given exclusively to the two or three main companies which each *jaebeol* designated as their core

Source: Lee (1998).

Fourth, the monopoly position of market leaders could be strengthened. A main theme of the swap deal is to make market followers give up their businesses and transfer them to the one or two market leaders. Necessarily, the outcome of the deals would be a significant increase in market concentration, which might cause price increases or other monopolizing practices.

Fifth, these government operations are always followed by some incentives for the participating companies. In the case of forcefully implemented restructuring, the parties to the deals have been compensated with preferential treatment such as privileged loans and tax exemptions. This time, as an incentive for taking part in the swap deals, debt/equity swaps are being provided to the companies.

In reality, these practices are nothing but "socializing" the private costs of firms. For bigger companies, the chance for preferential treatment becomes higher. In return for bailout funds, the government can legitimize its intervention in business decisions. In other words, a "helping hand" turns into a "grabbing hand."[11] In such an environment, close ties between political and business leaders can be easily formed.

Workout Program

The mid-sized *jaebeol*, mainly the 6-30 largest ones, are involved in so-called "workout programs" which intend to recover companies that seem promising in the long term but are financially constrained in the short term.

This type of corporate aid has a number of problems. The most severe problem is the nonclosure of inefficient firms due to the workout assistance. Technically nonviable firms subject to workout care are dumping their products at unreasonably low prices and waging unfair competition with their rivals who lack financial assistance. For example, some construction companies under workout programs are winning many project bids because their financial improvement through the help of their creditor banks has been evaluated highly by the project owners. Last year, Kia Motors, before selling-off, was criticized for having dumped its cars at unreasonably low prices; Hanbo did the same, raising much worry among rival steel makers.

---

11. See Shleifer and Vishny (1998) for details on the "helping hand" and "grabbing hand."

Table 6. Companies under Workout Program

(100 million won)

Company (number of subsidiaries)	Interest Rate Cuts	Interest Payments Waived	Debt-equity Swap	CB Conversion	Debt Write-off	Others	Total	New Loan
Donga Construction (1)	43,928	8,257	802				52,987	1,600
Geopyung (3)		824	748	111	3,048	3,953	8,684	0
Sepung (2)	4,605	92					4,697	225
Gapeul (2)	10,357	1,890	163	3,260	765		16,435	1,200
Kohap (4)	42,775	4,643	1,663	2,247			51,328	7,916
Shinho (3)	7,541	4,720	494	2,403			15,158	2,380
Pieoris (1)	540	58		50	65		713	0
Shinwon (3)	4,854	2,739	1,540	3,150	1,321		13,604	1,260
Jindo (3)	6,718	4,273	908	2,042			13,941	2,064
Kangwon Industry (4)	17,208	575					17,783	1,527
Woobang (1)	5,838	1,239	444	1,611			9,132	1,200
Hankuk Computer (1)	1,083	70					1,153	211
Pyuksan (3)	7,454	2,356	100	1,500			11,410	500
Daegu Dept. Store (2)	3,152	261		200	422		4,035	0
Dongguk Trade (3)	11,107	5,975	400	1,000			18,482	2,510
Ssangyong (2)	8,929	862	5,636			2,260	17,687	856
Anam (2)	10,747	6,313	1,419	1,081		9,194	28,754	500
Others	31,929	9,513	387	2,202	35	5,513	49,633	5,391
Total	218,765	54,660	14,704	20,857	5,656	20,920	335,562	29,340

Source: Corporate Restructuring Committee, June 1999.

Second, problems of moral hazard may occur. Creditor banks are more concerned with debt repayment from debtor companies than with ultimate recovery. Some of the banks are being criticized for having charged higher interest rates for their workout customers.

Third, the control rights of management are not rationally substituted. Managerial rights must be allocated according to the ownership structure. Companies under workout plans are very often given debt/equity swaps by banks. The essence of the exchange scheme is that debt-holders turn into shareholders. The banks, as controlling shareholders, should have legitimate control of management; however, in most workout cases, old management still maintains control.[12] This could yield the undesirable outcome of maximizing the interests of management at the expense of the banks and other shareholders. The existing owner-managers need to be responsible for management failures and be replaced unless shareholders prefer to keep them.

Finally, the government claims that creditor banks are leading the workout program, but in fact, the program has been guided by government agencies such as the Financial Supervisory Commission. If such intervention by the government continues, then the program will lose more autonomy. In the worst case scenario, it could degenerate into the outdated bankruptcy-protection accord that turned out to be a complate failure during the pre-crisis period.

Future Agenda for Corporate Restructuring

Since the onset of the crisis, the Korean economy has been carefully reformed in many ways. The astonishing speed at which it is returning to its normal state in every field is well evidenced. But behind the facade of success, the government's hand has been prominent. It must be noted that without strong intervention by the government, the current reform outcomes might not have been possible. Nonetheless, success in the past does not guarantee success in the future.

---

12. Of course, some exceptions exist, such as the Gohap Group. A new managment has been appointed, replacing the old one which had not kept promises such as foreign capital inducements.

Policy Recommendation

We are now in the second year since the restructuring of "Korea Inc." began, and the corporate restructuring policy requires fundamental changes. Forceful restructuring and the resulting property rights infringements might have been unavoidable in the early stages of the crisis, but should not be prolonged further. From now on, corporate restructuring must be firmly based on institutional reforms.

1. Transaction Cost Reduction

Both corporate and industrial restructuring policies need to adopt a fundamentally different paradigm from the old ones which became nonviable in the new business environment. In particular, while the government's policies of picking winners and targeting industries might have played a legitimate role in small and closed economies with stable demand and technology, in this era of rapidly changing open economies, such nonmarket allocation of resources will no longer be successful.

Hence, the future direction of industrial policy must be toward the reduction of transaction costs through the use of market mechanisms. Generally speaking, when transaction-related costs, such as taxes, are low and gains from transactions are great, trade occurs automatically. However, transaction costs are believed to be too high to facilitate restructuring in Korea.

		TC (transaction cost) targeting					
		Assets	Real estate	Equity (managerial right)	Production facilities	Inputs	Technology, patents
Industrial targeting	Industry 1		↓				
	Industry 2	→					
	Industry 3						
	Industry 4						

Source: Lee (1998).

Figure 7. New directions of industrial policies

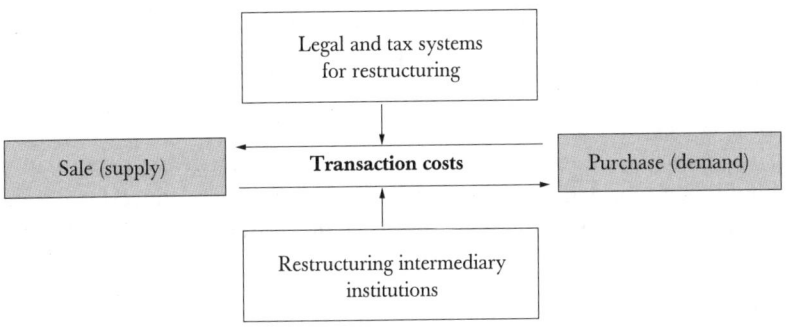

Source: Lee (1998).

Figure 8. Restructuring market and its transaction costs

If the tax burden for M&As is high, negotiations cannot proceed. For example, a high capital gains tax may prevent the active change in ownership of real estate, production facilities, equity, etc. If merging procedures are too complex, then deals can also stall. If gains from exchanges exist, and their transaction costs are not offset, then there is no need for the government to twist the arms of the transacting parties. Exchanges in the process of restructuring will occur voluntarily.

In this respect, those transaction costs necessary for corporate deals need to be curtailed on a large scale. Not only should restructuring-related taxes be lowered but temporary tax deferments should be changed to exemptions. The growing dissatisfaction among the companies is evidence of heavy tax burdens.

In other countries, systems for tax-free reorganization have been developed successfully. There exist many cases where M&As, spin-offs (split-offs and split-ups), and other reorganization procedures may be carried out without a tax burden. Holding company systems, once allowed, will enhance both the transparency and organizational efficiency of business groups. They need to be identified as just one of many organizational devices for corporate restructuring, not for the expansion of the *jaebeol*'s economic power.

Financial institutions specializing in restructuring brokerage functions need to be established as soon as possible. For example, the sooner the vulture funds, investment banks, "bad banks," mutual funds, and other financial devices and institutions are adopted, the better the performance of corporate rehabilitation will be. The recent introduction of mutual funds and its great impact on corporate capital structure is evidence of that. Such an outcome clearly illustrates how deeply the financial sector influences the real sector, and also how great a role the financial sector can play in corporate recovery.

To reduce transaction costs in general, a big push for deregulation should be advocated. Economy-wide deregulation in product, factor, and financial markets will provide a new stimulus to revitalize the economy.

2. Focus on Corporate Governance

The underlying focus of corporate restructuring must be on the corporate governance structure. The government has so far stepped up its efforts to accomodate the changes in the economic environment by making corporate laws more efficient and adaptable. This focus of the current governance policy is the distinguishing feature from past reform policies. It is true that the approach has had great success as we witness a rising tide of voices and suits from minority shareholders. The government needs to continue its concern about the evolving changes in corporate governance structure and ensure that the present policies are working properly.

The diversification issue does not concern the government, but only businesses. The government is not in a position to be fully informed of the benefits of diversification; the optimal level should be judged purely by businesses and their entrepreneurs. In this regard, the number of subsidiaries and the degree of diversification are the last issues for government involvement. However, much evidence clearly indicates that on the average, the *jaebeol* diversification level is beyond the optimal range. According to Markides (1996), the costs of group management are shifting upward, and the benefits are shifting downward, jointly lowering the optimal level of business expansion (see Figure 9).

Together with de-conglomerating, the de-leveraging of the capital structure needs to be carried out on a large scale. If corporate debt problems are pervasive and impose negative externalities on the economy at large, debt restructuring must be facilitated up to a certain level. It is understandable that government mediation between corporations and banks is warranted if there are market failures or other factors that inhibit banks from effectively leading debt restructuring. However, such intervention by government agencies must be done in a more transparent manner. One needs to remember that the tripartite "crony" relation-

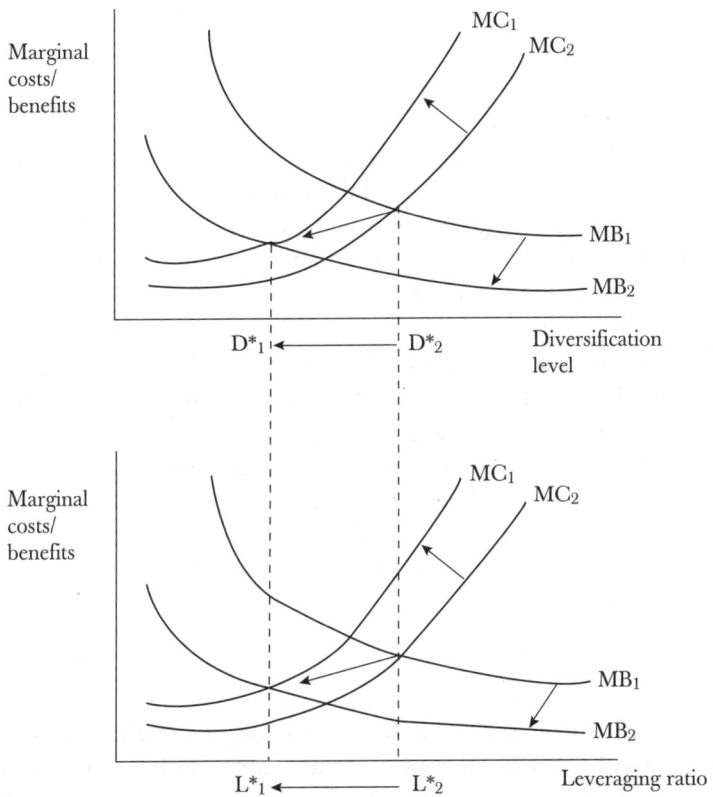

Figure 9. Adjustment of diversification and
corresponding capital leveraging ratio

ship between the government, banks, and businesses was a primary reason for the current crisis.

Particularly, the guideline for debt-to-equity ratio needs to be set independently of the government. The optimality of the 200% figure,
imposed as a benchmark by the government, has yet to be confirmed.
Optimal capital structures differ between borrowers and their projects. It
is imperative that banks should be able to judge the appropriateness of
the financial structure of each individual borrower.[13]

---

13. An economic survey of Korea also gives a critical evaluation of this issue. See OECD
    (1999).

Corporate Strategy

Recent changes in the corporate environment are so revolutionary that companies cannot survive the new competition without reshaping their strategies. The costs of group management, debt-financed expansion, and large shareholders' managerial dominance are all rising.

For example, cross-guarantees will be completely prohibited after March 2000. High interest payments and limitations in intersubsidiary cross-guarantees are significantly raising the inefficiency of old expansionist strategies such as LBOs (leveraged buyouts). Consolidated financial statements, which start in the fiscal year of 1999, will disclose the financial information of each group more transparently. Nonviable units will damage the credit of the group and will be shed immediately. Competition in the domestic market will be tougher in the wake of the abolition of the import-diversifying policy in late 1999. International competitiveness will be the criterion for whether or not a business should survive. Clearly, all these changes will negatively influence group management.

1. De-conglomerating

Khana and Palepu (1997), in a recent issue of the *Harvard Business Review*, argued that in emerging markets, diversification may be necessary to compete with established foreign companies. Focus or specialization is good advice in New York or London, but something important gets lost in the translation when that advice is given to groups in the emerging markets. Conglomerates including Korea's *jaebeol* can add value by imitating the diverse functions of several institutions that are present only in advanced economies.

Their paper illustrates the real incentives behind the formation of business groups underneath the allegedly greedy and expansionist behavior of *jaebeol*. However, these explanations cannot be used as excuses for the management failures of Korean enterprises. They have failed to adapt optimally to the above-stated changes in the business environment. Many studies argue that Korean *jaebeol* have been overly diversified, and that they need to refocus on core businesses (Booz Allen & Hamilton 1997; McKinsey Global Institute 1998). What implications do these results have regarding the *jaebeol*'s diversification behavior? Korean companies have to readjust their diversification level to match

number of subsidiaries

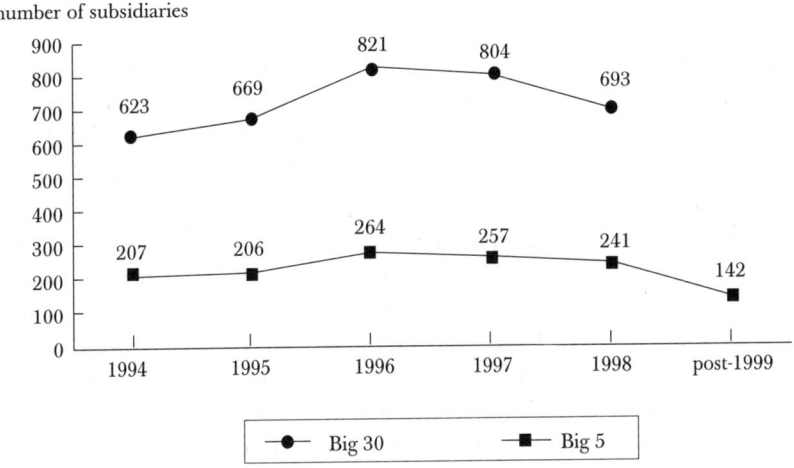

Source: Fair Trade Commission.

Figure 10. Change in the number of *jaebeol*'s subsidiaries

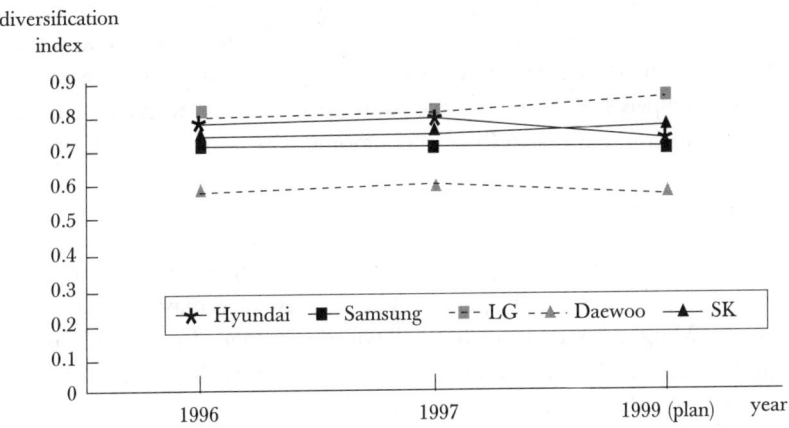

Source: Measures are based on annual sales of *jaebeol* subsidiaries and their restructuring plan.

Figure 11. Change in diversification measure of *jaebeol*

the new (marginal) cost and benefit curves of diversifying variables.[14]

Accordingly, the direction of business adjustments would be to focus more and diversify less. However, the course and extent of restructuring must be determined by the businesses themselves. It is the companies that best know what their core competence is and what to buy and sell. Big deals and the forced reduction of subsidiaries up to a certain number do not help companies restructure themselves.

Moreover, the conglomerates need to undertake business restructuring more voluntarily. We can evaluate restructuring plans and their performance so far. The number of subsidiary units will be significantly reduced by the end of 1999. In particular, the big five groups are all expected to shed, sell off, or merge more than 100 noncore units. However, in terms of the real measure of business refocusing efforts, they will not differ significantly from pre-restructuring times. The Bery index, a measure of diversification, will not drop significantly even after restructuring plans are fully implemented.

The experience of American enterprises in the 1980s deserves to be carefully examined in order to gain proper insights into restructuring. American conglomerates, overly diversified during the 1960s and 1970s, paid attention to refocusing their operations along core competence, streamlining their lines of business. Sell-offs, M&As, spin-offs, and other diverse strategies were used in restructuring. This aggressive restructuring has helped the American economy recover competitiveness. Surely, this lesson could apply to Korean conglomerates under restructuring.

2. De-leveraging

We have experienced the high risks of the historically deep-rooted debt financing practices of the *jaebeol*. The interest rate may fluctuate more widely. Market forces from outside will be stronger than ever. And the capital market, which is almost completely open, will take a more disciplinary role in monitoring companies.

To accommodate the new market conditions, firms must realign their capital structure from growth-oriented to efficiency (and profitability) oriented. To do so, they need to adopt so-called de-leveraging strategies, such as the reduction of business lines and external debt. It is a general

---

14. Markides (1996) first took this approach to derive an optimal level of diversification, which is an intersection of the MC and MR curves of diversification.

pattern that during booms, leveraging leads restructuring, while in recessions, de-leveraging takes the lead. It is important that companies find an optimal level of de-leveraging in order to maximize firm value.

In particular, as an effective way of de-leveraging, debt/equity swaps should be more enthusiastically pursued. Involuntary swaps are being carried out in workouts, while voluntary ones, such as issuing equities in the stock market and repaying debts, should also be recommended. It is imperative that Korean companies convert debt into equity to secure a more risk-free capital structure. In short, Korean corporate practices of debt financing must be rectified.

Delineation and Rearrangement of Property Rights

During the last 30 years of development, the corporate governance model of Korea has worked well to reduce agency costs. Owners, the controlling shareholders, have successfully accomplished their entrepreneurial function of enhancing corporate value. Therefore, the internal or external monitoring of management did not need to be significantly present. As the economy matures, however, the owner dominance system is producing many side effects, such as a distorted decision-making process, increasing inefficiency, and agency costs between large and minority shareholders. Naturally, the infringement of property rights, particularly of minority shareholders, stands out as a most severe problem.

To find a model of "good governance," we need to ask whether the present governance system is optimally structured to maximize shareholder value. A firm can be viewed as a set of property rights or nexus of contracts.[15] This theory indicates that if any contract or property right is severely infringed upon, the firm (and its nexus of contracts) will no longer be a "going concern." A corporate governance system represented by corporate laws is just a standard set of contracts that would have been voluntarily agreed upon by the stakeholders. It is built so as to minimize transaction costs (or agency costs) while establishing a nexus of contracts for a firm. In this regard, the optimal contract between stakeholders can differ from country to country, where socioeconomic environments are different. The OECD also confirms that each country

---

15. See a seminal paper by Jesen and Meckling (1976) and a book by Blair (1995) on this view.

has to have its own unique model of governance.[16]

The recent movements for small shareholders' rights represent the rising discontent and opposition of noncontrolling shareholders—these movements are gaining more public support than ever. The controlling shareholders must listen carefully to these voices from diverse stakeholder groups, otherwise they will not be able to gain cooperative support. In this respect, devising a good governance structure belongs to the realm of companies, not of the government. It is the corporations themselves that could be the biggest beneficiaries of successful governance reforms.

Conclusion

To "get property rights right" involves a simple but workable principle. To reform the corporate (and *jaebeol*) governance structure, property rights need to be delineated more clearly, and to do so, we need to "get the institutions right" first.[17] Without establishing an efficient system of corporate institutions, corporate restructuring cannot be carried out on a continual basis, but rather will end abruptly like a fad.

Clamoring for "solutions, now," the present administration hastened to undertake government-driven restructuring policies, as exemplified in the big deals and 200% debt ratio policies. However, a year and a half since the crisis began, we are now faced with a more formidable task. To acquire "problem-solving systems for tomorrow," we have to be more concerned with building up a set of corporate institutions that better support sustainable growth.

Under the parallel developments of the market economy and democracy under the Kim Dae-jung administration, the meaning of the former

---

16. Witherell (1999) explains the OECD Principles of Corporate Governance and says: "There is no single model of good governance. In light of the needs of individual firms and the variety of national institutional frameworks, it would not be useful to seek to establish a global standard of corporate governance."

17. Interestingly, Williamson (1994) considers property rights as one of the institutions. He suggests a desirable sequence of reform policies for transition economies, i.e. "get the institutions right" and then "get the property rights right," and, finally, "get the prices right."

has become ambiguous. The process of corporate restructuring has thus far led to a maze of complicated and political considerations that may even impede a speedy transition to a system in which property rights are clearly delineated and protected.

The system we are pursuing must be able to alter relative prices, which in turn will change the incentives of firms. Many institutionalist economists (North 1990; Williamson 1994, 1996) argue that "institutions truly matter," and the incentives (and behaviors) of corporate organizations almost take a one-to-one relationship with their surrounding institutions. Considering the importance of institutions, one can conclude that the core of corporate restructuring policies needs to be institutional reform, such as the transparent delineation of corporate stakeholders' property rights and the lowering of transaction costs using market mechanisms.[18] With the relatively low transaction costs of markets vis-à-vis hierarchical organizations, if markets were left to function smoothly, it would lead to expedient and voluntary restructuring. Then, firms would voluntarily try to readjust their business portfolios, setting up more globally standardized governance structures, and also aligning equity-based capital structures.

At times, establishing institutional systems conducive to corporate reforms may lag in yielding outcomes, but once set up, they can fundamentally transform corporate incentives, having deep and lasting impacts on business behavior.

---

18. Still, many corporate laws and regulations are unclear and might be subject to arbitrary discretion by bureaucrats. In some cases, taxes are charged, but in others they may be waived. The gaps between strict legal provisions and their weak enforcement must be narrowed, lowering uncertainty. Transparency in government matters in needed just as in private business.

REFERENCES

Blair, Margaret M. 1995. *Ownership and Control.* Washington, D.C.: The Brookings Institution.

Booz Allen & Hamilton. 1997. *Revitalizing the Korean Economy Toward the 21st Century.* Seoul: Maeil Business Newspaper Co.

Goold, M., A. Campbell, and M. Alexander. 1994. *Corporate-Level Strategy.* New York: John Wiley & Sons, Inc.

Hoskisson, R. E., and Michael A. Hitt. 1994. *Downscoping: How to Tame the Diversified Firm.* New York: Oxford University Press.

Hwang, In-hak. 1999. "*Jaebeol*-ui soyu-wa tongje" (The Ownership and Control of *Jaebeol*). Seoul: Korea Economic Research Institute.

Jang, Ha-Sung. 1999. "Corporate Governance and Economic Development: The Korean Experience." Paper presented at the International Conference on Democracy, Market Economy and Development organized jointly by the Republic of Korea and the World Bank, February 1999.

Jensen, Michael C., and William H. Meckling. 1976. "The Theory of the Firm: Management Behavior, Agency Costs, and Ownership Structure." *Journal of Finance* 3.

Jwa, Sung-Hee, and Huh Chan Guk. 1998. "Korea's 1997 Currency Crisis: Causes and Implications." *Korea Journal* 38.2 (summer).

Khanna, T., and K. Palepu. 1997. "Why Focused Strategies May Be Wrong for Emerging Markets." *Harvard Business Review* (July-August).

Koo, Bonchun. 1998. "Corporate Restructuring and Financial Reform in Korea." Working Paper, No. 9807. Korea Development Institute.

Korea Economic Research Institute (KERI). 1999. *Jaebeol bipan-ui silsang-gwa heosang* (Realities and Myth of Criticisms against *Jaebeol*). Mimeo.

Korean Stock Exchange. 1998. 2. *Sangjang gieop EVA bunseok* (EVA Analysis of Listed Companies) 98-1.

Lee, Jae-Woo. 1998. "Gieop gujo jojeong jeongchaek: junggan pyeongga-wa bowan gwaje" (Corporate Restructuring: Interim Evaluation and Complementary Agenda). In *IMF chejeha-ui gujo jojeong jeongchaek-ui jeomgeom-gwa gwaje* (Review and Recommendations of Corporate Restructuring Policies during IMF Management), edited by Lee Jae-Woo. Seoul: Korea Economic Research Institute.

————. 1999. "Corporate Restructuring in Korea: Experience and Lessons." Policy Workshop Proceedings. Korea Money and Finance Association.

McKinsey Global Institute. 1998. *Maekinji bogoseo* (McKinsey Report). Seoul: Maeil Business Newspaper Co.

Mankiw, N. G., and M. D. Whinston. 1986. "Free Entry and Social Inefficiency." *Rand Journal of Economics* 17.

Markides, C. C. 1996. *Diversification, Refocusing, and Economic Performance.* Cambridge, Mass.: MIT Press.

Modigliani, F., and M. H. Miller. 1958. "The Cost of Capital, Corporation Finance, and the Theory of Investment." *American Economic Review* 48 (June).

North, Douglas. 1990. *Institutions, Institutional Change, and Economic Performance.* New York: Cambridge University Press.

OECD. 1999. "Policy Brief." *Economic Survey of Korea* (July).

Shleifer, Andrei, and Robert W. Vishny. 1998. *The Grabbing Hand: Government Pathologies and Their Cures.* Cambridge, Mass.: Harvard University Press.

Stone, Mark R. 1998. "Corporate Debt Restructuring in East Asia: Some Lessons from International Experience." IMF Paper on Policy Analysis and Assessment.

Williamson, O. E. 1994. "The Institutions and Governance of Economic Development and Reform." *Proceedings of the World Bank Annual Conference on Development Economics.* Washington, D.C.: World Bank.

_____. 1996. *The Mechanisms of Governance.* Oxford: Oxford University Press.

Witherell, William. 1999. "Towards Principles of Corporate Governance." Paper presented at the International Conference on Democracy, Market Economy and Development organized jointly by the Republic of Korea and the World Bank, February 1999.

Yoo, Seong Min. 1999. *Corporate Restructuring in Korea: Policy Issues Before and During the Crisis.* Seoul: Korea Development Institute.

Restructuring and the Role of International Financial Institutions: *A Korean View*

Wang Yunjong

I. Introduction

On 2 July 1997, Thailand, which had been under continuous pressure to devalue the baht, finally abandoned its U.S. dollar-pegged system in favor of a freely floating exchange rate. The vulnerability displayed by Thailand quickly spread elsewhere as the financial crisis spread to Indonesia in October and further affected the economies of neighboring countries, including the Philippines, Malaysia, and Hong Kong. In the midst of this economic maelstrom, the Korean won quickly depreciated following a futile currency defense which cost Korea most of its foreign reserves. This forced Korea, the world's eleventh largest economy, to seek financial assistance from the International Monetary Fund (IMF) on 21 November 1997.

After reaching agreement on the restructuring program with the IMF on 3 December 1997, Korea was promised emergency funding of $10 billion from the International Bank for Reconstruction and Development (IBRD) and $4 billion from the Asian Development Bank (ADB), in addition to $21 billion from the IMF. Following the agreement reached with the IMF, Korea has swiftly implemented a wide range of economic reform measures. All of the measures have been directed towards

*Originally published in Vol. 39, No. 3 (Autumn 1999).

Wang Yunjong (Wang, Yun-jong) is Director of the Department of International Macro-economics and Finance at the Korea Institute for International Economic Policy. He received his Ph.D. from Yale University, and his main field of concentration is the liberalization of trade, foreign direct investment, and capital markets in Korea. E-mail: yjwang@kiep.go.kr.

rebuilding market confidence as well as expediting economic restructuring. Korea has now completed its first round of restructuring. Although foreign sentiment suggests that Korea's restructuring process is only slowly moving toward the right direction, the Korean economic recovery and the reform efforts made so far should not be overlooked as they have delivered some solid results. All international credit rating agencies have upgraded Korea's sovereign credit rating from "non-investment" to "investment" grade. This shows that Korea has not only committed, but also will continue to commit itself to changes and improvement.

Through these experiences, we can draw some lessons about the role of international financial institutions (IFIs). Certainly, the key question is whether the diagnosis of the IMF was correct and its policy prescription was relevant and effective. In evaluating the diagnosis, a balanced view of the root of the Asian financial crisis is needed. A predictably large amount of research and policy papers has been pouring out since the onset of the Asian crisis, with differing views leading to different policy implications. Academics have greater liberty to choose among various economic models or theories on which to base their analyses. However, policymakers have to be more cautious in implementing any policy measures by taking into account the reality and relevance of all findings and views.

For the sake of simplicity, academic circles may be divided into two basic camps. One camp, which focuses on the liquidity shortage of the Asian countries, emphasizes the vulnerability of the international financial market and the skittish behavior of international investors and creditors as a major triggering factor in the outbreak of the crisis. In this light, expanded financial support facilities through the IFIs, orderly capital market liberalization, and safeguards in the case of an emergency could be relevant policy proposals for building the new international financial structure. In addition, this view holds that the high interest rate policy and/or other austerity programs should be reconsidered as those policy measures may aggravate the situation rather than improve credibility in the eyes of international investors. The other camp, which focuses on the structural weakness of the country in question, and, in particular, the moral hazard problem in both the corporate and financial sectors, stresses the necessity of restructuring and growth sustainability based on a sound economic system.

This paper will discuss the role of international financial institutions by reviewing Korea's restructuring program and its process. Based on

Korea's experience of crisis management, this paper will address four issues. First, I will discuss the key question of whether or not the root of the Asian crisis should be attributed to regional structural weaknesses, or must be understood in the context of the inherent vulnerability of the global financial market. Second, the Asian crisis has ignited a lively debate on the necessity of including a restructuring program in the IMF rescue package. Because both internal structural weaknesses and external factors combined have caused the Asian crisis, fully overcoming the crisis will not be achieved without a successful completion of the restructuring process. Third, as the liquidity provision by the IFIs is by itself insufficient to resolve the immediate crisis, I will investigate whether there is a catalytic effect of lending by the IFIs. In light of Korea's experience, I will argue that the credibility and capital inflows are largely associated with the perceived strength of the government's commitment to economic restructuring rather than the IFIs' involvement per se. Finally, a brief comment will be made on the necessity of an "international lender of last resort."

The structure of this paper is organized as follows. In Part II, the nature of fund support by the IFIs will be briefly outlined. Part III describes conditionalities of the structural adjustment programs designed by the IFIs. Part IV explains the content of the restructuring program applied to Korea, while Part V discusses the current condition of the Korean economy. Finally, the role of IFIs will be reconsidered in the light of Korea's experience of crisis management.

II. The Nature of Fund Support by the IFIs

A Stand-by Agreement (SBA) enables IMF member countries experiencing difficulties with its short-term balance of payments to have access to funds within the previously agreed limit. In other words, the member countries, which conclude stand-by arrangements through the satisfactory conditionalities set forth by the IMF, may withdraw their credits from the IMF within the access limit at certain intervals. Such a method of granting access to funds was first introduced in December 1953.

The volume of the IMF assistance has drastically increased since the Latin American debt crises of the 1980s. As shown in Table 1, since the Mexican peso crisis of 1994-1995, the level of IMF assistance has steadily increased. The traditional assistance from a SBA was limited to three

Table 1. IMF's Commitment of Liquidity Support to the Crisis Countries

		As of January 1999 (Unit: $)
Country	Stand-by/ EFF	SRF
Mexico (1995)	17.8 billion (Stand-by)	–
Thailand (1997)	4.0 billion (Stand-by)	–
Indonesia (1997)	11.2 billion (Stand-by → EFF)	–
Korea (1997)	7.6 billion (Stand-by)	13.4 billion
Russia (1998-1999)	1.3 billion (EFF) in 1998	11.2 billion in 1998
	2.2 billion (EFF) in 1999	0.4 billion in 1999
Brazil (1998)	5.4 billion (Stand-by)	12.6 billion

Source: IMF.

times the country's quota, but this tradition was broken with the Mexican crisis. For Mexico, three times its quota amounted to $7.8 billion. However, the IMF underwrote an effort to put together $10 billion from non-G10 countries, but this never materialized. As a result, the IMF ended up pledging $17.8 billion to Mexico, of which about $12 billion was actually disbursed. This provided a precedent for the five times quota SBA for Thailand in August 1997.

The Supplemental Reserve Facility (SRF), a new fund facility, was created on 17 December 1997 during the Manila Finance Ministers' Meeting in order to stabilize the financial market through the provision of short-term, front-loaded financial support at higher interest rates than normal IMF funding through a SBA. In principle, any country may use the SRF. However, it is actually intended for situations where the effects of difficulty in one country may potentially destabilize the international financial system. The disbursement takes place when there is a chance of improvement in the balance of payments during a short period, based on bold restructuring policies and monetary policies. This facility was applied to Korea on 19 December 1997 just after its initial adoption. This decision was based on the fact that Korea had received a 20 times quota which far exceeded the typical credit limit of a 3 times quota. This figure constituted the largest IMF package ever. However, this was a major improvement in the problem of access limit, which became critically recognized following the 1994 Mexican crisis. Korea could become the first successful example of the use of SRF loans, as shown by the fact that the Korean government started to deliver repayments since December 1998.

In the cases of Thailand and Indonesia, SRF loans were not applied. In Thailand, a normal credit tranche of $4 billion was provided through the Stand-by Arrangement. Indonesia signed an extended arrangement with the IMF, which generally refers to the Extended Fund Facility (EFF). The EFF is an IMF facility that can be used when a longer credit withdrawal period and larger funds (in the case of Indonesia, borrowing from the IMF amounts to $11.2 billion) are necessary than that allowed under the SBA. The disbursement period is usually three years (may be extended to four years) and must be repaid within a disbursement period of four to ten years. It was intended to give support to developing IMF members and was not offered to Korea.

The original function of the World Bank was to provide different types of Project Loan or Structural Adjustment Loan (SAL) to aid the economic development of developing countries. As an exception, however, the World Bank provided Korea with $3 billion in Economic Reconstruction Loan (ERL) on 24 December 1997. Later, the ERL was followed by $2 billion of the Structural Adjustment Loan I (SAL I) as a second round of support on 27 March 1998. A third round of support, $2 billion of SAL II, was approved on 26 September 1998. Strict conditionalities were also imposed on both SAL I and SAL II.

The Asian Development Bank also promised loans totaling $4 billion. The first tranche of $2 billion was disbursed on 23 December 1997. Furthermore, a loan of $15 million for technical assistance was provided on 23 December 1997 in order to revitalize the financial sector. A disbursement of $1 billion was subsequently made on 6 January 1998, followed by a disbursement of $700 million at the end of 1998 and a final disbursement of $300 million will be made during 1999.

III. Conditionalities of the Restructuring Program

When a member country experiencing a currency crisis requests balance of payment support, the IMF has an obligation to provide such support. At the same time, the IMF has the responsibility to ensure the formulation and implementation of a structural adjustment program that will return the beneficiary to a stabilized economic condition. Thus, IMF financial assistance is, in principle, a conditional balance of payment support.

Prior to giving its support to a member country, the IMF has to assess the repayment capability of the member country to ensure that the IMF may provide support to future member countries in need. To this end, the IMF has to verify the recipient country's commitment to the structural adjustments that will result in an improvement of the balance of payments. The whole set of requirements surrounding the nature and content of the restructuring program is termed conditionalities.

The conditionalities for the IMFs fund support range broadly from general consultations for mutual cooperation to specific and quantitative formulations of economic policies. Prior to the first oil shock in the early 1970s, the conditionalities of the IMF's financial support were not very rigorous. However, as it became recognized that simple financial support was insufficient to help developing countries overcome their debt problems, the IMF started to heavily strengthen conditionalities in 1976. The conditionalities are set forth in the Letter of Intent and Stand-by Arrangement, which the member country submits to the IMF.

Along with the Letter of Intent, monetary authorities and policymakers of the member country draw up a Stand-by Arrangement and submit it to the IMF's Executive Board for approval. The Stand-by Arrangement stipulates the timetable for phased drawings and performance criteria, which are to be strictly carried out in each of the stages of economic restructuring. The performance criteria, which are derived from an understanding of the crisis country's policy, constitute the core of the IMF conditionalities. Hence, any failure to comply with the performance criteria results in the suspension or withdrawal of Fund support.

Unlike the understanding of policy, which may be more detailed and far-reaching, the performance criteria are generally limited to macroeconomic variables. One could observe from many of the Stand-by Arrangements with the IMF that performance criteria are typically applied to credit limits, money growth rates, amount of foreign assets, balance of payments, and foreign exchange guidelines, as mentioned above. In the case of Korea, the criteria for macroeconomic policies included a ceiling on the net domestic assets of the Bank of Korea, a ceiling on the reserve base, a floor on the Bank of Korea's net international reserves, and a ceiling on the consolidated budget deficit.[1] Furthermore, since the third Letter of Intent of 7 January 1998, the structural perfor-

---

1. Of these criteria, the upper limit on the reserve base is stipulated as an indicative limit.

mance criteria have been set according to quarterly reviews.

The IMF offers different types of credit facilities for the conditionalities that it proposes to the benefiting member country. The Fund also proposes conditionalities, which differ in terms of the structural adjustment programs and the size of the country's economy. If the country is supported by the general resources account, then the conditionalities are likely to increase in stringency the larger the financial support and the longer the maturity.

When concluding a Stand-by Arrangement with, or extending a Fund facility to a member country in support of its structural adjustment program, the IMF requires the member country to determine and implement new performance criteria on a quarterly basis.[2] The revised or added criteria are included in the subsequent Letter of Intent. For Korea, the performance criteria have been revised and quoted in each of the Letters of Intent since 7 January 1998. Stand-by Arrangements, which exceed a year in length, include review clauses through which the performance criteria may be changed in the member government's consultations with the IMF.

With the financial support from the IMF, Korea has been subject to Article IV annual consultations with the IMF, as well as performance reviews at least once every quarter. Considering the significant progress made in stabilizing and restructuring the economy, the IMF decided to change future reviews of the Stand-by Arrangement from a quarterly to a semi-annual basis.

IV. The Content of the Restructuring Program

The IMF structural adjustment programs for the crisis-affected East Asian countries, including Korea, are a mixture of traditional macroeconomic stabilization and restructuring policies, which have been applied to the transition economies in the past. There is no doubt that various inherent structural defects in each of the crisis-affected countries—the general lack of transparency, lax supervision and ineffective corporate governance, and the unsustainable level of short-term external debts—

---

2. The Enhanced Structural Adjustment Facility requires new performance criteria every six months.

played a major role in the crisis.[3] The IMF programs stress not only a tight short-term aggregate demand policy to stabilize the foreign exchange market, but also long-term structural reforms of the financial and corporate sectors, which were the underlying causes for the currency crisis. Such an approach underlines the IMF and Korean government's belief that structural reform, rather than a tight contractionary policy, is the key for Korea to recover its financial and economic health. However, structural reforms will be successful only if stability in the foreign exchange market is ensured.

The Korean government and the IMF have come to agree on nine Letters of Intent since 3 December 1997. The contents of the agreement can be separated into two categories: macroeconomic policies and restructuring measures. While the former stipulate specific quarterly and annual macroeconomic figures as the implementation guidelines or as the indicative targets, the latter contain general responsibilities for restructuring the economy.

The Korean government's macroeconomic policy goals at the outset of the IMF programs had targeted the stabilization of the foreign exchange market and the accumulation of foreign reserves through the maintenance of high interest rates and tight monetary policies. As a result, usable foreign reserves have increased from less than $3.9 billion in December 1997 to $64.0 billion as of 31 July 1999. Such a level of foreign reserves will serve as an effective buffer against any potential external shocks, including further currency instability in the region. Upon examining the Letters of Intent, the policy instruments for restoring stability to the foreign exchange market appear to have been the biggest concern during the early stages of the crisis. As the foreign reserves have increased to a substantial amount, the IMF programs have notably shifted their focus toward the specific implementation of the structural reforms.

The sixth Letter of Intent of 2 May 1998 served as a turning point for the focus of the Korean government's economic policy from overcoming the immediate crisis to targeting structural reforms in the financial and corporate sectors in order to prevent a future crisis. In particular, the

---

3. However, the Korean government also emphasized that the domestic bust cycle, which was amplified by negative external factors as well as the moral hazard and herd behavior of international investors, also contributed to the crisis. See more details in MOFE (1999).

IMF has agreed to relax the pressures that adversely affect the domestic credit crunch by lowering the high interest rates and resolving the financial difficulties experienced by the export sector. In addition, the specific details and deadlines for the introduction of sound banking standards, based on the Basle Agreement's Core Principles concerning financial soundness, were put in place in the sixth Letter of Intent. Also for the first time, detailed measures for corporate restructuring were confirmed; in effect, this was a break from the previous five Letters of Intent, which only discussed general principles.

From the onset of the crisis, the Korean government recognized the structural causes of the crisis and set out to restructure entire sectors of the economy. Structural reforms and restructuring measures have been actively carried out on four fronts: the financial sector, the corporate sector, the public sector, and the labor market.

Financial Restructuring

The 1997 financial crisis demonstrated how the development of Korea's financial sector had failed to keep pace with both the development of the economy and Korea's integration into the world financial markets. The granting of excessive credit for projects with limited or uncertain returns had weakened the financial sector and was a main contributing factor to the outbreak of the financial crisis. The restructuring program in this sector has focused on greatly expanding the market mechanism in the domestic economy and reinforcing the soundness of the financial sector. For this purpose, the Korean government enacted the first financial reform bills to establish the Financial Supervisory Commission (FSC), which is an independent, consolidated financial supervisory institution. The IMF also advised the Korean government to implement a plan to restructure ailing, unsound financial institutions and to close nonviable financial institutions which have no possibility of improvement.

Plans and procedures to eliminate nonviable financial institutions were developed to the satisfaction of international standards. The Bank for International Settlement (BIS) capital adequacy standards formed the basis for identifying financial institutions in need of improvement. The BIS capital adequacy ratio has been used for depository institutions such as banks, the operational net capital ratio for securities houses, and the solvency margin ratio for insurance companies. Institutions failing to satisfy the prescribed capital adequacy standards were required to submit management rehabilitation plans to the FSC.

The need to restructure the banking sector has taken precedence in government reform policies. The capital of the unhealthy Korea First Bank and Seoul Bank was written down to the minimum level. The banks then received a capital injection from the government and were put on the fast track for privatization where they will eventually be sold to foreign investors. The Korean government has signed a Memorandum of Understanding (MOU) with the Newbridge Capital consortium for the sale of Korea First Bank towards the end of 1998, and also signed a MOU with the Hongkong and Shanghai Banking Corporation (HSBC) for the sale of Seoul Bank on 22 February 1999. However, those deals failed to come to a successful close by their respective deadlines. In particular, since the two banks are Daewoo creditors, their long drawn-out sale will be further delayed or possibly aborted.[4]

Of the 27 existing commercial banks, the FSC has ordered the closure of 5 banks and the restructuring of 7 conditionally approved banks, whose BIS ratio had fallen below 8% at the end of 1997. Of the 13 remaining banks, voluntary mergers between Hana and Boram banks, and between Kookmin and Korea Long-Term Credit Bank (KLTCB), followed last September. Such mergers are likely to continue, but it is not only the banking sector that has experienced drastic changes. The FSC has also undertaken substantial measures for non-banking financial institutions. Thus, 16 merchant banks, 2 investment trust companies, 4 life insurance companies, and 6 securities companies have been either closed or suspended.

Non-performing loans (NPLs) have been on a steep rise since the end of 1997. The Korean government estimated that under the current asset classification standards, total accumulated NPLs stood at 60.2 trillion won at the end of 1998.[5]

---

4. Longstanding concerns about Daewoo's balance sheet—the group's total debts last year doubled to almost 60 trillion won ($50 billion)—came to a head on 19 July, when short-term debts worth 7 trillion won came due. At the urging of the Korean government, these were rolled over for six months, and creditors lent a further 4 trillion won against collateral of 10 trillion won, mainly in the form of unlisted shares held by Daewoo's founder chairman, Kim U-jung. With almost all the banks heavily exposed to Daewoo, the risk is that their own recent return to profitability in the first half of 1999 may be compromised if further write-offs or bailouts prove necessary.

5. On 4 June 1999 the FSC reported that NPLs of Korean financial institutions grew by 5.2 trillion won, from the end of 1998, to 65.4 trillion won as of the end of March 1999. The NPL ratio of the total loans stood at 11.4%.

This amount was comprised of 33.6 trillion won from the banks and 26.6 trillion won from the non-banking financial institutions. In order to clean up the non-performing loans and recapitalize the banking system, the Korean government has planned to spend 64 trillion won, which is approximately 15% of the annual GDP of Korea. The Korea Asset Management Corporation (KAMCO) and the Korea Deposit Insurance Corporation (KDIC) are the two organizations currently playing key roles in the banking sector reform. At the end of last year, 40.9 trillion won of fiscal support was provided. As a result of the financial restructuring, most remaining banks have recorded 10 to 12% BIS ratios, well above the BIS capital adequacy requirement (8%). The improved BIS ratios are a result of both government support and an easing of the credit crunch.

The Korean government successfully completed the first stage of financial restructuring at the end of 1998, with much of the efforts having been focused on the banking sector. Major steps were taken to revitalize the banking sector and normalize the credit flows through the injection of fiscal resources to dispose of the NPLs and recapitalize banks. At this moment, Daewoo's problems still remain a risk for banks; however, giving creditors control of the disposal of Daewoo, one of the top five *jaebeol,* would mark a new opportunity for banks to begin acting independently.

Corporate Restructuring

While the financial sector was given priority, given the tight linkage between the corporate and financial sectors, corporate and financial restructuring needed to be implemented simultaneously. Only through joint restructuring could the economic uncertainties arising from bad loans and the related credit crunch be minimized. The Korean government has developed market-oriented principles to drive the corporate restructuring process, much of which has already been implemented.

To facilitate the operation of the market mechanism by enhancing transparency, accounting standards and disclosure rules have been improved to meet the international standards. In 1998, the FSC organized a Special Committee to review the accounting and auditing systems, and the Committee recommended several reforms, including compliance with the international accounting standards. For the enhancement of transparency in corporate management, group-consolidated financial statements have been required beginning in 1999. In addition, penalties for fraudulent auditing reports–whether external or internal– have been strengthened significantly.

Prohibition of the affiliates payment guarantees for new borrowings and the reduction and elimination of cross guarantees also have been enforced. More specifically, new guarantees between the affiliates of the 30 largest *jaebeol* are now prohibited and the existing cross-guarantees must be resolved by March 2000. Furthermore, payment and loan guarantees among affiliates of the same top five *jaebeol* were eliminated by the end of 1998. Illegal intra-*jaebeol* transactions have been subject to continuous investigations of the Fair Trade Commission (FTC). As a result, the current convoy system of the large business conglomerates will be transformed into a united entity of independent and competent affiliates in the near future.

Capital structure improvement of the Korean *jaebeol* remains the foremost concern to foreign investors. The average debt-to-equity ratio of the 30 largest business conglomerates rose sharply to 518.9% by the end of 1997 from 386.5% in 1996. The FTC recently reported that the average debt-to-equity ratio significantly fell by 139.1% to 379.8% at the end of 1998. Nevertheless, this level of corporate debt is simply unsustainable. By December 1998, major creditor banks and the top five *jaebeol* had completed revising the Capital Structure Improvement Plan (CSIP), which entailed specific and feasible restructuring plans, such as the reduction of debt-to-equity ratios, the divestiture of the affiliates and assets, and the inducement of foreign investment.[6]

Unlike the top five *jaebeol*, which have the ability and capacity to pur-

---

6. On 27 April 1999, President Kim Dae-jung met with the heads of the top five *jaebeol* to discuss the progress made in corporate restructuring since the last meeting in December 1998. At this meeting, the FSC chairman reported that the top five *jaebeol* cut their debt-to-equity ratio without the effect of asset revaluation from 470.2% in 1997 to 386% by the end of 1998, but failed to meet the target of 320.1%. The top five *jaebeol* raised 81% of their target amount of 27.3 trillion won (a total of 22.1 trillion won) through asset sales and capital expansion from 1998 to the first quarter of 1999. *Jaebeol* that fail to implement their restructuring plans will face penalty measures including the suspension of fresh loans and the application of penalty interest rates. Slowly reforming *jaebeol* will also be placed under workout programs or court receivership. From now on, the major creditor banks will review *jaebeol*'s restructuring progress on a monthly basis instead of on a quarterly basis. Also, the FSC requested Hyundai and Daewoo to revise their quarterly restructuring plans.

sue restructuring through their own means, the remaining 59 *jaebeol* will have to enter into workout programs to improve their financial structure.

Most important in Korea's corporate restructuring is the large-scale reform of the top five *jaebeol*, given the size of their market share and, thus, their overwhelming economic influence. Restructuring the top five *jaebeol* should involve not only capital structure improvement, but also business restructuring. The Korean government has set an aggressive goal of reducing the average debt-to-equity ratio of corporations to less than 200% by the end of 1999. Asset sales, investment reductions, and debt repayments with the corporations' on-balance-sheet liquidity have already been initiated. Equity expansion, including the inducement of foreign capital, is just another way of improving the top five *jaebeol*'s financial structures. In 1998, the top five *jaebeol* had strengthened their financial structures through 11 trillion won in asset sales, 11 trillion won in new equity issues, and $8 billion in foreign capital inducement. In 1999, they have set even more aggressive goals to improve their capital structures.[7]

With the corporate restructuring program underway, nonviable companies will be forced to exit promptly, whereas the viable but financially weak companies will be given support through workout programs. The Corporate Restructuring Agreement (CRA), serving as the main vehicle for corporate workouts, was reached by 210 financial institutions on 25 July 1998 to coordinate the diverse interests of the creditor institutions and facilitate cooperation among them. Corporate workouts have been carried out through voluntary negotiations between creditor banks and corporate groups. The process resembles the London Approach, which was adopted by the United Kingdom to restructure its economy. In cases where creditor banks are unable to reach agreement on a workout plan, the Corporate Restructuring Coordination Committee (CRCC), which was set up pursuant to the CRA provisions, is to provide and govern the arbitration process.

Thus far, 248 affiliates of 16 *jaebeol* have applied for corporate work-

---

7. The handling of Daewoo's problems is seen as a crucial test case of the government's determination to pursue corporate reform. If the restructuring takes place within the proposed six months, other *jaebeol* will be required to carry out sound financial plans, and the economy will become more open, flexible and market-oriented.

outs. However, only 38 out of 248 affiliates were allowed to enter the workout processes. The remaining nonviable affiliates are undergoing resolution procedures through mergers, liquidation, or sell-offs. Most recently, three affiliates have dropped out of the workout processes primarily due to heavy resistance from major shareholders against the loss of their corporate control, which would force them to undergo the due resolution procedures.

As previously noted, each business conglomerate now has to identify and determine its core business areas, as described in its Capital Structure Improvement Plan. Noncore affiliates are to be reorganized through a variety of measures, such as spin-offs, management buyouts, and liquidation. Despite all of the propositions and conditions for improvement, *jaebeol* have made only half-hearted efforts toward carrying out the reforms. To remedy the situation, the FSC came up with a three-year plan to dismantle these *jaebeol*. Furthermore, with the government's guidance and mediation, the top five *jaebeol* are currently engaged in a collective restructuring program, known as the "big deals," which are designed to encourage *jaebeol* to streamline, to concentrate on their core businesses, and to reduce overcapacity by their own initiatives. Consequently, the top five *jaebeol* have finally announced that they will restructure seven business lines as part of their overall reorganizing efforts.[8]

This restructuring is to be achieved by the establishment of new business entities, asset transfers, mergers, and business swaps among the top *jaebeol* or other large corporations.

Moreover, to enhance the transparency of corporate management, external directors and external auditing systems have been strengthened. The legal scope on the liability of shadow directors has been broadened: that is, controlling owners are to register as directors and will bear any liabilities that may arise during the course of their management. As de facto major shareholders, institutional investors will be allowed to vote, which provides new checks against the management of companies. Minority shareholders' rights have also been strengthened to a significant extent through the revisions of related laws. The market for corporate control has also been developed to enhance the accountability of corporate management.

---

8. In the auto industry, Samsung Motors was recently put in court receivership, bringing an end to a "big deal" swap plan with Daewoo.

Public Sector Reform

Public sector reform is an urgent issue which has gained world-wide attention, with the recognition that the role of the state has to change to meet today's challenges. First of all, poor productivity and rampant inefficiency in the public sector have to be addressed. The Korean government has advanced public sector reform through privatizing and restructuring state-owned enterprises (SOEs) and downsizing governmental organizations. The government is proceeding with its plans to privatize 11 SOEs and their subsidiaries. The National Textbook Company, Korea Technology Banking Corporation, and Namhae Chemical Corporation have also been privatized. The recent sale of a 5.8% share in POSCO has reduced the government-owned share to 20.8%. Korea Heavy Industries will be offered for sale in early 1999, and Korea General Chemicals will be offered for sale later in that year.

Full privatization of four other SOEs (Korea Ginseng and Tobacco, Korea Gas, Daehan Oil Pipeline, and Korea District Heating) will occur in phases over the next four years. In addition, the government will offer for sale a 5% share in Korea Electric Power Corporation (KEPCO) in the first half of 1999. Korea Telecom has been publicly listed, and the government plans to reduce its share in the company to 33.4% by 2000.

Even in cases where the government retains ownership, drastic restructuring in the area of management is also taking place. Restructuring has been implemented to attack and eliminate all sources of inefficiency. Professional career managers have been appointed as top CEOs and have been given full authority over corporate management itself.

Downsizing of the government is also an important feature of the public sector reform. The government streamlined its organizational structure in February 1998, and plans to reduce its employees by 11%, or approximately 18,000 out of a total of 162,000 employees, by the end of 2000.

Labor Market Reform and Improving the Social Safety Net

To realize effective labor market reform, the Korean government is continuously working towards increasing labor market flexibility through the rigorous enforcement of labor laws against illegal strikes and other illegal labor practices. Simultaneously, the Korean government has been working to broaden the social safety net in order to ensure the maintenance of social cohesion and stability throughout the reform process. By 1 October 1998, unemployment insurance had been expanded from covering only displaced workers who lost their jobs at large corporations, to complete coverage of all displaced workers regardless of their previous employment. Furthermore, an excess of 10 trillion won has been allocated in the 1999's budget to various types of welfare benefits.

Unfortunately, throughout 1998, the restructuring process was accompanied by continued widespread economic difficulty. Since the onset of the financial crisis, Korea's economic growth rate has experienced sharp drops, while the rate of unemployment has continued to climb. However, no matter how difficult the current socioeconomic conditions may be, they will be more than offset by future benefits, which will be based on the solid foundation of the successful economic reforms.

V. Reform Gains Momentum: Do We Need Further Restructuring?

Korea's GDP grew by 5.0% in 1997, contracted by 5.8% in 1998, and grew by 4.6% in the first quarter of 1999–the first growth in five quarters. The economic growth performance was even more impressive as the GDP rose to a higher-than-expected 9.8% in the second quarter of 1999. This would be the first "V-shaped" recovery of any Asian country following the recent crisis.

Although the current economic situation has definitely turned around, participants in the Korean economy must safeguard themselves against the false notion that the ongoing restructuring process is no longer necessary. The sustainment of economic recovery will depend largely on the growth of private consumption and investment, and this requires successful restructuring of the financial and corporate sectors.

At this critical juncture, we should be carefully aware of three important economic developments. First, the labor situation is currently the most significant challenge to the Korean economy. Unemployment peaked at 8.6% in February 1999. Although the unemployment rate has dropped impressively to 6.2% in June 1999, the pace of restructuring will continue to be conditioned by the need to avert mass unemployment. As the economy rebounds, we can expect unemployment rates to continue to drop. Meanwhile, however, the government also has to accommodate the pressures of labor unrest by ensuring the adequacy of the social safety net, thereby reinforcing social stability and protecting the poor and needy until a genuine recovery is firmly established.

Second, throughout 1998, nearly 20,000 small- and medium-sized enterprises (SMEs) have lost ground due to the sharp fall in demand and the rise in interest rates. Given that this is the sector where job creation opportunities are most abundant, such a high level of business dissipation suggests that economic restructuring has failed to address a key need. The Korean government has a variety of sound and extensive programs to resuscitate the SMEs and encourage venture capital programs. Wiping out the *jaebeol*-oriented rigid economic system will promote the development and competitiveness of the Korean market as it becomes increasingly based on more creative and flexible SMEs.

Third, Koreans should not give in to any sense of euphoria or self-complacency. Again, the reform is not yet complete. Rather, they should look into the ways through which all of the economic participants—consumers, producers, businesses, labor, and the government—can come together to create the foundation of a more dynamic and competitive economic system. Thus far, the Korean people and the state have demonstrated that they are serious about and dedicated to the economic reforms. Koreans should take one step further and find ways to progress to the level of an advanced economy.

Since the true meaning of "graduating" from the IMF program is for Korea to rid itself of excessive uncertainties and risks, Korea's economic prospects depend greatly on the efficacy of its structural reforms. Continuing structural reforms will ensure the soundness of the corporate and financial sectors and bring in their wake a recovery of foreign investor confidence in 1999.

VI. The Role of International Financial Institutions

Looking back on the transitional path of the Korean economy since the outbreak of the financial crisis, we can draw some lessons about the role of international financial institutions (IFIs). With regard to the role of IFIs, four broad questions will be examined in this section.

- How relevant is the diagnosis of the Asian crisis by the IFIs?
- Do we need to restructure in accordance with the IMF conditionalities?
- Is there a catalytic effect of lending by the IFIs?

– Do we need an international lender of last resort?

How Relevant Is the Diagnosis of the Asian Crisis by the IFIs?

Certainly, the key question of the Asian financial crisis is whether the root of the Asian crisis should be solely attributed to regional structural weakness, or must be understood in the context of the inherent vulnerability of a global financial market which lacks an international lender of last resort. In this regard, the original assessment made by the IMF, that the Asian crises fundamentally stemmed from structural deficiencies but were exacerbated by illiquidity, has proven quite accurate.

Prior to the crisis, the IMF had made several recommendations to the Thai government that it undertake structural adjustment and abandon a futile defense of the currency. However, the Thai government ignored the recommendations, as it firmly believed that it could defend its currency. Its position was based on the assumption that if it devalued the baht, the external liabilities denominated in the domestic currency would increase and thus, servicing the debt would become unbearably difficult. In this sense, the Thai government justified its position by arguing that the hedge funds' currency attacks would be temporary and that their attacks were not due to fundamental economic principles.

Although the IMF had a strong sense of the growing difficulties in Thailand, there was little it could do to prevent the crisis. It was only after crisis struck that the Thai government gave in and requested IMF liquidity support. As for Korea, as late as mid-October of 1997, neither the IMF nor the Korean government expected Korea to become the next victim of the crisis. Despite the negative sentiment present in both the domestic and international markets, Korea, the eleventh largest economy in the world, was expected to remain solvent.

As shown in MOFE (1999), the emerging Asian economies were quite vulnerable to investor skittishness. Prior to the crisis, the net flow of private capital to the crisis-affected Asian countries increased from $24.9 billion in 1990 to $72.9 billion in 1996.[9] This surge of capital flows into the Asian region was due to both the international financial community's rapidly growing confidence in the continued growth potential of the

---

9. The crisis-affected countries include Indonesia, Korea, Malaysia, the Philippines, and Thailand.

Asian economy and its high interest rates. However, this was followed by the abrupt reversal of private capital flows in 1997. What triggered this sudden reversal of private capital movements? The explanations are numerous and diverse.

MOFE (1999)[10] explains that "After a decade of strength, the Japanese yen began to weaken in April 1995 vis-à-vis the U.S. dollar. This, in effect, significantly eroded the export competitiveness of emerging market economies of the Asian region. This resulted in a rise in current account deficits of other Asian countries, thus making the conditions ripe for the currency crisis in 1997. Another negative effect of the yen's weakening was its effect on the BIS ratios of Japanese banks. As yen-denominated assets lost their value, the corresponding drop in the capital adequacy ratios of Japanese banks forced many of them to pull their loans out of other Asian countries."[11] As clearly shown in the BIS reported data, total outstanding Japanese bank loans to the three crisis-affected countries of Asia diminished in 1997 from their level in 1996 by $4.3 billion in Thailand, $4.1 billion in Korea, but only by $17 million in Indonesia.

In Korea's case, the rise of the Japanese premium in the global financial market had prompted the withdrawal of short-term loans beginning in mid-October of 1997.[12] In addition to the decrease in Japanese lending

---

10. MOFE, *New International Financial Architecture: Korea's Perspective* (1999), p. 7.
11. Japan's leading international financial official, Mr. Eisuke Sakakibara, known as Mr. Yen in financial markets, recently pointed out that the U.S. and Japan had inadvertently put pressure on the other economies of Asia with their joint decision to weaken the yen in 1995. The weaker yen, by giving Japan's exports a price advantage in world markets, undermined the competitiveness of its Asian competitors. This led to a deterioration in the current account balance of the other Asian countries in 1996 and 1997. He said that the power of the yen's depreciation against the U.S. dollar was related to the fact that the others had pegged their currencies to the U.S. dollar.
12. Japanese banks, already fragile after the burst of the 1980s asset bubble and weakened by a stagnant economy in the 1990s, had heavily lent to other Asian economies. Given the very low interest rates in Japan, large-scale lending to the fast-growing East Asian countries was stimulated by the higher returns available outside Japan. In 1997, many of the Japanese banks suffered capital losses and were required to re-balance their loan portfolio in adherence to capital adequacy standards. Since the capital adequacy requirement is higher for international than for national lending, many banks chose to recall foreign loans and contain the magnitude of the domestic lending squeeze. Compared to the role of the U.S. in the Mexican crisis of 1994-1995, undoubtedly, the weakness of Japan in 1997 exacerbated the weak economic foundation in Asia and contributed to the currency crises. At the same time,

to Korea, the uneven financial liberalization also contributed to Korea's difficulties. Korea maintained many restrictions on its financial markets, even after it joined the OECD. However, other areas of the financial sector were being liberalized and this allowed a surge in borrowing by domestic banks to take place. As Japanese banks were facing increased difficulty in their own finances, they retreated from the Korean market, as did a number of other lenders to Korea. As much of this debt was short-term lending, this immediately led to a liquidity crisis. This demonstrates that in the case of Korea, the capital outflows of the portfolio investments were not a major triggering factor. Instead, a sharply declining roll over the ratio of short-term loans, particularly from Japanese banks, led to the cash flow mismatch.

In sum, the Asian crisis is considered to be "the biggest financial challenge facing the world in half a century," affecting two thirds of the world and putting nearly half of the global economy into recession. Even a senior IMF official publicly acknowledged, "The Asian crisis has been a painful learning process for everyone concerned, including the IMF." In coping with the Asian crisis, the IMF started to apply its orthodox prescription of macroeconomic stabilization and austerity measures along with rather drastic structural reform programs. Unfortunately, however, as the financially-troubled Asian economies did not improve as quickly as originally expected and, instead, the crisis spread throughout the world, the IMF adopted more flexible approaches to the problem as shown in the example of Korea.

Do We Need to Restructure in Accordance with the IMF Conditionalities?

The Asian crisis has ignited a lively debate on the necessity of a restructuring program as part of the IMF rescue package.[13]

---

the Asian crisis hit the vulnerable economy of Japan severely. See Corsetti et al. (1998) and DRI (1998) for further information.

13. Feldstein (1998) first made the criticism that, by including in the program a number of structural elements, the IMF was moving beyond its traditional macroeconomic adjustment. Stanley Fischer in his reply to Feldstein made the main counterargument. See Fischer (1998b). He asserted that "the basic approach of the IMF to these crises has been appropriate—not perfect, to be sure, but far better than if the structural elements had been ignored or the fund had not been involved."

The IMF has vigorously pursued both the policy goals of macroeconomic stabilization and economic restructuring. As part of its conditionalities in the affected countries, such corporate and financial restructuring programs have been well articulated. The appropriate policy prescription evidently rests on one's assessment of the crisis. If the problem is primarily one of illiquidity brought on by the panicked, herd behavior of international investors and creditors [as was asserted by Radelet and Sachs (1998),[14] and Chang and Valesco (1998a, 1998b, 1998c) in the case of the Asian crisis], liquidity should be injected into the crisis-hit economies at a much higher rate than is currently the standard practice. Failure to do so merely results in fire sales of domestic assets. However, if the cause of the crisis is one of moral hazard or structural weakness, then more drastic restructuring should be required as conditionalities for IMF financial support.

Both internal structural weakness and external factors led to the Asian crisis. While ascertaining whether structural weakness or external factors was the leading cause of the recent crisis might help in some respects, an approach that treats both causes with equal weight will likely bear greater results.

In order to resolve internal structural weakness, in particular, the moral hazard problem in domestic corporate and financial sectors, restructuring is an absolute necessity. Moral hazard is in no way limited to the three Asian countries receiving IMF assistance. While other countries have so far survived the financial turmoil without resorting to IMF assistance, they too will have to properly address structural weakness inherent in their economic system. For example, Japan and China, the world's leading holders of foreign reserves, are unlikely to have to resort to IMF funding. However, they are both unlikely to realize sustained future economic growth unless they too undergo successful restructuring.

According to Chang and Velasco (1998b), the economic and financial crises of Chile in 1982 and Mexico in 1994 support their argument regarding the disastrous effects of illiquidity. In Mexico and Chile, many investment projects which were left for dead once the crisis erupted, turned out to be perfectly sound once the economy returned to normal. Nonetheless, this should not be taken as proof that the only cause of the

---

14. Radelet and Sachs take the perspective that the currency crisis was a self-fulfilling prophecy. Along with Obsfeld (1996) and Sachs, Tornell, and Velasco (1996), their model allows for multiple equilibria.

crises was illiquidity. The reality is that once the Chilean government successfully accomplished corporate and financial restructuring, economic growth ensued. This tandem improvement of liquidity and financial and corporate structure, leading to renewed economic growth, explains that the two areas are both the causes and effects to not only the Asian, but also future crises.

Is There a Catalytic Effect of Lending by the IFIs?

The 1990s have experienced a rapid decline in the relative importance of official lending and a corresponding increase in the relative importance of private lending. However, since the onset of the Asian financial crisis, a sudden reversal of private capital movements has taken place, and official lending from the international financial institutions has started to fill the vacuum of private capital outflows in the emerging markets. The important question now is whether the strong commitment to conditionalities imposed by the international financial institutions will improve international investor confidence and thus see a remobilization of private investment in emerging markets. Although the IMF has emphasized the importance of its catalytic effect, the effect may be more pronounced in some countries than in others. Factors determining the degree of catalytic effect include the perceived commitment of the government to economic restructuring and the potential efficacy of reform and restructuring.

Dhonte (1997), in study conducted by the IMF, emphasized the role that IMF conditionality performs in signaling policy credibility. Latin America's renewed access to financial markets is claimed to be a response to changed policies which "IMF programs have been instrumental in stimulating." However, no matter how strong the commitment of the country involved in the IMF program, the gap between the receipt of IMF funds and inward flows of private investment is often large, regardless of the commitment of the country involved. Bird and Rowlands (1997) posit that the high interest rate policy, which was originally designed to stabilize the foreign exchange market, may also increase the likelihood of sovereign default to such an extent that the expected rate of return to capital falls. Moreover, not only will higher interest rates likely lead to economic recession, but they may adversely affect capital inflows in the form of direct and portfolio investment due to their destabilizing effect on the domestic economy.

As shown in MOFE (1999), the experiences of Korea and other Asian countries clearly illustrate that expanded liquidity support by the international community at the initial stage of crisis resolution would be a better alternative, in terms of economic costs, than the more common prescription of macroeconomic tightening. In fact, high interest rate policies imposed for the purpose of achieving currency stability led to a severe credit crunch, massive bankruptcies, and furthermore, deepened economic contraction and even social unrest. Such complications threaten to jeopardize any reform process, making recovery more difficult.[15]

The theoretical basis for the proposition of a catalytic effect based on IMF conditionality, therefore, is unclear. There may be a general consensus that policies designed to reduce fiscal deficits, rates of monetary expansion, and exchange rate overvaluation are generally useful in correcting a severe current account deficit. However, there remain doubts about the use of interest rate hikes, both in terms of their efficacy in achieving their stated policy objectives and in their consequences for subsequent capital flows.

Based on the demonstrated mixed results of crisis-affected countries, credibility and capital inflows largely appear to be associated with the perceived commitment of the government to economic reform and its strong economic potential to realize full recovery, rather than IMF involvement per se. Since the IMF and the Korean government agreed to undertake a more balanced approach between macroeconomic policies and restructuring, the growing signs of Korea's economic recovery have attracted foreign capital inflows.

Do We Need an International Lender of Last Resort?

The Korean government has asserted that "the international community needs to explore feasible ways of establishing an international lender of last resort. With the understanding that this is a long-term project, more

---

15. Nunnenkamp (1998) also critically asserted that more viable Asian firms and banks could have survived the crisis if the IMF had not insisted on harsh austerity measures. The argument for a lax monetary policy is termed a model of a currency/interest rate "Laffer curve": a fall of the interest rates would have strengthened the economy and restored confidence, causing the Asian currencies to appreciate. Regarding the "Laffer curve" argument, Paul Krugman replied that it is as silly as it sounds. See Krugman (1998b).

immediate emphasis should be placed on strengthening the role of the existing IFIs. As such, we would do well to resolve the issues surrounding the IMF's contingent credit line and the World Bank's partial guarantee facility so that these facilities can be put into place as soon as possible. Furthermore, to complement the role of the IFIs in providing emergency financial assistance, regional monetary cooperation, including the establishment of bilateral back-up facilities between central banks, should be pursued more vigorously."[16]

The debate on the need for such an institution dates back to the inception of the Bretton Woods System. J. M. Keynes put forward the plan to establish an International Clearing Union, which would issue new international money to be called bancor and provide automatic financing of current account deficits. The issue surfaced again in the 1970s when the international activity of commercial banks dramatically increased with the advent of the Eurocurrency markets and the need to recycle the sizeable surpluses of OPEC countries.[17]

The issue may be simplified into two questions. The first is whether there is a need for an international lender of last resort. If so, the second dimension is what institution, or group of institutions, should assume the responsibility. According to Kindleberger (1973, 1989), the international dimension of crises makes a case for the need of an international lender of last resort.[18] When a crisis is unfolding, countries may face limited access to capital markets even though they are implementing the appropriate policy corrections. However, economic historians challenge Kindleberger's interpretation of the interwar experience, on which he partially bases his argument, and also his assertion of the intrinsic instability of the world financial market without an international lender of last resort. They argue that the instability of the interwar period reflected inadequate international economic cooperation rather than any failure of hegemonic leadership. Monetary economists also reject the notion

---

16. See MOFE (1999), p. 12.
17. See De Bonis et al. (1999) for more details.
18. Charles Kindleberger is regarded as the father of the theory of hegemonic stability. According to his book, *The World in Depression 1919-1939*, the instability of the world economy during the interwar period reflected the absence of a dominant power with the ability and desire to stabilize the intrinsically unstable international system. His interpretation of specific historical episodes was generalized into a theory of hegemonic stability.

that markets are intrinsically unstable and need to be stabilized by an international lender of last resort. To the contrary, they argue that markets are intrinsically stable, efficient and smoothly operating and that contagion effects are negligible. They argue that an international lender of last resort would create greater problems, rather than solutions.[19]

While Kindleberger's detractors may be theoretically justified, the herd behavior of investors, volatility, and contagion continue to be the reality. Yet, even if Kindleberger's assertion of intrinsic market instability is valid, it remains unclear whether an international lender of last resort would effectively reduce the frequency and intensity of global financial crises and the extent of contagion.

The second dimension of the problem is also clearly pointed out by Kindleberger (1989): "With no world government, no central bank, and no international law, the question of where last resort lending comes from is a crucial one." Historically, such a role was informally performed by either the central bank or the most important financial institutions of the leading financial centers of the world. In 1945, the institutional setting shaped at Bretton Woods fell short of providing a full-fledged international lender of last resort. Instead, the IMF was created in order to provide financial assistance to member countries to correct external imbalances without resorting to trade and payment restrictions. However, it has been thought that the principles governing its lending activity can hardly be reconciled with the classic Bagehot rules of (a) lending freely to solvent borrowers; (b) against good collateral; and (c) at a penalty rate.[20]

In the aftermath of the Mexican crisis two important results were achieved towards strengthening several aspects of the IMF's capacity to cope with abrupt crises where there exists a risk of spillover to neighboring countries. The first has been the establishment of an Emergency

---

19. Schwartz (1986), Meltzer (1986), and recently Bordo et al. (1996) rejected Kindleberger's argument on two grounds. First, an international lender of last resort would exacerbate the risk of moral hazard by sovereign borrowers as well as by international banks. Second, the authority to create base money, the very raison d'être of a lender of last resort, remains within the purview of national central banks.

20. Fischer (1999) pointed out that the most famous lesson from Bagehot, "in a crisis, the lender of last resort should lend freely, at a penalty rate, on good collateral," could be traced back to Henry Thornton's 1802 analysis of monetary policy and the role of a lender of last resort.

Financing Mechanism (EFM)[21] by the IMF and the doubling of the lines of credit made available to the Fund by member countries. These were made possible through the General Arrangements to Borrow (GAB) and the New Arrangements to Borrow (NAB). In addition, the Supplemental Reserve Facility (SRF), as mentioned in Section II, has been instituted. Very recently, the IMF's Executive Board has agreed to provide Contingent Credit Lines (CCL) for member countries. Unlike the SRF, the CCL is a precautionary line of defense readily available against future balance of payments problems that might arise from international financial contagion. Moreover, with the provision of the CCL, the IMF's surveillance function will be strengthened by the Fund's careful monitoring of the reform measures.

At this moment, it is unlikely that the creation of an international lender of last resort in the form of an international central bank will be realized in the foreseeable future, even as the necessity of such an institution increases. According to Fischer (1999), two elements of Bagehot rules (penalty rate and the notion of lending freely) have been incorporated in the SRF, which enables it to make short-term loans in large amounts at penalty rates to countries in crisis. With regard to good collateral, as Fischer correctly indicated, the Fund and World Bank would be regarded as preferred creditors, and thus would require sufficient collateral.

In sum, the IMF appears to have the capacity to act as a lender of last resort to individual countries. Already, the IMF performs two roles as crisis lender and crisis manager. While the idea of creating an international lender of last resort is a long-term task, strengthening the role of the IMF along with the other IFIs as crisis lender and crisis manager will be increasingly important in the short term.

---

21. Critics have complained that the Fund is too slow in emergencies, but it has in recent years demonstrated the ability to respond very quickly, using the EFM. According to Fischer (1999), the main constraint on the IMF's ability to act in time is that governments delay too long in approaching it, in part because they hope to avoid taking actions that would be needed in a Fund program.

REFERENCES

Bagehot, W. 1886. "One Banking Reserve or Many." *The Economist* 24.

Bird, G., and D. Rowlands. 1997 "The Catalytic Effect of Lending by the International Financial Institutions." *The World Economy* 20.7: 967-991.

Bordo, M. D., B. Mizrach, and A. J. Schwart. 1996. "Real Versus Pseudo International Systemic Risk: Some Lessons from History." NBER Working Paper, No. 5371.

Chang, R., and A. Velasco. 1998a. "Financial Fragility and the Exchange Rate Regime." RR #"98-05, C.V. Starr Center for Applied Economics, NYU.

_____. 1998b. "Financial Crises in Emerging Markets: A Canonical Model." Working Paper. Federal Reserve Bank of Atlanta.

_____. 1998c. "The Asian Liquidity Crisis." NBER Working Paper, No. 6796.

Corsetti, G., P. Pesenti, and N. Roubini. 1998. "What Caused the Asian Currency and Financial Crisis?" NBER Working Paper, No. 6833 and No. 6834.

Dhonte, P. 1997. "Conditionality as an Instrument of Borrower Credibility." IMF Working Paper on Policy Analysis and Assessment.

De Bonis, R., A. Giustiniani, and G. Gomel. 1999. "Crises and Bail-outs of Banks and Countries: Linkages, Analogies, and Differences." *The World Economy* 22.1: 55-86.

DRI. 1998. *A Special Report: Asian Depression and World Recession.*

Giannini, C. 1999. "'Enemy of None but a Common Friend of All?': An International Perspective on the Lender of Last Resort Function." IMF Working Paper.

Feldstein, M. 1998. "Refocusing the IMF." *Foreign Affairs* (March/April): 93-109.

_____. 1999. "A Self-Help Guide for Emerging Markets." *Foreign Affairs* (March/April).

Fischer, S. 1998a. "The IMF and the Asian Crisis." Forum Funds Lecture at UCLA, Los Angeles, March.

_____. 1998b. "In Defense of the IMF: Specialized Tools for A Specialized Task." *Foreign Affairs* (July/August).

_____. 1999. "On the Need for an International Lender of Last Resort." Paper presented for delivery at the joint luncheon of the American Economic Association and the American Finance Association, New York, 3 January.

International Monetary Fund. 1999. *IMF-Supported Programs in Indonesia, Korea and Thailand: A Preliminary Assessment.*

Karminsky, G., and C. Reinhart. 1996. "The Twin Crises: The Causes of

Banking and Balance of Payments Problems." International Finance Discussion Paper, No. 544. Board of Governors of the Federal Reserve System.

Kindleberger, C. P. 1973. *The World in Depression, 1919-1939.* 2d ed. Berkeley: University of California Press.

_____. 1989. *Manias, Panics, and Crashes: A History of Financial Crises.* New York: Basic Books.

Krugman, P. 1994. "The Myth of Asia's Miracle." *Foreign Affairs* (November/December): 62-78.

_____. 1998a. "What Happened to Asia?" Mimeo. MIT.

_____. 1998b. "Will Asia Bounce Back?" Mimeo. MIT.

Meltzer, A. H. 1986. "Comment on Real and Pseudo-Financial Crises." In *Financial Crises and the World Banking System,* edited by F. Capie and G. Woods. London: Macmillan.

Miller, M., and L. Zhang. 1997. "A Bankruptcy Procedure for Sovereign States." Working Paper Series, No. 34. Global Economic Institutions.

Ministry of Finance and Economy (MOFE). 1999. "New International Financial Architecture: Korea's Perspective." Available at the website of the Ministry of Finance and Economy (www.mofe.go.kr).

_____. 1999. *The Road to Recovery in 1999: Korea's Ongoing Economic Reform.* Gwacheon: MOFE.

Nunnenkamp, P. 1998. "Dealing with the Asian Crisis: IMF Conditionality and Implications in Asia and Beyond." *Intereconomics* (March/April): 64-72.

Obstfeld, M. 1996. "Models of Currency Crises with Self-Fulfilling Features." *European Economic Review* 40: 1037-1047.

Radelet, S., and J. Sachs. 1998. "The Onset of the East Asian Financial Crisis." Working Paper. Harvard Institute for International Development.

Sachs, J., A. Tornell, and A. Velasco. 1996. "Financial Crises in Emerging Markets: The Lessons from 1995." In *Brookings Papers on Economic Activity,* No. 1, 147-198.

Schwartz, A. 1986. "Real and Pseudo-Financial Crises." In *Financial Crises and the World Banking System,* edited by F. Capie and G. Woods. London: Macmillan.

Wang, Y., and H. Zang. 1998. *Adjustment Reforms in Korea since the Financial Crisis.* Policy Paper 98-02. Korea Institute for International Economic Policy.

Mid-term Evaluation:
The Korean Financial Crisis

Yi Insill

Introduction

Due to the positive countermeasures implemented by the Korean government, the International Monetary Fund (IMF), and other international organizations, the possibility of another financial crisis in Korea now seems quite remote. Besides, major economic indicators show clear signs of recovery following the whirlwind of reforms and challenges of economic revival. However, one and a half years under the stewardship of the International Monetary Fund meant tumultuous and often painful changes for the Korean economy. For a nation that thrived on expansion and growth over the past 30 years, a contraction of the economy estimated at 5.8% in 1998 was disastrous. Bold restructuring of the financial and corporate sectors has so far left nearly 1.3 million people or 6.2% of the work force without a job, and the figures are not likely to decrease rapidly.

This convulsion of the economy was inevitable, as the main thrust of the Kim Dae-jung government's responses was to secure macroeconomic stability by means of tight monetary and fiscal policies. Financial and corporate sector reforms have been top priorities on Kim's reform agen-

*Originally published in Vol. 39, No. 3 (Autumn 1999).

Yi Insill (Yi, In-sil) is Director of Financial Studies at the Korea Economic Research Institute, Vice-President of the Korean Women's Economic Association and also serves on the Committee of the Fair Trade Commission. She received her Ph.D. in Economics from the University of Minnesota at Minneapolis in 1990. She has written "Capital Regulation and Korean Banks' Risk Taking Behavior" (2000) and "Korean Economic Reform: After the 1997 Financial Crisis" (1999). E-mail: insill@keri.go.kr.

da, as rapid progress in these areas is a prerequisite for returning the economy to a path of sustained growth. Confronting such challenges, Korea bravely pushed for sweeping reforms designed to take it into the twenty-first century as a thriving, not reeling, economy.

The Korean government pushed ahead with the restructuring and recapitalization of the financial sector, and the strengthening of prudential regulations and supervision. There also have been major steps taken to improve the institutional framework in order to facilitate corporate restructuring through market discipline, improve transparency, enhance corporate governance, liberalize mergers and acquisitions, and open to foreign investment. Banks are playing a central role in restructuring corporate debt and in strengthening the corporate financial structure. Furthermore, the layoffs as part of rationalization are now allowed, thus easing the rigidities of the labor market.

The Korean government's policies to restore financial stability have begun to regain the confidence of international investors. Along with the current account shifting to a massive surplus, usable reserves have increased to well above the pre-crisis level. However, the rapid restructuring process has also stirred up many problems, such as using large amounts of taxpayers' money and therefore raising the national debt to an unprecedented level. The impact of the crisis on the economy is still severe and difficult challenges remain ahead. Bankruptcies and unemployment are not decreasing to stable levels. The financial market showed signs of instability after the disclosure of the Daewoo Group's liquidity problems.

Furthermore, it seems to be getting more difficult to finance the extra resolution costs for restructuring the financial system. At this point it is not clear how much of taxpayers' money has to be put into the restructuring process. Moreover, global economic conditions still remain volatile and the Korean economy is now widely open. The Korean government's 1999 restructuring policies focus on the "software" aspects, meaning applications of global standards in the banking and corporate sectors, management renovation, and increased transparency. This marks a step forward from 1998, when the government focused on the "hardware" aspects, i.e., structural and institutional improvements. Internally, the establishment of a new economic paradigm warrants cultivation of an open mind-set and upgrading standards in all sectors of the Korean economy. Indeed, the challenges that lie ahead are both immense and complex.

It is too early to evaluate the results of the Kim Dae-jung government's reforms, since they have not yet come to fruition. It is, however, very useful to ask the following questions to gain some insights for future reform plans: "Is the ongoing reform process of the Korean economy headed in the right direction?" and "What did Koreans learn from this crisis?"

The present paper is structured as follows: Part II briefly reviews Korea's financial crisis including the current state of the Korean economy after the crisis. Part III overviews active reforms taken by the government following the crisis in four major sectors. Part IV conducts a mid-term evaluation and discusses the lessons from the recent reforms. The final part outlines a few open issues in assessing the implications of Korean-style reforms.

Korean Economy After the Crisis

Korea's Financial Crisis

Many economists believed that the immediate cause of the crisis was a combination of measures, rather than a single particular policy measure, undertaken by the Korean government in 1997.[1] The most important cause of the Korean financial crisis was the near depletion of foreign currency reserves. Needless to say, the latent structure of the crisis resulted from other more fundamental factors. The domestic origin of the crisis can be traced back to the long-standing structural weaknesses of the Korean economy, although one should acknowledge the exogenous effect of the Southeast Asian crisis.

Some economists further believed that the Korean failure to keep up with the rapid pace of globalization was one of the main reasons leading to the crisis. Korea was ill-prepared for the changes in the global economic environment. The country's over-exposure to short-term external debt made it particularly vulnerable to cyclical shocks as well as changes in market expectations. The Korean economy has long been plagued by pervasive problems of moral hazard. Under the umbrella of government protection, financial institutions indulged in questionable lending prac-

---

1. For a thoughtful review of what caused the Korean financial crisis, see Jwa and Huh (1998).

tices. Yet for every reckless lender, there was also a reckless borrower and reckless supervisors.

Korean corporations pursued excessively leveraged expansions into less profitable business areas and were consequently brought down by heavy debt burdens and substantial investment losses. This, in turn, resulted in the staggering accumulation of non-performing loans (NPLs) in the financial sector and the erosion of financial institutions' capital base. A series of *jaebeol* bankruptcies, starting with the Hanbo Group, began in early 1997. One immediate impact was the sharp loss of investor confidence. In fact, the abrupt outflow of short-term foreign portfolio investments between September and November 1997 initiated a sudden capital flight and resulted in the currency collapse. The won plunged 27.5% against the U.S. dollar in November 1997, and lost 40.3% of its value from the preceding year in December 1997.

Under such circumstances, it was inevitable for the Korean government to seek assistance from the IMF. An official request for an emergency liquidity arrangement was made on 21 November 1997. On 3 December, Korea finalized the Stand-by Arrangement with the IMF, and since then has had nine "Reviews for the Economic Program" as of February 1999.

IMF Programs in Action

The IMF attached a wide-ranging set of policy conditions to this emergency loan package. "The Policy Framework" section of Korea's Letter of Intent describes the basic tenets of those conditions. The aim of macroeconomic policies, agreed upon between the Korean government and the IMF, was basically to restore stability in the foreign exchange market. Table 1 shows the key items related to macro management of the economy agreed by the Korean government and the IMF. The IMF made some mistakes in addressing Korea's financial crisis in the initial stages of its development.[2] The main thrust of the early policy guidelines was to maintain a high-interest rate regime to restore confidence in the stability of the exchange value of the Korean won, and therefore stopping capital outflows. From another point of view, this meant that

---

2. For further explanation of these mistakes, see Jwa Sung-Hee & Huh Chan Guk, "Korea's 1997 Currency Crisis: Causes and Implications," *Korea Journal* 38.2 (summer 1998): 27-28.

Table 1. Changes in the Agreement between the Korean Government and the IMF

	1st (97.12.4)	2nd (98.1.8)	3rd (98.2.15)	4th (98.5.15)	5th (98.8.20)	6th (98.10.29)
Growth rate	3%	1–2%	1% (accepting 0% or minus growth)	–1% (possibly lower)	–4%	Plus growth in 1999
Prices	5%	9%	9%	One digit	9%	5% Current 4.3
Current account	4.3 billion dollar surplus (1% of GDP)	3 billion dollar surplus	8 billion dollar surplus (2.5% of GDP)	21–23 billion dollar surplus	33–35 billion dollar surplus	20 billion dollar surplus
Interest rate	Allowing 14–16% level of market interest rate	Removing interest rate ceiling, keeping yearly average 20% level	Consider to decrease cautiously and gradually when the exchange rate stabilizes	Decrease it flexibly and in a balanced way when the exchange rate stabilizes	Decrease flexibly if necessary	Flexible interest rate policy
Exchange rate	Yearly average 1,100	Yearly average 1,300	Yearly average 1,400	–	–	–
Monetary policy	Contractionary	Contractionary	Contractionary	Reducing contractionary policy	Reducing contractionary policy	Eliminating the money base constraint
Budget deficit/GDP	Balanced or small deficit	Allowing deficit	–0.8%	–1.75%	–4%	–5%

the IMF completely disregarded the structural characteristics of the Korean economy. Of course, everyone agreed that there was a need to restructure the business sector. However, the economic reality of firms with high leverage ratios was not reflected in the IMF's recommendations used in the formation of economic policy.

Table 1 also shows how the agreements have evolved since December 1997. The IMF provided recommendations on the basis of incorrect economic predictions and in disregard of economic indicators. It also overlooked the severity of the country's economic state. This fully exposes the IMF recommendations to critical review. Korean policymakers are also to blame, but the IMF failed to properly predict the economic growth rates that form the basis of all economic policies.

The Korean government's response was to follow the policy guidelines spelled out in the IMF agreement. Early on, the Korean government's policy responses were to put out the fire and prevent it from spreading. The key measures taken by the government included closing down insolvent merchant banks and providing wide-ranging deposit guarantees to prevent a potential bank run that could threaten the viability of the whole financial system. Also important was the completion of negotiations with international creditors about extending the maturity of various short-term loans coming due, which was completed in March 1998.

Following the initial round of crisis management, the government's priority was again placed on implementing various reform measures and supervising financial institutions more carefully, rather than on considering macroeconomic policy combinations. This was mainly because the stringency imposed on macroeconomic policy guidelines left little room for policymakers to maneuver. At the same time, the IMF emphasized the provisions for a social security net to mitigate the adverse impact of these rather constrictive macroeconomic policies on the poor.

Korean Economy After the Crisis

The high-interest rate policy regime imparted a huge negative momentum to the Korean economy amplified by the added financing burden borne by businesses that had relied on debt to an unusual degree according to OECD standards. The Korean economy started to experience the true extent of the adverse repercussions of the financial and foreign exchange market turmoil in 1998. Real GDP contracted by 5.8% in

1998 owing to a drastic fall in investment (–1.6%) and sharp cutbacks in private consumption (–8.9%). The unemployment rate, after remaining in the low 2% range over the past three years, started to rise in early 1998 and peaked at 8.7% in February 1999.

The adverse employment conditions have also been reflected in terms of the declining wage. For example, nominal wages for manufacturing sector workers fell 2.5% in 1998. One indication of the financial stress placed on the corporate sector since the beginning of the year is the extent of failure to meet short-term financial obligations. Figure 1 shows the trend in the rate of dishonored checks and bills since September 1997. There was a distinct peak during the December-January period and a discreet rise in the level since. A similar trend has been seen in the bankruptcy rates for the same period.

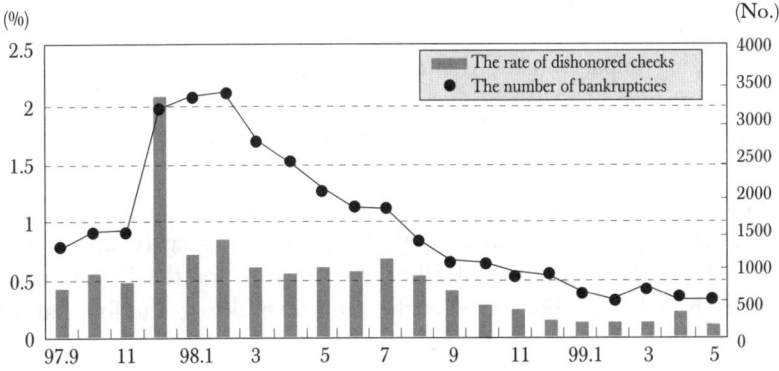

Figure 1. The rate of dishonored checks and the number
of bankruptcies (97.9 – 99.5)

Table 2 shows that the actual deterioration of macroeconomic conditions far outpaced those of the agreed-upon macroeconomic indicators, the only exception being the current account surplus. For example, the fifth agreement envisioned the growth rate for the year at –1% (or less), but real GDP shrunk by 5.3% in the first half of 1998.

The fall in the growth rate was somewhat mitigated by a rise in net exports caused both by the rising volume of exports, which benefited from the weaker won, and shrinking imports. The level of foreign exchange reserves started to rise in the beginning of 1998, bolstered by the infusion of IMF funds. More importantly, the steady growth in the current account surplus throughout 1998 contributed to the rebuilding of reserve holdings. The usable reserve amount stands well above average levels seen in the past, perhaps removing Korea to a safe distance from the lack of liquidity in the foreign exchange seen in December 1997 when the comparable figure stood at $8.9 billion. In March 1998, the exchange value of the won more or less stabilized at around 1,300 won per U.S. dollar after reaching a record low of 1,706.8 in January.

The weakening exchange value of the Korean won appears to have had positive effects on the external balance of payments mainly by reducing the amount of imports. As shown in Table 2, both exports and imports have been cut back in dollar terms when compared with the same period of 1998. However, the fall in the amount of imports has been quite sharp at 35.5% while exports went down only 2.8% in 1998. This resulted in a $40 billion current account surplus in 1998.

Large fluctuations in the exchange value of the won have also had a destabilizing impact on the domestic price of goods and services. The rapid depreciation of the won had an almost immediate pass-through impact on domestic prices, and the producer price index (PPI) rose 12.2% in 1998. The consumer price index (CPI) also rose 7.5% (year-over-year basis) in the same period. The initial inflationary pass-through effect has now subsided thanks in part to a fall in aggregate agricultural prices from the beginning of 1999. As a result, for the first time in Korea, the CPI in 1999 stayed at the same level during the first half of the year.

Over time people came to realize that the contraction in domestic aggregate demand was far worse than expected and rehabilitation of the banking sector would require a huge sum of public funding. Consequently, it became more obvious for all parties concerned that both fiscal and monetary policies needed to take a proactive role. At the same time, the exchange value of the won remained stable from the spring of 1998. Thus, the stance taken for both monetary (measured in terms of reserve money growth) and fiscal (measured in terms of budget deficit) policies has been somewhat more relaxed since the summer of 1998.

As a result of expansionary monetary and fiscal policies, according to macroeconomic projections for 1999 the growth rate is expected to reach around 7 or 8%. Interest rates continue to be stable, keeping the overnight call rate at under 5%, thereby the leading 3-year corporate yield rate is around 10% currently, after reaching 7.56% in April 1999 as

Table 2. Industrial Activities and Economic Indicators

(Unit: $ billion)

	1997	1998					1999						
		1st Q	2nd Q	3rd Q	4th Q	Ann.	Jan.	Feb.	Mar.	Apr.	May	Jun.	July
Production	6.9	-7.6	-11.7	-8.2	-0.7	-7.3	14.8	3.9	18.8	17.1	21.7	29.5	33.1
Shipment	5.0	-4.5	-11.8	-9.6	-2.2	-7.1	13.6	6.7	21.4	19.5	23.4	30.7	33.0
Inventory	5.3	-4.6	-8.0	-10.9	-17.3	-17.3	-16.9	-18.1	-18.5	-19.4	-18.0	-16.9	-15.2
Operation ratio	79.9	68.8	67.0	66.7	69.9	68.1	69.6	69.7	74.7	74.1	76.6	79.8	81.0
Whole and retail sales	3.2	-11.2	-16.0	-15.1	-8.3	-12.7	2.6	7.4	8.3	9.0	9.4	14.2	18.6
Shipment for domestic consumption goods	-1.8	-19.1	-25.4	-22.3	-18.4	-21.4	7.8	11.8	19.5	13.6	17.8	20.4	23.4
Machinery order received	3.3	-38.9	-43.8	-22.2	-10.9	-30.5	39.6	-1.0	15.8	23.6	40.5	51.1	29.4
Construction order received	4.7	-23.4	-53.4	-44.8	-44.9	-42.5	-20.5	-52.0	-51.1	39.3	89.6	-6.2	0.1
Unemployment rate	2.6	5.7	6.9	7.4	7.4	6.8	8.5	8.6	8.0	7.1	6.4	6.2	6.2
PPI	3.9	14.4	13.9	12.0	8.6	12.2	-1.8	-4.3	-4.3	-4.1	-2.6	-3.3	-2.9
CPI	4.5	9.0	8.2	7.0	6.0	7.5	1.5	0.2	0.5	0.4	0.8	0.6	0.3
Export	1,316.6	322.3	348.8	304.8	347.2	1,323.1	92.6	93.3	117.0	115.5	114.7	129.3	118.2
(Increasing rate)	(5.0)	(8.4)	(-1.8)	(-10.8)	(-5.5)	(-2.8)	(2.9)	(-16.8)	(-2.6)	(-4.3)	(1.5)	(12.3)	(17.9)
Import	1,446.2	236.6	235.4	214.6	246.6	932.8	86.3	76.3	93.0	90.9	94.5	102.0	97.6
(Increasing rate)	(-3.8)	(-36.1)	(-37.0)	(-39.9)	(-28.7)	(-35.5)	(15.3)	(-3.2)	(12.2)	(10.7)	(24.6)	(31.6)	(37.6)
Trade balance	-84.5	85.7	113.4	90.2	101.0	390.3	6.3	17.0	24.0	24.6	20.2	27.3	20.6

Note: Inventory is the end of period base.
Source: National Statistical Office.

the lowest monthly average. The exchange rate policy has remained somewhat flexible and (Bank of Korea) market interventions are limited to smoothing operations in the foreign exchange market. Usable foreign exchange reserves, already exceeding $64.9 billion as of the end of August 1999, continue to increase throughout the year.

Most of the current macroeconomic indicators cast a bright light on the future of the Korean economy. The latest figures of industrial activity bode well for economic recovery (see Table 2). Yet the high unemployment rate still remains a heavy social burden, while the recent number of unemployed workers slowly diminished to 1,349,000 people with an unemployment rate of 6.2% as of July 1999, down from a peak of 1,775,000 and 8.7% respectively in February 1999. However, there still remain uncertain ties about the Korean economy, such as the unstable financial market, sluggish exports, possible labor disputes, and rising inflationary pressure. Whether the current pace of recovery can be sustainable has yet to be seen.

Reforms in Four Major Sectors of the Economy

Under the difficult economic circumstances arising from the foreign exchange reserve depletion and the recession, the new government has been accelerating the reform efforts in four major areas. From the onset of the crisis, the Kim Dae-jung government, whose economic policies are rooted in the principles of democracy and market economy, understood the main causes of the crisis and set out to restructure entire sectors of the economy. Recognizing that dilapidation of loans and corrupt lending and borrowing practices were at the core of the structural failure, the new government prioritized the restructuring of the financial and corporate sectors simultaneously. In addition, labor and public sector restructuring has also been pursued to give each sector the flexibility and efficiency necessary to keep up with other sectoral reforms.

Financial Sector Reforms

1) Restructuring in Banks and Non-Bank Financial Institutions

The most pressing task for Korea was to restructure the financial sector. It was important to stop the vicious circle of corporate insolvency, which directly led to financial sector insolvency. With this in mind, the first thing the Korean government did was to restore intermediary functions based on voluntary credit screening and rebuild the financial system based on market principles, thereby minimizing the taxpayer's burden.

As an important step, the establishment of an independent and consolidated financial supervisory organization was agreed upon with the IMF. It has authorized the closure of defaulting financial institutions and assumed leadership for restructuring the financial sector. It has set a clear exit strategy and standards for loss sharing among parties to enhance the market's role in the financial sector. Merchant banking corporations, which were seen as the principal cause of the current crisis, were the government's first targets as far as closures were concerned. The next target was the commercial banks. The Financial Supervisory Commission used the capital adequacy ratio as one of its evaluation standards to check the asset soundness of all commercial banks. Banks that fell short of the 8% BIS ratio at the end of 1997 were required to submit recapitalization plans, which included timetables for reaching the ratio. Banks that did not pass the evaluation were forced to take drastic steps, such as M&As and liquidations.

Table 3 shows the results of the first round of financial restructuring. 171 financial institutions, including five banks, have either been closed down or had their operations suspended. The restructuring of merchant banks was most fatal, because they were reckless in dealing with short-term loans and in managing risky investments. As a result, 16 merchant banks out of 30 prior to the financial crisis, were either suspended or had their licenses revoked. Relatively comprehensive restructuring programs for leasing and insurance companies have also been implemented. Restructuring of investment trust companies is expected to be implemented in the near future.

Forcing insolvent financial institutions to exit the market provided a basis for reducing uncertainty and increasing efficiency. However, it has to be pointed out that only small financial institutions have exited so far and this does not help improve the competitiveness of the remaining financial institutions.

At the same time, financial institutions have intensified their own rehabilitation efforts. For example they reduced their personnel by 68,000, about 34% of total staff, and shut down 1,181 branches by the end of March 1999, as seen in Table 4. The most severe restructuring program in terms of reducing personnel has occurred in the leasing sector. More

Table 3. Major Reforms in Financial Institutions

	End of 1997	April 1999	Contents
Banks	33	24	• Exit of five banks through P&As • M&As involving nine banks including Chungbuk Bank • Two major commercial banks sold to foreign investors (Korea First Bank to New Bridge Capital and Seoul Bank to HSBC)
Merchant banks	30	12	• 16 merchant banks closed down • 2 merchant banks M&Aed with commercial banks
Security firms	36	30	• 2 security companies closed down • 4 security companies have their operations suspended
Insurance companies	50	45	• Exit of 4 insurance companies through P&As • 2 M&As • Management Improvement Notice to 16 insurance companies
Investment trust companies	31	25	• 2 investment trust companies closed down
Leasing corporations	25	21	• 4 leasing companies closed down • Assets and liabilities removed from 6 leasing companies by Bridge Leasing Company
Mutual savings & finance companies	231	208	
Credit unions	1,666	1,566	
Total	2,102	1,931	

Source: Ministry of Finance and Economy (1999).

than half of the supporting staff and managers in leasing companies lost their jobs. From the point of view of improving the efficiency of the financial industry, layoffs and downsizing can be considered successful. After restructuring, productivity increased in absolute numbers, though it remains uncertain whether it will lead to productivity increases in the medium and long terms.

The most tangible sign of financial reform was the government's deci-

Table 4. Downsizing of Korean Financial Institutions

			End of 1997	End of 1998	Changes
Banks		Managers	501	345	△156 (△31.1%)
		Supporting staff	114,118	75,259	△38,859 (△34.1%)
	No. of branches	Domestic	5,987	5,056	△931 (△15.5%)
		Abroad	190	127	△63 (△33.2%)
Merchant banking	Managers and supporting staff		1922	1,628	△294 (△15.3%)
Leasing companies	Managers and supporting staff		2,172	1,080	△1,092 (△50.3%)
Securities firms	Managers and supporting staff	Managers	362	271	△91 (△25.1%)
		Supporting staff	26,870	22,084	△4,786 (△17.8)
	No. of branches	Domestic	1,260	1,108	△152 (△12.1%)
		Abroad	89	41	△48 (△53.9%)
Investment companies	Managers and supporting staff		83,304	64,879	△18,425 (△22.1%)
Investment trust companies	Managers and supporting staff		6,230	5,004	△1,229 (△19.7%)
	No. of companies		31	24	△7 (△22.6%)
Mutual savings & finance companies	Managers and supporting staff		10,425	8,226	△1,229 (△21.1)
	No. of companies		230	209	△21 (△9.1%)
Credit unions	Managers and supporting staff		30,122	28,767	△1,355 (△4.5%)
	No. of companies		1,666	1,592	△74 (△4.5%)

Source: Financial Supervisory Service.

sion to sell its 51% stake in Korea First Bank and Seoul Bank to foreign investors, although it is quite uncertain at this moment whether this sale will take place.[3] The government-initiated sale of banks and insurance companies to foreign investors should result in more economic benefits

---

3. After six months of negotiations, the proposed sale of Seoul Bank fell through, despite the Korean government's efforts to sell the ailing firm. The Korean government and HSBC could not agree on how to evaluate Seoul Bank's assets and loan portfolio.

than simply attracting foreign capital and saving public funds. The efficiency of financial institutions can be improved by acquiring advanced financial techniques and management skills. The Korean government should consider the sale of financial institutions more rigorously rather than pouring public funds into the restructuring process. However, one should not underestimate that a moral hazard may arise in the process of selling financial institutions to foreign investors and using public funds to buy out non-performing loans.

2) Public Support for Financial Restructuring

Reducing the non-performing loans (NPLs) from the banking sector is a staggering task. The actual amount of cash involved in the implementation of NPLs riddance, however, is only a fraction of the total amount of NPLs. The Korea Asset Management Corporation (KAMCO) has been entrusted with the above-mentioned task. KAMCO, modeled after the U.S. Resolution Trust Corporation (RTC), purchases NPLs from banks at market value, which is only a fraction of the book value. However, KAMCO does not pay for the purchase in cash but in kind with its own issuance of bonds. The Korean government guarantees the KAMCO bonds and agrees to pay for the interest at maturity in cash. The banks welcome such an arrangement, since government-guaranteed bond holdings raise the BIS capital ratio.

The same strategy is employed in the recapitalization of banks. The Korea Deposit Insurance Corporation (KDIC), modeled after the United States Federal Deposit Insurance Corporation (FDIC), pays for the capital subscription of the bank not in cash but in kind with the issuance of its own bonds. The Korean government guarantees the KDIC bonds and agrees to pay for the interest at maturity in cash. The bank welcomes the receipt of the government-guaranteed bond, since such bonds also raise the BIS capital ratio.

In both of these NPL disposal and recapitalization operations, the amount of cash transactions should be brought to a minimum. KAMCO can resell its purchased NPLs to retrieve the cost of the purchase and minimize the eventual burden on the public. Likewise, KDIC also can sell its acquired equities in the banks to the foreign or domestic private sector. Therefore, KAMCO and KDIC should manage their assets to minimize the amount of fiscal support.

By the end of 1998, KAMCO issued 19.9 trillion won worth of government-guaranteed bonds to purchase 44 trillion won worth of NPLs from the banking sector, as seen in Table 5. KDIC by the same time issued 21 trillion won worth of its government-guaranteed bonds for recapitalization and depositor protection. Hence, KAMCO and KDIC together had financed a total of 40.9 trillion won for the sake of financial sector restructuring by the end of 1998. With an additional 23.1 trillion won in financing in 1999, total financing will amount to 64 trillion won (about $53.3 billion).

Out of those 64 trillion won, about 51.7 trillion won (about $43.1 billion) had already been allocated as of the end of August 1999 for recapitalization, the disposal of non-performing loans, P&A support, and the repayment of client deposits in the case of closed financial institutions (See Table 6). The Korean government expected to complete the financial restructuring process with 64 trillion won. However, it will be almost impossible to resolve all non-performing loans in the financial sector. Especially after the outbreak of the Daewoo Group's liquidity problem,

Table 5. Outline of Financial Sector Restructuring

(Unit: trillion won)

	Purchase NPLs	Recapitalization	Deposit Payment	Total
1977.11–98.12	19.9	13.2	7.8	40.9
1999	12.6	4.3	6.2	23.1
Total	32.5	17.5	14.0	64.0

Table 6. Injection of Fiscal Resources for Financial Reform

(Unit: trillion won ($ billion))

Allocation of Funds	Disposal of Non-Performing Loans	P&A Support and Deposit Repayment	Total Amount
For commercial banks	17.5 (14.6)	20.8 (17.3)	38.3 (31.9)
For non-banking sector	3.2 (2.7)	10.2 (8.5)	13.4 (11.2)
Total amount mobilized	20.7 (17.3)	31.0 (25.8)	51.7 (43.1)
Total amount left	11.8 (9.8)	0.5 (0.4)	12.3 (10.2)
Total amount planned	32.5 (27.1)	31.5 (26.2)	64.0 (53.3)

Source: Financial Supervisory Service.

the financial market showed signs of instability such as rising interest rates. This raises the possibility for additional public support for financial restructuring.[4]

3) Liberalization of Foreign Exchange Transactions and Capital Accounts

Capital account liberalization has been the most seriously considered issue for Korea ever since it joined the OECD. Korea has feared the drastic inflows of foreign capital due to the wide spread between the domestic and international interest rates may bring. The IMF agreement, however, included the bold implementation of capital account liberalization. In particular, the 6th Letter of Intent called for the opening of all capital markets, including the opening of the short-term capital market to foreigners. This also targeted the full liberalization of Korea's real estate market.

To overcome the foreign liquidity crisis, the Korean government liberalized the capital account sector ahead of the schedule arranged with the IMF. The Korean government also lifted the ceiling on foreigners' stock investment on 25 May 1998. The bond market has also been widely opened, which in turn led to a full opening of all short-term bonds on the same day. Implementing full liberalization measures, the new Foreign Exchange Transaction Act replaced the old Foreign Exchange Management Act. The new law that went into effect in April 1999 liberalizes corporate overseas borrowing, and establishes a futures market. In addition, Korea saw a significant expansion of the financial derivatives market. The Korea Futures Exchange (KOFEX) was inaugurated in April 1999.

The liberalization of foreign exchange transactions, however, also raises new challenges. Rapid, borderless transactions of short-term capital may destabilize the foreign exchange market and render the Korean won more susceptible to speculation. Therefore, the government should devise various measures to counter potential market instability. Reinforcement of regulations and supervision of financial institutions would

---

4. According to the Ministry of Finance and Economy, the comprehensive national debt/GDP ratio will reach 54% by end of 1999. The Korea Economic Research Institute has estimated, under reasonable assumptions, that 27 trillion won of additional public funds for financial restructuring may be needed.

be one such measure.

Capital market liberalization and the promotion of foreign direct investment (FDI) are also important aspects of the restructuring process. The Korean government's renewed zeal for attracting FDI is another case in point. The new Foreign Investment Promotion Act, drafted and legislated after months of intense deliberation, abolishes and replaces the old legal framework on FDI. The new FDI policy of "promotion and support" replaces the old "regulation and management" approach.[5] Local authorities now have greater discretion in attracting FDI in their own jurisdictions. Extensive tax exemptions are given.[6] Local authorities can give additional local tax breaks at their own discretion. The government's goal is to make Korea the most investor-friendly place for FDI in the world. Having attracted a record $8.9 billion in FDI in 1998, the government is confident that new inducements in 1999 will help reach the target of $15 billion.

Measures taken by the Korean government to promote FDI since the outbreak of the crisis reflect not superficial changes in the policy matrix, but more fundamental changes in the government's philosophy. Such measures include the complete removal of the foreign equity ownership ceiling (May 1998), the complete freedom for foreign investors to make hostile takeovers (May 1998), the complete freedom for foreigners to invest in local bonds and short-term money market instruments, and the complete liberalization of foreign exchange transactions (April 1999).

Corporate Sector Reform

1) *Jaebeol* Restructuring

The IMF pinpointed Korean conglomerates (*jaebeol*) as the culprits of Korea's structural weakness and stressed the need for rigorous corporate restructuring. High leverage ratios and a very poor use of capital in the Korean corporate sector prior to the crisis aggravated the impact of

---

5. The newly set up Korea Investment Service Center (KISC) at the Korea Trade Investment Promotion Agency (KOTRA) now provides a convenient one-stop service to all prospective foreign investors.
6. High-tech industry FDI, for example, is given full exemption from corporate and income taxes for the first seven years, and an additional 50% reduction for the next three years after that.

tightening liquidity on corporate cash flows and investment activities. Mutual debt guarantees between affiliates of conglomerates created massive debt levels prevalent in most conglomerates.

In early 1998, an agreement to improve the financial structure of the business sector was signed between creditor banks and the *jaebeol* under the "Five Principles of Corporate Restructuring" program. The agreement covered 1) enhancement of transparency of corporate governance; 2) strengthening accountability, such as allowing voting rights to institutional investors; 3) resolution of cross-debt guarantees; 4) improvement of financial structure; and 5) streamlining business activities (see Table 7).

Another element of the corporate restructuring process involves business swaps between the top five *jaebeol* to streamline overinvestment and enhance efficiency in such key industries as semiconductors, petrochemicals, aerospace, rolling stock, power plant equipment, vessel engines, and steel refining. In December 1998, the top five reached an agreement on many of the deals and are currently working on closing the rest of the deals.

President Kim Dae-jung vowed to implement three additional sets of measures toward *jaebeol* reform in his 1999 Liberation Day address, in addition to the five principles in Table 7. Since then, he has emphasized strong *jaebeol* reform, specially targeting their fleet-style operations. These three new reform measures aim to restrict the *jaebeol's* control of non-banking financial institutions, prevent them from making cross-subsidiary equity investments and insider trading, and put limits on illegal inheritances and transfers of wealth among *jaebeol* leaders' family members.

As a result of the government's push, thus far, the corporate sector has reduced cross-guarantees by 103.3% of the amount planned for 1998, and 48% of that for 1999. *Jaebeol* are taking steps to reduce their debt leverage ratio to 200% by the end of 1999 as part of their broader efforts to refocus on their core business areas and raise their returns in the process, thereby improving their financial soundness. Over the past few years, there has been a significant reduction in the debt-to-equity ratio for the five largest *jaebeol*, from 470.2% at the end of 1997, to 302.2% at the end of the first half of 1999. Through asset sales and capital expansion during the first six months of 1999, the top five *jaebeol* raised 17.3 trillion won or 117.7% of the targeted 14.7 trillion won. Had the troubled Daewoo been excluded from the group, the top *jaebeol* would have

Table 7. Five Principles for Jaebeol Reform

Objectives	Measures	Schedule
Enhanced transparency	• Adoption of consolidated financial statements	• FY 1999
	• Adoption of international accounting principles	• Oct. 1998
	• Strengthening the voting rights of minority share-holders	• May 1998
	• Compulsory appointment of outside directors	• Feb. 1998
	• Establishment of external auditors' committee	• Feb. 1998
Strengthed accountability	• Strengthening the legal liability of controlling owners	• Jun. 1998
	• Allowing voting rights to institutional investors	• Sept. 1998
	• Introduction of cumulative voting system	• Dec. 1998
Resolution of cross-guarantees	• Resolution of existing cross guarantees	• Mar. 2000
	• Prohibition of new cross guarantees between subsidiaries	• Apr. 1998
	• Prohibition of demand for cross guarantees from financial institutions	• Apr. 1998
Improved financial structure	• Agreement with banks to improve the capital structure	• Apr. 1998
	• Removal of restriction on capital infusion with consideration	• Feb. 1998
	• Exclusion of income tax deduction for interest payments on excessive borrowings	• FY 2000
	• Introduction of asset-backed securities	• Sept. 1998
Streamlined business activities	• Adoption of corporate-split system	• Jun. 1998
	• Improvement of M&A procedures	• Jun. 1998
	• Liberalization of foreign ownership of real estate	• Jun. 1998
	• Full liberalization of M&As	• May 1998
	• Streamlining bankruptcy procedures	• Feb. 1998

produced much healthier consolidated results, and otherwise, the restructuring of the other major *jaebeol* is progressing smoothly.[7]

---

7. Daewoo saw its debt ratio increase by 62% to 588.2% over the first half of 1999, as the group's debt burden increased by 1.9 trillion won due to prolonged restructuring.

Table 8. Top Five Jaebeol's Debt-Reduction

(Unit: trillion won, %)

	End of 1997	End of 1998	1999 Target	1999 1stH Target	1999 1stH Result
Debt	220.4	225.1	165.7	215.3	222.7
Shareholder's equity	46.9	58.3	83.6	64.1	73.7
Debt/equity ratio	470.2	386.0	198.3	335.7	302.2
(D/E ratio w/asset revaluation)		302.1		266.1	235.1
Restructuring effort (A+B)		14.7	48.8	14.7	17.3
Asset sales (A)		7.4	24.4	6.4	7
Capital expansion (B)		7.3	24.4	8.3	10.3
Foreign investment ($ billion)		2.70	14.66	2.35	2.67
Reduction of cross holdings			4.3	2.1	3.4
Rationalized affiliates			111	62	61

Source: Financial Supervisory Commission.

2) Corporate Workout Program and Nonviable Firm Exit

To initiate corporate restructuring, the government has launched a rather aggressive corporate reform package. One is the "big deal" operation for top five *jaebeol* as I explained above. The others are workout programs for mid-sized *jaebeol*, mainly the 6-64th largest *jaebeol*, and the exit of nonviable firms. The workout programs, which are unfamiliar to most Korean people, intended to help recover companies that are promising in the mid and long runs but are having financial problems in the short run.

In May 1998, creditor banks established a formal review committee to assess the viability of 313 client firms showing signs of financial weakness. Upon completion of their evaluation, creditor banks listed 55 firms as nonviable, of which 20 are affiliated with the top five *jaebeol*, and 32 with the top 6-64th. Outstanding loans to the 55 nonviable firms were approximately 5 trillion won. Creditor banks denied new credits and cross-subsidy bailouts to these firms to effectively wipe them out of the market. Legal proceedings for corporate rehabilitation and bankruptcy filing were simplified in February 1998 to facilitate the market exit of nonviable firms and to ensure better representation of creditor banks in the resolution process.

Procedural simplification for market exit also has important implications for corporate workouts, in that the presence of an expeditious exit scheme induces more efficient negotiations of workout programs between creditor banks and firms. The IBRD has been actively participating in the Korean workout program. The World Bank provided Korea with expertise and a Technical Assistance Loan of $33 million to employ outside experts as advisors for the design and implementation of the program.

Corporate workouts extend to small and medium enterprises (SMEs) as well. Creditor banks have evaluated the financial status of approximately 22,000 small and medium enterprises with outstanding loans of one billion won or more. Approximately 13,000 firms listed as viable were selected as candidates for workouts. So far, creditor banks concluded workouts with more than 11,800 SMEs.

3) Enhancement of Corporate Governance

To enhance the credibility of corporate accounting, from the fiscal year 1999 firms will be required to adopt more rigid accounting standards and to publish combined financial statements. The system of outside directors was adopted in order to rectify the practice of illicit control of firms through proxy equity participation. Appointed by the shareholders, outside directors represent the interest of minority shareholders and the public interest at large. All listed companies are required to appoint outside directors, and by October 1998, all 752 listed companies had appointed a total of 764 outside directors. Recently, the introduction of rather drastic changes in corporate governance is being discussed under the guidance of the state. These changes include the requirement that the top 30 *jaebeol* and all listed companies organize "independent audit committees" represented by minority shareholders and creditors as a way of increasing management transparency and accountability.

To accelerate the corporate restructuring process, measures to revitalize the domestic M&A market were developed. M&A activity, which involves foreign firms, has been promoted through the amendment of the Foreign Capital Inducement Law. Management efficiency was sought through the establishment of greater accountability to shareholders. Limits on the voting rights of institutional investors were lifted, and the rights of minority shareholders were strengthened. To facilitate the exit of insolvent firms, bankruptcy and corporate reorganization laws have been revised.

Public Sector Reform

Successful public sector reform requires a consensus on the need for and basic direction of change; without it, efforts toward reform will face enormous obstacles. Therefore, to create such consensus, it is crucial that the government explain the necessity for reform to the general public. Also, priority should be given to those areas where results can be seen by the public at an earlier stage. In this way, the government will be able to gradually expand the scope of the reform measures.

Public sector reform was an urgent issue. The Kim Dae-jung administration lost no time in setting three objectives for carrying out public sector reform. The first was to create a small but efficient government by streamlining governmental functions and vastly reducing its size. The second was to achieve a highly competitive government by incorporating the principle of competition among civil service organizations and personnel. The last objective was to pursue a customer-oriented government by fostering user-friendly behavior and attitudes on the part of public employees. To achieve these three objectives, Kim Dae-jung

Table 9. Objectives and Strategies of Public Sector Reform

Objectives	1. Principle of customer priority
	2. Entrepreneurial government management
	3. Flexible and transparent administration
Strategies	1. Redesign the government's role
	2. Promote competition in the public sector
	3. Introduce a responsible management organization
	4. Maximize the use of information
	5. Establish a competitive personnel compensation system based on ability
	6. Increase delegation of responsibility and authority to subordinates
	7. Transfer authority to local government
	8. Transparent administration
	9. Creation of responsible work ethics

Source: Ministry of Finance and Economy (1999).

administration has launched a wide-ranging set of programs.

The downsizing of the government is an important feature of the public sector reform to raise efficiency. Although the government streamlined its organizational structure in February 1998, the idea of restructuring emerged before the crisis. However, the crisis served to expose the weaknesses of governing infrastructures and made restructuring an immediate necessity. The three basic directions established for government reorganization were to consolidate redundant functions, to encourage competition in the private sector through deregulation and privatization, and to decentralize authority by giving more power to local governments. As for government restructuring, the Kim Dae-jung administration can take some credit for its policy designed to reduce the size of the bureaucracy. The government reduced the number of employees in the central government by 5.6%, or 9,084 people, in 1998. By 2001, it plans to reduce the number of government employees by 16%. Local governments also trimmed their organizations by reducing the total number of employees by 12% in 1998; they plan to bring that number up to 30% by 2002.

In conjunction with government reform, the quasi-government sector, including public institutions and various government-affiliated associations, has also been streamlined. Poor productivity and rampant inefficiency in the public sector beg thorough-going reform. In particular, state-owned enterprises (SOEs) require drastic overhaul by means of privatization and/or management reform. Twenty public institutions out of 109 SOEs were already privatized in 1998. More such actions are planned, as seen in Table 10. Eighty-nine subsidiaries of the 30 parent SOEs are also subject to privatization or management reform. The future status of the 21 subsidiaries of those SOEs scheduled for immediate privatization in 1999 will be determined by the new private management. Of the remaining 68 subsidiaries, 31 will be privatized either immediately or in a short period of time, while 37 will be restructured or consolidated.

Thus far, the privatization of state-run enterprises has been implemented as scheduled, probably contributing to increased efficiency within the public sector. A considerable amount of Korea Telecom, POSCO, and Korea Electric Power Corporation shares have been sold to foreign investors through the issues of depository receipts (DR). As well, the successful issuance of DRs in international financial markets has contributed to the rise of international confidence in the Korean economy.

Table 10. Reform Plan for SOEs

	Full/Immediate Privatization	Gradual Privatization	Management Reform and Restructuring
Deadline	By end-1999	By end-2002	Ongoing
Targeted SOEs	5 parent companies (including POSCO, Korea Heavy Industry & Construction, and Korea Technology Financing Corporation), and 21 subsidiaries	6 parent companies (including Korea Telecom, Korea Tobacco & Ginseng Corporation, and Korea Electric Power Corporation), and 31 subsidiaries	13 parent companies (including Korea Securities Printing & Minting Corporation, Korea Trade-Investment Promotion Agency, Korea National Tourism Corporation, and Korea Coal Corporation), and 37 subsidiaries

The elimination of excessive regulations is another important task in the public sector reform. The Regulation Reform Committee (RRC) has abolished 4,465 regulations, some 40% of the 11,125 total—23 laws were abolished, and 248 laws revised. These numbers seem to speak for the government's strong commitment to drastically reducing unnecessary regulations. The abolition of unnecessary regulations is also conducive to enhancing transparency in the corporate, financial, and public sectors. At the same time, the ongoing reforms will make Korea's regulatory system more in line with the frameworks of the World Trade Organization (WTO) and the Organization for Economic Cooperation and Development (OECD). In May 1999, the Civil Service Commission was inaugurated with the aim of making government personnel administration more efficient, and legal grounds for hiring civilians for government posts have been prepared. As well, the Korean government has planned to introduce competitive salaries and incentives for government jobs.

Labor Market Reform

One particular area in which dramatic change has taken place is the labor market. As a result of the sharp economic contraction that marked the onset of the economic crisis in 1997, the unemployment rate rose rapidly to unprecedented levels in 1998 and 1999. This was accompanied by a sharp fall in wage rates. Nominal wages fell by as much as 2.5% in 1998 after rising 15% on average per annum since the late 1980s. Such a drastic shift in general labor market conditions has also changed perceptions of what constitutes acceptable practices in the labor-business relationship.

Furthermore, Korea's labor market reform laid out by the Tripartite Accord also helped improve labor market flexibility, which was one of the factors that contributed to the deterioration in Korean export competitiveness and hence, the profitability of Korean businesses in the 1990s. Some potentially important changes were made to labor laws to increase flexibility in the labor market by removing barriers to large-scale layoffs. However, the actual implementation of layoffs remains extremely difficult. A clear result of developments following the economic crisis is the weakening influence and diminishing militancy of the labor unions, but once again, as with other reforms, the long-term effects of these changes in the labor market have yet to be seen.

One of the most crucial aspects of the national effort to overcome the current economic crisis is the effort to improve the working relationship between labor and management. In the belief that a new working relationship between labor and management is essential to economic recovery, the Tripartite Committee mandated that all parties concerned should be consulted before initiating the restructuring of certain companies (23 July 1998). The Tripartite Committee also agreed to push for the revision of laws governing political funds and the legalization of unions for the unemployed (28 September 1998). It also decided on the draft of a National Pension Act (1 December 1998), and agreed to hold public hearings regarding labor and management policies.

An important characteristic of 1998's labor-management compromise was the reasonable give-and-take between labor and management. At 4,357, or 84.5% of the 5,476 businesses employing 100 or more workers, labor took a pay cut or pay freeze in return for management's promise to limit layoffs to a minimum. At 308 companies, both labor and management agreed to bargain in good faith and to settle any differences at the negotiating table. This type of friendly working relationship is setting a new trend in the once acrimonious labor-management relations. The labor dispute at Hyundai Motors and its subsequent resolution in August 1998 showcased the social acceptance of the new principle of labor flexibility. However raucous the course of reaching compromise, neither side could deny the reality of the new labor practice. The same social acceptance of the new labor reality was confirmed in the subsequent labor disputes between the nine financially troubled commercial banks and their labor unions.[8]

Even during this current economic crisis, activities to promote labor rights are continuing. For example, a teachers' union and limited collective action by civil servants in the form of a workplace council have been legalized; a bonds system aimed at guaranteeing three months of wages for workers in bankrupt businesses is now in place. The Labor Standards Law now covers all workers, including those working for a company with four or fewer employees, putting another 1.6 million workers under its protection. Violation of the labor laws are being aggressively dealt with.[9] As employment adjustment was inevitable during the restructuring process, unemployment soared and had the potential to lead to social unrest. To minimize this risk, the Korean government and the IMF agreed on the need to design and implement an appropriate social security net. The Unemployment Task Force was organized under the jurisdiction of the Prime Minister's Office. Countermeasures were led by government's support of firms and the promotion of job relocation through job placement and job training programs. An employment insurance system has also been augmented to cover all regular, temporary, and daily employees. Funds to establish social programs, such as expanding employment insurance and job placement agencies, were allocated from the government's budget. In 1999, the government spent 7.7 trillion won, up from 5.7 trillion won in 1998, on various programs of unemployment protection. Recently, the Korean government unveiled a proposed 2.5 trillion won package comprising of tax deductions and subsidies to help reduce the burden of middle and low-income workers.

---

8. The two sides reached the agreement to reduce the workforce by 32% for managerial reasons.
9. As of 19 January 1999, a total of 886 workplaces had been inspected. Of them, 400 were cited for various unlawful practices and 376 have been prosecuted. Another 265 companies were ordered to correct minor breaches.

Mid-term Evaluation of Korean Reforms

Along with the efforts to overcome the financial crisis, the government pushed forward bold reforms in four major areas. As a result, the government seems to have overcome the crisis through a sharp increase in the country's foreign currency reserves and the stabilization of the foreign exchange rate. Still, at this moment, it seems a little bit early to say that the foundation for the revival of the nation's economy was laid with rising credit ratings and an improved environment for foreign investment; besides, the current macroeconomic recovery looks fragile. It is now time to look back and evaluate what the Korean economy has tried to achieve.

Reassessing the Government's Role

At the beginning, the 1997 Korean economic crisis was characterized as a short-term liquidity problem, but it soon became apparent that the basis of the problem was economic mismanagement by the Korean government. During the one and half years after the crisis, the primary concern in Korea was to overcome the financial crisis. The macroeconomic policies undertaken by the Korean government have been assessed as successful in the sense that the Korean economy has quickly recovered. Such impressive short-term success, at least in terms of macroeconomic variables, is mainly the result of the quick recognition by Korean authorities of the need for such measures. Authorities were well aware of the Japanese government's experience, whereby it failed to tackle problems in the financial sector in time, eventually leading to the long-term stagnation of the Japanese economy.

However, certain basic dilemmas still remain. On the one hand, as we have discussed, the crux of the structural problems beneath the current difficulties is the fact that the Korean government has played too active a role in all facets of economic life, leaving various market institutions weak. On the other hand, an active governmental role was inevitable during the crisis. Besides, there is a need for a responsible "monitor" that can ensure the implementation of genuine reform measures addressing past mistakes. Currently the government might be the only player in the position to step in and control the speed as well as the magnitude of economic recovery. Nonetheless, it is time to put the government back in its place by reassessing its role in preparation for the future.

The active role assumed by the government raised concerns in some corners, even with a strong consensus regarding the need for a substantive reform of the Korean economy. For example, active governmental participation in commercial bank credit allocation gave rise to the weak condition of the banking sector. Such government-led practices have provided an ideal background for a moral hazard problem. A firm blanket guarantee for the "safety" of banks' liabilities was not matched in terms of any prudent supervisory efforts to ensure the "soundness" of bank assets.

The major reason that the public sector reforms are in disarray is that the Korean government has vacillated between interventionism and free market principles. The government's basic stance regarding public sector reform and stimulative fiscal policy has been contradictory. The proposed public sector reform programs call for the privatization of some government organizations and the elimination of unnecessary regulations. Meanwhile, the government intends to keep its control over most aspects of both the economy and society. The absence of a clear-cut perspective on the government's role makes it difficult to have faith in the substance of the proposed reforms.

For example the privatization of SOEs has been delayed for several years, as the government cannot find a proper method. After the crisis, the Korean government started to sell SOE stock to the public, and announced that it would start privatization. However, it must be noted that selling stock to the public does not constitute privatization or an increase in management efficiency. To reap the maximum benefits of privatization, SOEs must be managed by private hands. The Korean government should not concentrate on the sale of SOE stock, but make plans to raise the efficiency of those firms. Just as the financial and corporate sectors try to maximize efficiency, the Korean government should do its best to expose SOEs to open market competition; the privileges and rents that bureaucrats have enjoyed should be eliminated.

Reestablishment of the Financial Sector

The measures taken thus far have been adequate to stabilize financial markets—they also have been instrumental in convincing international capital markets of a positive near-term outlook. By facing the non-performing loan problem squarely, the Korean government is not only cleaning up the financial sector's balance sheets but also is removing the key source of uncertainty regarding the fair valuation of Korean financial institutions for potential customers and investors. In the financial and corporate sectors, major changes have already been made to transform institutional settings with the aim of introducing a new paradigm for free market-based economic activities.

For instance, the function of the board of directors has been widened. Most Korean banks adopted a new system that segregates executive directors from the board of directors, which is comprised of a majority of non-executive directors. Now executive directors can carry out only what has been decided by the board of directors. In addition, the auditing function has been enhanced by introducing a separate audit committee which will help the auditor maintain a certain degree of independence. Other measures, such as explicit accounting rules and prudential regulations, have also been strengthened to the level of existing global standards. These new measures will most likely improve the governance of financial institutions. However, one has to realize that the most important thing is not the adoption of new measures, but their application. Despite the visible progress of financial sector restructuring, the following five problems can be pointed out.

First, we must worry that the fruitful effects of restructuring might be diminished due to the government's rash behavior. For instance, the government's impetuosity has been displayed well in the case of Korea Life Insurance (KLI). While dealing with the troubled KLI, the Korean government attempted to nationalize KLI by pouring in public money. Nonetheless, the government's decision to abolish the managerial rights of the troubled firm's major shareholders and its chairman has run into a roadblock. The court has ordered the Financial Supervisory Commission (FSC) to scrap plans to burn the outstanding stocks and replace the insurance company's management; it has pointed out that the FSC did not follow due procedures before issuing administrative orders. Despite this ruling, the FSC will proceed with its plan to nationalize troubled financial institutions such as Seoul Bank. However, the pace of restructuring will slow down, as the court ruled that the Korean economy was not in an emergency situation and therefore the FSC did not follow the proper rules in addressing the problem of these troubled financial institutions.

Second, in spite of the Korean government's firm intent to sell off ailing banks and complete the financial sector reform in 1999, the proposed sale of financial institutions such as Korea First Bank and Seoul Bank has been delayed. The main apparent reason for the delay is the disagreement regarding the real value of the banks' assets and the amount of bad loans. Furthermore, Daewoo's liquidity crisis not only defers but also threatens the deals. The more realistic reason for the delay is that Korean government officials do not want to be the target of criticism for selling financial institutions at such a discounted rate. No Korean wants to see domestic financial institutions sold at giveaway prices to foreigners. However, one should not underestimate the learning effect from foreign institutions or managers, and at any rate, the Korean government should acknowledge that the sooner it sells financial institutions to foreigners and/or the private sector, the more taxpayer money it can save.

Third, there were worries that political judgement would prevail over economic principle in the restructuring process. The concerns that general elections in April 2000 may distort the restructuring process are not too farfetched. The government's handling of Korea Life Insurance raised some doubts about political influences. Why the Korean government chose quick nationalization rather than sale to foreign or domestic buyers is not clear at this moment.

Fourth, it can be agreed that the Korean government's restructuring policy lacks consistency. The government has adopted different rules each time that important decisions were needed, using circumstantial necessity as an excuse. For example, the government announced plans to bring in foreign experts to manage Seoul Bank after breaking off talks with HSBC. The government explained that the purpose of selling financial institutions to foreigners is to learn advanced financial techniques and therefore, that either selling to foreigners and bringing in foreign experts are basically the same. Then, why was the Korean government trying so hard to sell Seoul Bank to foreigners at that time?

Finally, after the several M&As were encouraged by the Korean government to restructure the financial sector, the average size of financial institutions has increased. There were 5 cases of M&As among commercial banks and more are currently ongoing in other sectors. However, some of these M&As were not the result of market mechanisms or clients' demand, but the result of the regulatory commission's pressure. Therefore, there are doubts as to whether these M&As will really result in increased competitiveness and efficiency. Besides, these M&As failed to reflect the real value of the firms undergoing the M&A process. It does not improve the competitiveness of financial institutions targeted by M&As, since these M&As are not market driven.

The most important financial restructuring task in Korea is to make all three players—the regulatory commission, financial institutions, and the corporate sector—share a common vision. Made on a voluntary basis, this vision should work towards implementing the true market system. The boom in M&As in Europe and the United States, and the advent of various providers of new financial services are causing cataclysmic changes in the financial sector. Financial institutions in Korea must increase their capacity in order to survive in this globalized financial market. Not only must financial institutions clarify their strategic positions with a thorough understanding of their clients, but financial supervisors should move away from creating a cookbook of rules to follow, and instead return to prudential regulatory functions.

Korea has to establish an incentive system conducive to the formation of a group of investors that will monitor banks. With such a system, market players can internalize financial regulations through the decision-making process, and this will help to achieve the efficiency and stability goals of the financial system simultaneously. Recently, Korean financial institutions implemented a new board system as a way to strengthen internal monitoring and consulting functions. Most importantly, the Korean financial sector has to learn a way to survive in the new liberalized and globalized environment.

Corporate Sector Restructuring

While corporate sector reform has emerged as a key task since the onset of the 1997 currency crisis, much of the discussion surrounding the implementation of such reform has not been based on a systematic understanding of the corporate governance structure, which has a direct bearing on how businesses behave. Too much attention is paid to changing external symptoms rather than fixing the underlying institutional and incentive structures. It has to be pointed out that Korean corporate restructuring has proceeded under strong government guidance, and is reminiscent of the industrial restructuring attempts of the 1970s and 1980s.

For instance, the "big deals" were made under the guidance and the compulsion of the government. The government determined the acquiring and acquired firms in advance and gave them the guidelines and deadlines to be met. These big deals raise doubts about the consistency of government policies. First of all, they might lead to an increase in economic concentration rather than efficiency. After the completion of these big deals, there remains the problem of whether the government should allow new entries into the industries where big deals have occurred. If the government permits them, then it raises the question of why it ordered the big deals in the first place. If it does not, it has to offer a logical explanation for why it cannot.

Current efforts by banks and the government to improve financial conditions, such as eliminating cross-guarantees between group subsidiaries, will eventually help the corporate sector. However, the policy of lowering a firm's debt-to-equity ratio also fostered doubts about its propriety. The government applied a 200% debt-to-equity ratio guideline to each of the big five *jaebeol* and did not give any consideration to the diversity of each *jaebeol* and industry. Taking into consideration each *jaebeol*'s different business characteristics and managerial styles, it is highly questionable whether the uniform application of the same numerical target and deadline to each *jaebeol* can be effective. Besides, this approach also creates a problem of policy inconsistency. If the Korean government continues with the same guidelines after 2000, it will restrict the freedom of the firms in exercising their financial options.

To smoothen production capacity, firms should be provided with sufficient funds. However, in an environment where firms pose high credit risks and financial institutions are liable to merger or closure if they do not meet BIS capital adequacy ratios, the financial community cannot but be extremely cautious in extending credit. The dilemma here is that even a sound enterprise may fall victim to a temporary shortage of funds. The most efficient way of reducing this high cost is to shorten the period given over to structural reform. Once the shake-out in the corporate sector is complete and nonviable firms are driven out of the market, credit risks will decline, and this, in turn, should encourage financial institutions to expand their loans to the corporate sector, thus easing the credit crunch.

Above all else, corporate restructuring should proceed based on market principles. As such, the government needs to adopt a noninterventionist policy; in other words, the government should not bail out ailing firms as it did in the past. Instead, it should allow creditor banks to voluntarily evaluate the viability of firms and decide on debt restructuring. Transparency of corporate management through enhanced disclosure of business performance is the basis upon which management should be held accountable. In order to achieve this, the financial statements of listed companies have to satisfy international financial standards. For the affiliates of large business conglomerates, their consolidated financial statements are to be disclosed by the end of 1999.

The improvement of corporate governance and management transparency in the corporate sector has been promoted as specified in the "Five Major Tasks" for corporate restructuring showed in Table 7, which include the elimination of cross-guarantees, the establishment of core competence, and the improvement of the capital structure. In 1998, remarkable progress was made in the area of corporate governance: the accountability of *jaebeol* owners was increased considerably by forcing them to register as directors of their leading affiliates. As such, they will no longer be unaccountable for the consequences of management misconduct.

Korea merely laid the basic framework for improving corporate governance in 1998. From 1999 onward, more efforts should be made to solidify proper institutional settings. Institutional investors, including banks and other financial institutions, have started to exercise voting rights at shareholders' meetings. Previously, institutional investors, even in cases where they held a greater stake than the largest individual shareholder, were not able to use their voting rights to influence decisions. The appointment of more than a quarter of the total number of directors from outside was made mandatory for all publicly-traded companies, and moreover, minority shareholders' rights were strengthened. These new measures have proved to be efficient in advanced countries. During the course of corporate restructuring, corporate governance is expected to improve gradually either by sharing ownership with foreign firms or by transferring ownership to creditor banks through debt/equity conversions.

Financing Resolution Costs

The recent macroeconomic recovery was mostly attributable to the government's active countercyclical monetary and fiscal policies, but nevertheless the core problem of the restructuring process has not been solved. In addition to the banking sector, there are more financial institutions waiting for public funds, such as investment trust companies and insurance companies. The greatest difficulty facing structural reform is to find a way to finance the huge volume of resolution costs for restructuring the financial system. In May 1998, the government estimated that it would cost the public 64 trillion won to purchase bad loans, pay deposit liabilities on behalf of financial institutions, and participate in their recapitalization. This amount accounts for about 15% of the current GDP in 1997 prices.

The government plans to raise the needed resources by having the Non-Performing Assets Resolution Fund and the Deposit Insurance Fund issue public bonds in the market. However, the absorption of such a large quantity of bonds is not easy. If these bonds are issued in the domestic market, market interest rates would surge, pushing up firms' financial costs. Furthermore, it would not be easy for the fiscal budget to shoulder the burden of servicing the interest. The government is now attempting to come up with appropriate measures to solve this problem. For example, it is considering making payments in bonds when buying up bad loans or recapitalizing financial institutions. Along with this, it intends to recycle support funds by promptly selling off bad assets, and to secure sufficient money for servicing bonds by privatizing public enterprises and reducing government spending.

However, the total amount of bad loans to be cleared out during the entire restructuring period is likely to be higher than the government's initial assessment of 120 trillion won. The Korean government will introduce new standards for categorizing bad loans. Since the exposure of the problems of the Daewoo Group, if the loans on the "watch list" include those for which interest has not been paid for one to three months, the amount of bad loans will increase sharply. If the category of bad loans is extended to include normal loans which are given to businesses that will be unprofitable in the future, the amount of bad loans to be cleared out is expected to increase even more.

If the amount of bad loans increases, the estimation of the fiscal burden following financial reform rises sharply. Despite the improvement of the economic environment due to the rapid economic recovery and a reduction in interest rates, about 25-30% of total loans are estimated to be bad loans. If this is the case, about 30 trillion won of financial resolution cost are needed in addition to the initial 64 trillion won that the government established originally.[10] The total national debt/GDP ratio was 32.2% in 1998 and is expected to increase to 38% at the end of 1999. When we include the debt in the public sector and government

---

10. Nam and Kwon (1999) estimated that the additional amount of public resources would reach about 27 trillion won, under reasonable assumptions.

guaranteed payments, the total national debt/GDP ratio will reach about 50%, which is not low, and will act as a burden on the Korean economy and policymakers.

Lessons to Be Learned

Thanks to the government's efforts to overcome the short-term currency crisis, Korea can now afford to concentrate on economic recovery. Growth for 1999 is expected to be higher than 7%, compared to a 5.8% contraction in 1998, and usable foreign exchange reserves were substantially increased to record levels. Many analysts believe that the Korean economy had already bottomed out either in the fourth quarter of 1998 or in the first quarter of 1999. Either way the Korean economy is headed for a full recovery in 1999 and 2000, and the worst part of the currency crisis has passed without inflicting too much structural damage. Although at the early stages of recovery the high interest rate policy regime had a significant negative impact on the Korean economy, the macroeconomic situation, so far, has been positive enough to stabilize the economy and sufficiently influential in recovering international confidence. Cautious optimism for the future of the Korean economy is rising, although the global environment is still full of uncertainties and instabilities.[11]

Since this recent recovery is very dramatic, we can argue that the foundation of the Korean economy has not been severely damaged.[12] That is, an easy monetary policy along with a fiscal policy stimulus can play important roles in reshuffling all the nominal variables. The unprecedented low interest rates helped improve the financial status of the business sector. The National Assembly passed supplementary bud-

---

11. Troubled economic conditions in Latin America and Russia, the real possibility of a Chinese currency devaluation, and questions about the state of the American stock market pose threats to the world economy.

12. Cho Dongchul (1999) used the time-series methodology of Blanchard and Quah to show the decomposed magnitude of the demand shock in last year's recession. According to his analysis, 4% of the GDP's decline of –5.8% can be attributed to the aggregate demand shock. The implication of this decomposition is that an aggregate demand-driven recession can be cured rather easily through expansionary fiscal and monetary policies.

gets twice each year for both 1998 and 1999, increasing the budget deficit to more than 5% of GDP in two consecutive years. This increasing budget deficit also helped boost aggregate demand. Namely, the current economic recovery is sustained by this kind of governmental stimulus policy and could be a quite fragile one, not based on productivity increases and new investments. Therefore, it is very important to nurture the growth potential of the Korean economy, despite the pressing demands to solve immediate difficulties.

Keeping this in mind, what lessons can Korea draw from its harshest economic ordeal since the launch of industrialization in the early 1960s? Under the Kim Dae-jung government's policy of the joint development of a market economy and democracy, the meaning of a market economy has turned out to be ambiguous. The process of economic reform has so far led to a maze of complicated political considerations that may hinder a speedy transition to a new system. The most important lesson we can draw from the recent ordeal is that it is absolutely vital to construct and manage an economic system in tune with the imperatives of liberalization and globalization. Although Korea had pursued liberalization and market opening since the early 1990s, the sophistication of the economic system and the mentality of the economic agents had failed to keep pace with these trends; that is, the Korean economy has stumbled in the process of globalization. However, in historical perspective, the current crisis might be viewed as the necessary price of transition and renewal for the coming century. In that sense, what is happening in Korea is developmental in nature, and in some sense the Korean financial crisis can be a blessing for the future as long as the ongoing reforms continue to lay the ground for a new economic order. This new economic system should provide the basis for free competition in which all economic players will do their best for themselves and for society. The whole matter relies on how successfully Korea carries out true reforms in all the sectors concerned.

In the past, market principles necessary for liberalization and internationalization were not put into practice. The supervisory system for financial institutions, corporate governance, and exit procedures were ineffective so that they could not prevent moral hazard problems. In addition, there was a clear failure to understand the prevailing culture of international financial markets. Therefore, in order to ride out the current crisis and build up medium- and long-term growth potential, market principles should be established in the economy through the pur-

market-oriented policies. Similarly, systems to secure the efficient supervision of financial institutions and to ensure the transparency of corporate management must be prepared so that they can be put in place as soon as possible. Meanwhile, it is important to make an effort to cooperat with other countries' financial authorities, and keep international financial market participants well informed about current conditions in Korea by strengthening communications with them.

Another lesson learned from this crisis is a renewed recognition of the financial industry's importance to the overall economy. In the process of economic development from the 1960s, the basic functions of the financial industry, such as credit screening, had been largely neglected because the financial sector had been regarded simply as a means of supporting the "real" sector. This eventually became a cause of the crisis. When many large firms collapsed, it led to severe bad loan problems for financial institutions. Thus, the crisis has taught Koreans the importance of an efficient financial system.

Throughout the long haul of economic recovery, nonviable financial institutions have been leaving the market on an unprecedented scale. Financial institutions have been forced to stop practices that involve moral hazard and must now operate their businesses in accordance with market discipline, which requires transparent financial statements and profit-oriented, sound, and accountable management practices. Only the first round of financial restructuring has been completed so far; there still remain problems such as the need for more public funds.

While overcoming the economic crisis, both the financial and corporate sectors are now learning and realizing what direction the Korean economy should take. The Korean corporate sector, through the implementation of rigorous reform, has taken a step towards improving competitiveness in the future. In order for Korea to surmount the present crisis and regain the momentum of sustained growth, there seems to be no alternative other than swift and intensive structural reforms. However, reforms always go hand in hand with pain in the short run. In the process of putting reform policies into practice, various challenges and dilemmas may well arise. Therefore, a problem we must solve is how to minimize the painful side effects without wavering from the fundamental thrust of structural reform.

Many efforts need to focus on implementing any structural reform that is beneficial to the Korean economy in the long run. The recent experience heightened awareness about the need to reform various segments of the Korean economy. Indeed, one beneficial legacy of the financial crisis is that the experience will have increased the awareness of firms, the government, the press, and the general public of the need to improve efficiency in all areas. As I explain in this paper, Korea has undergone significant institutional changes since the implementation of the IMF package which would never have been enacted in the absence of such developments.

As the newly rejuvenated financial sector equips itself with more advanced management skills and the reshuffled organization of restructuring, the momentum built by the stimulus should be fueled by financial sector liquidity support, and should assist recovery into the second half of 1999. Nonetheless, Korea's will to reform should be adamant, and complacency should not be allowed to set in. In order for this to occur, reform and restructuring need to be progressively implemented. There is no reverting back to the old days of inefficiency, dilapidation of resources, and moral hazard. Onward and upward, the march must go on.

In conclusion, the general direction of the Korean government's economic reforms after the financial crisis seems adequate. However, the muscular role assumed by the Korean government despite the existence of a strong consensus regarding the need for substantive reforms remains troublesome. We clearly remember that active governmental participation in bank credit allocation led to a feeble banking sector. We also acknowledge that such government-led practices have provided the ideal ground for moral hazard problems. Even facing an immediate need for reforms, the government should not attempt to maintain control of most aspects of the economy and society. A clear-cut perspective on government's role is needed to successfully implement the proposed reforms.

The evaluation of the reform measures taken by the Korean government will also be valuable to policymakers and academicis both within Korea and abroad. The next crisis will almost definitely be of a different variety. Nonetheless, a through understanding of the experience of the Korean economy cannot but help give us an advantage in preparing for the future. Korea is drawing invaluable lessons from the current turmoil, even though it is footing the bill for the crisis. It is absolutely vital to construct and manage a sound economic system in tune with the current trends of liberalization and globalization. A final positive aspect is a renewed recognition of the importance of the financial industry which had been neglected for a long time. These lessons will serve as a recipe for Korea to construct a more advanced and efficient economic system.

REFERENCES

Cho, Dongchul. 1999. "A Year After the Korea Economic Crisis: What Next?" Working Paper, No. 9902. Korea Development Institute.

Corsetti, Giancarlo, Paolo Pesenti, and Nouriel Roubini. 1998. "What Caused the Asian Currency and Financial Crisis?" National Bureau of Economic Research Working Paper, No.6833-6834.

Hwang, Inhak. 1998. *Market Structure and Social Efficiency.* Seoul: KERI.

Jwa, Sung-Hee, and Huh Chan Guk. 1998. "Korea's 1997 Currency Crisis: Its Causes and Implications." *Korean Journal* 38.2: 5-33.

Jwa, Sung-Hee, and Yi Insill. 1999. "Korean Financial Crisis: Evaluations and Lessons." Paper presented at Australia and Korea into the New Millennium: Political, Economic and Business Relations Conference.

Kim, Dae Il. 1998. "The Social Impact of the Crisis in Korea." Paper presented at the EDAP Regional Conference on Social Implications of the Asian Financial Crisis organized by the KDI and UNDP, Seoul, Korea, July 29-31, 1998.

Choi, Kwang. 1999. "Public Sector Reform and Fiscal Policy in Korea." Paper presented at Australia and Korea into the New Millennium: Political, Economic and Business Relations Conference.

Ministry of Finance and Economy (MOFE). 1999. *DJnomics: A New Foundation for the Korean Economy.* Seoul: Korea Development Institute.

_____. 1999. "The Economic Crisis in Korea and the Role of Fiscal Policy." OECD/PUMA SBO Meeting, June.

_____. 1999. *One Year of People's Government.* Gwacheon: MOFE

Nam, Jooha, and Kwon Jaejung. 1999. "Estimating the Size of Non-Performing Loans and Public Supporting Costs after Korean Financial Crisis." Mimeo.

Planning and Budget Commission (PBC). 1999. *The Budget of the Republic of Korea—Fiscal Year.* Gwacheon: Planning and Budget Commission.

Massive Unemployment and Social Disorganization:

The New Face of High-risk Society

Seong Kyoung-Ryung

The End of a Miracle and the Beginning of Massive Unemployment

The global financial crisis began in late 1997 and struck the Korean economy, which had been experiencing rapid growth during the last four decades. The GDP of Korea that amounted to $484 billion in 1996 is expected to shrink to $310 billion at the end of 1998. These figures translate into a drop of the world's 11th ranked economy to 17th and a decrease of the per capita GDP from over $10,000 in 1996 to $6,600 in 1998. Thus, the state-led fast economic growth has come to an end and Korea has just entered a period of negative or slow growth, which will be difficult to get out of (Marvin 1998).

The unemployment rate that averaged around 2% during the 1990s increased to 7.6% in the July 1998 and is estimated to rise to the level of 8 or 9%. Such high unemployment never existed during the last several decades in Korea. More than 1.65 million unemployed workers (as of July 1998) and their families are suffering from this unexpected crisis. At

*Originally published in Vol. 38, No. 4 (Winter 1998).

Seong Kyoung-Ryung (Seong, Gyeong-ryung) is Professor in the Department of Sociology at Hallym University. He obtained his Ph.D. in Sociology from Stanford University in 1990. His publications include *Cheje byeondong-ui jeongchi sahoehak* (Political Sociology of Regime Changes) (1995) and *Gungmin gukga gaehyeok ron* (On Reforming the Nation-State) (1996). E-mail: krseong@sun.hallym.ac.kr.

the same time, many companies without high productivity and competitiveness are severely distressed by financial shortages and thus face the possibility of insolvency in the near future. As a result, more workers will be unable to escape layoffs due to the current and future structural reforms. Unfortunately, it is difficult to predict the end of the present economic crisis at this juncture.

However, the real problem is not the high rate of unemployment itself. Rather, a more serious issue is that many social problems, which have not been carefully addressed or discussed during the period of rapid economic growth, have emerged as urgent issues requiring immediate attention. Unemployment in Korea has caused serious psychological depression and mental frustration, which can lead to family conflicts. It is quite natural that this type of unhealthy situation will accelerate the dissolution of families and exacerbate the degree of social inequality, which may eventually break down the very basis of social integration. From late 1997 onwards, these problems materialized and various social conditions have deteriorated as a result of structural reforms, which will continue at least until the end of 1998. The situation has come to a point beyond control.

Considering that unemployment can be an extremely grave challenge to the general welfare of laid-off workers and their families in terms of health, security, and well-being, the outcome of a high rate of unemployment should be regarded as one of the fundamental social risks. But we should acknowledge that this type of social risk is different from what was experienced during the "rush-to development" period in the 1960s and 1970s, such as the building collapses and environmental disasters (Han 1998; Yee 1998). If those disasters of the last decades can be understood as the result of systemic malfunctioning or immoral corruption, this contemporary problem can be said to be the result of economic depression that seriously affects those who have worked hard and in fact had nothing to do with the causes of the problem.

However, recognizing that the current economic depression was primarily caused by excessive government intervention in the market and the structural expansion of business corporations supported by various types of loans, it is not very difficult to deduce that massive unemployment and its related social problems are the result of the same mechanism that caused the collapse of buildings in the past. In other words, the present crisis is the result of short-sighted activities within the public and private sectors and failure to consider the potential problems that arise from their short-term profit-maximizing activities. Based on this argument, this social trend is nothing but a harbinger of greater disasters in the future.

The reason why the high rate of unemployment is so critical to Korean society is because Korea is not equipped with a well-developed institutionalized system of social security. During the last period of the "rush-to development," the welfare of individuals has been left mainly to the responsibility of their families or their companies. The government played a limited role by providing minimal support only for those below the poverty line. Faced with massive unemployment, therefore, the government is not capable of offering any practical help to those in need. At the same time, due to the high rate of geographical mobility of the general population that once recorded over 25%, the disparity of Korean society is quite severe. Naturally, this social characteristic has hindered the development of civil society and the third sector (or voluntary sector). As a result, the social resources that can be used to help the poor and unemployed workers are quite limited (Institute for Social Development 1993; Seong & Kim 1997).

In addition, the contemporary trend of "the end of work" that replaces workers with automated machines is spreading throughout the world, and this can be said to be one of the causes of Korea's current problems (Rifkin 1994). Therefore, it is very difficult to expect that the economy will recover and solve the various social problems in the near future. Even if the economy starts to recover from the depression, there is still a possibility for Korea to enter the stage of "jobless growth" due to the emergence of the knowledge-based economy and the information age (see Marcos 1997, 67).

Korean society has entered the era of massive economic restructuring as a result of the financial crisis and moved into the next stage of social crisis. The only way to minimize losses and to overcome various socioeconomic problems is to understand the context of the crisis and to discover new developmental alternatives based on that understanding. Prescriptions based on this type of effort will provide us with a basic social security network to prevent future disasters.

The Current Situation of Unemployment and Its Prospect

At this point, it is best to take a brief look at the current unemployment situation. As Figure 1 clearly indicates, Korea had a very low unemployment rate of about 2.1% in October 1997. Then, it began to skyrocket in November when the government decided to obtain financial help from the IMF. In November 1997, the unemployment rate rose to 2.6% and continued to rise to 3.1% in December and 4.5% in January 1998. Finally in February 1998, the unemployment rate went up to 5.9%, which meant that the total number of unemployed workers exceeded one million.

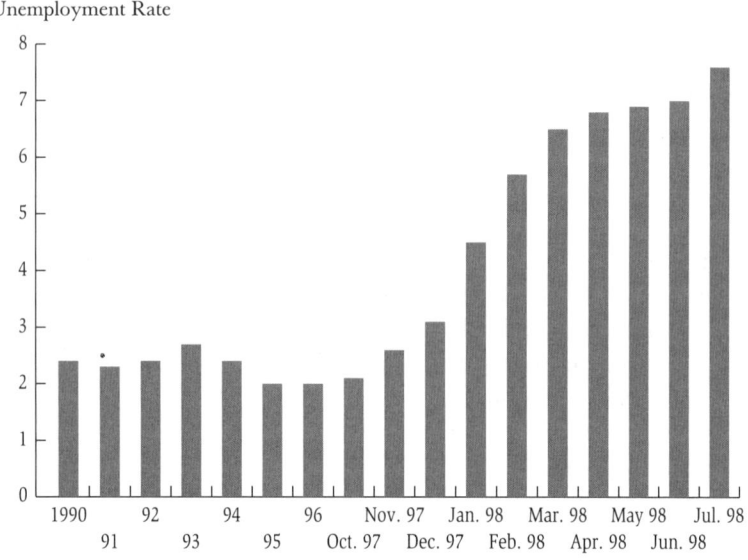

Figure 1. Unemployment rates in the 1990s

The unemployment rate rose to 7.6% in July 1998; that is, more than 1.65 million workers had lost their jobs. But the actual number of unemployed workers probably exceeds government statistics. Considering that there are more than 460,000 workers who work less than 18 hours per week, it is not very hard to conclude that the actual number of unemployed workers exceeds 2 million (*Chosun Ilbo*, 23 July 1998). At the same time, if those who have stopped searching for jobs in fear that they will not get one are included, the total number of unemployed workers can be well over 4 million.

Even if we accept the government's statistics, it is clear that the total population suffering from the current economic crisis definitely exceeds official calculations. According to the survey conducted by the Korea Labor Institute (1998a, 52), 43.6% of unemployed workers were heads of households. Considering that the average size of a household is 3.4, we can easily reach the conclusion that more than 3.5 million people are suffering from the unemployment crisis. If we add to this number the underemployed and the frustrated who gave up searching for jobs, the size is estimated to be four to five million, and this figure takes up about 10-15% of the total population. Unfortunately, however, all unemployment figures are expected to continue to rise even in the future. It is certain that this situation will get out of control if the total number of the unemployed exceeds over six million.

The general characteristics of the unemployed workers are as follows: Construction and manufacturing workers with simple manual skills are the most affected. Most of them are high-school graduates or have obtained lower levels of education, and are between the ages of 15 and 29 (Korea Labor Institute 1998a, 1-11). Female workers who lost their jobs during the last several months are not too different from their male counterparts, but due to the much higher number of women who were frustrated and thus gave up finding jobs, the general unemployment rate is about 2% lower than the male work force. Based on these figures, we can clearly see that the possibility of suffering from the present economic crisis quite differs from one group to another according to their socioeconomic status: workers with less education in the manual labor sector have a greater chance of losing their jobs.

As Rifkin (1994) indicated in his book, the problem of the present unemployment crisis is intimately connected to the ongoing social transformation that substitutes the human labor force with automated machines, and to the increasing "technical unemployment" of those who are less educated. In other words, with the onset of the economic crisis, many private and state-owned companies laid off workers in the process of factory automation. At the same time, they concentrated their investment in the fields of information and telecommunications, which reduced the need for a large labor force. Therefore, it will be more difficult for those who are currently unemployed and the potential job seekers to find jobs in the future.[1]

These workers can be referred to as the "surplus work force" in the era of postcapitalism, informational capitalism, or global capitalism, and they are facing an extremely high risk of being turned into the lumpen-proletariat (Marcos 1997, 67; Thurow 1996, 49-51).[2] Among the 1.65 million unemployed workers, only 6.6% are receiving unemployment insurance payments and 310,000 are temporarily supported by public aid, while more than 1.2 million are not receiving any form of assistance from the government or the third sector. Therefore, society should pay more attention to those who are helpless and deprived of all social aid.

The problem here is that it will be difficult to rectify the worsening situation of massive unemployment within the near future. As seen in Table 1, the hitherto unemployment regime of Korea was "Type C," i.e., "the low unemployment rate combined with a low rate of new entering and short-term unemployment. However, in the future, the characteristics of unemployment regime will change into "Type A": "high unemployment rate combined with a low rate of new entering and long-term unemployment."[3]

Of course, the unemployment situation will also be greatly affected by various external factors (e.g., the speed of structural reform, the inflow of international capital, the financial situation of other countries, and so forth), and it is very hard to clearly denote that the current unemployment crisis will remain a "Type A" situation for very long. However, considering the fundamental weakness of the Korean economy compared to other developed economies (especially, the gap of productivity

---

1. The distribution of the educational background of the current unemployed workers is as follows: 370,000 persons have middle-school diploma or less, 718,000 have high-school diploma, but only 218,000 have college education or higher. These statistics clearly show that unemployment affects those who have a high-school diploma or lower levels of education. The situation is expected to worsen in the future.

2. Regarding the notion of postcapitalism, informational capitalism, and global capitalism, see Drucker (1993) and Castells (1996).

3. Compared to many European countries with a solid social welfare system and good labor protection, Korea enjoys relatively less social welfare costs and a higher degree of flexibility in the labor market. However, the Korean economy has a very weak structural foundation for knowledge and information. At the same time, the structural reforms are currently taking place in both the private and public sectors. All these factors, therefore, are expected to entrench the "Type A" regime of unemployment in Korea.

Table 1. Types of Unemployment Regimes

Types	Unemployment Rate (1988)	Entrance Rate (%)	Duration (month)	Unemployment Rate (1988)
High and long unemployment regime				
France	11.1	0.6	21	12.5
Germany	6.6	0.4	16	9.6
Italy	23.6	0.2	105	21.6
Spain	23.6	0.2	105	21.6
High and short unemployment regime				
U.S.	5.8	2.2	3	5.4
Australia	7.8	1.4	6	8.6
Canada	8.3	2.6	3	9.7
Low and short unemployment regime				
Japan	2.6	0.5	5	3.3
Korea	2.4	0.8	3	7.6 ('98)

Source: Korea Labor Institute (1998a, 19).

and knowledge), the domestic resistance against structural reform, and the uncertainties of international economies (especially those of China and Japan), it is very hard to forecast that the situation will return from Type A to Type C within the next few years. As indicated in the McKinsey Report (1998), the unemployment rate will hover around 5% in the year 2010, even after the Korean economy is revitalized through a big bang in the service sectors.[4]

In this regard, it is highly expected that the unemployment regime of Korea will remain "Type A" for a long time. In this scenario, more people will suffer from unemployment, and the burdens of both the public and third sectors will be greater than ever before. As I have discussed above, however, the suffering will be most extreme for those who do not

---

4. The Hyundai Economic Research Institute predicted that in the worst-case scenario, the growth rate of the national economy will be –5.6% and –1.7% in 1998 and 1999 respectively. At the same time, the unemployment rate may rise to 11.3% in 1999 and will not drop to back to 5% until after 2003 (*Chosun Ilbo*, 27 July 1998).

have higher education and better skills, particularly the youth.[5] These are the people whom the society should pay more attention to and take care of with practical help.

Unemployment and Social Disintegration

As discussed thus far, the current problem of unemployment erupted within a very short period, and it is developing into a divisive factor that can disintegrate the moral and communal bases of Korean society. It is of great concern that, in the long run, this may be a corrosive factor that could break down social foundations. Therefore, in the following section, I will discuss three possible outcomes that could be caused by the long-term persistence of the current situation: individual suffering, disorganization of families, and social disintegration.[6]

Individual Suffering

When one loses his/her job suddenly, he/she initially feels extreme frustration and anger, followed by feelings of uneasiness, powerlessness, and inferiority. Finally, the person enters into a stage of being overwhelmed with a feeling of hopelessness and despair. From a psychological perspective, it is a general conception that most unemployed workers suffer from this type of extreme psychological instability mainly due to the recognition that he/she may not be able to find another decent job soon, or in the worst case, never. They know quite well that losing their jobs was not their fault, and their efforts will not do any good in securing their future unless the national economy improves.

---

5. In June 1998, the number of total unemployed college graduates was about 250,000. But considering that there will be more than 180,000 new college graduates by the end of February 1999 and that new openings of the thirty biggest private companies will only be 1,000 or less, the unemployed college graduates will exceed 400,000 (*Kyung Hyang Shinmun*, 14 August 1998). At the same time, unemployed workers whose ages range between 15 and 19 will double from 42,000 in 1997 to 98,000 in 1998.

6. Because it has only been ten months since the economic crisis first erupted, we do not have extensive studies regarding these issues. Therefore, the following discussion will be mostly based on the recent reports from daily newspapers.

Under these circumstances, some unemployed workers fall into alcoholism or drug addiction;·in the worst case, some consider suicide. According to a recent report in the *JoongAng Ilbo* (27 April 1998), among the 120 patients in a rehabilitation center located in Osan, about 30% of them became alcoholics after the economic crisis because they were laid off or had faced bankruptcies. At the same time, the institution received 20 phone calls a month to discuss drinking problems, and the number of calls has increased by 30% compared to the period before the economic crisis. Of course, this is a case of only one institution and so it cannot be seen to represent a general trend. However, this one example shows how people can easily fall into various types of deviant behaviors when they are affected by great stress resulting from sudden unemployment.

According to another recent report from the Office of the Attorney General, 6,974 drug-related criminals were arrested in 1997, which is an increase of 12.2% compared to 1996. In addition, during the first four months of 1998, more than 2,000 were arrested and this is an increase of about 45% compared to the same period last year (*Seoul Shinmun Daily*, 8 June 1998). It is believed that about 35% of the total drug addicts are unemployed while only 9% are employed. This clearly shows that there exists a high level of causality between the stress caused by unemployment and drug addiction. However, a more interesting fact is that the arrests amount to only 1% of actual drug addicts. This means that the actual number of total drug addicts is well over 700,000. And when the estimated 600,000 of those regularly using other substances such as glue, butane gas, etc. are added, the figure goes up to 1.3 million (*Seoul Shinmun Daily*, 8 June 1998). Therefore, the total number of drug addicts will increase drastically if unemployment continues to rise.

But becoming a drug addict or an alcoholic is not the only way to overcome the stress resulting from unemployment. Many decide to commit suicide due to frustration and despair. According to a Police Bureau report, the monthly number of suicides averaged 720 in 1996 while it increased to 900 from November 1997 to February 1998, that is, during the first three months following the onset of the economic crisis (*Munhwa Ilbo*, 27 March 1998). Based on a survey conducted by the "Phone of Love" (a voluntary civilian organization), more than 25% of the total 458 interviewees answered that they had an impulse to commit suicide due to the stress caused by the fear of being fired. Similarly, another survey conducted by the "Unemployed Fathers" in March 1998 revealed that 29% of the recently unemployed workers felt the impulse to commit suicide (Samsung Economic Research Institute 1998, 279).

In other words, most unemployed workers fall into various types of deviant behaviors, such as alcoholism, drug addiction, and suicide to escape from stress. In other cases, they turn to religion or become overly dependent on fortunetellers for reassurances to handle their psychological problems (Samsung Economic Research Institute 1998, 261-267).

When faced with debts or experiencing family conflicts, some simply decide to leave their homes and become homeless. According to a recent report from the Police Bureau, adults aged between 20 to 59 who left their homes totalled 11,075 in June 1998, and this is a 10% increase compared to the same period of last year. Of course, this figure refers to only reported cases and if we include unreported ones, the total number of adult runaways would be over 100,000 while the total homeless would be well over 3,000 (*JoongAng Ilbo*, 18 August 1998). Especially, many homeless people are losing their motivation to recover and become productive members of society. Instead, they fall into deviant behaviors, such as gambling, alcoholism, committing crimes, etc. This also means there is a great possibility for them to become permanent members of the "underclass."[7]

Based on this argument, the massive unemployment trend brings about panic to many unemployed workers who, in turn, try to escape from their problems through various types of deviant behavior.

Disorganization of Families

Similar to other societies, the family is the basis of Korean society and an important cohesive force that facilitates social integration. However, many of today's Korean families are disintegrating as a result of this severe economic crisis. Simply due to the worsening financial situation, there are more frequent fights between husbands and wives, and domestic violence has become quite common as well. In the worst cases, many married couples end up filing for divorce or choose to separate.

---

7. The total number of homeless people rapidly increased after the economic crisis from 2,000 in April 1998 to 3,000 in June 1998. The Ministry of Health and Welfare estimates that 94% of these people are recently unemployed workers, while the rest are vagrants from the pre-economic crisis period. The real problem is that more than 65% of the homeless do not want to return home. This means that there is a great possibility for them to become part of the lumpen proletariat in the long run.

According to a recent report from the Administrative Office of Legal Affairs, the total number of divorce cases increased by 64% (36,735 cases) during the first three months of 1998 from 22,324 during the same period of 1997 (*JoongAng Ilbo*, 26 June 1998).[8] If this trend persists, the total number of divorce cases for 1998 will be over 130,000. Considering that the total number of divorce cases in 1996 was 80,333, the ongoing social disintegration can be seen.

Another form of family disorganization is child abandonment or the passing of parental responsibility to orphanages. According to statistics from the Ministry of Health and Welfare, the total number of abandoned children was 4,876 during the first half of 1998, a 64% increase compared to the same period in 1997. Phone calls pleading with orphanages to take care of their children doubled from 1997. In addition, the abandoning of the elderly on the street or sending them into asylums is increasing more than ever. This is a very clear sign of the moral dissolution of our society caused by the economic crisis.

However, another serious case is the collective suicide of an entire family in despair. In contrast to the abandonment of children or the aged, this is the most extreme expression of familism that is emphasized over their own lives or human dignity. It means that when there are weak ties among family members, the economic crisis results in family disintegration, but in the opposite case, it may lead to the suicide of all the family members.

Even though less serious than the above problems, the rising trend of total unemployment brings about various negative effects on the formation of families. The most distinct tendencies include the delay of marriage and childbearing–such as increase in families without children or dinks (i.e., Double Income No Kids). It is generally known that most middle-class families spend between 300,000 and 500,000 won for their infants and even more in the case of kindergarteners. Therefore, it is quite natural for them to avoid the difficulties of the economic crisis by escaping from the burdens of raising children (Samsung Economic Research Institute 1998, 107). In any case, this can be a serious chal-

---

8. The Court of Family Affairs in Seoul recently announced that, in Seoul, the total number of monthly divorce cases increased as follows: 524 in January 1998 (505 in January 1977), 784 in March (569 in March 1997), 677 in May (531 in May 1997), 840 in July (596 in July 1997). *JoongAng Ilbo*, 18 August 1998.

lenge to society since it can reduce the size of the future population.

Delays in marriage and childbearing may not cause immediate problems to society, but other family matters such as divorce, domestic violence, the abandonment of children and the aged, and family suicide can be real threats and inflict direct social damage. Especially, if the familiar support system for children collapses as a result of divorce or separation, the individual family members can easily fall into deviant or even criminal behavior.

Social Disintegration

There are various types of sub-communities in Korean society, such as family-based communities, friendship-based communities, regional communities, and occupational communities. But due to individual inability to help others or to fulfill obligations in the economic crisis, the relationships among individuals formed within the above-mentioned communities become seriously challenged. As a result, the breakdown of these relationships becomes quite common and, in turn, can escalate into the breakdown of the entire society.

In a macro perspective, a factor accelerating community breakdown is the increase in criminal acts.[9] According to the Ministry of Justice, the total number of thefts increased to 14,501 and robberies to 941 during the first two months of 1998, which is a 37.4% and 55% increase respectively, compared to the same period of 1997 (*Chosun Ilbo*, 10 April 1998). At the same time, assaults, murders, and issuance of bad checks increased by 11%, 58%, and 10% respectively, while juvenile crime increased over 20%. As a result, the total number of prisoners in June 1988 was recorded at 70,300, which is over the national capacity of 66,000. This is well over the last two-year average ranging between 59,000 and 61,000, clearly showing a trend of increasing criminal behavior (*JoongAng Ilbo*, 3 July 1998).

---

9. In the U.S., when the unemployment rate increased by 1%, murder, assault, and property-related crimes also went up by 6.7%, 3.4% and 2.4%, respectively. In Korea, there do not exist such empirical studies, but in general, it is estimated that when the unemployment rate increases by 1%, the overall crime rate will go up by 5% (Samsung Economic Research Institute 1998, 305). Based on this estimation, with the increase of unemployment by 2%, the overall crime rate is seen to go up to 35%.

In addition, the rise in the crime rate has caused the expansion of the security industry. In 1998, it was estimated that the overall scale of security industry will exceed 1,000 billion won in total, including 330 billion won for security systems, 570 billion won for security guards, and 140 billion won for security equipment (*JoongAng Ilbo*, 20 July 1998). In the U.S., this industry is one of the fastest growing industries. According to Reich (1991, 269), the number of people working in the security industry is estimated to be about 2.6% of the total labor force, which well exceeds the total number of police. At the same time, Rifkin (1994, 285) noted that, in 1992, 16% of all households were equipped with electronic security systems and between 3 to 4 million people were dwelling in residential areas with protection fences.

In both Korea and the U.S., the reason for the rapid growth of the security industry is the increasing crime rate. The real issue behind the fast growing security industry, however, is that it increases segregation among people and communities and, ultimately, it destroys the social solidarity. Especially, the poor are being targeted by criminal acts more often than the rich. Since offenders and the victims mostly belong to the same class background, the casualties of economic hardship tend to be concentrated among the poor. More generally, however, a fundamental problem lies in the fact that the entire society becomes fragmented due to the increasing crimes which foster distrust and conflict as opposed to encouraging trust and solidarity.

The rapid growth of the security industry is also highly related to the increase in social inequality. In Korea, the economic crisis accelerated the bipolarity of income distribution. According to a recent study conducted by the Korea Institute for Financial Research, during the first half of 1998, the income gap among classes had widened a great deal. In 1997, while the middle class earned 74-76% of what the upper class earned, this dropped to 68% in 1998 and is estimated to be around 67.7% in 1999. In the case of the lower class, while they earned 31-32% of what the upper class earned in 1997, this is expected to drop to 28.55% and 28.4% in 1998 and 1999, respectively (*Chosun Ilbo*, 29 May 1998).

Reasons for the widening gaps among the classes is the rapid rise in the unemployment rate, salary cuts, and the devaluation of stock prices and real estate, all of which are the main sources of income for middle-class households. On the contrary, despite this worsening economic situation, the upper class enjoyed financial windfalls simply due to the high interest rates. In other words, the upper class was the only beneficiary of the economic crisis, while the rest of society suffered. In this sense, similar to other developed societies, we can easily notice that Korea is rapidly changing into another "20 vs. 80 society," transforming from an open to a closed society (Martin and Schumann 1996; Thurow 1996).

In this regard, it is easy to expect that those who have a lower education level and simple manual skills will find it more difficult to find a job and to earn a decent living. In addition, it is also a problem that the real income of most laborers, including many white-collar workers, will greatly decrease in the future due to the rapid automation and informatization. Thus, it is expected that the economic crisis will further increase the existing social inequality and weaken the status of most workers, especially those who are unskilled and not highly educated.

A riot is the worst case scenario that can result from the growing crime rate, which is related to the massive unemployment rate and the increasing social inequality. In Indonesia, right after the economic crisis, a large-scale riot took place.[10] Fortunately, in Korea there is no sign of such riots at this moment except for some strikes.

However, it is generally believed that if the unemployment rate reaches 8-9% and the economic crisis relapse lasts for 10 to 12 months, the critical points for a riot to occur (Samsung Economic Research Institute 1998, 27 & 336), the period between September 1998 through March 1999 is expected to be a "danger zone." An unemployment rate of 8-9% means that more than 6 million people will be affected, and after 10 to 12 months of economic crisis they will have exhausted their savings.[11] In this regard, we should pay serious attention to the metropolitan areas. According to recent reports, the unemployment rates in these areas have been higher than the national average in many cases, such as 9.3% in Busan, 8.6% in Incheon, 8.4% in Gyeonggi-do province, 8.1% in Seoul, Daegu, and Gwangju (Chosun Ilbo, 23 July 1998). Thus, practical solu-

---

10. One of the structural factors behind the Los Angeles riots was the high unemployment rate among black Americans. While the average unemployment rate was 10.4% in the LA area, that of black Americans was about 50% (Rifkin 1994, 283). Police brutality was only the triggering factor for the riot.

11. According to Bang's research (1998), unemployed workers can make their living with their severance pay for 1-2 months (34.7%), 3-5 months (35.9%), 6-12 months (7.3%), longer than 12 months (6.0%). This shows that about 94% of unemployed workers will not be able to survive longer than a year.

tions are needed right away to avoid potential dangers in these regions.

We should also worry about the possibility of a revival of chauvinism and extreme rightism as a result of the ongoing economic crisis. In many European societies whose unemployment rate has been kept over 10% for several years, the neo-Nazism targeting minorities and immigrants is drawing serious social concern. Especially, this kind of phenomenon is closely related to the high unemployment rate among adolescents or youngsters. These young people who cannot find decent jobs for a long period after graduation tend to blame the minorities and immigrants for their own difficulties and attack them. In addition, under these circumstances, many new political parties based on extreme racist sentiments such as the National Front and the Neo-Nazi Party can present a serious challenge to the social foundation of the political democracy. Hence, we should not ignore the fact that after World War I Nazism and Fascism rose as a result of economic crises with high rates of unemployment.

Korea has not yet entered this stage. However, because it is widely regarded as an appropriate behavior not to buy foreign products and many commercials appeal to patriotism by asking the public to buy domestic products, an extreme form of nationalism may arise in Korea in the near future. Above all, we should keep in mind that as long as the unemployment rate among the young is quite high, it is always possible for them to turn to political activism along the lines of chauvinism.

Therefore, if the current economic crisis persists for a certain duration of time, various actors of society may collaborate to form a political coalition based on extreme nationalism. All social actors such as *jaebeol*, who are under pressure of being more active in structural reforms, middle- and small-sized firms without international competitiveness, workers who want to keep their jobs safely under the blanket of economic protectionism, and finally, the large number of the unemployed suffering from extreme economic hardships can form a strong chauvinist political coalition. If this really occurs, it will be a great barrier to economic restructuring and democratic consolidation.

Creation of New Socioeconomic Orders

As discussed thus far, the current crisis is causing unprecedented disintegration in every aspect of Korean society. It is not only an economic crisis but also a social crisis to all individuals, families, and communities.

The society is gradually becoming more unstable, filled with dangers and risks. Many individuals are losing hope and questioning the meaning of life. Family bonds are disintegrating, while communities are being challenged by general distrust. Overall, society is losing its civility which forms the foundation of civil society, falling into anomie devoid morality and norms. Various types of deviant behavior such as suicide, crime, rioting, and extreme nationalism are a great possibility. Under this situation, do we have any viable alternatives to evade the predicament of a high-risk society and create a safer one?

New Policy Lines Based on Reform Liberalism

First of all, we should change the political, economic, and social systems along the line of reform liberalism. As we already know, Korean society has been a model case of centralism, interventionism, and strong nationalism (Seong 1998). The Korean economy has relied heavily on the collusion between the state and the banks. Korea did not develop a strong civil society or a third sector based on independence and a self-generating force. All of these resulted in state failure and economic failure that led to a massive scale of bankruptcy, unemployment, and social chaos. But the society was unable to handle the problems and now is about to enter the stage of "social failure."

In this regard, all the systems of state, economy, and society lack freedom, fair competition, autonomy, and communal foundation. Therefore, reform liberalism that includes policy prescriptions for both reform and liberalism will encourage freedom and accelerate competition in both the sectors of the state and economy, while in the social sector, it will strengthen self-governance and the communal foundation.

In the process of such structural reforms, the outdated paradigm in which the state plays an active role in facilitating economic growth and social integration should be cast aside. As proven by the successes of many developed nations, in which the functions and responsibilities of the state have been reduced, energy should instead be concentrated on encouraging partnerships among the state, private firms, and civil organizations to promote economic growth and social solidarity. Based on these partnerships, to maximize performance in the economic and social sectors, we must cut down on all sorts of unnecessary costs and in turn foster societal cooperation. In these days when globalization and information society proceed rapidly, no one will be able to deny the need to increase both external competitiveness and internal solidarity in order to pursue the new policy line of reform liberalism.

Building an Effective Social Security System

Despite the fact that the functions and size of the central government must be limited in order to build a new socioeconomic order, the responsibilities and efforts of the state in expanding social security and valuable human capital should be increased. This is mainly because the state welfare and its services are public goods.

In general, the social security system is composed of two basic functions: the first is the unemployment benefits and the second is a public aid program to prevent unemployed workers from falling into absolute poverty. However, as seen in both Tables 2 and 3, we face very serious problems in these two institutional programs. First, in the case of the unemployment benefits, as of May 1998, all of the recently unemployed workers, small business owners, workers in companies with four or less employees, part-time workers, daily workers, and family employees have been totally excluded from the benefits. In the case of those who are working at a workplace hiring five or more, only 5.72 million joined the program. This means that only 27.2% of the total number of workers are under the protection of the social security program (Korea Labor Institute 1998b, 6).

Table 2. Current State of the First Safety Net: Unemployment Insurance

	Recently Unemployed	Self-employed	Regular Workers	Part-time Workers	Daily Workers	Family Workers	Sum
Number of workers	–	595 million	738 million	405 million	180 million	187 million	2,105 million
Number of the unemployed	22 million (14.5%)	20.4 million (13.6%)	42.1 million (28.0%)	46.2 million (30.8%)	18.6 million (12.4%)	1 million (0.7%)	150 million (100%)
Whether covered by unemployment insurance	not covered	not covered	13.8% of the unemployed	not covered	not covered	not covered	572 million regular workers

In this regard, it is highly welcome that the state is planning to include 1.6 million workers who work at a workplace hiring four or less and 730,000 part-time or temporary workers as of October 1998 (*Chosun Ilbo*, 26 July 1998). However, even after this expansion of the social security program, daily workers and family employees will still be left unprotected.

Also, there are many problems in the second stage of the social security program. As seen in Table 3, the current program is not aimed at improving the living standard of unemployed workers and the poor based on the minimum cost of living, but is constructed to fit the annual budget of the Ministry of Health and Welfare. As a result, the program cannot be of practical help to the unemployed and the poor, thus losing its efficacy as a whole.

To solve this problem, the government recently increased the poverty line to a monthly income of 272,000 won with a 150% increase of total-owned property to include more people under protection (*Chosun Ilbo*, 30 July 1998). As a result, about 980,000 additional people will benefit from the program. In addition, for the unemployed workers who are excluded from this program but whose monthly income is at the margin, the government is planning to provide 60,000 won a month worth of food and an extra 20,000 won worth of emergency medical care for a limited period of three months. The government also decided to loan 5 million won to 190,000 households facing financial difficulties (*Chosun*

Table 3. Current State of the Second Safety Net: Public Aid

	Criteria		Number	Covered Protection
	Monthly Income	Property (household)		
Residential protection/ Institutional protection	220 thousand won	28 million won	509 thousand	living, self-help, education, child-birth, health, funeral service
Aid for self-help	230 thousand won	29 million won	1.03 million	education, health, self-help

*as of May 1998

Ilbo, 23 July 1998).

It is quite clear that, by leaving the responsibilities to families and the private sector and only taking care of those who are below the absolute poverty line, the government has not yet developed a practical social security system. However, it is worth noting that the government finally started to cover those who had been previously deprived of social protection.

Despite the government's recent efforts, however, there still remain several problems in terms of managing the social security system. First, although Korea has relatively good institutions and funds for unemployment benefits, there is a lack of relevant infrastructures to facilitate both vocational training and employment stability. Second, it is questionable whether the relief plan is well equipped with appropriate policies and whether it has been implemented effectively, especially when we consider that the plan was made and launched largely overnight during an emergency. The government has set aside 8.5 trillion won for the plan but, at the end of June 1998, it had spent only 27.5% of the total budget. The reason for this is that the actual amount and conditions of the relief package are too stringent and unrealistic. Third, the partnership network between the government and other private institutions, such as firms, higher education institutions, and private vocational training institutions, has not been well organized.

Therefore, to make the social security programs more effective, the government has to loosen the qualification requirements for beneficiaries and increase the budget for social security. At the same time, as I have already discussed, a partnership network should be constructed. Under this networking frame, the government should make an effort to provide more services to children, the aged, the handicapped, women, and single parents.

Of course, it is expected that the usual rent-seeking activities on the part of private institutions can be a problem in expanding the security network. Thus, the government should facilitate social environments for appropriate civilian activities and should invent a monitoring system to prevent such activities from occurring. Only through these measures can we guarantee the efficiency of the whole plan.

Civil Society and the Third Sector

At present, civil society and the third sector in Korea are very weak.

Especially, in regards to the nature of civil society, the biggest problem is that there are still too many government-funded semi-public associations that had been used as political tools to mobilize various social resources vertically and to increase the overall degree of social control in the past. Many government-funded organizations, such as the the National Council of New Community Movement in Korea, had been set up by the state and still exert a great impact on the society. Furthermore, these organizations basically monopolize the financial resources of the government.

Recently, the government adopted a new legal foundation, the so-called "Law to Support Civil Organizations" under the pretext of the "Rebuilding Korea" movement to dispose of state corporatism and to create a more liberalized and fair institutional environment (*Munhwa Ilbo*, 15 August 1998). In particular, this law will deprive government-funded organizations of all privileges and treat all nongovernmental organizations on an equal basis. At the same time, this will serve as a good initiating point to upgrade the quality of various civil social activities especially by providing necessary funds to those organizations.

The nature of the third sector in Korea is not much different from that of the civil society. As seen in Table 4, the size of the social welfare program worked out by the third sector is about $740 million. This is only about 5% the size of social welfare programs in most developed societies. While the proportion of those who participate in various types of volunteer activities out of the total population is 50% in the U.S. and 39% in the U.K., but it is only 2% in Korea. This clearly illustrates the weakness of the third sector in the society.

To facilitate the growth of the third sector, institutional reforms are needed. The government should make full efforts to increase the financial assistance from private firms, nonprofit foundations, and individuals to the third sector by relaxing tax exemption criteria. For this purpose,

Table 4. Size of the Third Sector

	Size of State Welfare	Size of Third Sector Welfare	Proportion of Volunteers
Advanced nations	20-30% of GNP	U.S.: $34.3 billion U.K.: $5.4 billion	U.S.: 50% U.K.: 39%
Korea	1% of GNP	$0.74 billion	2%

the government should also loosen tight legal controls, such as the "Law to Inhibit Mobilization of Private Contributions," which were initially designed to discourage civilian fund-raising activities. At the same time, the government should create the proper institutional environment to encourage volunteer activities by offering diverse incentives (e.g., extra points to college entrance, tax exemption, insurance coverage for injured volunteers). To demonstrate the importance of the third sector and to foster volunteerism as a part of the national agenda, the government should consider the possibility of making a special presidential advisory committee.

If the third sector expands in the long run, it can play a very important role as a social economy in solving problems caused by the fluctuation of market economy, such as large-scale unemployment (see Rifkin 1994, 315-319). A social economy is different from the market economy, which is based on pure utilitarianism. It is a socioeconomic system based on communal bonds within which individuals help one another. In developed nations, this system works efficiently in relieving the poor, providing basic medical treatment, educating adolescents, helping the handicapped, building shelters for the poor, and so forth. In the U.S., third sector activities take up about 6% of total GNP and 9% of total employment. The Korean government should utilize this type of social activities when we consider that more people will suffer from a decrease of real income due to a high level of unemployment which will extend for quite a long period.

A Ray of Hope: Overcoming the Myth of Statism

As we have discussed so far, it is a tragedy to have 1.65 million unemployed workers as a result of the economic crisis. However, there is still hope for a bright future if and only if we can build a new society based on reform liberalism that aims at liberalizing the market economy from state intervention on the one hand and at strengthening civil society on the other. The contemporary systemic crash has been caused by the old systems of the state, economy, and society. Unless we revise all these systems and adapt them to the rapidly changing global environment, the future will never be bright or favorable.

From a strategic point of view, the current economic crisis is a chance for us to restructure all those old systems and outdated paradigms. In this regard, the national effort should be concentrated on devising new systems and on improving the quality of operations of those new systems. For this purpose, the government should first get rid of the old conception that "the state should be in charge of everything," which is based on extreme statism. Of course, we cannot deny that, even today, most of the national authorities are in the hands of the government, still an important player in managing the national economy and securing the social order. However, we should also admit that a large part of the present economic crisis was caused by a series of state failures. So, to avoid repeating the same mistake, the government should transfer a large part of its power and responsibilities to the market economy and the civil sectors to increase both productivity and solidarity. It should also play the role of creating favorable socioeconomic environments to facilitate civil social activities.

In this regard, it is strongly believed that the authority, budget, and size of the government should be significantly reduced. At the same time, there should be a clear distinction between the steering and rowing functions of the government. Based on this division, a large part of the growing functions such as provision of public services should be transferred to the private sector or coproduced with it. By doing so, we may expect the private sector to provide local people with some public services, such as vocational training, welfare, health services, and lifelong education. Only the partnership between the public and private sectors can generate and deliver diverse public services more effectively to those millions of unemployed workers. In this way, both market economy and civil society can be strengthened simultaneously. Then, we can also expect that the efficiency and productivity of the whole Korean society will greatly improve.

Overcoming the myth of extreme statism is the only way to revive the vitality and dynamism of the market economy and civil society. Considering the seriousness of the current economic crisis, the solution should be fundamental and practical. If we continue to cling to the old paradigm and to attempt only minor revisions, it will be impossible for us to recover from this disastrous situation. If we sincerely long for a bright future, we can only achieve it by making concerted efforts to rebuild Korea by restructuring the political, economic, and social systems toward a new paradigm of reform liberalism and partnership.

REFERENCES

Bang, Ha-nam. 1998. *Siljik geullojadeul-ui gujik hwaldong mit saenghwal siltae-e gwanhan josa bogoseo* (A Report on Job-Searching Activities of the Unemployed Workers and the State of Their Living). Seoul: Korea Labor Institute.

Castells, M. 1996. *The Rise of the Network Society.* Malden, Mass.: Blackwell Publishers, Inc.

Drucker, P. F. 1993. *Post-Capitalist Society.* New York: Harper Business.

Han, Sang-Jin. 1998. "The Korean Path to Modernization and Risk Society." *Korea Journal* 38.1: 5-27.

Institute for Social Development, Seoul National University. 1993. *Simin undong danche hwalseonghwa bangan-e daehan yeon-gu* (A Study on Activating Civil Movement Organizations). Seoul: Seoul National University.

Korea Labor Institute (KLI). 1998a. *1999 nyeondo sireop daechaek bangan* (The Policy Direction of Dealing With Unemployment: The Year 1999). Seoul: Korea Labor Institute.

_____. 1998b. *Sahoe anjeonmang guchuk bangan* (A Study on Building Social Safety Net). Seoul: Korea Labor Institute.

_____. 1998c. *Current Labor Policies and Their Performance.* Seoul: Korea Labor Institute.

Marcos. 1997. *Je sacha segye daejeon-i sijakdoeeotta* (The World War IV Just Started). Translated by the Labor Institute of Chun Taeil. Seoul: Hanul Publishing Co.

Martin, H. P., and H. Schumann. 1997. *Segyehwa-ui deot.* Translated by Kang Su-dol. Seoul: Younglim Cardinal Inc. Originally published as *Die Golbalisierungsfalle* (1996).

Marvin, S. May 1998. "Death Throes."

McKinsey Global Institute. 1998. *Hanguk jaechangjo-ui gil.* Originally published as *Reinventing Korea.* Seoul: Maeil Business Daily.

OECD. 1998. *Labor Force Statistics* (Internet).

Reich, R. 1991. *The Work of Nations.* New York: Vintage Books.

Rifkin, J. 1994. *Nodong-ui jongmal.* Translated by Yi Yeong-ho. Seoul: Minumsa Publishing Co. Originally published as The End of Work.

Samsung Economic Research Institute. 1998. *IMF chunggyeok, geu ihu: byeonhwa-ui sidae-reul saraganeun 18 gaji sam-ui jihye* (The Impacts of the IMF: 18 Lessons to Survive in the Age of Great Transformation). Seoul: Samsung Economic Research Institute.

Seong, Gyeong-ryung (Seong, Kyoung-Ryung). 1998. "21 segi-ui byeonhwa jeonmang-gwa gukga gyeongyeong-ui sin paereodaim" (On a New Paradigm for the State Governance in the 21st Century). In *Gukga hyeoksin-ui bijeon-gwa jeollyak* (The Visions and Strategies for Innovation of the State), edited by the Korean Institute for Public Policies. Seoul: Samsung Economic Research Institute.

Seong, Gyeong-ryung, and Kim Ho-gi. 1997. *Simin undong-ui hwalseonghwa-reul wihan min-gan danche yukseong-e gwanhan yeon-gu* (A Study on The Ways to Support Civil Associations for the Activation of Civil Movements). Seoul: First Ministry to the President for Political Affairs).

Thurow, L. C. 1996. *Jabonjuui-ui mirae.* Translated by Yu Jae-hun. Seoul: Koreaone Press Inc. Originally published as *The Future of Capitalism.*

Yee, Jaeyeol. 1998. "Risk Society as a System Failure: Sociological Analysis of Accidents in Korea." *Korea Journal* 38.1: 83-101.

PART IV

THE ROLE OF GOVERNMENT IN A CHANGING ENVIRONMENT

The Role of Government in Economic Management:

Korea's Experiences and Lessons

Jwa Sung-Hee

Introduction

The goal of this paper is to shed light on the best possible role for the government in order to promote sustainable economic development led by private sector initiative.

The role of the government in economic management is basically an issue of defining the appropriate economic management borders between government and private sectors, and can be traced back to the debate on the feasibility of socialist economic calculations during the earlier part of the twentieth century. Accordingly, this paper briefly surveys the debates on the roles of government and market, beginning with the socialist calculation debate and moving up to recent discussions on the desirability and prospects of a government-led economic development strategy. In this paper, I argue that the debates on the role of the government can ultimately be reduced to a matter of market versus govern-

* Originally published in Vol. 37, No. 4 (Winter 1997).

Jwa Sung-Hee (Jwa, Seung-hui) is President of the Korea Economic Research Institute. He received his Ph.D. in Economics from University of California at Los Angeles in 1983. He has authored many books, including *A New Paradigm for Korea's Economic Development: From Government Control to Market Economy* (Palgrave 2001), *The Evolution of Large Corporations in Korea: A New-institutional Economics Perspective of the Chaebol* (Edgar Elgar, forthcoming), *Naesaengjeok geumyung jedo ron* (The Endogenous Financial System) (1995) and *Jinhwaronjeok jaebeol ron* (An Evolutionary Theory of the *Jaebeol*) (1998). E-mail: shj@keri.org.

ment failure. Market failure has traditionally been put forward as a reason for active government intervention, but I will show that market failure in most cases is a reflection of institutional failure which is, in turn, another form of government failure.

Next, this analysis extracts lessons from Korea's experiences of government-led development strategy of the past 30 years by reviewing policy patterns, defining their characteristics and, most importantly, delineating their legacies. Korea's experiences suggest that whenever government has intervened in endogenous decision variables, problems, such as a reluctance to economize on the part of the private sector and the impositions of unfair practices and regulations, have usually resulted. I argue that such intervention will inevitably be unsuccessful in the future because the size and complexity of the Korean economy has now reached a point where government information superiority over that of the private sector can no longer be guaranteed.

Finally, this paper will provide a basic framework in which to discuss the optimal role of government in a general context. I will apply the Hayekian philosophy of interpreting market competition as a discovery procedure moving toward optimal solutions to the economic problems of resource allocation. The paper concludes that the government role should be confined to preserving the spontaneity and endogeneity of the market order and to cultivating a better economic environment for the working of that order. In other words, the role of government is to determine exogenous variables for the proper functioning of the market order while leaving the determination of endogenous variables to individual firms in the private sector.

Overview of the Debates on the Role of Government

The government role in economic management has been a continuing but unresolved issue in discussions on economic policy. Debate began in the early twentieth century (1920-1940), particularly in the context of the feasibility of socialist economic calculation, and was led by Ludwig von Mises, Oscar Lange, Friedrich Hayek, and other eminent scholars of the Austrian school.

Mises argued that rational economic management in a socialist economy is impossible because of the nonexistence of market and price mechanisms. Lange disagreed with Mises and offered a concept of market socialism. Lange asserted that a central planning board could be a substitute for a market or the price mechanism, thereby acting as a coordinator of decentralized resource allocation problems. Lange's board would search for an optimal allocation or discover an equilibrium price vector through trial and error or successive approximation processes. Later, Hayek (1948) joined in this debate, contributing to the rise of the Austrian school as well as to the development of the concept of market competition as a dynamic discovery procedure. Although Hayek recognized the theoretical possibility of economic calculation by a central planning board in a socialist economy, he doubted whether such a system would be practical in view of the excessive information requirements. In the Hayekian world, no humanly conceived system is capable of discovering optimal outcomes of resource allocation without the process of dynamic competition.

During the 1940s and 1950s, the debates over the government role in economic management revolved around the desirability of a mixed economy and the welfare state. The Great Depression during the 1930s cast strong doubts on the automatic coordination function, and especially the macroeconomic coordination function, of a capitalistic free market economy.

As a result, the Keynesian anticyclical macroeconomic policy function of the government became the new subject for debate, overriding the issue of the mostly microeconomic nature of resource allocation which had dominated the socialist economic calculation debate. To remedy market failures at the macroeconomic level, especially the unemployment phenomenon, it was thought that the government should intervene in the market, thus giving rise to the argument for a mixed economy and the welfare state. Ironically, this new argument for government intervention in the macro economy was also strengthened by the development of the socialist planning theory which had come about in response to an earlier debate on the possibility of a socialist economic calculation.

However, government macroeconomic intervention–including fine-tuning macroeconomic policies–to maintain stable growth and employment turned out to be ineffective as is evident with various macroeconomic shocks of the 1970s and 1980s (such as oil price shocks and the misalignment of exchange rates). These experiences provided an environment for the revival of the liberal tradition that includes the rise of neoliberalism led by Hayek (1984a, 1984b, 1989), the birth of a public choice school led by J. M. Buchanan, and the surge of political conservatism led by Margaret Thatcher. In recent years, deregulation or liberalization of the private sector has come to the core of economic reform in most advanced countries, and the importance of long-term perspective in macroeconomic policymaking, such as a rule-based policy, has been reemphasized. In connection with this, it is argued that government failures are due not only to excessive informational requirements, as in the Hayekian framework, but also to the inherent nature of self-interest seeking government officials, as depicted by the Buchanan public choice framework.

An interesting debate on the role of the government in economic development has recently appeared on the scene, which originates his debate from somewhat different concerns than those of the earlier calculation debate. A prime focus of the debate considers whether a government in an underdeveloped capitalistic market economy can improve upon the market outcome of resource mobilization and allocation, and thereby expedite economic development. Therefore, the issue of this debate is ultimately reduced to discerning the relative degree of importance between market failures versus government failures.

Observing the remarkable success of economic development in East Asian countries like Japan, Korea, Taiwan, and other second-tier latecomers, adherents to the neoclassical view stress that setting the basics right is the most important lesson for economic development policy learned from East Asian experiences. They argue that the government should provide a stable macroeconomic environment and a reliable legal framework to promote domestic and international competition. Minimum intervention with the least degree of relative price distortion is seen as a virtue. In their view, Asian economies benefited mostly from strategies by which the government confirmed rather than led or directed the market.

On the other hand, a group of economists called revisionists find a greater significance in other aspects of the East Asian success story which have gone relatively unnoticed by neoclassicists. In their view, the government has taken a more active role in the economic development process than has been recognized by the neoclassicists and thus, they argue, East Asian governments have indeed led rather than simply conformed to the market. They even go further to suggest that the state, as observed during late industrialization stages, should set deliberately wrong relative prices in order to create profitable investment opportunities (Amsden 1989, 13). They point to the existence of market failures in developing economies such as the lack of relevant markets and market imperfections and argue that a positive government role is needed in order to remedy these failures. They contend that markets consistently fail to guide resource allocation needed for the highest growth in the overall economy. Amsden, one of the strongest revisionists, even suggests that macroeconomic stability should be sacrificed if the central bank has the priority to support its industries. According to Amsden, "whatever the relationship between inflation and investment in theory, in practice inflation did accompany Korea's push into heavy industry under government leadership in the late 1970s. . . . The pursuit of fast growth was not restrained in the interest of price stability" (Amsden 1989, 100).

Recently, the World Bank (1993) gave an answer to the revisionists' argument and, in doing so, reconfirmed a plain truth. "For interventions that attempt to guide resource allocation to succeed, they must address failures in the working of markets. Otherwise, markets would perform the allocation function more efficiently" (World Bank 1993, 11). We may observe that, in this argument too, macroeconomic stability is emphasized as the most important precondition for economic development.

In sum, the recent debate on the role of the government in economic development seems to center around the extent of market failures versus government failures. In this regard, it may be useful to reiterate a point made earlier: market failure generally reflects a failure of institutions and is, therefore, another form of government failure in that government has failed to provide adequate or appropriate institutions. Therefore, market failure, by its own defining characteristics, cannot be considered as an automatic justification for direct government intervention. Rather, government should try to introduce appropriate institutions as an environment for better economic performance (Vanberg 1991, 179). Furthermore, in most cases of apparent market failure it should not go unnoticed that government regulation or preferential treatment usually turns out to be the major cause of failure.

Korea's Experiences

Pattern of Economic Management

Korea has achieved remarkably high economic growth during the last thirty some years. Its economic development process during this period has been generally described as one following a government-led export promotion strategy. The government has been actively involved in almost every important aspect of economy-related decision-making and the private sector has closely followed the signals given by the government. Government-led order has always taken precedence over the spontaneous market order.

In the context of maximum utilization of economic resources, the economic development process usually entails two interrelated problems of resource utilization. One involves how to mobilize economic resources, and the other, how to allocate economic resources. Concerning economic resource allocation, there has been a lively discussion on the optimal degree of government intervention, and the consensus seems to be that the market order is superior to government allocation in general, except in special cases of so-called "market failures." However, practically speaking, it is very difficult to resolve the issues as to the extent and way government intervention should occur to optimally promote resource allocation for economic development. This, of course, has long been a subject for debate.

In allocating resources, the Korean government has a long history of intervening directly in microeconomic resource allocation through discriminatory policies, such as favoring certain sectors and certain groups of economic agents. The government controlled financial resource allocations by imposing regulations on interest rates and the lending activities of financial institutions. In the earlier stage of development—until the 1970s—large business groups and heavy and chemical industry sectors were favored, but now small- and medium-sized enterprises are relatively favored. Rather than allowing market competition to serve as a discovery procedure for making important allocation decisions regarding such things as what lines of business large business groups can engage in and what kind of businesses financial institutions can lend money to, the government has taken on this role itself. In recent years, direct government intervention in private decision matters has been reduced by increased liberalization processes in the private sector, but it has, nevertheless, generated far-reaching and lasting negative influences on the mind-set of policymakers regarding the role of the market order.

On the other hand, concerning the mobilization of economic resources, little attention has been paid to the possible side effects of stressing an active government role in resource mobilization. In general, mobilization drives tend to create a detrimental environment for macroeconomic management. Once priority is given to domestic resource mobilization, then even macroeconomic policies such as monetary, fiscal, and exchange rate policies tend to be "mobilized" as instruments to support economic development, thereby eroding a macroeconomic stabilization role. Low interest rates, base money creation, and tax-and-expenditure instruments all tend to be utilized to support policy loans for important industries. Exchange rate management also tends to be constrained by the concern for export promotion. Finding ways to mobilize available macroeconomic policy instruments to support economic development becomes the dominant concern rather than finding ways to improve macroeconomic stability.

Broadly speaking, it can be said that Korea has not been an exception in emphasizing the active role of government in resource mobilization even though the degree has, of course, fluctuated during the development period depending on the various situations faced by the country. In this process, Korea came up with a very peculiar macroeconomic management pattern. While the economy was subject to inflationary pressure stemming from base money and credit expansion resulting from a concern for maximum resource mobilization, monetary policy instruments such as the control of base money became inoperative. As a result, direct controls on important individual prices and even on economic activities within the private realm became widely utilized as the main instruments to maintain macroeconomic stability. In sum, macroeconomic policy function was performed by micro regulations.

However, in contrast to these and other similar legacies in the economic management pattern of government-led development, Korea's economic policy environment has undergone a drastic change in recent years. The Korean economy is becoming increasingly open and integrated with the global economy through financial liberalization including capital flow liberalization. Given the increasing openness of the economy, Korea can no longer rely on direct regulations for macroeconomic management. Furthermore, globalization and the increasingly borderless world economy will tend to limit the feasibility of the government's control of the domestic economy and will force the adoption of a market order-led economic management system. Globalization will also foster high international mobility of economic agents and resources such as firms, capital, and other economic factors. These, in turn, imply that any regulatory or discriminatory domestic economic policies will become ineffective since economic agents and resources subject to unfair treatment by any government's policy will simply go elsewhere. Therefore, economic policy should be based on the market mechanism in a nondiscriminatory way.

Characteristics of Government-led Economic Management

While it is generally accepted that the Korean government played a decisive role in the country's successful economic development over the last 30 years, one should be aware that it is very difficult to precisely define the concept of government-led economic management. In this paper, the concept is loosely and broadly defined.

A government-led economic management regime is an economic policy regime in which the government determines major endogenous economic variables within the realm of private economic agents by imposing its will on the market as an outsider rather than as a participant in the market process. In this regime, the government attempts to predetermine an outcome which would otherwise be determined endogenously through market processes.

Government-led economic management as defined here tends to exhibit the following characteristics. Government macroeconomic management relies on direct regulations such as credit rationing rather than open market operations for money supply control, and on wage-price controls over aggregate demand management for anti-inflationary policy. In addition, government microeconomic policy takes the form of picking the winners before the market process works itself out and of providing the means (such as financial support) necessary for the chosen to win.

However, in order for this type of economic management to be successful without causing distortions in resource allocation, the government must have informational superiority over private market participants and should have a complete set of solutions ready to be put into action against a host of difficult economic policy issues. But the requirements that must be fulfilled for government intervention to be beneficial are difficult, if not impossible, to satisfy, especially as an economy grows in size and complexity. Unless a complete recipe for solutions to various economic problems is readily available, the degree of government intervention needs to be reduced in order to benefit the economy. Korea now seems to have reached such a stage of economic development where active private sector initiatives must be cultivated, if development is to be sustained.

Legacies of Government-led Economic Management

More than 30 years of active government intervention in private economic matters have resulted in many legacies that pose serious stumbling blocks to a policy regime shift toward private sector activism.

Even as the informational requirements for efficient economic policymaking become increasingly daunting and impossible to satisfy, economic policymakers, including economists who are accustomed to the mind-set of the past regime, still think that they can and should manage the economy down to the finest details. This approach to economic management poses a serious stumbling block to economic reform and liberalization.

Ironically, some even think they can and should regulate the deregulation process. To compound this problem, many private economic agents have lost their sense of independence and fear that liberalization may create chaos. Therefore, they continue to seek government guidance and intervention, even in the affairs of the private sector, and ask the government to "control the process of economic liberalization."

In addition, active government economic management has created various barriers for entry into various markets and these have produced monopolistic and oligopolistic economic structures. The tendency to rely on direct regulations for economic management has also resulted in widespread regulation of prices and quantities, which created all sorts of distortion in the economic incentive structure. As a result, this tends to discourage the individual economic agent's will to economize and motive to innovate.

Finally, as government intervention has become more widespread, it has created needless demand for intervention beyond the government's true capability or necessity, and thus, the effectiveness of government intervention is rapidly declining.

Market Order and the Role of Government Economic Policy

Basic Framework

The basic viewpoint concerning the role of government economic policy proposed in this paper is based on Hayekian philosophy: there exists a market order in the economy that arises endogenously and spontaneously, independent of any outside intervention. Competition in the market order is a process by which optimal outcome is discovered. In other words one cannot discover or dictate the market outcome in advance of the competition process.

A direct implication of this view is that the government's role should be confined to preserving the spontaneity and endogeneity of the market order and cultivating a better environment for its working. To this purpose, the government should establish a regime of fair competition in the economic and social system so that the discovery function of the market order can be maximized.

Under this framework, the role of the government should be limited to defining the economic and social environments, that is, determining the exogenous variables for the market order, while freely leaving the endogenous variables to be decided by the private sector. If the government wants to influence endogenous variables, it must participate in the market order in the same manner as other private economic agents. If not, it must change the environment or incentive structure consciously in such a way as to influence endogenous variables in the desired direction. In any case, the government should refrain from directly intervening in the market order and dictating the endogenous variables.

Macroeconomic Stability as an Exogenous Environment

One of the most important economic conditions for the smooth functioning of the market order is the macroeconomic environment. Maintaining macroeconomic stability is understood as a precondition for efficient long-term economic decisions and, therefore, is regarded as the most important responsibility of the government. In the debate on the role of the government in economic development, the World Bank (1993) has consistently contended that the most important factor contributing to the East Asian economic miracle has been macroeconomic stability. One can also argue in the current context that maintaining macroeconomic stability is much like providing a better exogenous environment for the market order and should belong to the realm of active government policy function.

Globalization and the Role of the Government in Microeconomic Resource Allocation

Recently, national economies have become increasingly integrated into the global economy, moving from shallow integration under the GATT system to a deeper policy integration under the new WTO system.[1] In addition to such international efforts among national economies through official bodies of international cooperation, the private sector initiative for globalizing economic activities has always been an even more important driving force for economic integration. Thus, political and geographical borders of national economies are no longer effective hindrances to the international flow of economic activities. Globalization, via transformation in trade and investment, implies an expansion of economic activities beyond politically-defined national and regional boundaries through the increased movement of goods and services including labor, capital, technology, and information, via trade and investment.

What is the implication of globalization for national economic policy-making? Most importantly, it implies that any preferential or discriminatory policy will become increasingly ineffective under the globalized economic environment due to the increased mobility of economic goods and services, factors, and agents, as well as to the resulting inability of the national economic authority to hold these elements within its national boundary.

From this perspective, for example, the government-led economic development strategy and the policy instruments for it will also become increasingly ineffective. In this context, one can easily see that direct regulations to promote or protect targeted industries would become obstacles to further economic development. In general, the prospect of any economy being globalized implies that economic policymaking and implementation should be guided by the principle of nondiscrimination and the market mechanism. Futhermore, in the coming decades, as glob-

---

1. See Lawrence et al. (1994) for a detailed discussion on the possibility as well as the necessity of deeper policy integration under the new world economic order.

alization proceeds, domestic economic liberalization and reform will also gain a new dimension, with the result that economic management based on direct intervention in microeconomic resource allocation will tend to lose its effectiveness as it becomes inconsistent with the general philosophy of economic liberalization.

Recently, it appears popular for rational governments in developing countries to try to implement an industrial policy similar to those adopted by successful East Asian economies such as Japan, Taiwan, and Korea.[2] This tendency is even more conspicuous in discussions of the possible policy responses to the so-called "unlimited competition" resulting from globalization. An increasingly common view seems to be that government should help business firms successfully compete in the international market, that is, government should intervene in adjusting the industrial structure to the globalized competitive environments.

However, the basic stance concerning the role of government exemplified in this view suggests the following implications which are diametrically opposed to this new trend of industrial policy. Above all, it suggests that globalization is basically a diversified and sometimes conflicting phenomenon that has different economic implications depending on the context.[3] Therefore, it is especially difficult for a government to design a particular industrial structure *a priori*, which is supposed to be optimal for its economy. In this sense, one might further conjecture that the economists' search for an alternative industrial organization among the existing so-called American Fordist, German Craft, or even the lean and flexible production systems will not yield any definitive, single industrial organization structure.[4] Therefore, instead of adopting an active interventionist industrial policy that requires a tremendous volume of information and does not easily produce the desired solutions, an effective

2. Lengthy discussions on the nature and characteristics of the so-called industrial policies in those East Asian economies are found in World Bank (1993). This study suggests that while government intervention was helpful under certain conditions, the most important factors for the East Asian Miracle are macroeconomic stability and the market conforming economic policies adopted by these economies.

3. Oman (1993) identifies the globalization phenomenon as not only a market extension but also a mixture of market deregulation, the spread of new information technologies, the intermeshing of financial markets and the innovation of industrial and production systems.

4. Jwa (1997) analyzes the implications of globalization on the optimal industrial structure.

response to globalization might better be to let the market order prevail in discovering an optimal business structure and, to do this, the private sector must be free to decide on its course of structural adjustments.

Summary and Lessons

This paper has overviewed the debates on the role of its government in economic management, evaluated the Korean experience of its government-led economic development strategy in the past 30 years, and suggested an optimal role for the government in general. After arguing that debate on the role of the government can be reduced to the issue of market failures versus government failures, the paper emphasized that market failures in most cases are the reflection of institutional failure, which is nothing but another form of government failure. Korea's experience suggests that intervention into endogenous decision variables create many problems and will not be successful because the size and the complexity of the Korean economy are such that an informational superiority of the government cannot be guaranteed. Based on the lessons gleaned from the Korean experience, I argued that the government's role should be confined to preserving the spontaneity and endogeneity of the market order and to cultivating a better economic environment for the working of that order. Government should determine exogenous variables for the market order while leaving the determination of endogenous variables to the market.

If one applies this philosophy to the case of a search for an optimal industrial organization in the interest of post-Fordist alternatives to a Fordist mass production system, its main message may be that this search should not be the responsibility of the government. Instead, the government should lift, if any, all entry barriers, domestic as well as at national border, and deregulate the domestic economy. This should promote competition such that private firms can freely make a rational choice on the business and production system most suitable for the coming twenty-first century global market environment. I suggested that it is better to rely on active market competition among business firms rather than on government leadership in discovering alternatives to an outmoded production system.

REFERENCES

Amsden, Alice H. 1989. *Asia's Next Giant.* New York and Oxford: Oxford University Press.

Hayek, F. A. 1948. *Individualism and Economic Order.* Chicago: University of Chicago Press.

————. 1984a. "Competition As a Discovery Procedure." In *The Essence of Hayek,* edited by Nishiyama Chiaki and Kurt R. Leube. Stanford, CA: Hoover Institution Press.

————. 1984b. "The Use of Knowledge in Society." In *The Essence of Hayek,* edited by Nishiyama Chiaki and Kurt R. Leube. Stanford, CA: Hoover Institution Press.

————. 1989. "The Pretence of Knowledge." *American Economic Review* 79.6: 3-7.

Jwa, Sung-Hee. 1997. "Globalization and Industrial Organization: Implications for Structural Adjustment Policies." In *Regionalism vs. Multilateral Trade Arrangement.* NBER-East Asia Seminar on Economics Series. Chicago: University of Chicago Press.

Lawrence, R. Z., Albert Bressand, and Takatoshi Ito. 1997. *A Vision for the World Economy—Openness, Diversity, and Cohesion.* Washington, D.C.: Brookings Institution.

Oman, Charles. 1993. *Globalization and Regionalization: The Challenge for Developing Countries.* OECD Development Centre.

Vanberg, V. 1991. "Spontaneous Market Order and Social Rules: A Critical Examination of F. A. Hayek's Theory of Cultural Evolution." In *Friedrich A. Hayek: A Critical Assessments,* vol. 1, edited by John Cunningham Wood and Ronald N. Woods, 177-201. London and New York: Routledge.

World Bank. 1993. *The East Asian Miracle: Economic Growth and Public Policy.* New York and Oxford: Oxford University Press.

A Critical Look at the Korean Economy

Chung Un Chan

There are two perspectives when surveying an economy. One perspective is short-term macro and the other is long-term structural. A short-term macro perspective focuses mainly on a few macro variables such as growth rate, inflation rate, and the balance of payments. In contrast, the long-term structural perspective concerns varieties of micro factors such as the quantity and quality of human capital, the level of technology, market structure and the role of the government. To properly evaluate today's economy in Korea, we need to employ both perspectives at the same time.

On all counts, it is clear that the Korean economy is now facing enormous difficulties. From the short-term macro perspective, major indicators are not nearly as impressive as they used to be. GDP growth rate for the first quarter of 1997 was 5.4%, a disappointing figure compared to 1996's 7.8%. Equipment investment, one of the driving forces of economic growth, showed negative growth in the first half of 1997. Moreover, uneasiness about job security, which started to spread in 1996, is expected to increase since the unemployment rate rose by 1.1% point in the first quarter. Meanwhile, the current account showed a deficit of $11.2 billion for the first half of 1997, which is even worse than the $9.8 billion for the same period in 1996.

There is no doubt that the economy, which started to contract in the

* Origianlly published in Vol. 37, No. 4 (Winter 1997).

Chung Un Chan (Jeong, Un-chan) is Professor of Economics at Seoul National University. He is also President of the Korean Money and Finance Association. He received his Ph.D. in Economics from Princeton University. His publications include *Jungang eunhaeng ron* (A Tract on Central Banking) (1995) and *Hanguk gyeongje jugeoya sanda* (The Korean Economy–It Should Die to Live) (1997). E-mail: ucchung@dasan.snu.ac.kr.

latter half of 1995, is now in the course of a serious recession. In particular, continuing deterioration of the balance of payments is likely to set off a negative domino effect, including an increase in foreign debt, a decrease in foreign exchange reserves, and a rapid depreciation of the Korean won.

From the long-term structural perspective, the economy looks just as bad. It seems that the most important problem of the economy can be located in structural elements rather than in macro aggregates. For instance, research and development (R&D) investment focuses too much on short-term profits. Government-funded research institutes, whose mission is to develop basic technology, are not on the right track. Markets are more and more dominated by a handful of big businesses, and the financial sector has become a fetter to development. The efficiency and productivity of the public sector are poor when compared to those of major countries. Above all, the most fundamental problem is the absence of firmly established rules for economic activities; the survival of "the biggest" rather than "the fittest" has become the rule of the game. Businesses are, therefore, obsessed with making easy money from rent-seeking rather than from efficient management.

Conflicting Short-term Objectives

One of the critical problems of the Korean economy is the conflict among varieties of macroeconomic policies. Fiscal policy, monetary policy, policies on prices, exchange rate, and balance of payments conflict with each other, failing to coordinate themselves under a coherent economic perspective. The government tries to control prices while encouraging economic growth, seeks to promote investments while defending the balance of payments, wants to expand social overhead capital while tightening its budget, and tries to stabilize the exchange rate while increasing money supply.

What causes these conflicts? Above all, policymakers often want to achieve too many economic goals in too short a period. They tend to think that they can maintain high growth rate, stable prices, and sound balance of payments—all at the same time. It would be truly wonderful if one could kill so many birds with one stone, but the fact is that there is no normal way to achieve so many policy goals all at once.

In reality, policymakers have to make a choice between two different course of action. One is trying to achieve just one or two goals that are considered most urgent in the short term. The other is to take every possible measure, however unreasonable it may be, to achieve all the goals that are under consideration.

The first choice involves dealing with the problems at stake by employing macro measures as the occasion demands. This is possibly to give up, at least in the short term, those areas of the economy that are considered less important. But, inasmuch as macroeconomic policies are by nature short-term measures, it makes sense to focus on somewhat narrow objectives that are considered to be most urgent in the short run. To resolve the problem of high inflation, for instance, the government could control aggregate demand even though that would lower the growth rate. It could also encourage imports of cheap commodities even though that might increase trade deficits.

The second choice involves going all-out to take all available policy measures to achieve a larger number of goals. Nobody can deny that this course of action sounds great. But the problem is that it could actually create a number of distortions in the economic structure, especially through inconsistent and noneconomic actions. Whenever the government targets too many goals at the same time, it is likely to resort not only to short-term macro measures but also to long-term micro and sometimes even coercive measures. However, for long-term policy measures to be effective, they need to be taken according to their own principles and appropriate schedules. Otherwise, using long-term policy measures for short-term goals can have an adverse impact on the efficacy of economic policy as a whole.

Looking back, Korea has in most cases favored the second of these two courses of action, as can be seen from the occasional price controls. Needless to say, pushing mutually incompatible objectives can risk jeopardizing the national economy, especially when it should open up and become liberalized.

The government, however, seems to have recently changed its attitude to a certain extent. Its economic policy direction for 1997 declares that it "will concentrate all its efforts on stabilizing prices and the balance of payments, even if this might cause some sacrifices in growth rate." This announcement itself could be interpreted as the government's new approach toward economic problems; as far as it is true, policymakers will no longer pursue many economic goals at the same time.

Is the government truly departing from the practice of the past, that is, conflicting policies? Unfortunately, when judged from the policy mix chosen by the government right after the declaration, the answer appears to be "no."

In resolving the problems of high inflation and trade deficits, regardless of growth rate, tight money is a possible step, at least in theory. It would increase interest rates, decrease aggregate demand, stabilize prices, and reduce deficits. In addition, if the capital market is closed, policymakers may consider depreciation of currency. But recent practices in economic policy suggest the opposite course. For example, however unstable its foreign reserves may be, the Bank of Korea (BOK) has intervened to halt the rapid depreciation of the Korean won inevitably resulting from the balance of payment deficits. Moreover, its monetary policy has been aimed at lower interest rates. The BOK has lowered banks' reserve requirements and expanded the supply of money to minimize the impact of the recent collapse of the Hanbo Group in 1997. In short, the current policy can be said to be one that mainly intends to contain inflation by stopping depreciation, and at the same time to promote exports by lowering interest rates.

Obviously, this policy mix is risky. If the supply of money increases too rapidly, expectations of depreciation will dominate the market and foreign exchange dealers will tend to hold on to their dollars. This is contrary to the BOK's original intent. The BOK may be able to protect the won from falling for the time being, but if doubts arise about the BOK's ability to do so, Korea may encounter a serious foreign exchange crisis.

As is evident from this policy mix, the major problem with the government's macroeconomic policy is its conflicting goals. Admittedly, such policies worked well when the Korean economy was closed and the government could wield its ubiquitous power. With the Korean market being liberalized, however, the macroeconomic policy measures that the government can use are not as powerful as they used to be. What is important now is to determine policy priorities and to create a proper policy mix.

Problems of the Bubble Economy

Despite its structural problems, the Korean economy until 1995 showed amazing outcomes in terms of macro indicators. At the time, of course, many observers spoke of a bubble economy, but few probably really knew what the term meant or what its impact would be. What is a bubble? An economic bubble occurs when assets are overvalued compared to their fundamentals; the "bubble" may be interpreted as the difference between nominal and intrinsic value. It is not the result of rational behavior; furthermore, most people do not realize the irrationality of the bubble until after it bursts.

There are now a number of bubbles in Korea—in households, in colleges, in businesses, and in the government. Households are overconsuming, colleges and universities are expanding regardless of their capacity, corporations are moving into new business lines like predators going after prey, and the government is creating unnecessary posts.

In the late 1980s, the prices of assets, especially of real estate, skyrocketed. Stocks were no exception. As stock prices continued to rise sharply over several years, dreams of making a quick fortune prevailed, and the stock price index reached an amazing 1,000 points. These bubbles in the late 1980s were in part related to the excessive optimism following the 1988 Seoul Olympic Games. This optimism eventually hampered people's enthusiasm for work and stimulated overconsumption.

The rosy picture the government drew of the Korean economy right before the general election of 1996 was a repeat of the unfounded optimism of the latter half of the 1980s. Predicting that Korea would surpass Britain to become a member of the G7 by 2002, the government said that Korea would by then have become a good place to live, a good place to do business, and a good place to visit. Furthermore, when Korea was selected to co-host the World Cup Games in 2002, policymakers could hardly control their excitement over the chance to use the event to stimulate the economy.

Such vague optimism has led to the spread of economic bubbles, and consequently contributed to the economy's weakening foundation. Businessmen are more and more interested in windfall gains than efficient management. As the resources that otherwise would have been used in more productive areas have gravitated elsewhere, the accumulation of capital—the basis of growth—has been almost completely diverted. In addition, some corporations that overinvested in real estate have gone bankrupt under the burden of debts following the burst of the real estate bubble. This has put another strain on the economy.

Nevertheless, conglomerate-affiliated companies were in most cases able to ride out the bubble busts while others could not. This has inevitably made the gap between big and small businesses so wide that it is unlikely to be ever bridged. The basic capitalist rule, extolling the survival of the fittest, has been turned on its head, and a crude concept of the survival of the biggest now rules the economy. Those corporations that grew along with the bubble economy helped make the economy balloon while making themselves inefficient and wasteful in the process.

Seen from the long-term structural perspective, this bubble is mainly responsible for the inefficiency and imbalance that have made the economy weak. Therefore, it is not too much to say that the most serious problem facing today's Korea is its bubble economy.

Inefficiency of the Economic System

For an economy to grow over the long run, it is important to have a rationally and efficiently designed economic system as well as the individual efforts of economic agents. The financial system, the labor market, and government policies on education, science and technology are like a pond in which fish swim. Just as fish cannot live in polluted water, an economy cannot develop in an inefficient system.

Up to now, Korea has failed to move from the old system that has adjusted to rapid growth to a new one that will go with steadier growth. This has created a number of hardships: the recent commotion over the leading party's revision of labor-related laws is just one example.

The key elements of the old system include limited competition and the government-orchestrated allocation of resources. During the last four decades, the government controlled the economy by defining what areas businesses should enter, and assigning scarce resources. This control made rapid growth possible and brought about so-called condensed growth. But in this process, a few selected companies were virtually exempt from the forces of competition thanks to protective industrial policies, and they could concentrate on growth as directed by the government.

Over time, it became clear that this system could not continue. Businesses soon learned that once they used government resources for other purposes, such as real estate speculation, they could make quick money easily. This development was an unfortunate result of restricted competition.

In economic textbooks, income derived from limited competition is called "rent." One of the most serious problems with the old system was that it promoted rent-seeking activities. Rents do not go hand in hand with efficiency: the greater the rents, the less efficient the economy. It is, of course, rational for economic agents to prefer easy rental income to strenuous efforts in economic activities. Besides, rents create nasty competition between those who benefit from them and those who try to seize them. Moreover, firms that have once enjoyed rent benefits tend to try anything, be it normal or not, to gain additional rents. Businesses have thus become more involved in speculation than in their core businesses, while bribing banks and bureaucrats to get their way. Meanwhile, bureaucrats themselves seek to enact new regulations to secure their share of the bonanza by expanding their control. In this process, more and more people look for easy money instead of participating in normal economic activities, all of which make the economy even worse.

The most obvious example of such systematic problems can be found in the financial sector. It has played an important role during the period of rapid growth. The government has exercised control over industry through financial institutions by determining which industries should get financial resources, and by monitoring them as well. However, resource allocation through selective loans became less and less efficient, while scandals and rent-seeking activities prevailed. The natural result was huge non-performing bank loans. Now, Korea's banks are not capable of doing their normal businesses in a true sense, and there is little likelihood that this inefficiency will be resolved soon. It is because the banks cannot escape from the awkward situation unless the bad loans are settled. For example, faced with a big borrower's bankruptcy, a bank cannot but provide additional loans to keep it from collapsing, thus creating even more bad loans in a vicious circle. If banks are to be truly serious about their job of screening loan applications, they will first have to resolve the problem of non-performing loans.

Non-performing loans may be attributed partly to mistakes by the banks themselves, but most are the by-product of policy-oriented financing for rapid growth. Some are, of course, the result of loans made under political pressures, just like those loans discovered in the recent Hanbo scandal. I think that the government must take the lead in resolving these problems insofar as it has contributed to creating them. Furthermore, to expedite the process of financial liberalization, the government must lift unnecessary regulations, but sometimes it should also take more positive actions to build up prerequisites for liberalization.

The non-performing loan issue is exactly the area in which the government must take the initiative.

Imbalance Between *Jaebeol* and SMEs

With the emphasis on rapid growth, which has lasted more than 40 years, the Korean economy has made tremendous progress, at least in appearance. But little attention has been paid to social equality, and as a consequence, imbalances have sprouted in a number of areas. Imbalances between rural areas and urban areas, between the rich and the poor, between the southeastern (Yeongnam) provinces and the southwestern (Honam) provinces, and between big businesses and small ones have firmly established dualistic structures in every field. Among them, the most serious is the imbalance between the large conglomerates (*jaebeol*) and small- and medium-sized enterprises (SMEs).

Basically, the relationship between *jaebeol* and SMEs should be one of "complementarity and cooperation" and "confrontation and competition" at the same time. Without a sound foundation for SMEs, there is no way to nurture and cultivate the potential of the economy. SMEs have a greater possibility to reduce costs, improve productivity and develop new technologies.

The ongoing rapid innovation and demand diversification have shortened the life cycle of new products, and have also replaced the practice of mass production with that of small amounts with varieties of products. The quickness and flexibility of SMEs are, therefore, becoming increasingly vital in economic development.

Then, what made the SMEs so weak? The answer can be found in the fact that the rule of "the strong controlling the weak" has predominated in the relationship between *jaebeol* and SMEs. First, *jaebeol* companies often transfer their financial difficulties to SMEs by delaying payments or by issuing long-term bills. Because of this, even promising SMEs are often driven to financial ruin. In fact, it is difficult for small firms to borrow from banks, as banks require collateral or deposits in return for loans. Moreover, SMEs have to bear too many incidental expenses for noneconomic purposes. Even though banks are required to allocate a certain proportion of their loans to SMEs, this provision has often been ignored in various ways. On the other hand, *jaebeol* tend to encroach on the business lines of SMEs, sometimes recruit their best workers, and put pressures on them to lower their prices.

Even though SMEs are suffering from the tyranny of *jaebeol*, big businesses are not inherently evil, at least in theory. In other words, concentration of ownership is not necessarily harmful. In countries like the United States, where business ownership is well distributed, management could become unstable and overly sensitive to stock prices and short-term gains, that is, "principal-agent" problems could arise. But in countries like Korea, where ownership is too concentrated, where small shareholder's rights are ignored, and where business monitoring devices are of no use, there is not much concern over such "principal-agent" problems.

The shares of each *jaebeol* owner combined with those of his/her family typically amount to some 20% of total shares in the case of the top 30 *jaebeol* groups—and this figure does not include those concealed under other people's names. In addition, the owners of *jaebeol* groups virtually control more than 50% of total shares by having their affiliated companies invest in each other. Thus, handful of people can wield unchallenged control over a large portion of the economy, which, furthermore, will be handed down to their children. Now, Korea needs to solve the problem of how to check the power of the *jaebeol* rather than worry about principal-agent problems.

As the saying "absolute power corrupts absolutely" suggests, the combination of ownership and management, especially when it is outside the market mechanism, will definitely produce corruption. Scandals over secret funds from *jaebeol* almost always erupt toward the end of every President's term, as evidenced by the shocking revelations of Hanbo's secret funding, lobbying, and poor business performance. Perhaps not surprisingly, of all the major *jaebeol* groups, Hanbo had the largest proportion of total shares owned by one family—50% by chairman Chung Tae Soo (Jeong Tae-su), plus 30% owned by his relatives and close friends, and another 6% by affiliated companies.

The two large groups that have wielded the most power in Korea over the last 30 years are the military and the *jaebeol*. The military may be said to have gone back to their barracks, but *jaebeol* have become even more powerful during Kim Young-sam's regime. Rather than being reined in, their power is growing day by day, as political leaders either have failed to grasp the problem or have themselves become prisoners of *jaebeol*. The strong steps to stimulate the economy, as shown in the "New Economy 100-Day Plan" launched shortly after Kim's inauguration, and the subsequent reckless deregulation carried out in the name of internationalization and globalization have only added to the power of *jaebeol.*

Government policy on *jaebeol* has drifted aimlessly because the government has not taken a consistent stand. According to news reports, one senior government official called for lifting controls on *jaebeol,* saying that they "constitute the core of the economy but are looked at with disdain by the public." It seems that this view is shared by the majority of government officials.

The view that *jaebeol* are the core of the economy is a dangerous one. When Korea was working to raise itself from the ranks of underdeveloped countries, the concentration of government support on a few chosen *jaebeol* might have been effective, but now that the Korean economy has become large and complex, what is needed instead is intensive growth based on innovation and creativity. In fact, the dinosaur-like *jaebeol* have already come to impede economic growth. *Jaebeol* have made it impossible for their affiliated companies to go bankrupt, as they link themselves with mutual guarantees. Therefore, they have upset even the basic rule of the market economy, which must allow companies that should fail to fail, by in effect taking the whole economy hostage.

If the aim of economic policy is only to boost the economy in the short run, supporting the *jaebeol* might be effective, and all the more so if the aim is to keep the growth rate high and promote exports. Perhaps it is inevitable for the bureaucrats, whose minds are full of macro aggregates, to be lenient with the *jaebeol* which hold sway over the bureaucrats' destinies. Be that as it may, Korea should not sacrifice its long-term interests in securing short-term results. If Korea is really to strengthen its economic foundation, it must be ready to endure short-term pain, however painful it might be.

Future Tasks and the Role of the Government

During the last four decades of condensed growth, the Korean economy has achieved what took advanced countries more than a hundred years. What makes such rapid growth possible? First, in the 1950s and 1960s, foreign technology could be copied easily. Manpower was plentiful and business operations were simple. Besides, the international environment at that time was quite favorable to Korea. The United Nations' "Decade of Development" plan in the 1960s, the construction boom in the Middle East and the reflux of petrodollars in the 1970s, and the "three lows" of the 1980s (low interest rates, low international oil prices and the low value of the dollar against the Japanese yen) all worked to boost Korean economic growth. In addition, aggressive government policies played a significant role in promoting economic growth.

All of these elements started to disappear in the late 1980s. The reluctance of advanced countries to transfer technology has made it increasingly difficult to gain access to up-to-the-minute technology. Highly skilled labor is in short supply, wages are high and business operations have become increasingly complex. At the same time, the international environment has become uncertain.

These changes have forced the Korean economy to attempt ever more fundamental reform than that of the past. In reality, however, things still remain unchanged for the most part, further weakening the economy. From the short-term perspective, economic policies lack consistency. From the long-term perspective, the inefficient economic system remains unchanged. So do the problems of imbalance between *jaebeol* and SMEs, and bubbles. If Korea really wants sustained growth, it must resolve the side effects of rapid growth, and it must create and nurture intensive growth. To put it simply, Korea needs to carry out a truly fundamental reform program.

Economic reform must start with institution building. The Korean economy has been directed by government initiative rather than by economic rules. The competition in seeking hidden rents under complex regulations has also shaken the economy. Now the target of Korea's reform should be directed toward tearing down this inefficient structure. Where should reform begin? It seems to me that the answer is the financial sector, where the working of the most basic principle of capitalism—the survival of the fittest—could begin. In a capitalist economy, the flow of funds always follows the flow of goods and services. As such, the maldistribution of resources, which lies at the core of every economic problem, can be prevented by normalizing the financial system so that funds may flow properly. Normalizing the financial system may not be the only reform necessary to fix the economy, but it is clearly the most important. In particular, the resolution of non-performing bank loans requires urgent attention.

One way to do this might be to create a special bank and have it accept all existing non-performing loans, which would allow the existing banks to start with a clean state. Since the non-performing loan problem is a product of government policy, the new bank could be established with public bonds and the backing of the government. A second way might be to have the BOK provide special loans to the banks. This could be interpreted as giving special favors to debt-ridden banks, but it is still worth considering when taking into account the seriousness of the problem.

Finally, debt resolution might take the form of swapping, whereby creditor banks would give up loan claims in exchange for corporate stocks, even though this may invite strong resistance from firms opposed to surrendering their stocks. Whatever method is adopted, the problem of non-performing loans needs to be cleared up as soon as possible, and the affected banks must restructure themselves by every possible means including specialized manpower training. To improve the health of Korea's banks in the long run, the focus should be on competitiveness instead of supports from outside.

Moreover, Korea must come up with long-term and short-term measures to eliminate those bubbles that now prevail in every field of the economy, and to remedy the inefficient structure of its markets. To do this, true competition must be introduced into all sectors of the economy, which will put a stop to rent-seeking activities. In fact, the problem posed by the growth of the *jaebeol* also has much to do with the rent-seeking activities of monopolies and oligopolies, which indicates that creating fair competition is much more crucial than it may have seemed.

When considering the medium- and long-term needs to improve Korea's economic structure, increased investment in R&D and human resources cannot be ignored. Foreign technology and royalty payments now cost Korea more than $2.5 billion a year. Such a burden cannot be overcome without R&D investment. R&D is undoubtedly costly and takes a long time to produce returns. It is also difficult to make accurate predictions on expected profits from R&D investment. At present, technology-related loans provided by banking institutions account for just 1% of all loans, which shows how reluctant banking institutions have been to extend loans with future profitability.

On the other hand, R&D is not something that will succeed just because there is enough money for it. The more fundamental reason R&D has lagged is that there have been few opportunities for people with creative minds and little reward for their achievements. To be successful, R&D efforts should be backed by well-developed basic science, efficient manpower, a competitive atmosphere, and economic conditions that ensure rules to be fair—all at the same time. Therefore, even though foreign technology imports might be desirable in the short run, more emphasis should be placed on fostering creative minds by improving the educational system and investing in human resources in the long run.

Last but never least, to restructure the economy, Korea needs a forward-looking, thoughtful blueprint, rather than a quick fix. If trees are planted on poor soil, what will come of them? However long it may take, now is the time for fertilizing the economy. This can only be done with the joint efforts of the government, businesses, the financial sector, and the Korean people.

The Korean Economy in a Borderless World

Yoo Jungho

I. Introduction

The world economy is becoming increasingly integrated, and its pace seems to be accelerating. In a way this is a historical continuity; since prehistoric times forces have been continuously at work to merge neighboring economies. The world's population was once scattered in small, self-sufficient villages, separated from each other by geographical distance, language barriers, animosity, and so on. As means of transportation developed, we can assume, trade also developed between villages, linking essentially independent economies and eventually binding them together into mutually dependent systems.

Yet, the current processes of world economic integration appear to be more than just an extension of long-term historical trends. Integration has proceeded to such an extent that the world economy is on the verge of becoming a "borderless world" in the sense that national borders become economically meaningless. International movement of diverse factors in a "borderless world" will bring about fundamental changes in

* Originally published in Vol. 37, No. 4 (Winter 1997).

Yoo Jungho (Yu, Jeong-ho) is a senior fellow of the Korea Development Institute (KDI). He recently served as the Vice President of the Institute. He received his Ph.D. from the University of Wisconsin in 1978. He is the author of *Han · Jung · Il su-ip uijon gujo bigyo* (Comparative Study of Import Structure of Korea, China and Japan) (1995) and co-author of *Industrialization and the State: The Korean Heavy and Chemical Industrialization Drive* (1995) and "*Jaebeol* Capitalism and the Currency-Financial Crisis in Korea" (2001). E-mail: yoojungho@hotmail.com.

the nature of national economies that trade in goods and services has not.

To Korea this change in the world economic environment represents a challenge for which it is not yet fully prepared. While an "outward oriented" development strategy is in principle embraced by all, to many a fully open economy is too idealistic a prescription for the country. Protectionism continues to run high, often under the guise of patriotism, even though the country owes much to international trade for its economic achievements over the past thirty years. At the same time, political authoritarianism is strong, and the government's paternalism is widely accepted by the populace.

This paper is an attempt to anticipate changes the movement toward a borderless world will cause to the nature of national economies, and to discuss their implications for policy. It is organized as follows: Part II considers the trends that strengthen the tendency toward world economic integration and their significance. Part III attempts to foresee the changes in the nature of national economies that will be brought about by the tendency of world economic integration, and Part IV considers the policy implications of such changes from Korea's point of view. Part V concludes the paper by discussing what role the government should play in the new world economic environment.

II. Trends toward a Borderless World

Three big changes have recently taken place in the world economy. They are both the effect of past integration and the cause of further integration in the future. First, international trade rules have recently undergone sweeping changes, as the Uruguay Round was successfully concluded and the World Trade Organization launched. Worldwide, tariffs have been lowered. Coverage of the international trade rules is now extended to agricultural products and services. Multi-Fibre Arrangement will be phased out. Rules regarding subsidies have been clarified, and rules have been introduced on trade-related investment measures. Individual countries' trade policies will be regularly reviewed, and dispute settlement arrangements have been strengthened. Protection of intellectual property rights will improve. Such strengthening of liberal trade order and multilateralism was achieved in the midst of rising protectionism in major trading countries.

Another big change in the world economic scene is "globalization," a phenomenon of an increasingly large number of firms expanding their activities to reach foreign markets and engaging in international production. The main players of globalization are large multinational firms based in industrial countries, but small- and medium-sized firms as well as large ones in developing countries are becoming active. Consequently, in recent years there has been rapid growth in foreign direct investment (FDI) and intra-firm trade.

Direct foreign investments have long been prevalent. Yet, globalization seems to be more than just an extension of this trend. According to an OECD report, thanks to the convergence of computer, communication and control technology, "[i]t has now become technically feasible for [Multinational Enterprises], banks, industrial and service firms to install intra-corporate worldwide information networks, through which headquarters' management can link together production and marketing facilities around the world."[1] The report also notes that an increasing fraction of total value and wealth the world produces will be produced and distributed through the intra-firm and inter-firm networks covering the entire globe.

Third, the need for so-called "deep integration" is rising, as national economies come into closer and more frequent contact with one another. When trade accounted for only a small part of a country's economic activities, the distinction between domestic and international matters was clear. For example, a country's international economic policy dealt with tariffs or non-tariff measures affecting its interaction with the rest of the world. Domestic policy dealt with matters that are usually, or should be, of no concern to the outside world such as domestic tax, environmental protection, regulations concerning product standards or worker safety, government budget, and so on.

As countries are linked with each other by increasing trade, investments and related economic activities, what used to be regarded as domestic matters of a country came to affect other economies more directly, and with greater impact. Countries having economic ties with each other may be likened to families living next to each other, separated not by, say, a ten-minute walk but by an apartment wall. They simply

---

1. OECD, "Technology and Globalization," chap. 10 in *Technology and the Economy: The Key Relationships* (Paris: OECD, 1992).

cannot remain indifferent to how the neighbors handle their domestic matters. This gives rise to the necessity that they somehow have to come to terms with one another.

These trends will tend to weaken the autonomy of national government, especially its power to control at the border the in- and outflow of goods, services, factors of production, and so on, while accelerating the pace of integration of the world economy. First of all, what the new international trade rules mean is very clear. Under the new WTO system countries are supposed to open their service markets as well as goods markets. Border measures discriminating against foreign goods and services and domestic measures doling out favors to some industries in discrimination of others will, for the most part, be illegal.

Globalization will also weaken the government's power to control the border. This will happen as globalization weakens the government's position vis-à-vis firms. Governments will find themselves in a position of waiting to be selected as the site of operation by multinationals' investment decisions rather than giving foreign firms permission to make direct investments in the country. For, as globalization proceeds, whether or not a country can attract foreign direct investments will make a big difference to economic performance.

What is likely to make such a prospect a reality is the tendency, mentioned earlier, that an increasing fraction of the total world output will be created and distributed through the global networks within and among firms. If a country is attractive enough to be chosen as a site of these global networks, it will benefit from the tendency; otherwise, it will have to compete for the rest of the world output produced outside the global networks, which will account for a smaller and smaller proportion of the total.

Countries already compete against one another to attract foreign firms and direct investments, and the competition will only become more intense. An important consequence is that the power of governments to restrict the movement of goods, services, labor, capital and firms will be drastically weakened, since an exercise of power contrary to foreign investors' interests will certainly make the country an unattractive site for multinationals' location. Governments will think twice before they exercise power to control the border.

Thus, national borders of the future will become like a low fence with many big holes that goods and people can go over or through it without having to utilize the gate. The world is effectively becoming economically borderless.

"Deep integration" is another reason why the autonomy of the government will weaken. The negotiation between the U.S. and Japan in the 1980s called "Structural Impediment Initiative" (SII) is an example of what "deep integration" between two economies requires. In the two countries' negotiations, complaints were made regarding such "domestic" matters as fiscal policies or saving behaviors, and each demanded the other party to take remedial action. The next round of multinational negotiations is likely to include one or more matters regarding the environment, labor standards, and competition policy. The need for multinational negotiations on these subjects arises out of inevitable, ongoing "deep integration," and it will surely further weaken the autonomy of the government.

Regionalism appears to present an exception to the long-term tendency toward world economic integration. Since 1987, when the EC resolved to turn most of the European continent into a single economic unit by 1992, many wondered if this was the beginning of a "fortress Europe"–an inward-oriented Europe raising trade barriers against outsiders. After that came NAFTA, and many wondered if the world economy was going to be fragmented into trade blocs.

While there are some grounds for worry about their effects on the world trade order, regional trade arrangements do not represent a reversal in the long-term tendency toward an integrated world economy. Referring to the "EC92" movement, Giovanni Agnelli, a former Italian industrialist and chairman of Fiat said, "Ironically, it was politicians who in 1957 first conceived the idea of a common market often over the objections from the business community. Now the situation has been reversed: it is the entrepreneurs and corporations who are keeping the pressure on politicians to transcend considerations of local and national interest."[2] In other words, the business community would like to engage in international operations unhampered by the national borders that are becoming obstacles to efficient operation.

---

2. Giovani Agnelli, "The Europe of 1992," *Foreign Affairs* 68 (fall 1989).

III. The Changing Nature of the National Economy

The ongoing world economic integration represents a change in any country's economic environment. The nature of the national economy is not likely to remain the same. The greater such changes, the more dependent a country is on its foreign sector. But, how the national economies will be affected and what policy changes, if any, are required are not at all certain. This section attempts to predict the nature of the national economy in the borderless world, a theoretical extreme to which the world is approaching as the trends considered in the previous section continue.

The Economic Characteristics

In the standard international trade model, factors of production such as capital and labor are assumed to be internationally immobile. They determine a country's economic characteristics, which in turn determine the country's pattern of trade and in- and outflows of investments. For example, a labor-abundant country exports labor-intensive goods while importing capital-intensive goods, and vice versa. Thus, economic characteristics of a country are given by the abundance or scarcity of immobile factors of production.

Not all factors are equally immobile. Some intrinsically have little or no mobility, while others are mobile, the international mobility of which is restricted by the government. Once these restrictions are lifted, mobile factors will cease to determine a country's economic characteristics, as they will begin to move from where they are abundant to where they are scarce. Only for those intrinsically immobile factors will the factor rewards differ between countries and, consequently, continue to be the determinants of a country's economic characteristics. For example, capital that is supposedly more internationally mobile than labor, will determine a country's characteristics to a lesser degree than labor.

The discussion regarding future determinants of a country's economic characteristics will become more meaningful if one recognizes that there are varieties of capital, labor, and other factors of differing international mobility, which may be regarded as factors of production in a broad sense. For example, scientists and engineers are much more internationally mobile than average workers. Land and its associated wealth is completely immobile; as are social overhead capital, the level of a given country's science and technology, social institutions, customs, culture, and so on.

Lack or abundance and the qualities of these broadly defined, immobile factors of production will determine an economy's characteristics. Consequently, these factors will have greater influence on the pattern of trade in goods, services, and on foreign direct investments between countries than internationally more mobile capital or scientists and engineers.

Emergence of Local Economies with Distinct Characteristics

Another likely consequence of a borderless world and the government's weakening power to control the border is that localities within the same country will develop distinct economic characteristics. Furthermore, they may develop closer economic ties with foreign localities than they do among themselves. This will depend on how much government power weakens.

The reason why such development is expected is that the economic characteristics of a locality will be determined by the factors that are immobile, as a country's characteristics are. Thus, in the extreme case where all governments in the world lose the power to control their borders, internationally mobile factors will be the only set of determinants of the national and local economic characteristics. Put differently, that a locality, legally or politically, belongs to a particular country will have no influence on its economic characteristics.

As the world economy becomes increasingly borderless, what used to be the common economic characteristics among various localities of the same country will gradually disappear, and the difference in economic characteristics between localities in the same country will become more pronounced. Indeed, it is a possibility that the economic difference between localities within the same country become more pronounced than the difference between countries. Thus, in a borderless world, the trade or investment relations between two countries will simply be the sums of respective relations between the localities belonging to the two countries. The economic interactions between localities will depend entirely on the economic characteristics of the localities, not on those of the countries.

It may also happen that two localities from different countries will become more dependent on each other than they are on another locality from the same country. For example, the Seoul-Incheon area may develop closer economic ties with the east coast of China than with the Busan area, which in turn may develop closer ties with Japan than with the Seoul-Incheon area.

Inter-industry Relations

In a closed economy, domestic demand can only be met by domestic supply. The demand for inputs by an industry for its production must be met by other industries' production in the same country. This need not be the case in an open economy. Inputs can come from abroad, and outputs may not all be consumed within the country.

Thus, as government power weakens and markets open up, industries in the same country will become less dependent on each other and more dependent on foreign industries. This loosening of inter-industry linkages implies that backward- or forward-linkage effects will become weaker. Also, a given amount of fiscal or monetary stimulus will have a smaller multiplier effect as leakages become more numerous and greater in magnitude. As the world economy becomes borderless, something similar to what occurs in relations between industries will occur between localities of the same country. The economic linkage among them will weaken.

The Concept of Nationality

Conventional nationality will increasingly follow the territorial principle instead of the personal principle. Korea, which has been following the personal principle, will experience a big change in society's concept of what a nation is. Whether or not an individual is a Korean is in principle decided by the nationality of the parents, and similarly a firm is considered Korean, if it is owned by Korean(s).

This will inevitably change as people and firms can move, more or less freely from country to country. Given a Korean affiliate of a multinational firm based in a foreign country and a foreign affiliate of a Korean multinational, it would be a mistake to regard the latter as Korean and the former as foreign, as one would under the personal principle of nationality. It seems rational to consider a person one of "us," if the person's allegiance is to "us" and the impacts of what the person does is favorable to "us." Often, firms of foreign nationality operating in Korea are of greater benefit to Koreans than Korean firms operating in foreign countries. Also, the allegiance of Koreans and Korean firms operating in foreign countries is not entirely to Korea alone. Korea must share or compete for allegiance with the countries where these firms are operating.

IV. Policy Implications for the Korean Economy

Market Opening and Nondiscrimination

The most obvious implication of the launching of the World Trade Organization for Korea is opening of both service and goods markets and further liberalization of the rules on foreign direct investments. Korea has been liberalizing its trade regime and opening its markets, especially since the early 1980s; however, liberalization was undertaken often passively and reluctantly under pressure from abroad.

It would be futile and contrary to Korea's best interests to delay market opening under the new circumstances. Futile, because Korea has become too important a trading country for its trade partners to remain indifferent to the speed or the extent of its market opening; and contrary to its best interests, because Korea can grow rapidly, as the country's own growth experience shows, by utilizing the world market not just through exports but through imports as well.

In addition, to abide by the WTO rules, Korea should refrain from providing selected industries with preferential treatment in fiscal, financial, and other policies. In accommodating international rules on subsidies, the best approach need not be the one that retains the most past practices with the least violation of the new rules. Past practices for assisting domestic industries through protection and subsidies are becoming costly and ineffective. Korea should first decide what the best direction is for trade and industrial policies in the new world economic environment. Then, based on the policy direction, it should decide on the best scope, sequence, and speed of accommodation with the least violation of international rules. In other words, Korea should, in principle, not discriminate against foreign goods, services, and firms in favor of domestic ones. Nor is it advisable to discriminate in favor of select domestic industries against others.

It is interesting to note that, in light of the changes in national economic characteristics, nondiscrimination also seems to be most appropriate for the future world environment. In view of the earlier discussion of the change in the concept of nationality, discrimination against foreign nationals defined according to the personal principle will increasingly be less justifiable. For example, discrimination against a Korean subsidiary of a Japanese parent company in favor of competing Korean firms may harm the Korean economy, especially if the former is more efficient. Moreover, it is not at all certain that a policy favoring a Spanish subsidiary of a Korean parent company benefits Koreans more than the Spanish. What makes better sense is to follow the territorial principle, namely, a policy of nondiscrimination from the viewpoint of the personal principle, for such a policy will encourage the efficient firms and discourage the inefficient ones, regardless of nationality. In addition, it will attract firms and factors of production to Korea.

Loosening of inter-industry linkage also renders the rationale less compelling, if it ever was, for favoring some selected domestic industries. The main reason advanced for selective favor was the positive externalities some industries generate, directly by benefitting other industries or indirectly by forming a core of industries which are necessary for "balanced" development of the economy. This proposition becomes less tenable as the outputs of "key" or "essential" industries become available at no unfavorable price in international markets as the world economic integration proceeds.

The possibility that localities of different economic characteristics and interests coexist within the same country, as discussed earlier, is another reason why the principle of nondiscrimination should be upheld. What is appropriate in one locality with a certain set of industries may not be in other localities with a different set of industries. Trade and industrial policies by nature favor some and discriminate others. Thus, as the world economic integration proceeds, trade and industrial policies will become increasingly inappropriate. More generally, the set of policies which may be regarded as beneficial to all sectors and localities of the economy tend to shrink.

Macroeconomic policies geared to stability and growth of all sectors in the economy will continue to be necessary and welcome, but discriminatory policies in terms of industries, nationalities, and localities will become inappropriate. Nondiscrimination against foreign goods simply means doing away with protectionist policies. It is well established that the protectionist policy is not advisable in both theory and practice because of its bias against exports and its smothering of competition in domestic markets. The objection to nondiscrimination in this sense often arises from a concern for noncompetitive industries. However, it would be a big mistake to attempt to make all industries competitive before market opening. It is not logically possible for all industries to be competitive, as the theory of comparative advantage testifies. What is possible is for all individual economic agents to become competitive. This is what the policy should attempt to achieve. For this reason, the role and function of the central government must be reexamined and reestablished.

Resource Attraction

The most obvious implication of the world economy becoming borderless is that a country's economic performance will depend on resource attraction as well as resource allocation. When resources are mostly immobile between countries, the economic problem is how to obtain maximum output from the fixed amounts of endowed resources. Theoretically, the answer is to allocate resources to different uses so that the efficiency with which the output is produced in different uses may be equalized. However, if some factors of production and firms are internationally mobile, the amount of resources need not be assumed fixed. Rather, the amount may be augmented by attracting firms into the country. Depending on how successful a country is in attracting resources from abroad, a country's economic performance may differ substantially. Thus, resource attraction will become an important responsibility of the central and local governments, and the competition among countries to attract resources from abroad will intensify.

Governments will be drawn into the competition for resource attraction, as the firms' competition against one another becomes more intense in the more integrated world economy. In order to survive, firms will seek the best business environment, over which they have little control, which more or less only government can provide. The search for the best business environment will prompt governments to make efforts to provide it. In this way, governments will be drawn into competition.

For some time governments have been making efforts to attract foreign direct investments by providing various incentives such as tax breaks, tariff exemptions, industrial parks, etc. However, provision of special preferences applicable to only foreign firms will have a limited effect in the future world of economic integration. Building global intra-firm and inter-firm networks involves not only searching for a country with low wages and abundant labor to move assembly lines or manufacturing facilities; it is also a matter of locating sites for headquarters, R&D facilities, design units, financing units, and so on. It involves moving a variety of mobile factors such as capital, managers, scientists and engineers. Consequently, firms will look for countries that can offer the best set of complementary immobile factors.

Also, what should concern policymakers is not just the inflow of foreign resources. They should be equally concerned with the outflow of domestic resources. If the business environment is not favorable, domestic firms will also look elsewhere, possibly other countries, and will relocate. What does matter is the quality of a country's immobile factors in all aspects. It is in a country's best interests to provide, at the least cost, the best combination of immobile factors that would attract the kinds of foreign firms and other resources deemed most desirable. The increase in international mobility of high quality workers, capital, and firms raises an interesting possibility. For example, in obtaining management talent, scientists, and engineers, a country may opt for a direct route of investing in the training of nationals or for an indirect route of investing in the upgrading of immobile factors, thereby attracting foreign nationals of desired qualifications. The indirect route will never entirely replace the direct one. However, the increased international mobility of factors implies that, if faced with a choice between raising the quality of average workers and training scientists and engineers, a greater emphasis should now be placed on the former. Similarly, it is becoming more important to upgrade the technology level of society in general than to have a cutting-edge technology introduced in some "key" sectors of the economy. Furthermore, the provision of social overhead capital becomes more important than, say, assistance to a particular industry to acquire the latest capital equipment.

The Rules of the Game

Quality of broadly defined, immobile factors of production will become increasingly more important. Among them, factors whose quality is most difficult to upgrade are social institutions such as the legal system, government regulations, fiscal and financial systems, customs and practices, and so on. Here, social institutions, as such, include fair or unfair application of the laws and regulations as well as the written laws and regulations themselves. Social institutions, in other words, are a set of "the rules of the game" (ROG) of a given society. The ROG prescribe, for example, what one has to do unofficially to obtain certain permits or licenses from the government as well as what the legal requirements are. It also shows who is likely to get a promotion within the government or in a private firm, what types of firms are likely to get bank loans, what one has to do to get fame as a singer, poet, and so on.

Life may be likened to a game where, from birth to death, people pursue wealth, power, and fame in competition with each other, if one disregards religious goals. To ignore the ROG of a society is to incur some costs or inconveniences. It is unreasonable to expect individual economic agents to act in violation of the rules in order to be patriotic or to live up to a certain moral standard, as they are often exhorted to do. Just as the behaviors of players in sports are determined by the rules and the referee's application of the rules, as well as by the players' skill and desire, an economic agent's behaviors are also determined by the ROG as well as by its talents and desire.

For the economy as a whole, the ROG are its *modus operandi*. They are the way the market operates, and they govern the competition that determines how the resources are allocated among economic agents. Thus, the performance of an economy depends not only on the amount of resources at its disposal but critically on the nature of the society's ROG. One of the reasons why the newly industrializing countries (NICs) were able to achieve rapid growth was that they could import what they lacked, be it capital equipment, industrial law materials, technology, or management skills. However, ROG are not easy to import or copy. Therefore, if a society's ROG are not propitious to a market economy, it will sooner or later run into problems.

For a market economy to thrive, the ROG have to be fair and transparent. Fair ROG provide everyone with equal opportunities ex ante and evaluate individuals' abilities and efforts by the same standards ex post. ROG are transparent when anyone who wants to has a way of knowing what the rules are. Under fair and transparent ROG, what one gets depends mostly on one's ability and efforts. Thus, individuals will try to find the best application of their own talents and assets, and in this way the economy will be led to realize its potential. Under unfair and nontransparent ROG, individuals will try their best to acquire other means, such as family connections, school ties, hometown connections, and so on, which will help them get an advantageous position in resource allocation. Distortion in resource allocation and waste are inevitable, and the economy's maximum potential will not be realized.

ROG seem to provide the reason why the Korean economy is ranked year after year as one of the lowest in competitiveness among developing countries, while at the same time the economy is expected by others to continue its rapid growth to become the seventh largest economy in the world by 2020. These widely divergent evaluations by the international community do not necessarily contradict each other but reflect two different aspects coexisting in the Korean economy. On the one hand, Korea has a great potential as indicated by the size of the population and the performance of the past three decades. On the other hand, the ROG are unfair and nontransparent, and this is the reason why Korea falls behind in competitiveness among other developing countries, especially in the financial sector and the government.

For the Korean economy to maintain its dynamism, the most crucial task is to establish fair and transparent ROG. Success in this will determine how well Korea survives and prospers in the new world environment. This can be better appreciated by reviewing the difficulties facing the Korean economy.

Wages more than doubled in real terms during the ten years up to the mid-1990s. Land prices and rents have always been high by international standards, and the interest rate has also been higher than in the comparable countries. The highways are crowded, and the port facilities have a hard time coping with the increasing volume of trade. The shortage of social overhead capital is becoming an important reason for the inefficiency of the country's distribution system, weakening the competitiveness of its exports.

These difficulties certainly weaken the competitiveness of Korean firms in the world market, but it needs to be recognized that they are to a large extent the consequences of rapid economic growth of the past, and of Korea's lack of natural resources. The wage rate rose rapidly mainly because the demand for labor exploded with the rapid economic growth. Land prices and rents are high in Korea simply because land is in short supply. The high real interest rates in Korea, after an allowance is made for the country risk, reflect the existence of better investment opportunities in the country than abroad. Thus, no easy remedy can be found to cure high factor costs and shortage of social overhead capital, and they are problems not just for some particular firms or industries, but for all sectors of the economy.

Since the supply of factors of production cannot be easily increased, a way must be found for the Korean economy to better utilize the resources it has. This is nothing but a classical problem of resource allocation. Since resource allocation in a market economy is determined by competition and competition is governed by the ROG, establishment of fair and transparent ROG is the most important task for the Korean economy for better utilization of resources.

This raises a question: How can one explain Korea's rapid growth in the past, and why has it suddenly become so important to establish fair and transparent ROG? The relatively low wage rate, compared to productivity, was the main source of export competitiveness which made possible rapid economic growth. Although unfair practices in resource allocation and corruption had raised the cost of production, this could be absorbed by extra profits generated by low wages without affecting the competitiveness of Korean exports. However, this slack was wiped out by the wage hike. From now on, the rise in costs due to unfair and nontransparent ROG will directly and adversely affect the competitiveness of Korean exports.

V. Conclusion: The Role of the Government

To briefly summarize the argument presented thus far, I have discussed the significance of three big changes in the world economy. Globalization of firms' economic activities, strengthening of the liberal trade order and multilateral trade system under the WTO, and ongoing deep integration are expected to weaken the autonomy of the national governments in policymaking, especially, its power to control the cross-border flow of goods, services, and factors of production. Thus the world is becoming increasingly borderless in an economic sense.

I also considered how the nature of a national economy changes as the world becomes economically borderless. A country's economic characteristics will be determined by factors of production that are intrinsically immobile such as the land, social overhead capital, a country's technology level, ROG, culture, and so on. It is these broadly defined factors of production that will determine the pattern of a country's trade and other economic interactions with the rest of the world. Within the same country, localities with distinct economic characteristics will coexist. The inter-industry linkages among domestic industries will loosen.

The convention determining nationality will increasingly follow the territorial principle rather than the personal principle.

In examining the policy implications of the changes in the nature of the national economy, the importance of further market opening and stronger commitment to the principle of nondiscrimination with respect to nationality and with respect to industries became clear. Another policy implication of the freer international movement of resources is that resource attraction will become an important factor in determining a country's economic performance. This section discusses what the role of the Korean government should be in the future world economic environment in light of discussions from the previous sections.

International movement of the mobile factors of production represents a search by firms for the best combination of immobile factors. Thus, the ability to attract foreign and domestic resources depends on the quality and quantity of the immobile factors, such as social overhead capital, technology level, ROG, culture, etc. Among these, the factor most critically requiring upgrade would be the ROG, since they cannot be simply imported or copied from other countries. This points to the importance of establishing fair and transparent ROG.

The discussion on the nature of a national economy in the future world environment raises an interesting proposition. It concerns what may be termed "reference units" in resource allocation, and states that industries become increasingly irrelevant as reference units while individual economic agents, including firms as well as persons, become more relevant.

The reference units here refer to the objects among which an economy's resources are to be allocated. The units could be real goods and services, such as rice, automobiles, education, etc. Having real goods and services as the reference units in resource allocation, however, implies setting target amounts of individual goods and services to be produced in the economy. This is meaningful only in a planned economy and needs not concern us here.

Instead, industries such as agriculture, automobile, education, etc. could be the reference units. But, all the anticipated changes in the nature of a national economy suggested that the principle of nondiscrimination should be more thoroughly applied in government policies, especially with respect to industry. Even if a certain activity generates positive externality, subsidy for the industry in which this activity takes place becomes harder to justify, as the inter-industry linkages become loose and as the probability increases that some localities may benefit while others suffer. In contrast, the case can continue to be made for the subsidy to the individual(s) whose activity generates the externality. Thus, it becomes more appropriate to view resource allocation as a problem of allocating resources among individual economic agents rather than among industries. In other words, individuals become more relevant reference units.

Interestingly, this highlights the importance of the ROG. As it becomes inappropriate for the government to allocate resources among different uses (real goods and services, or industries) and impossible to be directly engaged in resource allocation among individual economic agents, the allocation has to rely on competition among individuals. Hence, the ROG that govern competition matter much more in the borderless world.

When the ROG governing the competition are fair and transparent, competition will lead individuals to find the best application of their talents and assets and to make their best efforts, since how much wealth, power, and fame they can achieve will be largely determined by their abilities and efforts under the ROG. This way the economy will be led to realize its potential to the fullest extent. Individual economic agents in pursuit of their personal interests will perform socially desirable functions without realizing it, as if led by an "invisible hand."

In summary, the future world environment calls for more open domestic markets and more thorough application of the principle of nondiscrimination with respect to industry and locality as well as nationality. It also increases the importance of immobile factors of production. This, together with the tendency for individual economic agents to become increasingly more relevant as the reference units in resource allocation, calls on the government to establish fair and transparent ROG which are a prerequisite of efficient resource allocation through competition.

This prescription asks the government to do little else in the way of managing the economy besides providing public goods. It should be noted that the broadly defined, immobile factors of production including the ROG all share the characteristics of public goods. The prescription is little different from that of classical economics of Adam Smith. This is not surprising, since the domestic economy will more closely resemble the pure form of market economy as market forces will be less fettered by government regulations and interventions in the domestic markets in the future world of economic integration, and competition from within and without will become more intense.

Two final points need to be made about the prescribed role of the government. First, it is not the same as a laissez-faire policy advocating a minimalist government. In fact, it is recognized here as the responsibility of the government to establish fair and transparent ROG rather than regarding ROG as something to evolve as the market economy develops.

Second, the prescription is not a trivial proposition for the Korean society and government, as it calls for sweeping changes in the economy's constitution. In the past, the government heavily intervened in the market mechanism of resource allocation as if it knew better than the market. The government made development plans and forced, if it felt necessary, the private sector to follow. Now the function of the government should be changed so that the resource allocation that used to be under the government's control may be made by the market. Critical in this change in *modus operandi* is that the government policy, or its will, be replaced by impersonal ROG as the determinant of the resource allocation. The government should be allowed to intervene in the market only when there is a case of market failure and, even then, only if the intervention can make an improvement in resource allocation.

This is the greatest challenge facing Korean society. Because government intervention in the market has been pervasive in the past years of rapid economic growth, the conviction that market order is the feeding hand is not firm. Confidence in the international division of labor is not strong, either, even though the Korean economy could not have achieved rapid growth without it. Yet, for the market economy to thrive, it is necessary to reduce the resource allocating role of the government, to establish fair and transparent ROG and have them take over the resource allocating role that the government previously played, and to allow the government to be the servant of the market order that will develop under the new fair and transparent ROG.

REFERENCES

Agnelli, Giovanni. 1989. "The Europe of 1992." *Foreign Affairs* 68 (fall 1989).

Hayek, Friedrich A. 1982. *Law, Legislation and Liberty.* London: Routledge.

_____. 1988. *The Fatal Conceit.* London: Routledge.

International Institute for Management Development. 1995. *The World Competitiveness Report.*

Kuznets, Simon. 1966. *Modern Economic Growth: Rate, Structure, and Spread.* New Haven: Yale University Press.

North, Douglas. 1995. "Institutions and Economic Development." *Taiwan Economic Review* (National Taiwan University) 23.1 (March).

OECD. 1992. *Technology and the Economy: The Key Relationships.* Paris: OECD.

Smith, Adam. [1937] 1776. *An Inquiry into the Nature and Causes of the Wealth of Nations,* edited by Edwin Kennan. Reprint, New York: Modern Library.

Yoo, Jungho. 1990. "Industrial Policy of the 1970s and the Evolution of the Manufacturing Sector in Korea." KDI Working Paper, no. 9017.

Index